EUROPEAN FOREIGN POLICY AND THE EUROPEAN PARLIAMENT IN THE 1990s

To my parents, Natalina Scambia and Francesco Viola, for their love and support, and in loving memory of my grandmother, Agata Bucarelli.

In the belief that the pursuit of the 'grand European design' is of vital importance to our own and future generations.

European Foreign Policy and the European Parliament in the 1990s

An investigation into the role and voting behaviour of the European Parliament's political groups

DONATELLA M. VIOLA
London School of Economics and Political Science

LONDON AND NEW YORK

First published 2000 by Ashgate Publishing

Reissued 2019 by Routledge
2 Park Square, Milton Park, Abingdon, Oxon, OX14 4RN
52 Vanderbilt Avenue, New York, NY 10017

Routledge is an imprint of the Taylor & Francis Group, an informa business

© Donatella M. Viola 2000

All rights reserved. No part of this book may be reprinted or reproduced or utilised in any form or by any electronic, mechanical, or other means, now known or hereafter invented, including photocopying and recording, or in any information storage or retrieval system, without permission in writing from the publishers.

Notice:
Product or corporate names may be trademarks or registered trademarks, and are used only for identification and explanation without intent to infringe.

Publisher's Note
The publisher has gone to great lengths to ensure the quality of this reprint but points out that some imperfections in the original copies may be apparent.

Disclaimer
The publisher has made every effort to trace copyright holders and welcomes correspondence from those they have been unable to contact.

A Library of Congress record exists under LC control number:

ISBN 13: 978-1-138-70317-9 (hbk)
ISBN 13: 978-1-315-20332-4 (ebk)

Contents

Detailed Table of Contents	*vi*
List of Tables	*xii*
List of Illustrations and Charts	*xiv*
Preface	*xvi*
Acknowledgements	*xvii*
List of Abbreviations	*xviii*

Introduction		1
I	European Foreign Policy and the European Parliament	12
II	The Responses of the European Community and the European Parliament to the Gulf Crisis	46
III	The Role of the Political Groups in Forging the European Parliament's Stance on the Gulf Crisis	73
IV	The Responses of the European Community and the European Parliament to the Yugoslav Crisis	147
V	The Role of the Political Groups in Forging the European Parliament's Stance on the Yugoslav Crisis	179
Conclusion		242
Epilogue		263
Appendix		*265*
Bibliography		*293*

v

Detailed Table of Contents

Introduction	1
1. General Context of the Research	1
2. Research Objectives	4
3. Methodology	5
4. Overview of the Case Studies	7
5. Academic Contribution	8
6. Outline of the Book	9
I European Foreign Policy and the European Parliament	12
1. The European Parliament and its Political Groups	13
2. The European Parliament's Configuration and Political Groups' Composition	15
3. The Nature and Role of Political Groups in the European Parliament	20
4. MEP Allegiances and Freedom of Conscience	21
5. The Foreign Affairs Activities of the European Parliament and its Political Groups	23
6. Reasons for the Participation of the European Parliament in Foreign Policy	27
7. The Development of the Powers of the European Parliament in the Context of Foreign Policy	29
7.1 Community Treaties	
a) External Relations	29
7.2 Single European Act	
a) External Relations	30
b) European Political Cooperation	31

vi

7.3 Treaty on European Union

    a) External Relations — 33
    b) Common Foreign and Security Policy — 34

7.4 Treaty of Amsterdam

    a) External Relations — 36
    b) Common Foreign and Security Policy — 37

8. Decision-Making in Foreign Policy: the Role of the European Parliament and its Political Groups — 39

Conclusion — 43

II The Responses of the European Community and the European Parliament to the Gulf Crisis — 46

1. Brief Historical Background on the Gulf Crisis — 46
2. The European Community and the Gulf Crisis — 51
3. The European Parliament and the Gulf Crisis — 58
    a) Pre-War Stage — 59
    b) War Stage — 64
    c) Post-War Stage — 68

Conclusion — 70

III The Role of the Political Groups in Forging the European Parliament's Stance on the Gulf Crisis — 73

1. Political Groups' Positions vis-à-vis the Gulf Crisis — 76

1.1 The Socialist Group
    a) Pre-War Stage — 76
    b) War Stage — 79
    c) Post-War Stage — 82

vii

1.2 The European People's Party
    a) Pre-War Stage — 84
    b) War Stage — 85
    c) Post-War Stage — 86
1.3 The Liberal Democratic and Reformist Group
    a) Pre-War Stage — 88
    b) War Stage — 90
    c) Post-War Stage — 91
1.4 The European Democratic Group
    a) Pre-War Stage — 93
    b) War Stage — 94
    c) Post-War Stage — 95
1.5 The Greens
    a) Pre-War Stage — 97
    b) War Stage — 100
    c) Post-War Stage — 102
1.6 The European Unitarian Left
    a) Pre-War Stage — 105
    b) War Stage — 108
    c) Post-War Stage — 109
1.7 The European Democratic Alliance
    a) Pre-War Stage — 110
    b) War Stage — 112
    c) Post-War Stage — 113
1.8 The European Right
    a) Pre-War Stage — 114
    b) War Stage — 117
    c) Post-War Stage — 118
1.9 The Rainbow Group
    a) Pre-War Stage — 120
    b) War Stage — 122
    c) Post-War Stage — 123
1.10 The Left Unity
    a) Pre-War Stage — 124
    b) War Stage — 126
    c) Post-War Stage — 127

2. Level of Transnationality in Political Groups' Voting Behaviour on the Gulf Crisis — 131
3. MEP National Allegiance versus Political Group Loyalty — 133
4. Political Groups' Voting Similarity on the Gulf Crisis — 134

viii

5. Intergroup Cooperation in Shaping the European
Parliament's Stance on the Gulf Crisis 136

Conclusion 142

IV The Responses of the European Community and the European Parliament to the Yugoslav Crisis 147

1. Brief Historical Background on the Yugoslav Crisis 147
2. The European Community and the Yugoslav Crisis 153
3. The European Parliament and the Yugoslav Crisis 164

a) Pre-Recognition Stage 164
b) Post-Recognition Stage 172

Conclusion 175

V The Role of the Political Groups in Forging the European Parliament's Stance on the Yugoslav Crisis 179

1. The Political Groups' Positions vis-à-vis the Yugoslav Crisis 181

1.1 The Socialist Group 181
   a) Pre-Recognition Stage 181
   b) Post-Recognition Stage 185
1.2 The European People's Party
   a) Pre-Recognition Stage 189
   b) Post-Recognition Stage 192
1.3 The Liberal Democratic and Reformist Group
   a) Pre-Recognition Stage 195
   b) Post-Recognition Stage 197
1.4 The European Democratic Group
   a) Pre-Recognition Stage 199
   b) Post-Recognition Stage 201
1.5 The Greens
   a) Pre-Recognition Stage 203
   b) Post-Recognition Stage 205

ix

1.6 The European Unitarian Left
    a) Pre-Recognition Stage — 207
    b) Post-Recognition Stage — 208
1.7 The European Democratic Alliance
    a) Pre-Recognition Stage — 210
    b) Post-Recognition Stage — 212
1.8 The European Right
    a) Pre-Recognition Stage — 213
    b) Post-Recognition Stage — 215
1.9 The Rainbow Group
    a) Pre-Recognition Stage — 216
    b) Post-Recognition Stage — 218
1.10 The Left Unity
    a) Pre-Recognition Stage — 220
    b) Post-Recognition Stage — 221

2. Level of Transnationality in Political Groups' Voting
Behaviour on the Yugoslav Crisis — 225
3. MEP National Allegiance Versus Political Group Loyalty — 226
4. Political Groups' Voting Similarity on the Yugoslav Crisis — 228
5. Intergroup Cooperation in Shaping the European
Parliament's Stance on the Yugoslav Crisis — 229

Conclusion — 239

Conclusion — 242

1. The Gulf and the Yugoslav Crises — 242
2. The Response of the European Community to the Gulf and
Yugoslav Crises — 243
3. The Response of the European Parliament to the Gulf and
Yugoslav Crises — 244
4. The Political Groups' Positions vis-à-vis the Gulf and Yugoslav
Crises — 246

4.1 Political Groups' Levels of Absenteeism — 246
4.2 Political Groups' Indices of Agreement — 248
4.3 Political Groups' Indices of Transnationality — 249
4.4. MEP National Allegiance versus Political Group Loyalty — 250
4.5 Political Groups' Voting Similarities — 252

5.	Intergroup Cooperation within the European Parliament	252
6.	The European Parliament and Foreign Affairs	256
7.	Towards a Supranational European Parliament and European Political Parties?	257
8.	Future Developments	261

Epilogue 263

Appendix 265
Bibliography 293

xi

List of Tables

Chapter I

Tables 1a-1f   European Parliament: Group Composition and Index
of Transnationality (ITc) June 1990 - July 1992   16

Chapter III

Tables 2a-2c	List of EP Roll-Call Votes on the Gulf Crisis	74-76
Table 3	Political Groups' Voting Similarity on the Gulf Crisis	134
Table 4	Breakdown of Adopted and Non-Adopted Motions for Resolutions on the Gulf Crisis	137
Table 5	Intergroup Cooperation: Adopted Joint Resolutions on the Gulf Crisis	138

Chapter V

Tables 6a-6b	List of EP Roll-Call Votes on the Yugoslav Crisis	179-180
Table 7	Political Groups' Voting Similarity on the Yugoslav Crisis	228
Table 8	Breakdown of Adopted and Non-Adopted Motions for Resolutions on the Yugoslav Crisis	235
Table 9	Intergroup Cooperation: Adopted Joint Resolutions on the Yugoslav Crisis	236

Appendix

Table 10	Key for Index of Agreement and Level of Absenteeism	267
Table 11	Chairmen/Women of the Political Groups between June 1990 and June 1991	268
Table 12	Adopted Joint Resolutions according to PG Contribution on the Gulf Crisis	271
Table 13	Individual PG Non-Adopted Motions for Resolutions on the Gulf Crisis	272
Table 14	Adopted Joint Resolutions according to PG Contribution on the Yugoslav Crisis	273

Table 15	Individual PG Non-Adopted Motions for Resolutions on the Yugoslav Crisis	274
Table 16	Socialist Group Voting Trends: Gulf Crisis	275
Table 17	EPP Group Voting Trends: Gulf Crisis	276
Table 18	LDR Group Voting Trends: Gulf Crisis	277
Table 19	ED Group Voting Trends: Gulf Crisis	278
Table 20	Green Group Voting Trends: Gulf Crisis	279
Table 21	EUL Group Voting Trends: Gulf Crisis	280
Table 22	EDA Group Voting Trends: Gulf Crisis	281
Table 23	ER Group Voting Trends: Gulf Crisis	282
Table 24	Rainbow Group Voting Trends: Gulf Crisis	283
Table 25	LU Group Voting Trends: Gulf Crisis	284
Table 26	Independent Members' Voting Trends: Gulf Crisis	285
Table 27	European Parliament Voting Trends: Gulf Crisis	286
Table 28	Socialist Group Voting Trends: Yugoslav Crisis	287
Table 29	EPP Group Voting Trends: Yugoslav Crisis	287
Table 30	LDR Group Voting Trends: Yugoslav Crisis	288
Table 31	ED Group Voting Trends: Yugoslav Crisis	288
Table 32	Green Group Voting Trends: Yugoslav Crisis	289
Table 33	EUL Group Voting Trends: Yugoslav Crisis	289
Table 34	EDA Group Voting Trends: Yugoslav Crisis	290
Table 35	ER Group Voting Trends: Yugoslav Crisis	290
Table 36	Rainbow Group Voting Trends: Yugoslav Crisis	291
Table 37	LU Group Voting Trends: Yugoslav Crisis	291
Table 38	Independent Members' Voting Trends: Yugoslav Crisis	292
Table 39	European Parliament Voting Trends: Yugoslav Crisis	292

xiii

List of Illustrations and Charts

Chapter I

Illustration 1	The European Parliament's Configuration and Political Groups' Composition	15

Chapter III

Charts 1a & 1b	Socialist Group's Index of Agreement and Level of Absenteeism: Gulf Crisis	83
Charts 2a & 2b	EPP Group's Index of Agreement and Level of Absenteeism: Gulf Crisis	88
Charts 3a & 3b	LDR Group's Index of Agreement and Level of Absenteeism: Gulf Crisis	92
Charts 4a & 4b	ED Group's Index of Agreement and Level of Absenteeism: Gulf Crisis	97
Charts 5a & 5b	Greens' Index of Agreement and Level of Absenteeism: Gulf Crisis	104
Charts 6a & 6b	EUL Group's Index of Agreement and Level of Absenteeism: Gulf Crisis	110
Charts 7a & 7b	EDA Group's Index of Agreement and Level of Absenteeism: Gulf Crisis	114
Charts 8a & 8b	ER Group's Index of Agreement and Level of Absenteeism: Gulf Crisis	119
Charts 9a & 9b	Rainbow Group's Index of Agreement and Level of Absenteeism: Gulf Crisis	124
Charts 10a & 10b	LU Group's Index of Agreement and Level of Absenteeism: Gulf Crisis	129
Charts 11a & 11b	EP Index of Agreement and Level of Absenteeism: Gulf Crisis	130
Chart 12a	PG and EP Indices of Agreement: Gulf Crisis	130
Chart 12b	Political Groups' Level of Absenteeism: Gulf Crisis	130
Chart 13	PG and EP Indices of Transnationality: Gulf Crisis	132
Chart 13a	EP Index of Agreement by Nationality: Gulf Crisis	133
Chart 14	PG Contribution: Gulf Crisis	139

xiv

Chapter V

Charts 15a & 15b	Socialist Group's Index of Agreement and Level of Absenteeism: Yugoslav Crisis	188
Charts 16a & 16b	EPP Group's Index of Agreement and Level of Absenteeism: Yugoslav Crisis	195
Charts 17a & 17b	LDR Group's Index of Agreement and Level of Absenteeism: Yugoslav Crisis	199
Charts 18a & 18b	ED Group's Index of Agreement and Level of Absenteeism: Yugoslav Crisis	203
Charts 19a & 19b	Green Group's Index of Agreement and Level of Absenteeism: Yugoslav Crisis	206
Charts 20a & 20b	EUL Group's Index of Agreement and Level of Absenteeism: Yugoslav Crisis	210
Charts 21a & 21b	EDA Group's Index of Agreement and Level of Absenteeism: Yugoslav Crisis	213
Charts 22a & 22b	ER Group's Index of Agreement and Level of Absenteeism: Yugoslav Crisis	216
Charts 23a & 23b	Rainbow Group's Index of Agreement and Level of Absenteeism: Yugoslav Crisis	219
Charts 24a & 24b	LU Group's Index of Agreement and Level of Absenteeism: Yugoslav Crisis	223
Chart 25a & 25b	EP Index of Agreement and Level of Absenteeism: Yugoslav Crisis	224
Chart 26a	PG and EP Indices of Agreement: Yugoslav Crisis	224
Chart 26b	PG and EP Levels of Absenteeism: Yugoslav Crisis	224
Chart 27	PG and EP Level of Absenteeism: Yugoslav Crisis	226
Chart 27a	EP Index of Agreement by Nationality: Yugoslav Crisis	227
Chart 28	PG Contribution: Yugoslav Crisis	237

Appendix

Charts 29a-29b	EP Composition by Political Group: June 1991-July 1992	269
Chart 30	EP Composition by Nationality: June 1990 - July 1992	270

xv

Preface

This book aims to unravel whether joint policies and supranational solutions can be forged within the *sui generis* 'laboratory' of the European Parliament (EP), enabling a European collective identity to emerge rather than simply the sum of national sentiments, preferences and ambitions. In particular, it intends to ascertain whether vested national interests expressed by the various Members of the European Parliament (MEPs) have been overcome within their respective political groups, on the way to becoming effective and cohesive parties at European level. In order to validate or refute the above hypothesis, foreign policy, traditionally regarded as a sacred domain and stronghold of the nation state, is taken as a yardstick.

Whilst bearing in mind the EP's limited competence in this field, the question at the heart of the book is whether the European Parliament is likely to become a genuine international actor or whether it is likely to remain a forum for discussion, functioning as the 'voice of conscience' and 'dissent' of the Community and its member states. As such, the research explores the parliamentary dynamics behind the definition of a common position vis-à-vis two major events of the 1990s: the Gulf and the Yugoslav crises. A qualitative investigation into the role of the political groups combined with a quantitative analysis of MEP voting behaviour is carried out in order to assess the interactions within and between the political alignments of the polychromatic Europarliamentary spectrum with respect to the aforementioned cases. Whereas the political groups reached a level of internal cohesion vis-à-vis these crises, the views of the European Parliament appeared rather ambiguous due to intergroup divergences.

It is the contention of this book that the political groups have come to constitute embryonic transnational political parties which are deemed to play an increasingly important role in the development of the European Parliament, in the evolution of party politics at European level as well as in the European Union's policy-making.

xvi

Acknowledgements

I wish to express my sincere gratitude to the former President of the European Parliament, Enrique Barón Crespo, the former Secretary-General of the Liberal Group, Massimo Silvestro, and all MEPs and officials of the European Parliament who kindly agreed to be interviewed. I am indebted to the staff of the Secretariat of the European Parliament and political groups in Luxembourg and Brussels for the openness with which I have been received, in particular the Secretary-General of the European Parliament Enrico Vinci, Karen Jepsen, Katerina Berry, Michail Liokaris and Jacques Schouller. I am especially grateful to Dr Thomas Grunert for his expert advice. I would also like to acknowledge the kind assistance of Avis Furness of the London office of the European Parliament.

A special word of thanks should go to Professor Christopher Hill for his invaluable guidance and constant support throughout the writing of this book.

This research has greatly benefited from conversations and correspondence with Professor Fulvio Attinà, Professor Fred Halliday, Professor Stanley Henig, Dr Carsten Holbraad, Professor Juliet Lodge, Professor Gordon Smith, Professor Paul Taylor, Professor William Wallace and Professor Joseph H Weiler, as well as Dr Liza Burdett, Dr Simon Hix, Dr Talal Nizameddin, Dr Tapio Raunio and Dr Roger Scully.

I want to express my deep gratitude to Mary Bellamy, Sanja Carolina, Martin Hedemann-Robinson and Keith Wickens for their help and support.

Finally, I wish to acknowledge the European Commission for providing the financial foundation for my employment as a *Marie Curie Fellow* at the LSE and the British Foreign and Commonwealth Office for awarding me a *Chevening Scholarship*.

List of Abbreviations

ASEAN	Association of South East Asian Nations
CFSP	Common Foreign and Security Policy
CSCE	Conference on Security and Cooperation in Europe
ECSC	European Coal and Steel Community
EC	European Community
EEC	European Economic Community
EFTA	European Free Trade Association
EPC	European Political Cooperation
EU	European Union
EURATOM	European Atomic Energy Community
IA	Index of Agreement
IGC	Intergovernmental Cooperation
ITc	Index of Transnationality of Composition
ITv	Index of Transnationality in Voting
JNA	Yugoslav People's Army *Jugoslovenska narodna armija*
LAP	Latin American Parliament
NATO	North Atlantic Treaty Organization
RCV	Roll-Call Vote
SEA	Single European Act
SFRY	Socialist Federal Republic of Yugoslavia
TEU	Treaty on European Union
UN	United Nations
VSP	Voting Similarity Percentage
WEU	Western European Union

Political Groups

EP	European Parliament
PG	Political Groups
SOC	Socialist Group
EPP	European People's Party
LDR	Liberal Democratic and Reformist Group
ED	European Democratic Group
V	Greens
EUL	European Unitarian Left
EDA	European Democratic Alliance
ER	European Right
LU	Left Unity
RB	Rainbow Group
MEP	Member of the European Parliament

Introduction

1. General Context of the Research

In the wake of the phenomenon of globalization, due *inter alia* to the development of technology, mass communication and international trade, national boundaries are gradually being transcended in economic, political and cultural terms. The traditional distinction between domestic and foreign policy has slowly, but inevitably, become more and more blurred.

As the former President of the European Parliament (EP) Klaus Hänsch maintains, "[w]e have reached the point where (...) foreign policy has in fact become domestic politics" (Hänsch, 1996, 344). The close interface between international and national spheres has generated greater public interest in international affairs. As a result, although its reins remain securely in the hands of governments' leaders, EP attention has increasingly been turned towards foreign policy.

The active participation of national parliaments in the international arena is still viewed sceptically by many constitutional lawyers, politicians and specialists in the field of international relations. The possible involvement of the European Parliament in foreign policy-making is seen as an even more unlikely and remote prospect. Cynics point out that it is vain to assess the views of the political groups (PGs) or individual Members of the European Parliament (MEPs) since their declarations are not legally binding and are often "so futile in terms of bringing results" (Coombes, 1979, 117). The weakness of the EP along with the absence of a fully-fledged European foreign and security policy have often discouraged MEPs from even attending relevant debates and voting sessions. Nevertheless, some consider that this state of affairs has conferred a new impetus to the urgency for a wide programme of institutional reforms, with special emphasis on the EP's quest for greater powers in order to combat the democratic deficit within the European Union (EU). As defined by the EP, this deficit consists of "the combination of two phenomena: (i) the transfer of powers from the Member States to the EC and (ii) the exercise of these powers at Community level by institutions other than the European Parliament, even though, before the transfer, the national parliaments held

1

power to pass laws in the areas concerned" (*Toussaint Report*, 1/2/1988, 10-11). Karlheinz Neunreither distinguishes three elements of democratic deficit. The first is the lack of a balance of powers between the executive and the legislative branches at European level, whereby the executive is not elected by a majority of Parliament and is not accountable to it. The second is the lack of accountability to its citizens that a powerful union of democratic states, such as the EU, might be expected to display. The third is the absence of genuine European political parties and pan-European media, with the consequence that it is only with great difficulty that citizens can get objective information (Neunreither, 1994, 300). This deficit is deemed to persist as long as crucial policy areas, including foreign policy, remain outside the realm of Europarliamentary and, therefore, public accountability.

One of the premises underlying this book is that the EU member states have to decide whether they intend to forge a supranational political entity which would enable the EU to play a leading role on the world stage, bearing in mind that this decision would entail substantial adjustments to the systems of governance both at European Union and member state levels. Parallels can be drawn with the critical stage in the mid-1980s when the EEC was working towards the completion of the internal market ideal. In its White Paper of 1985, the Commission of the European Communities boldly stated:

> Europe stands at the crossroads. We either go ahead - with resolution and determination or we drop back into mediocrity. We can now either resolve to complete the integration of the economies of Europe; or, through a lack of political will to face the immense problems involved, we can simply allow Europe to develop into no more than a free trade area (COM (85) 310fin, pt. 219).

The question at the heart of this book is whether the European Parliament is likely to become a real international actor or whether, conversely, it is likely to remain a 'voice of conscience' and 'dissent' for the European Union and member state policies.[1] The first possibility stresses

---

1 According to Gunnar Sjøstedt's definition, an international actor consists of a unit in the international system which possesses 'actor capability' being 'discernible from the external environment', and having a minimum degree of internal cohesion (Sjøstedt, 1977, 6-13). However, when referring to the

the factor of *efficiency*, asserting that the aim of the EP should be to project a united and consistent image in order to make an impact on EC/EU decisional institutions, and thus, to exert a degree of influence on third countries' governments and parliaments as well as on international organizations. The former chairman of the Socialist Group, Rudi Arndt, highlights the fact that originally the two largest political groups, the Socialists and the Christian Democrats, used to be at loggerheads, wishing to "display pure ideology" and "to show the other political camp how clever our own ideas were and how wrong theirs were", rather than pursue a large majority (Arndt, 1992, 65). Subsequently, the need to reach a consensus within the House was acknowledged as being the only viable solution which would enable the EP to exert its rather limited constitutional powers and to prevent "overblown verbiage" from becoming the very embodiment of what the philosopher Gustave Thibon defines as "the reflection of [an] atrophied reality" (Antony, 23/10/1990, 79). During the so-called 'meeting of the giants' held just before the beginning of the second EP legislative period, the two groups decided that, for pragmatic reasons, "there was no point in a mutual flexing of ideological muscles" and that "the only sensible strategy was to achieve the appropriate majorities". Since then, what Martin Westlake calls "the Socialist-Christian Democrat Oligopoly" has effectively dominated EP proceedings (Westlake, 1994b, 186).

This view contrasts with that of the opposing camp which emphasizes that the EP needs to focus on *democracy* by simply remaining a forum for discussion where pluralism and diversity should be encouraged in order to ensure that all distinct opinions of society are fully represented. As the former EP President Pierre Pflimlin claims, "Parliament's role is not to produce majorities, but to state positions clearly", especially on issues of international politics (Pflimlin, 1992, 70).

The paradox raised by these two fundamental but opposing concerns - *efficiency* and *democracy* - remains unsolved, inevitably determining a state of perpetual tension within the European Parliament. The different cultural and political backgrounds of MEPs may lead to dramatically diverse

---

relationship between actorness and the democratic deficit, it must be borne in mind that were the European Union to become a real international actor, a democratic deficit could persist. Conversely, the deficit could be overcome and the European Union could still fail to become an international actor. This uncertainty has impelled the EP to carve its quest to increase its international status.

expectations as to the performance of political groups and the European Parliament in EU policy-making. Two extreme situations are represented in relation to the EP: at one end, *dictatorship* and, at the other, *anarchy* (Westlake, 1994a, 25). The first, underpinning constitutional conservatism, results in stability while the second, symbolizing parliamentary incoherence, results in instability. Both consequences are, however, undesirable. Dictatorship would lead in the medium and long-term to a stalemate, denying Parliament the most relevant dialectical and dynamic prerogatives that stem from exchanges of views and verbal confrontation. Anarchy would lead to chaos and prevent Parliament from functioning, undermining its bargaining power vis-à-vis the other institutions in order to influence EU policy (Westlake, 1994a, 25). To avoid such extreme degeneration of efficiency and democracy, it is important to look closely at the internal dynamics of such a unique and multinational parliamentary body to assess whether and how these concerns can be accommodated to a degree of mutual satisfaction. A premise for the book is the need for an appropriate 'trade-off' between these apparently irreconcilable necessities when dealing with issues of foreign policy, traditionally regarded as a crucial policy area and one where nationalist sentiments are likely to emerge (Lodge, 1996, 205).

2. Research Objectives

The general aim of the book is to assess whether, within the *sui generis* 'laboratory' of the European Parliament, joint policies and supranational solutions can be forged by pursuing a holistic approach that emphasizes a collective European identity, rather than simply the sum of national sentiments, preferences and ambitions.

The research intends to discover whether a 'Europeanization' process has been taking place within the European Parliament and to appraise whether the EP succeeded in transcending conventional state frontiers or whether conflicting national interpretations were still at the heart of the parliamentary debate.

Furthermore, by gauging the specific involvement of the respective PGs against their claimed allegiance to 'European' as opposed to 'national' interests, it is possible to assess whether they are becoming effective and cohesive parties at European level. The research appraises the level of cohesion within the European Parliament and political groups, the extent of intergroup negotiations, the frequency of compromise and coalition-building, the level of affinity between political groups as well as the level of transnationality within the various groups, with respect to two key cases.[2] In order to confirm or refute the argument underlying this Europeanization process, foreign policy, regarded as one of the most sensitive policy areas, is taken as a yardstick. This can also assist in clarifying whether "the territorial/national dimension" or the "party/ideological dimension" dominated the pursuit of political groups' goals (Hix, 1993, 45).

3. Methodology

As Fulvio Attinà argues, parliamentary debates over topical international issues have symbolic rather than functional connotations, given the limited competence of the EP in foreign policy. The level of affinity in the attitudes and voting patterns of the EP political groups on foreign affairs are generally high, due in part to the negligible value of the texts of virtually cost-free resolutions which are therefore easy to agree on (Attinà, 1990, 572). Nevertheless, as Luciano Bardi remarks, when the content of resolutions involves more critical issues, as in the defence sector, such a large consensus undoubtedly decreases (Bardi, 1994, 369). An investigation into MEPs' attitudes vis-à-vis two major international crises is an excellent analytical tool to indicate the effective level of cohesion and transnationality reached within the European Parliament and PGs, and to validate or refute the above assumptions. The two cases are examined using a three-tiered analytical framework: the first briefly outlines the EC's position while the second and the third levels of analysis, respectively, focus on the EP and its sub-units, the PGs.

This investigation is undertaken through a review of all the relevant Europarliamentary debates, significant EP political and legislative resolutions as well as motions for resolutions on the Gulf and Yugoslavia.[3]

---

2 The formulae employed for calculating the indices of agreement, similarity and transnationality are explained in detail in the Appendix.

3 The EP acts consist of two formal categories on the basis of the impact they have on the EC decision-making process: legislative and budgetary acts which fall under the Community legal framework and the so-called own initiative political resolutions which do not belong to the EC structure and, therefore, are

Gathering some of the motions was made highly problematic due to the unfortunate parliamentary practice that texts of non-adopted motions are not kept in any libraries, not even those of the EP; they are often discarded by the political groups themselves. The archives of the Translation Division of the Secretariat of the European Parliament based in Luxembourg have been a mine of information. It was here that, after carrying out thorough searches, most of these texts were eventually located. Testimony has also been provided by some MEPs and officials who closely followed the political and economic developments in the Gulf and former Yugoslavia.

This research follows a combined qualitative-quantitative methodological approach through a qualitative analysis of the debates and a quantitative analysis of MEP voting behaviour in order to counteract the anomalies of each approach when taken separately. Specifically, a qualitative analysis may be tainted by the researcher's subjective perception when reading through debates, resolutions and explanations of vote. A quantitative analysis of roll-call votes (RCVs)[4] may be misrepresentative of the real level of cohesion within groups not least due to the long preparatory stage the motion for a resolution undergoes prior to voting and the symbolic rather than politically concrete value of a vote that carries with it the weight of public accountability (Bardi, 1996, 104).

The cohesion of the various political groups is measured with the index of agreement (IA), elaborated by Fulvio Attinà from a variant of Stuart Rice's formula (Attinà, 1990, 564, Rice, 1928, 208-209).[5] Tables are calculated on percentages of the roll-call votes of each group for individual and joint motions for resolutions, amendments and paragraphs drafted over the period between September 1990 and May 1991 for the Gulf crisis, and between February 1991 and July 1992 for the Yugoslav crisis. The empirical validity of this analysis rests on the central proposition that

---

    not legally binding. These texts are drafted on the initiative of groups or individual members on urgent and topical problems, sometimes following oral questions or as responses to statements issued by the Council or Commission.

4   Roll-call voting consists of a process whereby the names of MEPs and their modalities of votes are recorded. This information is made available to the Parliament, political groups and the general public since it is published in the Official Journal of the European Communities - Series C 'Information and Notices'.

5   Attinà's formula has been used by other researchers such as Bay Brzinski (1995), Raunio (1997) and Scully (1997) in their respective RCV analyses of the European Parliament.

cohesion provides stability in groups and is a sign of the development towards identifiable European parties.

The voting affinity between groups is assessed by employing Stuart Rice's index of voting likeness, also illustrated in the Appendix, but referred to in this book as voting similarity percentage (VSP) (Rice, 1928). The composition of the groups is taken into consideration in order to evaluate what impact the more or less heterogeneous configuration of the PGs may have on their level of cohesion. Any modification incurred between 1990-1992 is therefore duly registered and taken into consideration. Indices of transnationality of voting behaviour (ITv) are compared to the index of transnationality of composition (ITc) in order to assess whether and to what extent PG voting behaviour proves to be more transnational than PG composition and to demonstrate whether foreign policy functions as a catalysing factor of transnationalization within the group or, on the contrary, whether it perpetuates and consolidates the traditional tendency towards a nationalist approach. The ITv-s on the Gulf and Yugoslavia policies are calculated on the highest modality of vote, which is assumed to represent the official position of each political group, with respect to the examined RCVs. A comparison of the data of this index of transnationality with those of the cohesion coefficient serves to judge whether group heterogeneity represents an inhibiting factor for reaching internal cohesion, undermining members' ability to achieve consensus. Two formulae based on Douglas Rae's index of fractionalization are used to compute ITc and ITv-s with regard to the cases (Rae, 1967).

4. Overview of the Case Studies

The international political scene over the last decade has witnessed two major events: the invasion of Kuwait by Iraq and the conflict in former Yugoslavia. The Gulf crisis marked the end of the Cold War era, showing the concurrent dangers and the challenges posed by the sudden disappearance of one of the superpowers, the Soviet Union. As such, it represented the first major test for the New World Order. The crisis in former Yugoslavia, which was the first outbreak of sustained military fighting on the European continent since the end of the Second World War, has been selected for its geographical proximity to the Community, the magnitude and duration of the conflict as well as the human, political and economic consequences for Europe. Both cases, commonly regarded as

7

proving grounds for European Political Cooperation (EPC),[6] seriously challenged the ability of the then Twelve in the management of international crises. The periods examined are August 1990 until May 1991 for the Gulf crisis and January 1991 until July 1992 for the Yugoslav crisis. These time frames were chosen, in the first case, to include the invasion of Kuwait in August 1990 until the beginning of the withdrawal of the allied troops from Iraq in the post-war period and, in the second case, the escalation from economic and constitutional crisis to war up to a few months after the recognition of independence of Bosnia-Herzegovina.

Christopher Hill has argued that "[t]here are, of course, contrary arguments about the value of case-studies, from those who believe on the one side that the case-approach does little more than dress up history, without transcending the limits of all phenotypical work, in producing non-commensurable results, and on the other that cases inevitably miss the deeper, more impersonal forces of long duration which shape choice without always being revealed at the point of surface decision" (Hill, 1991, 5). However, pursuing the case-study path could provide impetus for developing a broad survey and generating a more general debate on the internal dynamics of the European Parliament with respect to foreign policy.

5. Academic Contribution

Although the literature on both the European Parliament and European foreign policy has proliferated in recent years, becoming overwhelmingly vast and rich in content and diversity, the above areas of research have rarely been combined in a systematic analysis. Virtually no studies have focused on the interface between the EP, especially its political alignments, and foreign policy since EPC's formal inauguration under the 1986 Single European Act (SEA). Despite the welter of studies on the European Parliament, only a few publications have focused on the European Parliament and Foreign Policy, notably Gaja (1980), Weiler (1980),

---

6   European Political Cooperation (EPC) was an intergovernmental forum for discussion, consultation and the coordination of member states on foreign policy issues. It was introduced in 1970, institutionalized by the Single European Act in 1986 and superseded by the Common Foreign and Security Policy (CFSP) created by the Treaty of European Union in 1992.

Fontaine (1984), Lodge (1988) in her contribution to Sondhi's book, Penders (1988), Neunreither (1990) in his contribution to Edwards and Regelsberger's book, Elles, J. (1990), Millar (1991), Monar (1993), Prout (1992, 1993, 1994), and two unpublished theses: Stavridis (1991) and Dupagny (1992). In a wider context, Bardi (1997) also examines the powers of the European Parliament, the desirability of EP transnational party cooperation and the future of European security and defence policy. With reference to EP political groups, an interest was expressed by Geoffrey and Pippa Pridham (1981). After some years of neglect, research into the PGs has been revived by the studies of authors such as Lodge (1983a), Delwit and de Waele (1995), Westlake (1994a) and jointly by Jacobs, Corbett and Shackleton (1992, 1995), Julie Smith (1995) and Bardi (1996), to quote just a few. Yet, only Neunreither (1990) and Lodge (1988) have looked more specifically at the trinomial 'EP-PGs-foreign policy'. Attinà has pioneered the study of EP voting behaviour analysis (Attinà, 1995, 39), subsequently undertaken by Bay Brzinski (1995), Raunio (1997), Hix and Lord (1997) and Scully (1997). Attinà and Raunio have both referred in their respective works to foreign policy, yet due to the wider range of areas examined, they devoted only part of their research to this aspect, without testing their statistical data against an in-depth examination of the parliamentary debates.

Neither inter- nor intrapolitical group behaviour has so far been explored in depth, whether on a separate or a comparative basis with regard to the chosen cases. This book attempts to fill such a lacuna by breaking new ground with a qualitative-quantitative analysis of parliamentary reaction towards the above foreign policy issues. As such, it could be regarded as a contribution to both research areas, while also trying to give a new stimulus to the debate on the democratization of foreign policy through an examination of the 'efficiency versus democracy' dilemma.

6. Outline of the Book

The book begins by constructing a detailed profile of the internal structure and relevant organization of the European Parliament as well as its constituent political groups, with reference to foreign policy.[7] After a short

---

7   The chapter stresses the exceptional character of the constituent political

introductory section on the reasons for the desirability of a greater participation of the European Parliament in the formulation and supervision of a common foreign policy, the development of the EP's role in European foreign policy is then outlined from the advent of the Paris and Rome Treaties in the 1950s to the signature of the Treaty of Amsterdam in June 1997.[8] The external relations of the European Community/Union, which are subject to the supranational regime of EC Law as well as the intergovernmental structure of European Political Cooperation, renamed as the Common Foreign and Security Policy (CFSP) under the Treaty on European Union (TEU), are considered.[9] Chapters II and IV set out brief historical backgrounds and general appraisals of the Community's political, economic and military involvement in the Gulf and former Yugoslavia. The multifaceted attitude of the European Parliament towards these events is then ascertained, providing examples of the EP relating to and working within the EPC and, occasionally, the EC environment.

Chapters III and V aim to shed some light on the stances taken by the political groups of the European Parliament in the Gulf and Yugoslav crises, respectively.[10] After addressing the specific contributions of the PGs and, therefore, their levels of influence in defining the EP's responses, these chapters turn towards the analysis of voting behaviour in order to measure the level of internal group cohesion as well as the extent of transnationality and voting similarity between groups. The chapters represent the analytical *loci* of the book, the core of the research pertaining to intragroup

---

      groups in the European Parliament, gathering representatives from member states' sister parties, naturally inclined to bring their own political and ideological traditions and experiences, which sometimes are hardly comparable with one another. The history and the character of Western European political parties reveal that deep-rooted national differences exist between them since they are founded on distinct historical and social backgrounds. See von Beyme (1985), Ware (1996), Allum (1995), Smith, G., (1972), Hancock et al. (1993), Mair, P. and Smith, G. (1990), Keating, M. (1994), Urwin and Paterson, eds. (1990) and Katz and Mair, eds. (1994).

8   This comprehensive examination has been conducted in order to give an updated insight on the development of European foreign policy. However, it is important to bear in mind that both case studies analyzed in this dissertation fall within the pre-Maastricht legal and political framework.

9   The CFSP constitutes the second of the three pillars on which the Europe Union is based.

10   For the list and composition of the political groups within the European Parliament during the 1990-1992 period see Tables 1a-1g in Chapter I.

cohesiveness and intergroup cooperation aimed at designing common strategies to influence and determine the EP's official position.

By summarizing and comparing the specific results which emerged in the qualitative and quantitative analysis undertaken in the above cases, an assessment can be made as to whether there is a general trend towards the formation of a genuinely supranational European Parliament and whether the EP political groups are likely to be raised to the rank of European political parties.

I   European Foreign Policy and the European Parliament

The chapter looks at the largely *sui generis* Europarliamentary environment, its configuration and organization with particular regard to its international activities. A brief outline of the reasons for the participation of the EP in the formulation and supervision of EC/EU international affairs follows. The competence gradually acquired by the EP in this field is then analysed through the following stages:

1) The Treaties of Paris and Rome
2) The Single European Act
3) The Treaty of Maastricht
4) The Treaty of Amsterdam

This examination covers the increasingly interwoven areas of EC/EU External Relations and European Political Cooperation (EPC), later replaced by the Common Foreign and Security Policy (CFSP)[11] which, in

---

11 External Relations refer to the EC/EU relations with third countries and international organizations in economic and trade issues. EPC/CFSP refers to the EC/EU political relations with third countries and international organizations, where sovereignty is fundamentally retained by all participating member states. It is appropriate to underline that, whatever the terms used External Relations versus European Political Cooperation and its successor the Common Foreign and Security Policy, Economic Relations versus Foreign Policy, and Low Politics versus High Politics, the basic distinction remains the same: while the development of foreign economic relations is derived from the provisions of the Community Treaties, the political aspects of external relations and its agreements are not contemplated in the Treaties in their original and subsequent amended form (Weiler, 1980, 154). There is a vast literature on EPC and its evolution into CFSP that includes Allen, Rummel and Wessels, eds. (1982), Allen and Pijpers, eds. (1984), Hill (1983a, 1996), Holland (1991), Ifestos (1987), Nuttall (1981-1987, 1992a, 1993), Pijpers et al., eds. (1988), Ginsberg (1989), Schoutheete (1980, 1986) and Regelsberger et al., eds. (1997).

line with the so-called *consistency* principle,[12] constitute the basis for a broad and holistic European foreign policy (Ginsberg, 1989).[13] And yet, this distinction is maintained in the chapter to reflect the diversity of the EP's functions in the Community and EPC/CFSP jurisdictions, respectively. By way of conclusion, a general appraisal of the progress EP and PGs have achieved in both areas is provided.

1. The European Parliament and its Political Groups

Among the European and international assemblies which have been created throughout history, such as the Nordic Council, the Atlantic Assembly, the Western Union Assembly and the United Nations General Assembly,[14] all of which are still in existence and operating, the European Parliament is by far the most progressive in its ambition to become the prototype of a genuine *transnational* democratic institution (Jacobs, Corbett and Shackleton, 1995, xxi). One of the EP's peculiarities is the adoption and the evolution of a group system based on political rather than national allegiance.[15] This institutionalized process of coordination of policy positions by political groups, gathering members of the same ideological tendency often from different countries, within the broad framework of the European Union, represents a significant catalysing factor for the integration process and a step forward in finding a solution to the democratic deficit of the European Union (Pridham and Pridham, 1981).

---

12 Article C of the Common Provisions of the TEU states: "The Union shall in particular ensure the consistency of its external activities as a whole in the context of its external relations, security, economic and development policies".

13 In Roy Ginsberg's words, "Foreign policy activity in the EC is a process of integrating policies and actions of the member states toward the outside world. The resulting EC policies and actions are generated toward non-members and international organizations on political, diplomatic, economic, trade, and security-related issues" (Ginsberg, 1989, 1).

14 For a historical survey of the evolution of the party groups in these assemblies, see Henig and Pinder, eds. (1969), Haas (1958, 1960) and Merkl (1964).

15 This structure was first introduced within the Common Assembly of the European Coal and Steel Community (ECSC) in 1953, the forerunner of the European Parliament, but the political groups assumed authentic political form and visibility only following the 1972 first enlargement of the European Communities and after the 1979 first direct election to the European Parliament, as it was referred to from 1962.

Despite numerous weaknesses, the political groups represent, as John Fitzmaurice argues, "an inevitable fact of modern political life", the core and the essence of parliamentary activities (Fitzmaurice, 1975, preface, xiii). With the exception of EP Rule 29, no mention was made of the existence of the PGs either in the texts of the original Treaties or in the Single European Act. Official recognition came only with the 1992 Maastricht Treaty, with the introduction of Article 138a which states that:

> Political parties at the European level are important as a factor for integration within the Union. They contribute to forming a European awareness and to expressing the political will of the citizens of the Union.[16]

Although suggesting that transnational parties enhance the process of integration by creating a new European awareness which may supersede national and nationalist thinking, this article makes only a cautious reference to the action of political parties at European level leaving "the matter of their possible setting up and operation to the discretion of civil society".[17] However, as Richard Corbett notices,

> Although the Treaty article has no direct legal consequences on the status of European political parties, its existence gives encouragement and legitimacy to the process, already underway (albeit very gradual), of strengthening the structures and procedures of transnational party political cooperation [in the European Union] (Corbett, 1994, 219).

Subsequently, the *Tsatsos Report*, which was adopted by the EP on 10 December 1996, sought "to set forth and clarify the 'constitutional' mission and framework defined by Article 138a of the Treaty for the emergence of European political parties and the manner in which their continued

---

16 The proposal of including the above article in the TEU text was advanced only at a late stage during the Maastricht negotiations by the Chairmen of the European party political federations, the former Belgian Prime Minister Wilfried Martens for the European People's Party, Guy Spitaels for the Confederation of Socialist Parties and Willy de Clercq for the Federation of the European Liberal, Democrat and Reformist Parties (Corbett, 1994, 218).

17 This view was also expressed by a minority within the Institutional Affairs Committee of the European Parliament opposing the adoption of the Tsatsos Report on the constitutional status of the European political parties of 30 October 1996.

development can be encouraged by the institutions of the European Union". The EP Report/Resolution stressed the need for regulating the legal status of the European political parties and defined the political parties as political associations represented in the European Parliament that voice opinions on aspects of European policy and international policy and are "involved in the process of expressing political will at European level in some other, comparable way" (EP 10/12/96).

2. The European Parliament's Configuration and Political Groups' Composition

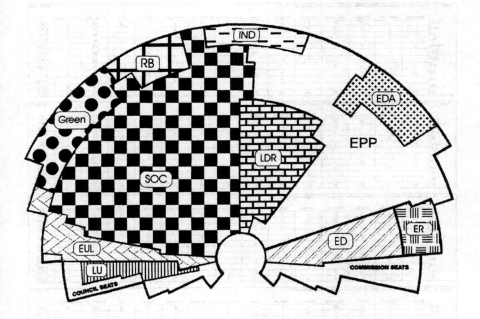

Over the years the number and the size of the political groups within the European Parliament have varied also to reflect the changes within the European Community/Union, in particular following the accession of new member states (Jacobs et al., 1992, 1995). The present EP configuration extends to 626 members from 15 countries gathered in 8 political groups, except for the Independent members. However, since the case studies analysed in the thesis cover the period between 1990-1992, this section focuses on the PGs' configuration in that specific time frame.

Tables 1a-1f   European Parliament: Group Composition and Index of Transnationality (ITc)
June 1990 - July 1992

As illustrated in Tables 1a-1f, the 1990-1992 EP spectrum was populated by 10 political groups (except for the Independent members). The *Socialists* were the most numerous and gathered MEPs from far left state interventionist to more moderate social democrat parties. In terms of size, it was closely followed by the Christian Democrats, the *European People's Party (EPP)*. Having been historically dominated by the German *Christlich Demokratische Union (CDU) Christlich-Soziale Union (CSU)* and Italian *Democrazia cristiana (DC)*, after 1989 it became far more open to the inclusion of other Community groups within its ranks. As could be expected, due to the large size of both groups, their members were representative of all 12 states of the Community. The third largest group, albeit considerably smaller, was the *Liberal, Democratic and Reformist Group (LDR)* with members of 10 different nationalities. Ideologically it was also rather heterogeneous with a combination of members from centre-right parties and a left oriented minority. It should be noted that, on 12 December 1991, the liberal leader Valéry Giscard d'Estaing left to join the Christian Democrats, after his failed attempt to establish closer links between the LDR and EPP and create a more solid centre-right within the European Parliament.[18]

However, the goal of strengthening the centre and centre-right forces, especially with a view to gaining seats in the 1994 European elections and the prospect of EU enlargement towards European Free Trade Association (EFTA) was achieved by the *European Democrats (ED)*. Consisting almost exclusively of British Conservatives, they joined the EPP as affiliated members on 1 May 1992 (Kohl, EPP Conference, 7/1991). This took place some eighteen months after the resignation of Lady Thatcher as Prime Minister and party leader in Britain, and would have been inconceivable otherwise, given her anti-federalist view and the 'rod of iron' with which she ruled. The *European Democratic Alliance (EDA)*, dominated numerically by the French Gaullists, also included members of the Irish *Fianna Fáil* party along with a few Spanish and one Greek MEPs.

Stemming from ideological schisms, the extreme left wing of the European Parliament was split into two groups the *Left Unity (LU)* and the

---

18 Other French members of the group, Alain Lamassoure, Jeannot Lacaze and Robert Hersant, followed the liberal leader into the EPP.

European Unitarian Left (EUL).[19] The former comprised members of the French, Greek and Portuguese communist parties and one MEP from the Irish Workers' Party. They shared an orthodox communist ideology and overall were hostile towards further European integration. The latter was composed essentially of members of the Italian Reformist Communist Party, the *Partito Comunista Italiano (PCI)*, which represented a strong opposition force in the complex Italian political scene at the time. In February 1991, following the Rimini conference, the party embraced new concepts of political democracy as well as a new socialist doctrine and renamed itself as the *Partito Democratico della Sinistra (PDS)*, the Democratic Party of the Left. While the German, French, British and Spanish Socialists recognized the new-born party, the Italian Socialist Chairman Bettino Craxi refused to recognize the PDS, vetoing its incorporation in the Socialist International for fear that it would interfere with the strategy of the *Italian Socialist Party (PSI)*. This prevented the EUL from merging with the Socialist group within the European Parliament right up until the beginning of 1993. This eventual increase in members of the Socialist group was aimed at counterbalancing the British Conservatives' move to the EPP group.

In addition, there were the *European Right (ER)* and the *Rainbow group*, the so-called technical groups, which incorporated members from different parties, and in the case of the latter, with even dissimilar political convictions, who joined simply in order to be able to benefit from certain administrative and economic facilities and procedural rights exclusively available to official political groups. The ER consisted almost exclusively of members from Jean-Marie Le Pen's *Front National* and the Italian *Movimento Sociale Italiano (MSI)* up until 1989, when due to the admission of a German Republican MEP with differing views over the South Tyrol issue, the MSI broke away to sit as independents. During the 1990-1992 period, it consisted of Le Pen's followers along with a few German and Belgian right-wingers. Due to their extreme nationalistic views, condoning and promoting strict immigration regulation and discriminatory laws, the ER was almost completely ostracized by other EP groups.

---

19 The two groups had experienced a difficult cohabitation within the Communist group in previous legislations, as reflected in the low level of voting cohesion of the group (Attinà, 1990).

The Rainbow group gathered members from eight different nationalities and represented a very loose political grouping, from anti-market Danes to Lombard regionalists, *Lega Lombarda*, Flemish federalist party, *Völksunie* and one Irish Independent Member. As a result, it had little political coherence and most members often spoke in their own names rather than on behalf of the group.

Following the 1989 EP election, the *Greens* made a smooth transition from being *Green Alternative European Link (GRAEL)*, a contingent of the Rainbow group, to a new independent political group in the European Parliament. Being biased towards ecological rather than political concerns, it was difficult to classify this group within the traditional left-right spectrum. Its party members were more closely aligned to left-wing elements within the EP over social issues, whilst being more closely aligned with right-wing elements in resisting further European integration.

Between June 1990 and June 1991, the configuration of the LDR, ED, Greens, EUL, EDA and LU remained unaltered while that of the EPP and Socialists varied negligibly and those of the Rainbow and the ER changed slightly.[20] Between June 1991 and July 1992 major changes occurred within the EPP with the entry of 5 French and one Spanish MEPs, followed on 1 May 1992 by the merger of the European Democrats with the EPP enlarging the group by 32 British and 2 Danish MEPs. With regard to the Socialist group no major change took place with the departure of only one Portuguese MEP, as shown in Table 1e of EP composition of April 1992. The LDR registered a decrease of 4 MEPs with 6 French deserting the group, marginally compensated by the joining of one Spanish and one German MEP. Some marginal changes occurred within the Greens which went from 29 to 27 members, the European Democratic Alliance from 22 to 20 members, the European Right from 17 to 14 members, the Rainbow Group increased from 14 to 15 and then 16 members while the number of the Independent MEPs oscillated throughout the whole period from 10 to 9 and finally 12 members.

---

20 As shown in Tables 1a-1f, the marginal numeric variations in group composition between June 1990 and July 1992 did not affect significantly the various indices of transnationality on PG composition (ITc). For the formula of ITc see Appendix.

3. The Nature and Role of Political Groups in the European Parliament

Commentators, such as Knut Heidar and Ruud Koole, refer to political groups as "organized group[s] of members of a representative body who belong to the same (extra-parliamentary) political party organization" (Heider and Koole, 1996, 6). Yet, this model becomes highly problematic when applied to the European Parliament where the majority of the PGs, not only of the so-called technical groups, "are loosely coordinated umbrella organisations linking representatives from like-minded parties but with few formal structures, no real mechanisms for party discipline, and little internal cohesion" (Marsh and Norris, 1997, 155). Unlike the national parties, PGs are not directly answerable to the electorate for their actions and EU citizens are therefore deprived of their rewarding or punishing prerogative, based on the evaluation of the PGs' performance and effective commitment to represent their own interests (Attinà, 1994, 3). As Euro-elections are still essentially based on national political affiliation rather than EP political group membership, the only constraints on the MEPs derive from their respective national party. This explains the reason why members generally look after their relationships with their home parties more attentively than with their political groups in the European Parliament (Attinà, 1995, 39). However, by virtue of a process of socialization,

> [MEPs] feel increasingly more at home within the family of their European-minded group, and isolated in their own party at home. On many issues a British Conservative MEP is nearer to a French or German Socialist of the European Parliament than to a Conservative MP from Westminster, and a French Gaullist in the EP is nearer to his Christian Democrat colleague there than to a French Gaullist at home (Ionescu, 1996, 353).

Although the political groups within the EP can be seen as the embodiment of the distinct opinions of the European citizens, an excessive party polarization can be detrimental for parliamentary efficiency and its influence on policy definition since internal disagreements may diminish the EP's ability to pressurize the Council and the Commission. For this purpose, in the 1960s and 1970s the traditional left-right dimension was discouraged as a deliberate move of "neutralizing ideology" within the

European Community and of preventing the replication of traditional national cleavages at the European level which might hamper the integration process (Weiler, 1992, 33). In addition, it was felt that in order to gain more influence and play a propulsive role in policy-making, the EP should become more cohesive rather than engage itself in a hopeless ideological struggle between its groups. Even the Socialists and the Christian Democrats recognized this fundamental need by agreeing to cooperate. The resulting oligopoly inevitably raised protests from other groups that feared remaining at the fringe of political dialogue whenever their views did not conform to the Socialist and Christian Democrat policy line. This danger appeared to have been mitigated over the period considered in this book, 1990-1992, by the fact that the ED, LDR and the EDA were politically close to the EPP, with the ED eventually joining, while the Greens and the Italian Communists held very similar views to the Socialists. As such, these groups could exert their influence by tipping the political scales (Westlake, 1994b, 187-189).

However, as strongly argued by Robert Ladrech, the striking left-right omission in the parliamentary environment, initially based on historical and functional exigencies, needs to be readdressed in order to become more visible and identifiable to the EU citizens:

> In the light of the heterogeneity of the groups and the absence of a government-opposition polarity, the left-right division could serve as the means by which public opinion comprehends not only the role of party groups within the EP but EU policy issues in general (Ladrech, 1991, 295).

4.   MEP Allegiances and Freedom of Conscience

A paradox is inherent to the office of Euro-parliamentarian between four distinct and sometimes antithetical needs: the exercise of individual political conscience in fulfilment of the principle of independence, regard for the opinion of constituents, loyalty to national party and loyalty to the political group. The last requirement, reflected in the level of group cohesion, is the object of study in Chapters III and V which investigate PGs' voting behaviour on the Gulf and Yugoslav crises, respectively.

Instructions, especially on critical votes are issued by the groups, although the so-called free vote is accepted in some cases, particularly within small groups (Jacobs et al., 1995, 92). Overall, MEPs enjoy more

21

freedom than their national counterparts and in the European Parliament there is a far less rigid whip system than in national legislatures.[21]

Rule 2 of the EP Rules of Procedure proclaims that:

> Members of the European Parliament shall exercise their mandate independently. They shall not be bound by any instructions and shall not receive a binding mandate (EP Rules of Procedure, 2/1996).

MEPs have the right to deliver their opinions by also taking into serious consideration the views of their constituents. Having faced a similar dilemma in their own time, two eminent politicians Edmund Burke and Robert Peel criticized the practice of authoritative instructions or *mandates* which represented "a fundamental mistake of the whole order" by requiring members to obey, to vote, and to argue for blindly and implicitly, regardless of "the clearest conviction of [their] judgement and conscience" (Burke, 3/11/1774 in Hill, B.W., 1975, 158). The office of parliamentarians should not be held under "servile tenure" or any other obligations but "those of consulting the public interests and of providing for the public safety" (Peel, cols. 92 and 95).

The central authority of the national political parties has extended to the European Parliament's environment due to the strong links between national and European political platforms. National parties can therefore exert their sanctioning power of expelling members and deselecting them for the following elections at national and European level. In January 1998, two Labour MEPs, Ken Coates and Hugh Kerr were expelled from the Socialist group of the European Parliament following their application to sit with the Greens as a protest against the planned welfare cuts announced by the British Labour Prime Minister Tony Blair (Butler, 17/1/98).

Again from the words of Peel, it may be seen that party dominance is not only a phenomenon of contemporary parliamentary systems:

---

21 The whip system, which stemmed from the Anglo-Saxon parliamentary tradition, is widespread in national legislatures. It aims at ensuring parliamentary attendance and supervising members' voting behaviour. (The word 'whip', originally belonging to fox-hunting terminology, refers to the rider who has the task of inducing the others to keep hunting the same fox).

..I am under a personal obligation for holding the great office which I have the honour to occupy. I see it over and over again repeated, that I was placed in that position by a party, and that the party which elevated me to my present position is powerful enough also to displace me...

Already torn between loyalty to the national party and freedom of conscience, Europarliamentarians also have to consider their relation with their political group and bear the consequences of their unjustified absences from important votes or rebellious acts, by facing disciplinary measures which may range from the exclusion from such key tasks as rapporteurs or as members of delegations to the payment of fines. While traditionally power is centralized in the case of Socialist, Communist and the Christian Democratic and Conservative parties, it appears rather diffuse in the case of the LDR, EDA and Green groups. By assessing the level of group cohesion in the Gulf and Yugoslav cases, this book also indirectly tests the accuracy of the above general statement.

As regards the conflict of loyalty between national and European obligations, it can be resolved through the logic of subsidiarity that foresees three levels of competence: local, national and European. The German MEP Klaus Hänsch and former President of the European Parliament states that he is "a European deputy, elected in Germany, in a certain region of Germany" with specific interests in his constituency, similar to those of any national deputy, and if necessary particular German national interests. And yet, he firmly believes that "the best way to serve national interests, German interests, is in cooperation and joint European policies in certain fields" (Hänsch, cited in Ionescu, 1996, 354).

5. The Foreign Affairs Activities of the European Parliament and its Political Groups

During the week before a plenary session, the national components of the political groups decide among themselves over what official position to take and if they intend to comply with their respective government's policy line (Lodge, 1988, 129). Their decisions are then discussed within the political groups in order to reach an agreement. In order to have an impact on the EP arena, individual political groups need to present a strong and unified position. This presupposes overcoming internal divisions and achieving party cohesion (Nugent, 152-153). The groups then decide who among their representatives should speak at the plenary sessions by taking into consideration the interests and expertise of individual MEPs, membership in specific committees, hierarchy principles, rotation and other general factors. It must be noted that the amount of speaking time afforded to MEPs is relatively limited if compared to that granted to representatives of most national legislative assemblies.[22] This is mainly due to the vast number of political alignments present in Strasbourg and to the fact that the EP operates in periodic as opposed to permanent sessions.[23] At the end of the debate members can make brief personal statements on certain topics in order to reply to remarks that have been unfairly addressed to them, to clarify their position or to notify the House of a change of attitude in the light of new factors which have emerged (Rule 108 EP Rules of Procedure).[24] Sometimes the plenary session can be suspended when additional elements arise in order to enable the political groups to debate them. In fact, as Karlheinz Neunreither highlights, "no important matter is treated in plenary sessions without having been discussed previously by the political groups" (Neunreither, 1960, 484).

At the end of these meetings, the leaders of the various groups convene to consult each other over the various major topics on the agenda and to

---

22 The President, in agreement with the Chairmen of the PGs, allocates a fixed speaking time for each debate prior to the opening of the part-session. Rule 83 of EP Procedures set the guidelines (based on the d'Hondt system) for such distribution between members with a first small fraction of time equally divided among political groups and an additional and larger fraction allocated in accordance with the size of the political group. Time is awarded to the Independent MEPs on the basis of the percentage given to the other political groups. This is then doubled in order to take into consideration the different opinions of these members. See Corbett et al., 1995, 145.

23 Further sessions can exceptionally be convened by the President, at the request of one third of MEPs or at the request of the Commission or the Council.

24 Rule 85, EP Rules of Procedures, February 1992 now Rule 108 Rules of Procedures, February 1996 (unmodified text) states:
"1. A member who asks to make a personal statement shall be heard at the end of the discussion of the item of the agenda dealt with or when the minutes of the sitting to which the request for leave to speak refers are considered for approval.
2. The Member concerned may not speak on substantive matters but shall confine his observations to rebutting any remarks that have been attributed to him, or to correcting observations that he himself has made.
3. Unless Parliament decides otherwise, no personal statement shall last for more than three minutes".

negotiate the list of the urgent and topical questions to be discussed. This debate which takes place on Thursdays, represents an opportunity for MEPs to express their views on current international issues and attracts the attention of the media as well as the governments of the third countries concerned. In addition, it is noteworthy for privileging the role of political groups to that of the committees: by virtue of Rule 47 of the EP Rules of Procedure, a political group or at least 29 MEPs can request a debate on topical and urgent subjects if linked to a motion for a resolution regarding human rights, natural disasters and international crises. Although the choice and order of these issues is usually the result of compromise between the large groups, it is not impossible even for a small group to object (Jacobs et al., 1995, 157, 273).

By this stage, common texts are often agreed between the various groups, showing that the coalition-building process starts much earlier than the actual submission of the motions for resolutions at the plenary, in order to facilitate their adoption and generally to improve parliamentary efficiency in view of the EP's increased workload (Grunert interview, 24/1/1996). No group individually can reach a majority in the European Parliament, hence coalitions are necessary for any decision. Whilst this does not imply necessarily that coalitions have to be built prior to submitting any text to the plenary, previous consultations certainly ease the process and enhance the prospect of the motion being approved (Rocard written interview, 22/7/1995). This necessity is especially felt by small groups, as the Greek left-wing MEP, Alexandros Alavanos, confirmed (Alavanos written interview).

Negotiations are carried out, debates held, working parties occasionally established and meetings between groups' leaders also organized to find out whether joint resolutions can be drafted. Political groups can request roll-call votes in order to record their positions on specific issues, to monitor members' compliance with the group line or to embarrass other groups by forcing them to reveal their opinions publicly (Jacobs et al., 1995, 160, Westlake, 1994b, 189). Roll-call votes can also bear the symbolic function of celebrating parliamentary consensus on certain questions (Attinà, 1986, 138).

The main objective of the political groups is to formulate stances encouraging the House to translate them into the European Parliament's official policy. If strong intragroup and intergroup discrepancies persist and cannot be healed, the ability of the European Parliament to influence the Council is greatly weakened. By contrast, the chance that a parliamentary resolution may become the object of real interest by the Council can be increased if the House reaches a substantial majority (Lodge, 1988, 129). In this sense, the creation of political groups can assist to promote the achievement of parallel national, supranational and international political aims, through a process of 'Europeanization' and socialization.

PGs also play a decisive part in the internal organization of the European Parliament, particularly in the appointment of the members of the Standing Committees and of inter-parliamentary delegations. There are three committees and two subcommittees which cover various aspects of the EU foreign policy: the Foreign and Security Committee, previously known as Political Affairs Committee with its Subcommittees on Security and Disarmament and on Human Rights, the External Economic Committee and the Development Committee. The first can draft recommendations to the Council in its areas of responsibility after obtaining authorization from the Conference of Presidents and upon receipt of a proposal tabled by a political group or at least by 29 members (Rule 46). In urgent cases, the authorization from the Conference of Presidents is provided by the President who can also authorize an emergency meeting of the committee concerned (Rule 92). The Subcommittee on Human Rights prepares a detailed yearly Report on the situation of human rights in the various regions of the world (Jacobs et al., 1995, 106, 108-109, 289). The External Economic Committee deals with trade and commercial agreements with third countries, whilst the Development Committee monitors EU policy with developing countries, the application of the Lomé Conventions with ACP countries, tables resolutions calling for emergency and food aid and for a more open North-South dialogue (Westlake, 1994b, 210-211). Although often their activities overlap, a net division of competence is maintained between committees, reflecting the Community/CFSP pillar structure.

Proposals for recommendations enclosing brief explanatory statements and, if relevant, the opinions of the committees consulted are then submitted to Parliament prior to being forwarded to the Council (Rule 46). In order to express its opinion in foreign policy, the EP often requires an in-depth study on a specific subject, a task which is imparted to competent committees.

The European Parliament also accommodates delegations that represent important parliamentary bodies closely involved in the EU international activities through consultation - mainly with members of the parliaments of third countries. These delegations, which meet regularly in the country concerned or in the Union, represent a valuable source of information: they represent what David Millar defines as "the eyes and ears of the European Parliament" (Millar, 1991, 148). The members of the delegations are selected in order to include representatives of most political groups. Unlike the committees, delegations do not have the right to accede or present reports to plenary, but they can introduce reports to the Conference of the Presidents which forwards them, for information, to the competent committee (Neunreither, 1990, 172). While the plenary sessions remain as "a publicity vehicle for the EP", decisions are informally but effectively negotiated by the political groups at committee level (Miles, 12).

In the fulfilment of their functions, the members of the political groups are assisted by officials who pursue administrative tasks, draft working documents and liaise with sister parties of the various members states or even with third countries (Jacobs et al., 1995, 88). Despite the introduction of EP direct elections, the different electoral procedures of the various member states and the drafting of national lists have so far hindered the realization of the Europeanization process.

6. Reasons for the Participation of the European Parliament in Foreign Policy

More than forty years after the establishment of the Treaty of Rome and almost twenty years after its first direct elections, the European Parliament remains obscure to many of its citizens who feel distanced from the European political platform. Popular indifference, reflected in the poor turnout to the EP election, is largely the direct consequence of the minimal attention devoted by national media to the EP activities, particularly with regard to foreign affairs. And yet, advances in technology, allowing instant media coverage from the remotest corners of the world, have led to

> [an] increase in influence of the masses of people over governments, together with greater awareness on the part of leaders of aspirations of people, brought about by the new dimension for foreign policy operation. Certain foreign policy objectives can be pursued by dealing directly with the people of foreign countries, rather than with their governments. Through the use of modern instruments and techniques of communications it is possible today to reach large or influential segments of national populations - to inform them, to influence their attitudes, and at times

perhaps even to motivate them to a particular course of action. These groups, in turn, are capable of exerting noticeable, even decisive, pressures, on their government (88th US Congress Report, 1964).

This statement, delivered in April 1964 by the US Congress, seems to be accurate now more than ever before. Since it is important that European citizens' views are taken into account whenever crucial foreign and security issues are at stake, the European Parliament has the task of giving voice to popular concerns and of exerting its influence over the Council and the Commission in both external economic and political relations of the European Community/Union (Grunert interview, 24/1/1996).

Yet, despite the changes introduced consecutively by the Single European Act, the Maastricht and Amsterdam Treaties, the EP remains at the margin of decision-making on international affairs, due in part to the nature of foreign policy and security "whose characteristics, confidentiality and rapidity, are difficult to reconcile with the functioning of a parliamentary body" (EP Institutional Affairs Committee, 21/1/1992, 23). For these reasons, most national legislative assemblies have resigned themselves to playing a limited role in their governments' conduct of international affairs. In some member states, such as Great Britain and France, the impact of national parliaments on foreign policy can be even more modest than that of the European Parliament (Viola, 1997, 112-114). However, as Jörg Monar aptly observes, the absence of effective parliamentary participation in foreign affairs at the national level can be counterbalanced by the fact that mono-coloured governments not relying on a significant majority of their own party representatives and, in particular, coalition governments relying on the support of various political alignments, normally avoid adopting foreign policy positions contrary to the opinion of their respective parliaments for fear of being censured (Monar, 1993, 1). Conversely, the EP is deprived of such a power over the Council. As such, any shift of power from national to central government can appear as a threat to sovereignty and democracy within the member states (Weiler, 1980, 157-158). It can be argued that the need for developing the European Parliament's scrutinizing powers on the executive for the sake of democracy seems pointless because democratic control is already exerted at the national level where members states' governments are still responsible to their own parliaments. However, when decisions are taken collectively by governments at European level, especially with the wider use of majority voting, it is exceedingly difficult for national

28

parliaments to exert any form of effective control. Increased EP supervisory powers become vital to guarantee the democratic accountability of this policy-making process and to compensate the loss of accountability to national parliaments (Williams, 1991, 155). Unfortunately, the EP strives to increase its influence have been viewed suspiciously by other EC-EU institutions and regarded by national legislatures as an attempt to encroach on their already rather limited powers (Monar, 1993, 1). Similarly, MEPs from various political groups have sought to develop relationships with their national counterparts, but their communication channels have often been sabotaged by antagonistic attitudes taken by national parliamentarians (Lodge, 1996, 202, 203).

The absence of an official government-opposition structure can be, nevertheless, an advantage as there is no parliamentary engagement to assist the Council and its members can express freely their views on international issues by either supporting or criticizing the stances taken by the Council and the Commission (Attinà, 1994, 3, Monar, 1993, 4, Viola, 1994, 5).

7. The Development of the Powers of the European Parliament in the Context of Foreign Policy

7.1 Community Treaties

a) External Relations
The Paris and Rome Treaties of 1951 and 1957, respectively establishing the European Coal and Steel Community (ECSC), European Economic Community (EEC) and European Atomic Energy Community (EURATOM), initially granted a very confined consultative role to the Common Assembly over the conclusion of association agreements under Article 238 EEC. Subsequently, in order to respond to parliamentary demands for a closer involvement in the process of concluding agreements the *Luns* and *Westerterp* procedures were introduced in 1964 and 1973, respectively whereby the European Parliament would hold a debate prior to the opening of negotiations of association and trade agreements with third countries, the Commission would regularly inform Parliament and competent committees on the progress of the negotiations of association and trade agreements and the Council would communicate to Parliament

29

the content of the agreements prior to their conclusion (MacLeod, 1996, 98, Nuttall, 1992, 57).

In 1982, the two procedures, simply referred to as the *Luns-Westerterp procedure*, extended to the negotiations of accession treaties and all international agreements which had important repercussions on the formulation and application of Community policies, even if not explicitly indicated by the Community Treaties. Finally, in the event of strong EP opposition to the conclusion of these treaties, the Council agreed to open a political discussion between the three institutions.

7.2 Single European Act

a) External Relations

Under the Single European Act, the role of the EP remained predominantly that of non-binding consultation, except for the conclusion of commercial agreements where no EP involvement was foreseen. The Council was expected to adopt international agreements in the field of research and technological development in cooperation with the Parliament (Art. 130q §2 EEC). However, when in 1986 Parliament revised its Rules of Procedure to incorporate the SEA provisions, it sought to expand its consultative powers to all international agreements by adopting a wide interpretation.

The SEA also introduced the *assent procedure* under which the EP had a final say on the conclusion of association agreements (Article 238 EEC) and membership agreements (Article 237 EEC). The Parliament's decisions, if reached by an absolute majority of its component members, were regarded as fully binding. Certainly, this represented a turning point for the EP in its struggle for power in the EC's international affairs. This assent procedure proved to be an important instrument for Parliament to assert its political priorities and as a bargaining tool to exercise influence over the decisions of member states' foreign ministers on EPC topics. Over the years, the EP made use of this power, rejecting on the ground of human rights violations the adoption of several financial protocols to association agreements with Turkey in December 1987, Israel following the events in the West Bank and Gaza in March 1988, Morocco in February 1992 and Syria twice, in February and October 1992 (Corbett, 1988).

Despite the progress achieved, the SEA failed to resolve an important issue relating to external relations: the EP's right to request directly the

European Court of Justice (ECJ) to deliver its opinion on the compatibility of concluded international agreements with EC Law (Article 228 (1) EEC). Yet, during the negotiations leading to the signing of the European Economic Area Treaty (EEA), strong pressure from the EP succeeded in forcing the Commission to refer the draft Treaty to the Court of Justice for an opinion as to whether it conformed with the constitutional principles of the Treaty (Prout, 1992, 3).

b) European Political Cooperation
By the beginning of the 1970s, member states started to realize that it was increasingly unrealistic to pursue external economic relations without any harmonious and parallel agreements on political and diplomatic aspects. A process of information, consultation, concertation and joint action, known as European Political Cooperation (EPC) started to take shape among the member states.[25] However, it was not until the signing of the Single European Act (SEA) in 1986 that EPC was formally institutionalized and the need for the EP to be "associated" with EPC proceedings recognized:

> The High Contracting Parties shall ensure that the European Parliament is closely associated with European Political Cooperation. To that end the Presidency shall regularly inform the European Parliament of the foreign policy issues which are being examined within the framework of Political Cooperation and shall ensure that the views of the European Parliament are duly taken into consideration (Title III, Art. 30.4 SEA).

Due to pressures exerted by Parliament in the various reports, among which were the *Vedel, Blumenfeld, Elles and Martin Reports,*[26] member states' governments agreed to confirm some pre-existing procedures relating to EPC such as the Presidency's address to Parliament covering both EC and EPC issues at the beginning and the end of its term-in-office as well as after each European Council meeting; Annual written report to Parliament on progress achieved in the EPC sphere; Council Presidency's colloquia with the EP Political Affairs Committee, renamed as the EP

---

25 For an extensive discussion on the EP's role in European Political Cooperation from the latter's inception in the 1970s up to the ratification of the Single European Act see Stavridis, 1991, 331-343.

26 Vedel Report of 1972, Blumenfeld Report of 1977, Lady Elles Report of 1978, Martin Reports I, II and III of 14 March 1990, 11 July 1990 and 22 November 1990, respectively.

Committee on Foreign Affairs and Security from January 1992, and Presidency's replies to EP oral and written questions on EPC (EPC Bulletin, Doc. 86/090). However, this final EP right was effectively 'discovered' as a means of obtaining an official reaction to parliamentary views only in 1989. The Presidency, represented by his foreign minister, was required to answer oral questions posed by parliamentarians at Question Time, which was extended to foreign policy issues in 1975 (Lodge, 1983a, 33). The European Parliament succeeded in inducing the Council to provide some feedback to MEPs on international questions following EPC/CFSP meetings. In the event that the Presidency was unable to answer all the questions on the agenda, replies were to be given in writing and published in the Annex to the Official Journal of the European Communities.

In addition, the possibility was introduced of convening special meetings at ministerial level with the appropriate parliamentary committee on specific EPC issues. However, in practice, only a few ever took place due, inter alia, to the difficulty of arranging additional meetings on the already overburdened agenda of Foreign Ministers. Finally, the Presidency committed itself to transmit swiftly to the EP all declarations adopted in the context of EPC, a task that was subsequently facilitated by the creation of the EPC Secretariat in 1987.

As regards the expression "due consideration" contained in Article 30 SEA, the Danish President-in-office Uffe Ellemann-Jensen made clear in September 1987 that it was to be interpreted only in the sense of taking notice of EP resolutions, without any obligation of the member states to comply with EP opinions. This view was not shared by the Spanish EC Presidency, in office during the first semester of 1989, which expressed its intention to look more attentively at EP views on foreign policy issues by organizing special information meetings between the EP Political Affairs Committee Bureau and the Political Director of the Presidency and by sending to the EP written observations with respect to parliamentary positions on EPC topics (Monar, 1993, 2-3, Dupagny, 1992, 26-27). Another important step to enhance the parliamentary cause was taken in November 1989 when, in a joint session with Chancellor Kohl, François Mitterand addressed the European Parliament on foreign policy, "the first serving President of the European Council to do so" (Clark, 1992, 158, Note 14).

Despite the progress in the Parliament-Presidency dialogue over EPC, most of the improvements introduced by the SEA depended entirely on the willingness of the Presidency without involving definite mutual legal and official inter-institutional commitments. The European Parliament could "not oblige the Foreign Minister of the Presidency to be present at topical debates on foreign policy issues" (Nuttall, 1992, 57). In order to be able to address oral or written questions to Ministers, MEPs had to submit them at least five weeks prior to the opening of Parliament's sitting (EP Rule 58.2, Rule 59.1). Replies to written questions were relatively slow in arriving and often far too general. The three-monthly colloquia with the Political Affairs/Foreign Affairs and Security Committee represented the occasion for obtaining more substantial information. These colloquia could not serve any purpose since the Foreign Minister divulged information only after the events had taken place (Penders, 1988, 43). Finally the outcome of these meetings was strictly connected with the personal attitude of the ministerial interlocutor and Parliament was still unable to influence topical foreign policy issues (Nuttall, 1992, 57).

7.3 Treaty on European Union

a) External Relations
The Maastricht Treaty confirmed the consultation procedure as the basic form of EP participation in External Relations. The European Court of Justice specified that failure on the part of the Council to consult Parliament when requested by the Treaty represented a clear procedural breach. In principle, the Council had to take into account parliamentary opinion and required a fresh consultation in the event that the text finally adopted varied substantially from the text submitted to Parliament.

Under the TEU, parliamentary assent, reached by an absolute majority of votes cast, was extended from the association agreements to a wider category of treaties which involved a close cooperation with third countries and had important financial implications for the Community. However, the value of parliamentary right of assent was reduced by allowing the Council to suspend agreements to which the EP had assented without previously consulting it.

By virtue of its financial powers, the European Parliament could reject the annual budget and amend non-compulsory expenditure, impelling and even determining financial priorities in the context of External Relations and the financing of aid projects to third countries.

33

b) Common Foreign and Security Policy

Whilst reiterating many of the rules previously established under the European Political Cooperation mechanism, the Treaty on European Union sought to bring about improvements in this sphere, by replacing it with a new framework named the Common Foreign and Security Policy (CFSP).

> The Presidency shall consult the European Parliament on the main aspects and the basic choices of the common foreign and security policy and shall ensure that the views of European Parliament are duly taken into consideration (Article J.7 TEU).

However, the vagueness of the expressions 'main aspects' and 'basic choices,' left the application of the consultation mechanisms open to wide interpretation. In addition, no clause specified that this consultation should take place prior to Council's decision, as implied by Parliament and at least accepted by the Portuguese Presidency of 1992, which also seemed inclined to assume that the Council was obliged to ask EP opinion on specific issues before taking a decision. In its resolution of 23 October 1992, Parliament stressed that it should be informed not only on the majority of the Council's positions prior to their adoption, but also on all related information. Nevertheless, the EP acknowledged the peculiar nature of foreign policy and its requirements for immediacy and secrecy, by suggesting the involvement of the Committee of Foreign Affairs and Security and its Bureau rather than the plenary to ensure prompt EP response to Council's positions without jeopardizing their confidentiality (Annex VII, EP Rules of Procedure, 10/1993).[27]

In a subsequent resolution of 2 February 1993, Parliament specified that "the Council should consult the Committee on Foreign Affairs and Security in advance, possibly via the committee's bureau, on the joint positions it intends to adopt and the joint measures it plans to take", giving thereby the Parliament "the opportunity of expressing reservations on a particular text before it is made public" (*Roumeliotis Report*, 2/2/1993). The European Parliament deplored the fact that the TEU provisions relating

---

27 Annex VII of the EP Rules of Procedure states that if proceedings at committee level are declared confidential the number of people present can be restricted, documents shall be distributed at the beginning of the meeting and collected again at the end without any note taken and that the minutes of the meeting shall make no mention of the item discussed under the confidential procedure.

to the CFSP were "based on an intergovernmental approach which reduced [its] involvement to the mere right to be heard and informed and to the possibility of making non-binding recommendations to the Council.." (*Poettering Report*, 1994, 9).

With the introduction of Article 228a EC, the Treaty on European Union provided for the Council's adoption of economic sanctions and therefore "the interruption or reduction of relations with a third country [in order] to force or encourage that country to take or desist from a course of action" (MacLeod, Hendry and Hyett, 1996, 352). Sanctions, regarded by far the most effective instrument of EC external relations under international law, were adopted by the member states under the remit of the TEU as a CFSP measure, clearly highlighting the overlap between the two areas. Although the reason for such a course of action is strictly a matter of foreign and security policy which therefore falls outside the Community sphere, the means of achieving these measures belong to the commercial field which falls within Community competence. Nonetheless, EP opinion was still not required. In addition, it became evident that although the quantity of information made available to the EP had increased under the CFSP mechanism compared with the EPC one, its quality had not improved substantially, remaining often vague and imprecise. Whilst the CFSP structure was seen as "mitigating the absence of a European foreign policy" and despite the bridges between the two pillars, the EC and the CFSP, regarding collective action, the problem of parliamentary accountability remained unresolved (Prout, 1992, 11).

As a way to increase its weight in the domain of foreign policy, the EP could use other instruments in its possession such as budgetary powers on the CFSP administrative and possibly operational costs[28] (Monar, 1993, 4). The EP could resort to its power of dismissal against the Commission which shares with the Council the right of initiating issues in the context of international politics. Theoretically, it could even use the motion of no-confidence against the Commission as a sign of retaliation against Council and the member states that appointed the Commission. Although the *Verde I Aldea Report* stressed the strategic importance of effectively using this power, in practice, however, the EP never resorted to such a

---

28 Article J 11 (2) TEU stated that CFSP administrative costs will be charged to the EC budget, while the operational costs will be charged either to the budget of the EU member states or, upon unanimous decision of the Council, to the EC budget.

drastic measure which requires the approval of a two-thirds majority (*Verde I Aldea Report*, October 1992). It is unclear what would happen if it were exercised and if the EP objected to the reappointment of the same Commission by the members states, generating an impasse. In addition, parliamentary ability and inclination to proceed against the Commission is narrowed by the fact that the EP and the Commission consider themselves as natural allies sharing an interest in the supranational EU development.

In its Resolution on the European Council report for 1991 on progress towards European Union, the European Parliament drew attention "to the significant shortcomings in the Treaty (..), whose structure, based on 'pillars', fails to incorporate into the EC Treaty the common foreign and security policy." Overall, the CFSP did not differ to a very great extent from EPC, nor did the position of the European Parliament change significantly in the two areas of EU's foreign affairs: External Relations and CFSP.

The Treaty on European Union did not address the relationship between the legislative and the executive, where the executive was represented by two institutions, the Commission and the Council. The decision to maintain the Commission as the official representative of the European Union regarding the negotiation of economic and trade agreements with third countries and the Council when dealing with CFSP issues, contributed to the confusion surrounding the EU institutional framework and diminished the credibility of the Union.

7.4 Treaty of Amsterdam

"The long night of Amsterdam closed on a note of bitter disappointment" for those who expected far more daring and radical steps towards to the realization of a federal Union (Dini, 1997, xxvii). The Treaty that emerged from the European Council Summit in June 1997 was formally signed in October 1997 and entered into force on the 1 May 1997 after ratification by all member states' national parliaments. The text epitomized the talent of politicians "for bridging seemingly unbridgeable (..) differences (..) or papering them over" (*Common Market Law Review*, Vol. 34, 1997, 767).

a) External Relations
Pursuant to Article 300 TEC (ex Article 228), the parliamentary right to information is extended to any decision in the field of external trade policy,

including the provisional application and the suspension of agreements with third countries. In addition, the Article provides for parliamentary consultation of international agreement However, as *Mendez de Vigo and Tsatsos Report* stresses, EP consultation is envisaged only after the Council has reached a decision with no chance for Parliament to exert any kind of influence (*Mendez de Vigo and Tsatsos Report*, 5/11/1997, 41, 43). Overall, the EP's involvement in the formulation and negotiation stages of international agreements remains marginal as well as its ability to influence their principle and content.

b) Common Foreign and Security Policy
The attempt to develop further a European foreign policy failed since the CFSP's intergovernmental essence remained unaltered. During the 1996 Intergovernmental Conference (IGC), Parliament proposed its own designs and strategies and stressed the importance of gradually replacing intergovernmental procedures of the CFSP with Community ones based on a qualified majority voting in the Council rather than unanimity (*Poettering Report*, A3-0109/94). In the EP's view, the revision proposed in Amsterdam was "confined to *enhancing,* up to a certain point [its] *right to information and nothing further"*. No effective change occurred with regard to its involvement in Common Foreign and Security Policy, which remained largely outside its sphere of influence and therefore not "subject to fully democratic and controllable decision-making procedures" (EP Resolution, 11/3/1993, 39).

In compliance with the new obligation pursuant to the inter-institutional agreement on the CFSP finance, parliamentary consultation is introduced to the Council's annual document on the main aspects and basic choices of the CFSP, including the financial implications for the Community expenditure. Being realistic, the EP did not seek codecision power in the CFSP or the right of dismissal over foreign ministers. And yet, ironically, its modest attitude was not rewarded considering that even a parliamentary request for obtaining an effective power of consultation, especially on the Presidency's negotiation of agreements on behalf of the EU was not fully met in Amsterdam.

> Just as the EP is assigned an insignificant role in the CFSP decision-making process (merely an enhanced right of information), the new Treaty totally ignores the EP - as usual - when agreements are being concluded in the intergovernmental sphere. Obviously, this is unacceptable

37

for the EP, and only a change in the legal nature of this pillar can really resolve the problem (EP Report, 15/7/1997, 39).

This change would imply a merge of the two pillars and a single external representation of the Union. From the European Parliament perspective the Commission would be preferable because of its accountability to the European Parliament while the Presidency of the Council could easily evade serious parliamentary scrutiny at national and supranational levels (Allott, 1997, 13). This along with other reforms strongly advocated by the European Parliament, was ignored by the member states who decided instead to maintain the separation between the two areas and to assign the Presidency, assisted by the Secretary-General of the Council, the task of representing the Union in the sphere of the CFSP (Article 18 TEC, ex Article J.8).

In relation to general responsibility on revenue, Parliament did not make any progress in terms of achieving full equal rights with the Council. Yet, it managed to prevent the adoption of the proposal of including the CFSP operational costs under compulsory expenditure, which would have resulted in a significant reduction of its power (Mendez de Vigo and Tsatsos Report, 5/9/1997, 46). Although substantial limits persist on its capabilities in the CFSP, EP may still make use of those devices and levers, such as assent power over association and cooperation agreements and the budget power, previously mentioned, to persuade and bring pressure on the Council and the Commission and maximize its influence on EU foreign affairs. Finally, the European Parliament can resort to its 'ace', legally non-recognizable yet politically powerful, that is, acting as a moral force and conscience in the international society. It can offer an international and official platform for foreign leaders, public figures or members of opposition parties from totalitarian countries, allowing them to denounce facts and events which would otherwise remain unknown to the political world and the general public.

After instructing the appropriate committees to carry out investigations and its delegations to undertake visits to the countries concerned, the EP can take overt and critical stances against EU member states' as well as third countries' governments. These can be a cause of great embarrassment to the latter and damage EU member state governments' general reputation for competence. To provide just two examples: the Dalai Lama's address to the European Parliament raised public awareness of the Tibetan question and attracted world condemnation of the Chinese government, while the speech of Yasser Arafat, the leader of the Palestinian Liberation Organization (PLO), increased sympathy for the sufferings of the Palestinian population in Israeli occupied territories (Neunreither, 1990, 177, Elles, J., 1990, 72).

8. Decision-Making in Foreign Policy: the Role of the European Parliament and its Political Groups

The fundamental problem of the European Parliament in aspiring to participate in foreign policy-making consists in the largely declamatory character of its functions in international relations. Although it might seem wishful thinking and, to a certain extent, advantageous for the European Council Presidency to be sustained by the EP over foreign affairs, this support is neither legally nor politically required. Parliamentary opinions and resolutions in this domain are not binding on the European Council which is not accountable to the European Parliament. Notwithstanding the progress achieved in the relationship between the Council and the Parliament in terms of briefing and communication, as previously seen, there continues to be a substantial information and consultation deficit between the two institutions as the Council is still far from taking into consideration parliamentary opinion. Political groups working on their account either in competition or in cooperation with others can fill, to a certain extent, this lacuna (Lodge, 1988, 127-129).

As to the method and the modalities according to which the major party groups operate in order to influence foreign issues, it emerges that the various groups compete among themselves to determine the EP's official policy or to sway a committee in a certain direction by requesting an urgent debate, where a good knowledge and insight into issues in question can be an advantage. In addition, "the mere existence of a party group does not imply that it will be easy to secure consensus within that group as to what the official party line should be" (Lodge, 1988, 128). Within the political groups it is possible to reconcile differences of views and temper extreme opinions in order to achieve a consensus based on political rather than national terms. Their efforts to overcome national barriers by an exchange of views among its MEPs are maximized when dealing with foreign affairs issues, since the individual members' contributions derive from distinctive cultural, historical and geopolitical sensitivities to the questions at hand (Silvestro, 1974).

39

As Simon Hix argues:

> When the EU agenda includes [foreign] questions, (..) a system of articulation in the main decision-making arenas based on national government representation is inadequate [to respond to external challenges and to link] between public wishes and political outputs. This is where transnational parties could play a role (Hix, 1995b, 537).

The presence of political parties constitutes a key factor for enhancing a process of politicization within the European Union. On several occasions, the EP political groups have played a major part in foreign policy. For example, the Socialists have developed links with sister parties outside the EC and contacts with member states' national parties within the ambit of the Socialist Confederation. Even prior to the EP direct elections, they sent delegations to Sweden, Norway, Austria, Portugal and Malta, providing financial assistance to Portuguese and Spanish Socialist parties in their respective election campaigns to restore democracy (Pridham and Pridham, 1981, 72).

EP political groups have direct and frequent contacts with their Latin American fraternal parties, sharing historical, cultural and ideological traditions (Neunreither, 1990, 172-173, 175). With the aim of promoting "a pluralistic society based on free elections" and "respect of human rights" in the area, the PGs stressed the necessity of establishing a parliamentary interlocutor in the region during a series of visits to various Latin American countries. Since 1974, delegations of the European Parliament and the Latin American Parliament (LAP) have gathered to address topical subjects, although the latter gained its official status only in 1987 (Neunreither, 1990, 175-176).

As the British Conservative MEP James Elles argues, another "example of the informal but emergent foreign policy role of the European Parliament" can be found in its relationship with the Congress of the United States of America, which has developed a similar kind of dialogue only with the Canadian and Mexican Parliaments (Elles, J., 1990, 72). Since 1979 biannual meetings have taken place alternately in Europe and the United States between the European Parliament and the American Congress in order to exchange opinions on three major areas: trade, security and institutional matters. During these visits to Washington, the EP delegation also meets representatives of US Administration as well as members of the Trades Unions (Palmer, M., 1981, 49-50).

Since the creation of the ASEAN[29] inter-parliamentary organization meetings with the European Parliament take place annually alternating the site between ASEAN countries and the EU (Neunreither, 1990, 177). Periodic meetings also take place between representatives of the Japanese Legislative Assembly, the Diet, and the Parliament (Budd, 1991, 144). Despite the absence of official parliamentary contacts with the Arab world, members of numerous political groups have regular meetings with Arab parliamentarians within the Euro-Arab parliamentary intergroup session (Monar, 1993, 5). While the validity of these meetings has yet to be proved, they remain important for the European Parliament given the scarcity of information about the activities of the numerous regional committees of the Council in Latin America, the Middle East and other areas, provided sometimes only through leaks or via the Commission (Grunert interview, 24/1/1996).

Visits of Socialist and later Christian Democrat MEPs to several Central and Eastern European countries contributed to opening the dialogue between the European Community and the countries of the former Warsaw Pact, laying the basis for the signature of the EEC-Comecon (CMEA) common declaration of 25 June 1988 (Groux and Manin, 1985, 70). In the absence of certain necessary preconditions, for instance the mutual diplomatic recognition between the then European Economic Community and the seven countries of the former Eastern bloc, the European Parliament was prevented from acting in any official capacity. Against this background, the unofficial role of the political groups was crucial in preparing the ground for this recognition by the Central and Eastern European countries and for a new attitude of the then Soviet bloc to European integration (Neunreither, 1990, 173). Finally, in September 1988, Lord Plumb, who was at that time President of the European Parliament, was able to make his first official visit to the Supreme Soviet (Silvestro, 1989, 309). Since EEC recognition and especially following the fall of the communist régimes in Central and Eastern Europe, formal parliamentary relationships have developed and intensified with these countries with the aim of assisting them in their democratization process and of guiding them in the preparatory stages for acquiring full EU membership.

Most political groups cultivate relationships with NGOs in many countries to support campaigns against the violation of human rights. They

---

29 Association of South East Asian Nations (ASEAN).

represent a key factor in developing and deepening links with corresponding parties in third countries as well as channels of information. On the basis of this accurate and constant flow of news, the PGs and ultimately the EP can take positions condemning the policies of countries responsible for human rights abuses and attempt to exert pressure for the release of political prisoners as well as to save human lives (Silvestro, 1996, 4).

Political groups share the ambition of defending human rights and fundamental freedoms. For instance in 1973, following General Pinochet's coup in Chile, the EP President, reflecting the combined concerns of all political groups, expressed deep "concern at the events" and called for a return to democracy. Chile's situation was condemned along with, "the restrictions on civil liberties in the [former] Soviet Union" (OJEC Annex 165, 8, cited in Gaja, 1980, 199). This strategy of denouncing at the same time violations of human rights in various parts of the world, preferably belonging to different geopolitical areas, is adopted to accommodate concerns arising from both wings of Parliament (Gaja, 1980, 199-201). In the past while the Socialists tended to focus their criticisms primarily on right-wing totalitarian régimes of Latin American countries, such as Argentina, Chile and Nicaragua, the Christian Democrats censured mostly the communist dictatorships of Central and Eastern European Countries (Silvestro interview, 1996). Resolutions on human rights seem to enjoy a wide agreement due perhaps to the EP's determination to project externally an image of a united and coherent institution capable of exerting a moral force (Attinà, 1992, 120-124). Inevitably, the priority given to the factor of 'efficiency' as opposed to 'democracy' can obscure party identity and alter the voting behaviour of its members:

> in [these] circumstances, intra-group cohesiveness as such may lose most of its meaning, at least as an indicator of Euro-party institutionalization, particularly because inter-group differences would themselves be blurred (Bardi, 1994, 368).

These general considerations may be useful in the analysis of the reaction of the EP and PGs to the Gulf and Yugoslav crises which follows in the next chapters.

Conclusion

The above portrayal of the European Parliament has highlighted the unique character of this institution, different from any typical national parliament or international assembly. As Richard Corbett emphasizes, the European Parliament is the forum

> *par excellence* where politicians from different Member States are in regular contact. No other group of politicians in Europe is in such constant contact with colleagues from other Member States. Inevitably, exchanges of ideas between political parties of similar views, between members interested in the same issues and between the political élites generally, pass through the EP (Corbett, 1998, 71).

The combination of unofficial initiatives pursued by political groups and official measures taken by the European Parliament make it a resourceful and privileged body which relies on instruments and opportunities other institutions do not enjoy (Neunreither, 1990, 184). As such, the European Parliament can support and foster the evolution of this politicization process and ensure a more incisive and effective impact on European policy-making in all areas, not least in foreign affairs (Lodge, 1983a, 40).

By contrast, an Italian axiom reveals the other side of the coin of party politicization where political parties, which represent the quintessence of Europarliamentary life, become 'a necessary evil' (un male necessario) or even an 'incurable illness' (un male inguaribile) common to contemporary democracies (Silvestro interview, 1996).

In addition, the chapter confirms the old prejudice surrounding governments' exclusive role in foreign policy, to be exercised in total secrecy and away from the 'intrusions' of representative organs and the public eye. EU Ministers exercise their foreign policy-making independently from the European Parliament, especially in the field of CFSP which is still a broad framework rather than an inclusive system. This has triggered MEPs' demands for a more transparent and democratic process. A paradox arises between the EP's expectation of being fully informed and duly consulted over foreign policy issues and the necessity for secrecy required by the Council as a strategic negotiating tool and as a way to avoid embarrassment deriving from public disclosure of differences of opinion among its members (Nuttall, 1992, 59). While at national level this low profile in the definition of foreign policy is somehow compensated by general rights of supervision and censure over the executive, at the European level the Council of Ministers remains unaccountable to the European Parliament.[30] By exercising direct and indirect pressures over the Council through its national political parties, the EP political groups can attempt to counterbalance the absence of EP's official power in foreign policy. They can operate as intermediaries, channels of information and communication as well as meeting points between national and European political stances.

The Single European Act and the Treaty of European Union enhanced parliamentary involvement in European foreign policy, by introducing a right of assent on many international agreements and the need for the Council to take into account EP's views on EPC/CFSP issues. Nonetheless, the various reforms have often been interpreted by the Council in minimalist terms, highlighting the facts that no legal revision can make up for the lack of political will and that the decision over complying with these rules ultimately rests with the member states. The Intergovernmental Conference, which culminated with the signing of the Amsterdam Treaty in June 1997, has not changed this reality. It even failed to endorse on paper parliamentary requests for the establishment of an international personality for the Union, the incorporation of the CFSP in the Community pillar in order to bring together all provisions concerning the various aspects of European foreign policy and the fundamental question of establishing an effective parliamentary scrutiny over the Council. The extension of majority voting in the context of CFSP, agreed in principle by the Fifteen, plus the renewed commitments to inform and consult the EP will once again rely on the states' genuine willingness to fulfil them. Against this background, the task for the EP remains that of denouncing shortcomings and unsatisfactory institutional developments in order to achieve a more democratic European Union.

In conclusion, the European Parliament is still deprived of the legal and political instruments to become a real player on the international scene. The absence of effective powers granted to the European Parliament has inevitably shaken public interest and weakened its credibility in the eyes of the electorate to the extent that this situation might simply become

---

30 Dominated by the executives, most national parliaments have ceased to be a meaningful mechanism of accountability. This represents certainly an aberration in a modern and democratic society (Viola, 1997).

untenable in the future (Harrison, 1990, 146). In an era of internationalization and democratization, a more decisive role of the European Parliament and its political groups in European foreign policy seems crucial to remedy this 'democratic deficit' within the European Union. Mechanisms could be introduced to guarantee Parliament's right to information and consultation over Council and Commission's activities in the field of External Relations and CFSP.[31] And yet, only with the extension to the CFSP of the same competencies enjoyed in the area of External Relations or with the incorporation of the CFSP into the Community pillar, will the EP be able to perform a role consistent with the responsibilities of an international actor. As William Wallace and Julie Smith eloquently state, the European Parliament is still "hobbled by the looseness of its constituent parties, by the diversity of the electoral systems and the national campaigns through which it is constituted and by the resistance of the majority of national governments to any substantial increase in its authority. If there is any reconciliation to be found between popular consent and European integration, however, that reconciliation will have to include both greater visibility and greater authority for this directly elected Parliament of 'European peoples' " (Wallace and Smith, 1995, 154).

---

31 Joseph Weiler distinguishes between formal or legal legitimacy and social legitimacy. The EU has legal legitimacy in so far as all member states consensually allow a certain degree of sovereign powers to be surrendered to the EU. There are those that claim that democratic deficit can be overcome if more powers are passed to the EP, ensuring far greater parliamentary scrutiny of the executive. However, if the institutions still fail to gain popular support, they would fail to gain social legitimacy (Weiler, 1992, cited in Wallace and Smith, 1996, 152).

II The Responses of the European Community and the European Parliament to the Gulf Crisis

Having dealt with the general part of the book, its analysis of the composition and organization of the European Parliament and the political groups and its historical account of parliamentary involvement in the wider context of foreign policy, the focus of the research now turns to the two case studies. This chapter, in particular, provides a brief overview of the main events that occurred in the Gulf region between August 1990 and May 1991 and analyses the resultant attitudes within the European Community and European Parliament. This aims to set the scene for an investigation into the various positions assumed by the European Parliament's Political Groups, which is undertaken in Chapter III.

The Iraqi invasion of Kuwait amounted to an important challenge to the new world order established in the aftermath of the Cold War era as well as a major test for the European Community's ability to coordinate action between its members in the framework of European Political Cooperation. The crisis erupted at a crucial time for the Twelve on the eve of the Intergovernmental Conference which was aimed at revising the EC Treaties and especially for Germany at the final stage of negotiations with the United States, Soviet Union, United Kingdom and France over its reunification.

1. Brief Historical Background on the Gulf Crisis

The Gulf crisis erupted on 2 August 1990 when the Iraqi army crossed the Kuwaiti border and occupied the small Emirate. The invasion was allegedly motivated by the Iraqi claim on Kuwait's territory as a part of the Basra region which, together with two other former Ottoman provinces, had been unified to form Iraq at the end of the First World War. The breakdown of the Jeddah talks to settle the dispute diplomatically offered Saddam

Hussein the pretext for taking up arms. Relations between the two states were exacerbated by the Gulf states' refusal to support Iraq's economy following its eight-year war against Iran and, in particular, by Kuwait's rejection of the Iraqi request to restrict its oil production in order to keep prices high and therefore to maintain or even increase Iraqi oil income. Saddam's personality and ambition to extend his political leadership beyond Iraq's borders were also significant factors. Yet, the official reason given by the Iraqi government for the occupation was to support an alleged *coup d'état* against the ruling al-Sabah family.

Reaction from the international community was not slow in coming: on the same day, at the request of Kuwait and the United States, the United Nations (UN) Security Council convened and, discounting the absence of Yemen, unanimously adopted Resolution 660 which fiercely condemned the Iraqi aggression and requested the immediate and unconditional withdrawal of Iraqi troops from Kuwait.[32] On the following day, the American Secretary of State James Baker and the Soviet Foreign Minister Eduard Shevardnadze issued a joint statement from Moscow, urging Iraq to comply fully and immediately with the UN Resolution. The US President George Bush, the British Prime Minister Margaret Thatcher and the French President François Mitterand announced respectively that American soldiers would be dispatched to Saudi Arabia, that British naval units and aircraft would be sent to the Gulf region and that the French aircraft-carrier *Clemenceau* as well as other naval units would join US and UK contingents (WEU Assembly, 1992, 16-26). Saddam's proposal for a wider settlement of the crisis, also entailing the withdrawal of Israeli forces from Palestine, Syria and Lebanon as well as the retreat of Syrian troops from Lebanon was adamantly rejected by the US Administration, whilst causing divisions in the Arab world. Meanwhile, Baghdad announced that the Western hostages taken during the invasion would be sent to Iraqi and Kuwaiti military bases in order to deter allied air strikes. This manoeuvre was unreservedly condemned by the UN Security Council which demanded that "Iraq take no action to jeopardize the safety, security or health of [third countries'] nationals" (UN Resolution 664, 19/8/1990).

Eager to show the French public as well as the Arab world his distinctive approach, Mitterand presented before the UN General Assembly

---

32 In August 1990, in addition to its five permanent members, the UN Security Council consisted of Canada, Colombia, Cuba, Ethiopia, Finland, the Ivory Coast, Malaysia, Romania, Yemen and Zaire.

on 24 September 1990 a four-point plan, in the hope that the logic of peace would prevail over the logic of war. According to his plan, Iraq would withdraw from Kuwait under the supervision of the international community and, after the restoration of the sovereignty of the Emirate, general elections would be called. Furthermore, an international conference would be convened to discuss other problems in the Middle East, including the Palestinian question. Finally, the issue of establishing a collective security system would be addressed with the purpose of reducing weapons procurement (WEU Assembly, 1992, 20). The plan was not accepted by Britain and the US, but Mitterand's gesture seemed to be appreciated by Saddam who authorized the release of all French hostages by the end of October. This 'generosity' on the part of the Iraqi leader was considered as belying the intention of breaking international and European solidarity over the hostage issue. Against the commitment "not to send representatives to negotiate with Iraq" made by the Twelve on 28 October 1990 (*Europe*, 28/10/1990), other member states' governments decided, under strong domestic pressures, to authorize or, at least, to close their eyes to the 'pilgrimage' to Baghdad of many politicians, public figures and private citizens.

On 29 November 1990, the UN Security Council passed Resolution 678 granting Iraq a final chance to withdraw from Kuwait and to implement fully by 15 January 1991 all eleven UN Resolutions on the crisis, guaranteeing in return that retaliatory measures would not be taken. Should Iraq not comply, the Council authorized "the use of all necessary means (..) to restore international peace and security in the area". On the following day, President Bush extended an invitation to the Iraqi Foreign Minister Tariq Aziz for a meeting in Washington and proposed to send Baker to Baghdad. To convey this message and show to the public that no peaceful avenues had been spared, a summit was held between Aziz and Baker in Geneva on 9 January. However, the seven-hour discussion did not produce the desired results due to the inflexibility of both parties (Freedman and Karsh, 1993, 1994, 260).

On 14 January 1991, the eve of the expiry of the ultimatum, Mitterand presented before the Security Council a last-minute initiative which entailed a commitment of non-reprisal from Iraq's Arab neighbours, support for further negotiations regarding Kuwait and the settlement of the Arab-Israeli conflict in return for the announcement and commencement of a full-scale exit of Iraqi forces from the Emirate, in accordance with a pre-planned timetable. The US rejected the French initiative on grounds that ties between the Kuwait and Palestine questions were unacceptable, whilst the British drafted a much more hard-line text which risked dividing the Security Council. Yet the feared split did not occur as Saddam refused all the proposals, including Mitterand's 'olive branch', which proved to be the epilogue of all the attempts to resolve the crisis peacefully (Freedman and Karsh, 1993, 1994, 274).

On 17 January 1991 at 3 a.m. Gulf time, *Operation Desert Storm* commenced with US, British, French, Italian and Saudi air forces engaging strategic targets such as power stations, oil installations, telephone exchanges and roads as well as nuclear, chemical, biological research establishments and military bases, also causing civilian casualties. In February 1991, a new peace plan was drafted by the Soviet President Mikhail Gorbachev who proposed a more flexible timetable for the withdrawal, a ceasefire at the start of the evacuation, the suspension of sanctions, a guarantee of non-aggression and a loose undertaking regarding an international settlement to the Palestinian issue. As the Soviets waited for a formal Iraqi response, the French cold-shouldered the Soviet proposal (Freedman and Karsh, 1993, 1994, 381), whilst Britain and the United States objected to the initiative, not least because of its linkage with Palestine and the impact that a ceasefire might have in strategic military terms. On 21 February, Saddam delivered a speech which seemed a prelude to a clear Iraqi rejection of the proposal, so that when the Iraqi Foreign Minister presented in Moscow an official response, the Soviets were surprised to receive a conditional acceptance of the plan. Iraqi withdrawal would commence two days after a ceasefire and as soon as two-thirds of Iraqi forces had left Kuwait, sanctions against Iraq should be lifted. Washington ignored Baghdad's acceptance of Gorbachev's plan, deflected the Kremlin from submitting the proposal to the UN Security Council and delivered an ultimatum to Saddam to start leaving Kuwait by 23 February and to complete the evacuation within one week. Washington's conduct, which in the past would have infuriated Moscow and shaken the world, did not lead on this occasion to an irreconcilable wedge being driven between them and, instead, produced only mild Soviet criticism. On the morning of 24 February, the land offensive began with allied bombers attacking an entire Iraqi convoy, still armed and loaded with plunder, retreating from Kuwait City and proceeding north towards Basra. Although the attack was an unmitigated military success, forcing Saddam to comply with the UN Resolutions and accelerating the conclusion of the war, accusations rose of an inhumane and unnecessary US slaughter against the Iraqis (Freedman and Karsh, 1993, 1994, 244-245). On 26 February, Kuwait City was liberated and two days later, the war between the Allies and Iraq officially ended.

One of the consequences of the Gulf War was the brutal repression inflicted on the Kurdish people in reprisal for their rebellion against Baghdad's totalitarian régime, which led to a large-scale migration of refugees towards Turkey and Iran. Margaret Tutweiler, the Spokeswoman for the US Department of State under the Bush administration, stressed that Washington had no intention of interfering in Iraqi domestic affairs, concluding that the overthrow of Saddam Hussein was not one of the aims of the international coalition. Tutweiler's declaration, which contradicted previous statements by the British Prime Minister John Major, who had taken over from Margaret Thatcher in November 1990, and President Bush, rejected allegations that the United States and, in general, the international community had abandoned them after instigating rebellion against Saddam's régime (Freedman and Karsh, 1993, 1994, 411-413).

On 3 April 1991, the Security Council passed the lengthy Resolution 687 which laid down the conditions imposed on Iraq for peace, reiterating the inviolability of the border with Kuwait, which would be demarcated with UN assistance and monitored by UN peacekeeping forces. Iraq was expected to decommission its chemical, biological and conventional ballistic weapons - and associated research and manufacturing plants - as well as accept periodical UN inspections.

At the United Nations, a French proposal to provide armed protection for the Kurds was rejected by the United States, China and the Soviet Union. However, later in the month, the Security Council adopted Resolution 688 which introduced into international law the notion of the right to intervene in a sovereign state for humanitarian reasons. The United States insisted that Iraq should refrain from taking any military action north of the thirty-sixth parallel, warning that any attempt to obstruct international assistance to the Kurds would be firmly resisted. *Operation Provide Comfort* was launched to distribute medical and food supplies while the EC plan for a safe haven for the Kurdish population was created. In early May, allied troops withdrew from southern Iraq.

2. The European Community and the Gulf Crisis

On the same day of the Iraqi invasion, the Twelve meeting in Brussels within the framework of European political cooperation issued a statement condemning "the use of force by a Member State of the United Nations against the territorial integrity of another state" (*Europe*, 2/8/1990). This was followed on 4 August by an agreement to suspend the Generalized System of Preferences for Iraq and occupied Kuwait, to freeze Iraqi and Kuwaiti assets and to impose an embargo on oil imports (*Europe*, 4/8/1990, 4). Four days later, the Council adopted, under Article 113 EC, a regulation banning trade with Iraq and Kuwait[33] (Resolution 2340/90/EEC). The prompt reaction of the Twelve was noteworthy given that the crisis erupted during the summer recess. By the end of the month, the Community had allocated some funds to provide humanitarian and emergency relief to refugee camps in Jordan and to cover the repatriation costs of over 100,000 foreign workers from Iraq and occupied Kuwait. The hostage question was a central and crucial matter of concern for the Twelve who warned the Iraqi authorities that "any attempt to harm or jeopardize the safety of any EC citizen [would] be considered as a most grave offence directed against the Community and all its Member States and [would] provoke a united response from the entire Community" (EC Bulletin 7/8/1990, 124). On several occasions, the Twelve confirmed their intention to contribute to the settlement of the pending problems in the region with the objective of attaining security and stability as well as promoting fairer social and economic development.

The hopes raised for a swift and non-violent settlement of the crisis with the release of some hostages were dashed in early September 1990 with the Iraqi violation of Belgian, Canadian and French embassies and the arrest of their diplomats following the official annexation of the Emirate as Iraq's nineteenth province on 28 August 1990. The condemnation of such an infringement of the most basic principle of diplomatic immunity was unanimous among the Twelve, as was the decision to take the retaliatory measures of expelling Iraqi military attachés as well as monitoring and restricting the liberty of Iraqi diplomatic personnel. The Twelve sought to keep open their embassies as long as possible in Kuwait and, for the first

---

33 Resolution 2340/90/EEC prohibited imports to the Community of all commodities and products from Iraq and Kuwait and exports to those countries.

time, their embassies were required to take over the responsibilities of other EC member states when unable to fulfil their tasks[34] (*Europe*, 17-18/9/1990, 3). This system of joint protection outside the Community "was a clear sign of European citizenship", revealing that, beyond all its reprehensible repercussions, the Gulf crisis had served involuntarily as a catalysing factor for the unification process (Andreotti, 12/9/1990, 98-103).

Meanwhile, as public anxiety grew, distinguished politicians, among them the former British Prime Minister Sir Edward Heath and former German Chancellor Willy Brandt, went to negotiate the liberation of British and German nationals along with a few Italian and Dutch citizens. The Belgian government also undertook negotiations for the release of hostages in exchange for an imprisoned Palestinian terrorist and the concession of an entry-visa for a spokesman of Abu Nidal's Fatah Revolutionary Council who was eventually expelled. In particular, the Belgian government temporarily refused to provide ammunition to Britain so as not to jeopardize the outcome of the negotiation, causing a major row between the two countries. During November 1990, many other German, Italian, Dutch, Swedish, Belgian and Soviet hostages were freed and, finally, on 4 December the Iraqi authorities announced that all remaining foreigners detained in the country would be released by 15 January (Gnesotto and Roper, 1992, 188). The hostage issue, tactically used by Saddam, wrecked hopes for solidarity between the EC members.

In line with the policy pursued since 1980, the Twelve reiterated, on several occasions, the necessity to convene an international Middle East conference to address the Palestinian and Lebanese questions (Poos, 21/1/1991, 9-11). As Martin Landgraf claims, although it is not feasible to ascertain the direct causal nexus between the above intention of the Twelve and the critical attitude taken by the majority of the Arab states vis-à-vis Iraq, there was some kind of EC influence on their decision not to uphold Saddam's foolish ambition of undertaking a 'holy war' against the West (Landgraf, 1994, 81-82). The Community keenly sought strategies for preventing the eruption of further crises in the Gulf region and more widely in the Middle East, not least due to its geographical proximity and its members states' oil dependence (Coëme, 1991, 8).

---

34 Such diplomatic assistance was formally recognized and enshrined by virtue of the Treaty of the European Union, Art. 8c EC, Part II, Title II.

In December 1990, following the announcement of the UN deadline dictated by Washington, the EC President stressed that the period of time up until the fixed date was not to be interpreted as a "countdown to zero hour for the military option", but as "a goodwill pause" aimed at encouraging dialogue (De Michelis, 11/12/1990, 64-67).

On 4 January 1991, the French Foreign Minister Roland Dumas presented a peace plan to the EPC which included the following seven steps:

1) Baghdad's announcement of the acceptance of the UN Resolutions
2) Assurance that if Iraq withdrew no armed intervention would occur
3) Acknowledgement of Bush's offer of talks with Iraq
4) Meeting to be arranged as soon as possible between the EC President and the Iraqi Foreign Minister, even if the US-Iraq summit would not materialize
5) Establishment of talks between the EC Troika[35] and the Presidency of non-aligned countries
6) Organization of a post-crisis international Middle East conference
7) Convening of a general conference on security in the Mediterranean.

The expectations of achieving a united EC front were soon dashed when the Twelve failed to reach agreement over the most controversial points (3, 6 and 7) of the French proposal. Italy, France and Spain were determined to curb the prospect of military intervention and explore further peaceful paths despite the winds of war blowing from across the Channel and the Atlantic. On the contrary, Britain and Denmark adamantly opposed taking any initiative independently of the United States other than an appeal to Iraq to abide by the UN Resolutions. The former were favourable to a meeting with Tariq Aziz prior to the US-Iraq summit, while the latter, whose caution eventually prevailed, rejected this idea for fear that it could be interpreted as evidence that the Community and the American Administration were pursuing conflicting policies (*Europe* 19/12/1990, 7-8/1/1991, 3-4). The Twelve were also faced with another dilemma over

---

35 The EC Troika consisted of representatives from Luxembourg which held the presidency, Italy, its predecessor, and the Netherlands, its successor. The purpose of the Troika was to ensure a certain continuity at the level of the EC Presidency.

whether to "convey the agreed coalition message, which would be pointless, or convey (..) a distinctive European sentiment, (..) which risked a split in the coalition" (Freedman and Karsh, 1993, 1994, 261). Once again, loyalty to the United States overcame the desire of the Twelve for political emancipation so that the Community lost credibility as a potential peace broker (Dury, 1991, 10). Against this background, it was not surprising that on 8 January Iraq declined the Council's invitation for a meeting in Luxembourg, on the grounds that the Community did not have an autonomous external policy, being instead totally dominated by the United States (*Europe*, 7-8/1/1991). The Iraqi Foreign Minister emphasized in his Geneva press conference that talks with the Community could still be arranged if the Troika would travel to Baghdad ready to offer more concessions. The Iraqi refusal demonstrated that, in Saddam's eyes, the Community seemed to be little more than a small speck on the political map.

After a careful evaluation of the previous unsuccessful attempts at negotiation by the international community, including that of the Secretary-General of the United Nations, Javier Pérez de Cuéllar on 13 January 1991 (Freedman and Karsh, 1993, 1994, 270-271), Luxembourg's Foreign Minister Jacques Poos, who had taken over the EC Presidency from Italy at the beginning of the year, declared that the climate did not allow a new peace initiative.[36]

In an atmosphere of deep frustration and disappointment at EC passivity, France did not abandon the idea of pursuing its unilateral course of action and, as seen previously in the chapter, on 14 January, President Mitterand submitted to the UN Security Council a last-ditch proposal. Despite Soviet support, the plan failed not least due to renewed US and UK opposition over a link between the Kuwaiti and the Palestinian questions. This effectively swept aside hopes to hold back the tide towards overt military confrontation: "soon after this last attempt, the Gulf crisis became the Gulf war" (Closa, 1991, 8).

The French initiative, introduced without consulting the other EC partners, represented a contravention of Article 30 SEA,[37] which called for

---

36 Based on a six-month period, the European Community's Presidency rotates among the Member States.

37 This article relates to the establishment of European Political Cooperation in foreign policy and the subsequent determination of EC member states to formulate and jointly achieve a European foreign policy.

a coherent stance on foreign policy matters, and regrettably revealed that the positions taken in the UN Security Council by the two permanent members, France and Britain, were not subject to prior agreement at EPC level (Lucas and Usborne, 23/1/1991). Following the launch of air strikes, the Twelve voiced their deep regret at the recourse to arms, concluding that all efforts had been made by members of the international community, including Arab countries, to avert the offensive that Saddam had brought upon himself. They strongly condemned Iraq's missile attack on Israeli territory and expressed sympathy for the victims, emphasizing that "under the present circumstances, every restraint displayed by Israel [should] be interpreted as a sign of strength and not of weakness" (*Europe*, 18/1/1991). The EC member states expressed concern about the consequences of the war with respect to the "traditional links of friendship between the Community and the Arab countries" (*Europe*, 17/1/1991). EC Commissioner Abel Matutes highlighted

> the risk of destabilizing certain moderate Arab regimes, such as Egypt and Morocco, or those of other countries which belong to the international coalition, due to the pro-Saddam Hussein attitude of a part of their ill-informed populations (Matutes, 21/1/1991, 11).

On 23 January, John Major deplored the different levels of military participation among the various EC countries. In Germany's case, due to its historical legacy rather than constitutional impediments to military action, Bonn preferred to maintain a low profile. However, to reciprocate American, British and French solidarity shown with regard to its unification process, the German government offered a large financial contribution to US-UK missions and EC humanitarian initiatives, the use of its naval and air bases and a tightening of controls on arms exports (Dury, 1991, 25, Kaiser and Becher, 42). In comparison with the US, UK and French deployments, Italian military involvement appeared modest, yet deserves mention for the determination of its government not to hide behind a perfectly plausible constitutional obstacle. Alan Sked argues:

> It is instructive to contrast Germany's self-inflicted constitutional crisis over the Gulf with Italy's more positive approach to its real constitutional difficulty (Sked, 1991, 9).

55

Specifically, Article 11 of the Italian Constitution stipulates that:

> Italy repudiates war as an instrument of aggression against the freedom of other peoples and as a means of resolving international controversies. It agrees, on conditions of equality with other states, to such limitations of sovereignty as may be necessary for an order ensuring peace and justice among nations: promotes and encourages international organizations which share such objectives.

An interpretation *strictu sensu* of the constitutional predicament would fully justify a non-interventionist policy. Instead, the sentence referring to repudiation of "war as an instrument of aggression" was seen as backing Italy's condemnation of Iraqi invasion of Kuwait, while participating in security operations under the UN aegis as a means to achieve international order, "peace and justice" (Guazzone, 1992, 86).

In view of the intensification of air raids on Iraq and Kuwait, Luxembourg authorized the United States to use its airport for the transit of supplies, troops and wounded, committing itself to bear the entire costs of these operations. The Dutch government announced that it was prepared to dispatch eight Patriot anti-missiles batteries to Israel.

The initial cohesion of the Twelve had already started crumbling when increasingly pressing circumstances arose, such as the question of hostages and the issue of military intervention. In February 1991, the Community and its member states welcomed the Kremlin's appeal to Baghdad, although once again they strove to balance internal and external pressures, trying not to irritate the US and the UK, which remained sceptical over the effectiveness of diplomacy with Saddam (*Europe*, 19/2/1992). Among the Twelve only France, Britain, Italy and Germany were directly informed of the plan with the result that the Ministers of Foreign Affairs meeting the next day could only discuss its content in very vague terms. The importance of achieving a stable solution in the Middle East was reiterated and, for this purpose, the decision was taken to send the Troika to meet Israeli and Palestinian representatives (Dury, 1991, 22).

> The Community and its member states "deeply regret that Iraq has failed to respond positively to the appeal of the international coalition" and acknowledged the American decision to launch its ground offensive trusting that the liberation of Kuwait would be rapidly realized "with a minimum of loss in human lives on both sides" (*Europe*, 24/2/1991).

The EC members greeted with jubilation Kuwait's liberation during the last days of February 1991 and the official announcement of the cessation of hostilities in the Gulf on 28 February. The Council adopted a regulation lifting the sanctions previously imposed on Kuwait (Regulation 542/91). However, the Twelve reproached Saddam's ruthless repression of the Kurds in the conviction that "only the path of dialogue with all the parties concerned will allow the shaping of a renewed Iraq, united and respectful of the legitimate aspirations of the population groups of which the country is made up" (*Europe*, 28/2/1991).

On 8 April 1991, the EC Ministers meeting in Luxembourg adopted the British plan for the creation of a safe haven in northern Iraq to protect the Kurds from Saddam's attacks. A few days later, the European Community, following the plea from the German Foreign Minister Hans-Dietrich Genscher to seek ways in which the Iraqi President could be called personally to account for his invasion of Kuwait, genocide against the Kurds, alleged use of chemical weapons and mistreatment of prisoners of war, vainly stated once again to put Saddam on trial for crimes against humanity (Buchan, 1/4/1991, Usborne, 16/4/1991). In addition, on the EC initiative, the UN acknowledged the right of intervention for humanitarian reasons on the ground that "national sovereignty cannot be an alibi for tolerating massacres of population" (Barón Crespo, 16/4/1991, 99).

Lastly, it could be argued that EC's adoption of a programme of sanctions as well as emergency aid to those countries most affected by the crisis proved that, when authorized, the Community could function operatively (De Michelis, 1991, 48). And yet, these positive steps were overshadowed by disagreements between the EP and the Council of Ministers, for instance, over the allocation of the Community's contribution in the Gulf with the result that it took more than two months to commit their share of money. Inevitably, the Community remained marginal to international decision-making, failing to find an alternative to the UK-US inclination for rapid military action. "It was left to the Anglo-Saxon powers, working on the basis of the old London-Washington 'special relationship', to set up the mechanisms of response" (Johnson, P., 1991, 31).

Criticisms of the EC's inability to coordinate the actions of its member states and the delay in responding to the American request for military and financial contribution, albeit justifiable, were often too simplistic as they failed to recognize that within the intergovernmental EPC framework the pace of response on most issues depended totally on the political will of each member state government.

Hence, two diametrically opposed conclusions were drawn from the Gulf lesson: the first affirmed that the "hopes for a new world role for a united Europe [seemed to].. run into the Arabian sands", pointing to the reemergence of old national postures and diverging interests among the EC member states (Binyon, 17/9/1990). In the second view, the crisis had highlighted EC political weakness, thus reinforcing the case for an institutionalization of common foreign policy-making that would eventually boost the quest for unification (Ascherson, 3/2/1991, 19).

3. The European Parliament and the Gulf Crisis

As the Gulf Crisis erupted during the parliamentary summer recess, it took several weeks before official discussions were held on the Iraqi invasion of Kuwait. The complexity of the procedures for arranging extraordinary parliamentary sessions accounted, in part, for the delay.[38] However, as the Liberal leader and former French President Valéry Giscard d'Estaing commented:

> Cumbersome though the procedure for convening an extraordinary sitting may be, this was an event that could have justified convening the House especially (Giscard d'Estaing, 12/9/1990, 109).

This overview of the European Parliament's role in the Gulf issue is organized on the basis of three stages. The first stage extends between 2 August 1990, when Iraq invaded Kuwait, and 15 January 1991, the expiry of the UN deadline. The second stage extends between 16 January when *Operation Desert Storm* started and 28 February when fighting ceased between the Allies and Iraq. The third and final stage covers the period

---

38 Article 139 (2) of EEC Treaty states that extraordinary sessions can be arranged at the request of the majority of its members or at request of the Council or the Commission. The final decision is vested in the President of the European Parliament who, after consulting the then named Enlarged Bureau (including the President, the Vice-Presidents and the Chairmen of all political groups), can convene the House.

between March and May 1991 when the Kurdish question hit the headlines.

a) Pre-War Stage

As acknowledged by its own members, the European Parliament had proved to be the weakest and the slowest among the EC institutions in responding to the events in the Gulf, to the extent of waiting forty days after the Iraqi aggression before convening. Not even an urgent meeting of the Enlarged Bureau to show at least some kind of parliamentary concern was called until 29 August 1990. On that occasion, it was decided that, upon Giscard d'Eistaing's proposal, the EP would devote the whole day of 12 September to debate the crisis (LDR Communiqué de Presse, 29/8/1990). A prompt response from the EP, for instance the convening of an emergency session, would have bolstered its cause for more powers in foreign policy. By contrast, parliamentary apathy gave weight to the case against such involvement and more justification for the often criticized procedure which does not require, due to the urgency of such action, parliamentary consultation over the application of sanctions (MacLeod et al., 1996, 353-357).

A positive element was introduced, however, by the participation in the debate of the EC President-in-office, Giulio Andreotti, following the practice initiated by the Spanish and pursued by the French Presidency. As a result, the meeting assumed a more solemn and official character whereby no other parliamentary meeting was concurrently held and a vote on a Joint Resolution was organized in the same evening at the conclusion of the debate (Cattet, 30/8/1990).

Since the Iraqi invasion, the House had been regularly informed of the Council's action by the EP Delegation on the Relations with the Gulf countries as well as the EP Political Affairs and External Economic Relations Committees (Andreotti, 12/9/1990, 98). Moreover, as Andreotti emphasized, his presence was intended to go beyond giving a simple account of the Council's views and to establish, in conjunction with the EP, the necessary strategies to settle the crisis.

The EP Vice-President, Roberto Formigoni, reported on the visit of the *ad hoc* delegation to the Gulf and the meetings[39] with the Egyptian

---

39 The visit was undertaken on the behalf of the EP Enlarged Bureau by a small parliamentary delegation including Roberto Formigoni and Andrea Bonetti (EPP, Italy), Claude Cheysson (Socialist, France), Peter Crampton (Socialist, UK) and James Moorhouse (ED, UK).

President Husni Mubarak, the Saudi Arabian King Fahd Ibn-Abd-al-Aziz, the Jordanian Crown Prince Hassan, as well as other political authorities, such as the PLO leader Yasser Arafat, the Secretary-General of the Arab League Chadly Klibi and representatives of the Kuwaiti government in exile. During the journey, the members of the delegation were notified by the EC Presidency, which had provided them with an aircraft for their *shuttle diplomacy*, of the opportunity to extend their mission to Baghdad. Yet, despite the willingness of the Labour MEP Peter Crampton and the French Socialist MEP and former Minister of Foreign Affairs Claude Cheysson, the invitation was declined by three votes to two (Crampton interview, 31/1/1996). Although the mission would not have changed the course of events, this refusal seemed to go against the EP's ambition of becoming an actor on the world stage and to contradict the essence of parliamentary tradition and "desire for dialogue, for discussion with all peoples of the world, (..) reflecting with absolute clarity [its] views (..), with an awareness and a desire to understand and appreciate the views of others.." (Formigoni, 12/9/1990, 106-107). In Tunis, Cheysson also secretively spoke with Aziz, in the presence of Arafat, stressing that negotiations would not be undertaken until all hostages had been freed and Iraq announced its intention of retreating from Kuwait (Freedman and Karsh, 1993, 1994, 171).

In September 1990, Parliament unanimously condemned the Iraqi aggression against Kuwait and the detention of foreign civilians for use as human shields against possible attacks on strategic Iraqi sites. However, it was split over the "additional" steps to be taken if neither the search for a diplomatic solution nor economic sanctions proved sufficient to handle the crisis. The centre-right endorsed the military option and pushed for a stronger commitment from the Community in case of a war while the left rejected the use of force and opposed any Western military action other than for defensive purposes (Crampton interview, 31/1/1996). Despite parliamentary insistence that the "responsibility for dealing with the crisis should .. remain in the hands of the Security Council" (*OJEC* C 260/1990, 81), it soon appeared that there was little alternative but to transfer the command of forces and control over the conduct of war from the United Nations to the United States. The European Parliament also urged the EC member states to refrain from undertaking separate initiatives for the release of their nationals and called for airlifts in order to provide humanitarian assistance to refugees. Finally, the international community was asked to admit its responsibility for having armed Iraq as well as other countries in the Gulf and Middle East. On 13 September 1990, the EP President Enrique Barón Crespo called an emergency meeting of the Political Committee with representatives of the Commission and the Council of Ministers to discuss further the development of the crisis.

At the sitting of 11 October, none of the 13 Motions for Resolutions on the Gulf was put to the vote for failing to reach the required number of participants, following the request to ascertain whether a quorum was present.[40] This legitimate act was widely perceived by the others as a boycott perpetrated by ER members. However, the next day, after the Commission's statement on oil prices, the Socialists, supported by the Rainbow Group, requested a debate on the matter and succeeded in putting to the vote at least this important aspect of the crisis (Dury, 1991). The EP passed two Resolutions,[41] urging steps to be taken to end speculation on the price of oil which had doubled since August 1990. MEPs across the political spectrum expressed their intention to strengthen EC support for those developing countries threatened by the catastrophic repercussions of the Gulf War.

At the second October session, the EP unanimously adopted by RCV a report, drafted by Crampton on behalf of the Political Affairs Committee, pertaining to the Community's extension of a total embargo to Iraq and occupied Kuwait in accordance with UN Resolutions 661 and 670 (*OJEC* C 295/1990, 645, 695). The application of Article 235 of the EEC Treaty was recommended as a legal base for this measure, rather than Article 113 EEC, which did not envisage any parliamentary involvement in the decision-making process. The roll-call vote, requested by the European Democrats, revealed the amazingly low number of 23 members present in the Chamber.

In November 1990, the leader of the French *Front National* and of the ER group in the European Parliament, Jean-Marie Le Pen, undertook a

---

40 OJEC 284/90 states that more than thirteen members rose in support of the request for a quorum check, although according to Raymonde Dury (Socialist, Belgium), the European Right was deemed responsible for this quorum check (OJEC 3-394/90, 324). However, Rule 89 (3) of the EP Rules of Procedure of the time envisaged that: "A request that it be ascertained whether the quorum is present. (..) must be made by at 'least thirteen Members'. A request on behalf of a political group is not admissible". As such the ER, as a group, could not make this request.

41 Resolution B3-1843/90 (Socialist Group) and Resolution B3-1844/90 (Socialist, EPP, LDR, ED, Green, EUL, LU and Rainbow Groups).

journey to Baghdad where he was successful in obtaining the release of French and also of other European citizens. This act was fiercely condemned by the vast majority of his colleagues as "a sordid piece of political theatre" involving the manipulation of hostages and their relatives (Ford, 22/11/1990, 249) with the aim of deriving a political advantage for [his] party". Le Pen's behaviour was regarded as unacceptable and unethical, not least "for the impression .. given that the EP was behind [this initiative]" (Sainjon, 22/11/1990, 251). As a result, many members requested that the EP disown Le Pen's trip and condemn "his shabby opportunism" (Pérez Royo, 22/11/1990, 250). Finally, a suggestion was made, albeit in vain, to set up a delegation of representatives from all PGs, preferably led by the EP President, to travel to the region to persuade the Iraqi authorities to release all detainees (Ferri, 12/9/1990, 162-163).

In its Resolution of 22 November 1990, the EP condemned the attempt by Iraq to destroy Kuwaiti national identity by invalidating all Kuwaiti passports and replacing them with Iraqi documents as well as through its plans for mass relocation and deportation to Iraq (*OJEC* C324/1990, 200-201). On the following day, the House passed, by way of RCV, another report drafted by Crampton on behalf of the Political Affairs Committee, on a Proposal for a Council regulation on financial aid for the countries most directly affected by the Gulf crisis (*OJEC* C 12/1990, 326-327). Crampton's amendments to the original text, particularly the granting of more aid to Jordan, were endorsed by the Council, with the European Parliament succeeding on this occasion to impose its own views (Crampton interview, 31/1/1996).

On 12 December, the EP welcomed all diplomatic initiatives, including the proposed visits of the American Secretary of State to Baghdad and the Iraqi Foreign Minister to Rome, following his visit to the United States. It reaffirmed support for all UN Security Council Resolutions on the Gulf crisis, including Resolution 678, stressing, however, that the military option was not "an automatic consequence" of the adoption of this UN Resolution and calling "for no military action to be taken while there [was] the prospect of a peaceful solution to the crisis" (*OJEC* C 19/90, 76-77). In addition, while acknowledging the initiatives already taken by the Council, the EP urged the Community, and in particular the Council, to initiate a peace plan and to establish a Euro-Arab dialogue (*OJEC* C 19/90, 76-77).

As the UN deadline approached, the divisions within the EP became more noticeable with the left including the majority of the Socialist Group "not resigned to the inevitability of war" opposing the centre-right which acknowledged that, in light of the events, war had become unavoidable (Comfort et al., 11/1/1991). The former supported a ceasefire as soon as Iraq began its evacuation while the latter required completion of Iraqi withdrawal operations before halting the hostilities.

On 9 January 1991, on the initiative Christine Crawley (Socialist, UK), Eva Quistorp (Green, Germany) and Christa Randzio-Plath (Socialist, Germany), 42 women parliamentarians of different nationalities from the Socialist, EPP, Green, EUL and Rainbow groups signed an appeal for peace in the Gulf, "call[ing] for the intensification of negotiations and the exploration of all possible avenues to avoid war and to end the crisis" (Women MEPs' Appeal, 9/1/1991).

The EP Political Affairs Committee expressed concern at the failure of the US-Iraqi summit and disappointment at the refusal of Tariq Aziz to meet the EC Troika after his meeting with the American Secretary of State. The committee urged the Ministers of Foreign Affairs meeting in Political Cooperation to assess all existing peace plans in order to avoid an armed confrontation in the Gulf region through close cooperation with the countries of the Arab League and the US Administration (Doc PE 147.883/BUR, 10/1/1991). Finally, it required all necessary steps to be taken to ensure a more direct involvement of the Parliament in the EC decision-making through consultation with the other EC institutions before the UN deadline of 15 January.

During the week preceding the UN ultimatum, Barón Crespo met Jacques Poos and exchanged views with some representatives of the US Congress and the Soviet ambassador. Concurrently, in a letter to Sa'di Mehdi Saleh, the President of the Iraqi National Assembly, the EP President declined an invitation to Baghdad to open a dialogue between the two parliaments, on the ground that the Iraqi government had refused to meet the EC Troika before the fateful day of 15 January, urging the Iraqi Parliament to impress on its executive to reconsider the issue (Barón Crespo's Letter, 9/1/1991). Furthermore, the Iraqi invitation to the EP President could be seen as part of Saddam's general strategy of opening up divisions within the European and the Western camps. Whatever the reasons for this decision, Parliament, nonetheless, lost another opportunity to take an autonomous view and test its mediatory powers at the international level.

After failing to convene an EP extraordinary plenary session, the Presidency authorized for 14 January an extraordinary meeting of the Political Affairs Committee, regarded as the most appropriate parliamentary organ to follow the evolution of the crisis (Barón Crespo's Letter, 10/1/1991). A final appeal was therefore launched to the Iraqi government to express its intention to comply with the UN Resolutions and to the international community to promote other peace initiatives (EP Doc 14/1/1991). A meeting of the Enlarged Bureau, open to all MEPs and the representatives of the Council and Commission, was convened on 16 January 1991 to discuss the evolution of the crisis.

Towards the end of this first stage of the crisis, a major bone of contention emerged between the left and the centre-right of the House with respect to the question of whether sanctions had to be allowed more time to work or whether the UN should intervene without delay in order to prevent Saddam Hussein from refining his military strategy and organizing further his troops. Just before the expiry of the UN deadline, on the initiative of Brigit Cramon Daiber (Green, Germany) and Dieter Schinzel (Socialist, Germany), the European Parliament made an appeal to members of both the US Congress and the Soviet Parliament "to find a solution other than the war for the Kuwait question" as well as "to prepare a more long-term conference on security and cooperation in the Middle East". This was intended to reach the American Congress before its vote on a Resolution authorizing President Bush's military plan in the Gulf (MEPs' Appeal to US and USSR Parliaments, 9/1/1991). On 12 January 1991, the Congress endorsed the decision to use force by 250 to 183 votes in the House of Representatives and 52 to 47 in the Senate, showing that the EP had failed to influence the final outcome (WEU Assembly, 1992, 22). Giscard d'Eistaing's assumption that no debate in the EP or in any other parliament could forge a policy over Kuwait proved inaccurate, since the Congress had, nevertheless, the potential to influence a decision and therefore could have changed the course of the events (Giscard d'Estaing, 20/2/1991, 122-123).

b) War Stage
By mid-January 1991, the prospect of air strikes became inevitable when it appeared that sanctions alone could not rapidly achieve the desired effect, or rather that the US was not prepared to wait at least for one year to see the results, the time predicted by William Webster, the Director of the American Central Intelligence Agency. Realistically, the 'index of the parliamentary scale' gradually moved towards a pro-military approach. On the day of the start of *Operation Desert Storm*, members from the left of

the EP, including the European United Left, the Left Unity, the Greens, the Rainbow and a faction of the Socialists, gathered to express their concern

> about the loss of human lives among military personnel and the civilian population, as well as ecological damage and the consequences that this attack will have on any efforts at peace in the Middle East. [They expressed their] support for peaceful demonstrations against the war in Europe and the United States and - even at this late date - [they] call[ed] for the cessation of military operations to facilitate the peaceful implementation of the United Nations Resolutions. [They] also request[ed] that immediate steps be taken to organize an international conference on all the problems of the Gulf region and the Middle East, in particular the Palestinian question (*European Report*, 17-19/1/1991, 3).

This declaration, followed by a torchlight procession through Strasbourg by MEPs and officials as a sign of protest for the beginning of hostilities, was received with suspicion by the United States Administration and with hostility by Israel (Palmer, John, 22-24/1/1991). Objecting to the continuation of the onslaught on the Iraqi population, MEPs spelled out that "a collision between one million-plus armed men, using the most modern military technology, would restore neither peace nor security" to the Middle East. The EP animatedly debated the EC's failure to agree on more than broad principles on a common policy vis-à-vis the Gulf and the new unexpected French initiative which clearly exposed the limitations of "turning the Community into a geopolitical actor in its own right" (Johnson, Boris, 23/1/1991).

On 21 January, on the initiative of the Italian Green MEP Eugenio Melandri, the Assembly observed one minute's silence in honour of the victims from both sides in the Gulf War. Disappointingly the House rejected his request, made along with 13 other MEPs, to devote the whole day of 22 January to a "serious and detailed debate on the Gulf War" in addition to the discussion following Council statement on the Gulf scheduled for 21 January (Melandri 21/1/1991, 3). The main motive for such a decision was, as Price remarked, that Parliament did not need "a long debate over one day and a half but to monitor events as they develop[ed] during the next month" (Price, 21/1/1991, 3).

Frustration was expressed by members, such as Derek Prag (ED, UK), Enrico Falqui (Green, Italy), Vassillis Ephremidis (LU, Greece) and Eva Quistorp (Green, Germany), at the cancellation of an extraordinary plenary session with just a few hours' notice and the postponement of a meeting of the Enlarged Bureau, scheduled for 16 January in Brussels. These revocations, meaning that Parliament could not make its views known prior to the actual outbreak of the hostilities, were ostensibly justified by the absence of the representatives of other EC institutions and that "it would achieve too little too late" (Brock and Guildford, 18/1/1991). In reality, they were motivated by a French-inspired campaign to avoid the precedent of holding parliamentary sessions in Brussels rather than in its traditional Strasbourg venue. It seemed that, "no matter that the Gulf was in flames", the dispute between France and Belgium about the EP seat overrode the political question, risking the paralysis of parliamentary activities (Claveloux, 8/2/1991).

Eventually, against all the conventional rules, MEPs agreed to hold two special sittings in Brussels on 30 January and 6 February 1991, despite French MEPs' opposition,[42] who argued that these meetings were worthless since no electronic voting system was available in Brussels and no vote could therefore be taken (B3-0120/91). Moreover, on 30 January, the EP convened in Brussels a meeting of its Enlarged Bureau open to all its members with the mandate to follow the events in the Gulf more closely. The additional plenary sittings provoked new protests from some French MEPs who raised once again the question of the legality of the decision to convene a parliamentary meeting in a seat other than the official one established in Strasbourg (Dury, 1991, 21).

Despite these internal wrangles, however, MEPs were united in their condemnation of Saddam, who was considered solely responsible for the war, and in their support for the actions of the UN and the allied forces. They also collectively suggested extending controls over the arms trade and developing European economic, commercial, political and cultural cooperation with the Middle East. Among the EC institutions, only the EP officially backed a proposal for convening a permanent Conference on Security and Cooperation in the Mediterranean (CSCM) based on the CSCE model, at the conclusion of the Gulf crisis (Landgraf, 1994, 82-83).

By the beginning of the second stage, a cacophony of voices was resounding within the House, opening up old divisions between left and centre-right, preventing the creation of a united parliamentary stance. The Greens, the European Unitarian Left, the Left Unity and the Independent

---

42 All French MEPs voted against the convening of these additional sittings with the exception of the Green MEPs Didier Anger and Solange Fernex.

left-wingers with a faction of the Socialists unrelentingly opposed the war and called for an immediate ceasefire and even the withdrawal of the allied troops from the region. By contrast, the Christian Democrats, the Liberals, the British and Danish Conservatives as well as the Gaullists along with some Socialists supported the continuation of air strikes, by taking the view that negotiations should not be resumed prior to Saddam's conformity with UN Resolutions or the defeat of Iraq. In the tragi-comic plenary session of January 1991, even the search for a compromise expressing the lowest common denominator among political groups seemed doomed to fail. Due to deep tensions between and within its constituent political groups, the European Parliament was nearly prevented from voicing its response to the grave developments in the Gulf. Finally, after using all political channels, sounding out all possibilities, endeavouring to circumvent ideological preconceptions and obstacles, the EP succeeded in incorporating the two disputed references and in formulating a common, if vague policy. This delay in reaching an agreement, nevertheless, discredited the European Parliament in the eyes of other EC institutions and, more generally, in the eyes of the public, as well as attracting harsh criticism from the press.

Parliament called on Iraq to withdraw its troops from Kuwait under "a binding and rapid timetable [which] would make possible an immediate cessation of hostilities and the resumption of negotiations" (*OJEC* C 48, 25/2/1991, 116). While reiterating its belief that the recourse to the use of force reflected a failure, the EP recognized that responsibility for the outbreak of hostilities lay with President Saddam Hussein who had rejected all peaceful initiatives. However, Parliament considered as a priority to try "to contain the war and to bring it to a rapid conclusion with minimum casualties" (*OJEC* C 48, 25/2/1991, 116). Finally, it called the Council to implement a Community political, economic, commercial and cultural cooperation policy on the Middle East.

As the prospect of land warfare loomed, the divide within the EP deepened further, if not along national lines. This culminated on 21 February in total parliamentary disarray which was caused by Saddam's speech, with the withdrawal of a joint text together with numerous individual motions for Resolutions (*OJEC* C 72/91, 125-127). Finally, Parliament made its final appeal to all parties to seize the historic "opportunity afforded by the Soviet Government's offer" (*OJEC* C 72/91, 141). It also called on the Commission to introduce emergency measures to face the economic and social consequences of the crisis in the maritime and air transport sectors (*OJEC* C 72/91, 131). The most extraordinary aspect of the EP's reaction to the Gulf crisis, even when the land war was raging, was its focus on the future: on the post-crisis era and the role of the Community in the settlement of other conflicts in the region, a clear indication of its impotence on the *hic et nunc* (Levi, 1990, 627).

c) Post-War Stage

On 28 February 1991, the day which marked the cessation of hostilities, the Political Affairs Committee called upon the Community to take an active part in establishing a lasting peace in the region, based on respect for human rights and with due consideration for political, social and ecological factors (Info Memo No. 41, 26/2/1991 cited in EPP Report, 7/1990-7/1991, 28). In the following month, the EP passed a Resolution which raised hopes that the Iraqi régime would be based on democratic, peaceful and just principles and that the Palestinian question would be finally settled. In particular, the Commission was asked to submit a proposal for reconstruction in the Gulf region. Regarding its extraordinary meetings, the EP blamed the Council for boycotting two sessions that were supposed to be held in Brussels in order to monitor Community actions on the Gulf crisis more closely. In a Resolution tabled by the Socialists, the EP reminded the Council that it was obliged to take part and respond to MEPs' requests for information concerning its activities. Parliament also reaffirmed its right to decide the place of its meetings. A majority believed that the EP had to be in immediate proximity to the other European decision-making institutions, namely the Council and the Commission, both based in Brussels (Dury, 1991, 23).

On 18 April, the EP passed a Resolution on the situation of the Kurds, whereby it condemned "the attempted genocide against the Kurds by Saddam Hussein's regime and the repression of the Iraqi population as a whole". As such, it urged the EC member states' governments "to bring the matter before the International Court of Justice to ensure that these acts of genocide are acknowledged and condemned in accordance with the [1948] Convention". The Resolution also stressed the necessity for the United Nations "to develop the means of preventing totalitarian regimes from perpetrating genocide" (..) if necessary by amending the UN Charter" (*OJEC* C 129/91, 141-142). The proposal of putting Saddam on trial for war crimes was also raised at talks held at the EP in Strasbourg between Jacques Poos and Pérez de Cuéllar. However, the British Foreign Office Minister Tristan Garel-Jones argued that as long as the Iraqi leader remained in power there was no possibility of realizing this plan (Usborne, 16/4/1991).

The EP condemned Saddam's persecution of the Kurdish and Shi'ite minorities, urged the creation of safe havens under the UN aegis and requested the allies not to withdraw before receiving guarantees for the safety of the Kurds (EPP Report, 7/1990-7/1991, 29). At this session, following the invitation extended by President Barón Crespo, UN Secretary-General Pérez de Cuéllar addressed the House which, like the assemblies of representatives elected by peoples, has "natural affinities [with] the United Nations, an organisation of peoples inspired by democratic values" (*OJEC* 3-404/91, 100). With regard to the Gulf War, he stated that it was not a United Nations war and that "the victory of the allied or coalition countries over Iraq [was] not a United Nations victory" (*OJEC* 3-404/91, 100). He also claimed that the new world order should take place within the UN framework and not under the false pretence of a multilateralism "camouflaging the pursuit of national or regional interests". He then stressed the need to achieve peace in the Middle East and in the world. Finally, the UN Secretary urged parliamentarians to use their influence and power to promote some of the necessary steps to achieve this goal, such the reduction in arms trade and a total international ban on chemical weapons (*OJEC* 3-404/91, 100-101).

In the following month, the question of emergency relief for the Kurds triggered a dispute between Parliament and the Commission. The EP was accused of having delayed humanitarian aid on previous occasions, for instance in the case of Russia. Most parliamentarians expressed their disappointment with such an unfair misrepresentation, concluding that Parliament had proved to be willing to award financial assistance as rapidly as possible even beyond the extent proposed by either the Commission and the Council (Lenz, 15/5/1991, 140).

The Gulf crisis was the focus of intense parliamentary activity prior to, during and after the outbreak of the War, between September 1990 and May 1991. Stunned and bewildered by the Iraqi occupation of Kuwait and the outbreak of war, the EP reflected, as a kaleidoscope, the myriad of distinct attitudes taken by national governments, parties and the public (Freedman and Karsh, 1993, 1994, 358). Over the length of the crisis, the EP also had exchanges of view with the Iraqi Assembly, often via the Iraqi embassy in Brussels.

69

Conclusion

Iraq's sudden invasion of Kuwait inevitably threw into disarray the new international order emerging in the post-Cold War period, challenging the European Community's aspiration to make its début as a political actor on the world stage. Iraqi aggression was condemned as a flagrant violation of territorial sovereignty, but solidarity and cohesion were undermined by contrasting views over whether to take diplomatic or military measures against the Iraqi leader. However, Saddam's final refusal to leave Kuwait on the eve of the UN deadline of 15 January 1991 and his disregard of all diplomatic efforts eventually convinced the Twelve to endorse US military strategies. In the crucible of the Gulf War, the EC member states were collectively reduced to the rank of secondary actors and failed to cross the threshold of 'high politics'. Their faltering, ambiguous and sometimes opposing stances attracted attention as well as inevitable criticism from the media. However, deprived of rapid, centralized and efficient ways of making major decisions pertaining to the sphere of foreign policy and defence, the Community could have no real impact as a political entity. In this context, the EC institutions had to carry out the delicate and demanding task of coordinating separate national responses rather than initiating joint policies (Moïsi, 1991, 11). The European Community was "one of the casualties of the Gulf War" revealing a landscape dominated by member states' divergent political responses and the absence of coordination as regards both diplomatic proposals and appropriate military solutions (Giscard d'Estaing, 20/2/1991, 122-123).

However, while accepting many of the above criticisms, it should be recognized that the EC's response to the occupation of Kuwait, with the swift adoption of a total embargo against Iraq, was exemplary in terms of effectiveness and rapidity, even preceding the United Nations and the Arab League (Andreotti, 12/9/1990, 99). Its aid policy in favour of the refugees and the frontline countries also proved that the Community could be efficient where it had clear and full authority to act. Lastly, the Twelve promoted diplomatic solutions, supported the adoption of UN Resolutions and contributed, albeit to a far less significant degree, to the US-led military operations.

Inevitably, the question of the definition of a common foreign policy emerged, in particular in the context of the debate on Europe's future transatlantic relationship. Confirming the axiom that politicians tend to fit any evidence to suit their own predilections, the war became a tool to stress either the impossibility of or the need for the creation of a European Political Union. According to the realists, the Twelve's slow and inconsistent reaction to the invasion of Kuwait reinforced the argument that the European Community could never attain political authority in international affairs.

Conversely, the advocates of European integration believed that the weakness of the EC edifice was responsible for the failure of an effective policy over the Gulf conflict. For this reason, and so as to acquire both internal and external credibility, the need was stressed for establishing a common European foreign policy and security structure in order to enable the Community to gain the political, legal, and financial resources to shoulder its international responsibilities.

As regards the European Parliament's response to the crisis, Barón Crespo stressed that from the outset the EP had firmly condemned Iraqi aggression as well as fully supported the personal initiatives of the UN Secretary-General and those of the UN Security Council. Furthermore, long before Saddam's attempt to link the invasion of Kuwait with the Palestinian issue, which had been used by the Iraqi leader "as a distraction to inflame emotions throughout the Arab, and indeed the Moslem world", the European Parliament had called for the gathering of an international conference to solve the Arab-Israeli problem (Barón Crespo's Speech, EUI, 4/2/1991).

Nevertheless, despite the numerous parliamentary messages to the Iraqi authorities, the consultations with member states' governments and national parliaments as well as exchanges of views with the US Congress, the EP's stance carried little weight. In fact, the European Parliament 'cut a sorry figure' over the Gulf War. Some among its own members recognized Parliament's inability to act as a political entity and deplored its unconvincing attempt to "disguise in texts lacking direction the internal conflicts of political groups" (De Montesquiou Fezensac, 13/3/1991, 77). The resulting image of the EP was of a sort of academy where opinions were formulated "tardily and bureaucratically" (Fontaine, 13/3/1991, 83).

The reasons for this marginalization of the EP from the political centre can be attributed to the lack of powers and poor cohesion within the parliamentary forum itself, which had prevented the building of a solid bloc capable of exerting influence on the other EC institutions. Responding to the criticism of poor EP cohesion on Gulf events, President Barón Crespo argued that a comparison of the debates of the European Parliament in Brussels and Strasbourg with those of the US Congress in Washington, revealed that before 15 January the former was slightly less divided than its American counterpart (Barón Crespo's Speech, EUI, 4/2/1991).

Furthermore, against the old prejudice that foreign policy is not a parliamentary concern, as Andreotti stressed, the crisis "required complete awareness and involvement on the part not only of governments and political forces, but all citizens who must be enabled thoroughly and clearly to comprehend the reasons which impel us, so that they are then able to give their consent to decisions and, where necessary, the required sacrifices." On the assumption that the European Parliament represents the will of the people of Europe, "it is from this Assembly, therefore, that the most profound statements and influential encouragement must come" (Andreotti, 12/9/1990, 98).

On the page of history opened to 2 August 1990, the European Parliament, and indeed the Community as a whole, was only able to write a few words in invisible ink. Their performance in relation to the crisis, however, has to be examined in the light of many extenuating circumstances connected to inadequate institutional mechanisms and powers. What remains to be assessed is whether and to what extent this institutional hiatus has effectively prevented the forging of a European common approach or rather whether the absence of political will and the dominance of national constraints effectively represent the "insuperable obstacles" (Hill, 1983b).

III The Role of the Political Groups in Forging the European Parliament's Stance on the Gulf Crisis

In order to unveil fully the multifaceted Europarliamentary outlook on the Gulf crisis during its three stages - the build-up to war, the war itself and the immediate aftermath of the war - it is necessary to look closely at the positions taken by the political groups. This is achieved through a review of relevant parliamentary debates, Motions for Resolutions, substantiated by interviews with MEPs and an analysis of roll-call votes (RCVs). An attempt is also made to discern whether and when dissenting voices emerged, and to measure the levels of cohesion and transnationality within the various political groups. An examination of the level of similarity or discord between the various groups is also carried out by comparing and combining the respective RCVs of PGs. Finally, since "no group operates in a vacuum; each react[ing] to what other groups do and [being] in its turn reacted to", the chapter attempts to unravel the complex process of group interaction and to detect whether a particular PG or coalition made any significant impact in terms of defining or influencing the EP official policy vis-à-vis the Gulf crisis.[43]

---

43 The methodology followed for such qualitative and quantitative evaluation has already been explained in the Introduction, whilst the formulae are illustrated in detail in the Appendix.

Table 2a List of EP Roll-Call Votes on the Gulf Crisis
Pre-War Stage

Date	Resolution	Recital / Paragraph	OJ	Page
12-Sep-90	Joint Resolution on the Gulf Crisis B3-1600, 1602,1603, 1604, 1623	Recital A	C260	105-106
		Recital H		106-107
		Paragraph 6		107-108
		Paragraph 11 first sentence		108-109
		Paragraph 17 excluding first sentence		109-110
		Paragraph 17		110-111
		Paragraph 20		111-112
		Paragraph 21		112-113
		Paragraph 24		113-114
		Whole		115-116
23-Nov-90	Crampton Report A3-321	Whole	C324	421
12-Dec-90	Joint Motion for a Resolution B3-2182, 2185, 2187 & 2196		C19	186-187
12-Dec-90	Joint Motion for a Resolution B3-2188, 2189 & 2232	Recital A-D	C19	187-188
		Recital E		188-189
		Paragraph 1, Part 1		189-190
		Paragraph 1, Part 2		190-191
		Paragraph 1, Part 3		191-192
		Whole		192-193
12-Dec-90	Motion for a Resolution B3-2190		C19	193

Table 2b List of EP Roll-Call Votes on the Gulf Crisis
War Stage

Date	Resolution	Recital / Paragraph	OJ	Page
23-Jan-91	Joint Motion for a Resolution B3-108, 109, 111 & 115	Amendment 2	C48	36-37
		Whole		37-38
23-Jan-91	Joint Motion for a Resolution B3-108		C48	38-39
23-Jan-91	Joint Motion for a Resolution B3-111		C48	39-40
23-Jan-91	Joint Motion for a Resolution B3-113		C48	41-42
23-Jan-91	Joint Motion for a Resolution B3-115		C48	42-43
23-Jan-91	Joint Motion for a Resolution B3-117		C48	43-44
23-Jan-91	Joint Motion for a Resolution B3-119		C48	44-45
23-Jan-91	Joint Motion for a Resolution B3-123 & 127, tabled by SOC and RB	Amendment 2	C48	45-46
		Amendment 1		46-47
24-Jan-91	Resolution B3-120 on the Baltic States and the Gulf		C48	188-189
24-Jan-91	Motion for a Resolution B3-125	Recital A & B	C48	188-189
		Amendment 1		193
		Recital C-F		194
		Amendment 2		194-195
		Paragraph 1		195-196
		Paragraphs 2 & 3		196-197
		Paragraph 4		197-198
		Paragraph 5 & 6		198-199
24-Jan-91	New Joint Resolution B3-123 & 127, tabled by SOC, EPP, ED, RB	Amendment 1	C48	199-200
		Whole		200-201
21-Feb-91	Motion for a Resolution B3-333 on Ecological Disaster in the Gulf		C72	150-151
21-Feb-91	Joint Resolution B3-387, 388, 389 & 392 on the Situation in the Gulf.		C72	151

75

Table 2c List of EP Roll-Call Votes on the Gulf Crisis
Post-War Stage

Date	Resolution	Recital / Paragraph	OJ	Page
14-Mar-91	Resolution B3-398, 402, 426, 429, 450 & 466	Amendment 17	C106	136-137
		Amendment 18		137
		Amendment 19		137-138
19-Apr-91	Joint Resolution replacing B3-552, 555, 562, 564, 565 & 660 on Arms Trade	Whole excluding Paragraph 8	C129	154-155
		Paragraph 8, Part 1		155
		Paragraph 8, Part 2		155-156
18-Apr-91	Joint Resolution replacing B3-566, 560, 618, 619, 619, 620, 621, 622, 622, 623 & 624 on the Situation of the Kurds	Amendment 1, Part 1	C129	156-157
		Amendment 1, Part 2	C129	157

1. Political Groups' Positions vis-à-vis the Gulf Crisis

1.1 The Socialist Group

a) Pre-War Stage
As early as September 1990, the group recognized that the Iraqi occupation of Kuwait was the first real threat to international peace in the so-called New World Order and that a weak response to Iraq's defiant behaviour might well set a dangerous precedent encouraging other countries to emulate Baghdad. Support was given to the adoption of an international embargo on oil imports from Iraq as well as on exports of all goods, including agricultural products other than those permitted for humanitarian reasons under UN Resolution 661. The Socialist Chairman Jean-Pierre Cot also stressed the need for the European Community to participate in the UN operations aimed at enforcing the Resolutions adopted by the Security Council in order to induce Iraq to withdraw from Kuwait (Cot, 1990a). The group appeared split over the so-called "additional measures" to be adopted in the Gulf, as indicated in the September EP Resolution, because about 80 MEPs remained implacably opposed to the war, being influenced by the Greens. This lack of internal cohesion made the Socialists more than ever aware of the necessity of seeking a compromise with other PGs (Crampton interview, 31/1/1996).

No negotiations should be undertaken before an unconditional Iraqi departure from Kuwait, the re-establishment of the latter's legitimate government and the freeing of all hostages. The need was also stressed to avoid engaging in separate negotiations which, even if successful, would undermine the chances of the remaining detainees. In the group's view, the Community should give assistance to war refugees and to the populations in Egypt and Jordan who were suffering from the effects of the sanctions imposed on Iraq and occupied Kuwait. Solidarity with these countries should be subject to full compliance with the embargo against Saddam (Cot, 12/9/1990, 107-108).[44] In addition, the Socialists spelled out the need to address the conflicts in the Middle East, the crucial issue of arms trade and finally the need for the EC member states to improve their political cooperation in the field of foreign policy (Woltjer, 12/9/1990, 164-165).

The group appeared fairly cohesive throughout the RCVs leading to the adoption of the September Resolution.[45] The final roll-call vote on the whole text, which was requested by the Socialists along with the Christian Democrats and the Greens, revealed that out of a total number of 145 Socialist members participating in the vote, 136 were in favour, none against and 9 abstained, among whom were 8 British Labour and one Belgian Socialist members.[46] As the British MEP Alfred Lomas explained, he refused to "give comfort to those who support[ed] Iraq by voting against [the] Resolution". However, due to the omission in the text of an unequivocal rejection of war a solution to the crisis, the failure to ban further arms trade to the Middle East and to condemn other, similar violations of territorial sovereignty, he could not but abstain from voting (Lomas, 12/9/1990, 158-159).

In early October, the Socialists focused on the humanitarian effects of the crisis, expressing concern about the hostages and the Kuwaiti population and urging the Commission to establish a task force to look closely at the repercussions of the crisis in the Community's industrial sector (McMahon, 11/10/1990, 273-274). Attention was also given to the disastrous financial consequences of the oil price rise for developing

---

44 See also Paragraphs 11 & 12 of the Joint Resolution B3-1600, 1602, 1603, 1604, 1623 of 12 September 1990, OJEC C 260/90, 81.
45 For the indices of agreement of the individual RCVs see Appendix.
46 Within the Socialist group, the following British Labour members Falconer, Hindley, Lomas, MacGowan, Newman, Stewart, Smith A., West as well as the Belgian Socialist MEP van Hemeldonck abstained from the vote.

77

countries, already burdened by a heavy public debt. The repayment of the loans of African, Caribbean and Pacific countries equivalent to 1,300 billion dollars should be written off to prevent further their economic deterioration (van Putten, 11/10/1990, 274). The Socialists urged the Community to bear the repatriation costs of the thousands of Filipino workers who had to flee from Iraq, with serious economic consequences for their country which had also been hit by a major earthquake on 16 July 1990 (Visser, 11/10/1990, 274-275).

As the French MEP Gérard Caudron pointed out, the Gulf crisis had given cast-iron proof not only of Saddam's totalitarian régime, but also of an "even more evil" dictatorship imposed by certain multinational companies. Hence, the Commission should take swift and effective measures to control the oil sector, re-establish order to the market and penalize speculators. In addition, energy-saving policies should be adopted and the use of alternative energy sources promoted (Caudron, 11/10/1990, 284). The majority of the Socialists advocated a diplomatic solution, to be carried out at international level rather than via a unilateral EC action (Woltjer, 23/10/1990, 81-82). In December, the Socialists welcomed, as a step in the right direction, Saddam's decision to free the hostages and finally to comply with the conditions established by the UN Security Council. They also welcomed the Council's invitation to the Iraqi Foreign Minister to stop in Rome on his return from Washington (Sakellariou, 11/12/1990, 69-70). The group's cohesion seemed to decline further with regard to the UN ultimatum to Iraq, which was considered a mistake by the majority who opposed military intervention, in the belief that the sanctions would eventually force Iraq to yield (Cheysson, 74-75, Crampton, 76-77, 11/12/1990, Newens, 150, Crawley, 151, McGowan, 152, Tongue, 153, Falconer, Hughes, 154, Green, 155, Coates 155-156, Elliot, 156, Crampton, 160, McCubbin, 161, Romeos, 162, 23/1/1991).

The Socialists, together with the European Unitarian Left and the Left Unity, tabled a Motion for a Resolution which was passed by the House on 12 December, after 5 roll-call votes requested by the British Labour MEP Alexander Falconer and 23 other members (*OJEC* C 19, 28/1/1991, 53). Of the 127 Socialist members present, 121 supported the Joint Motion, while 6, specifically 3 British Labour, 2 German Social Democrats and one Belgian Socialist members abstained from the vote. During the same session, the group almost unanimously, with the exception of the Spanish MEP Francisco Javier Sanz Fernandéz and the German MEP Rolf Linkohr, opposed the approval of the text jointly presented by the Christian

Democrats, the Liberals and the British Conservatives (*OJEC* C 19, 28/1/1991, 53). The outcome of the RCV on Recital E "Whereas the military option is not an automatic consequence of the adoption of Resolution 678" displayed a very high index of agreement, 98.40 percent, with 124 votes in favour and only one dissenting vote cast by the British MEP David Bowe. The expression "[The EP] calls on the United Nations to continue to manage this conflict and *calls for no military action to be taken*" (emphasis added) was endorsed by 124 members while only one member rejected it and 2 preferred to abstain from voting reaching an IA equal to 95.28 percent.

The initial response of the Socialist group, which changed by the end of the pre-war stage, was founded on the premise that war should be averted at any costs and that every effort should be made to reach a settlement of the crisis through political negotiations and economic sanctions. Emphasis was put on full compliance with UN Resolutions and a commitment by the international community to address the crucial problem of economic disparities in the region and to find a definitive settlement to the Palestinian question (Cheysson, 11/12/1990, 74-75). Throughout this stage, the Socialists registered a very high level of agreement in the RCVs, at 91.21 percent. The low level of absenteeism within the group, equal to 29.96 percent, also deserves mention.[47]

b) War Stage
On 16 January 1991, Jean-Pierre Cot together with the Chairman of the European Unitarian Left, Luigi Colajanni, issued a common declaration supporting the 'last-minute' initiative by President Mitterand (Cot and Colajanni, 1991, PE/GC/08/91). Saddam's disregard for this new peace proposal induced the Socialist leader to deem legitimate the military option, albeit strictly limited to the liberation of Kuwait. He then criticized the European Community for "cut[ting] a sorry figure in the Gulf crisis", stressing the importance of preparing an international conference on the Middle East (Tutt, 1991).

A few days later, at the January session, controversy arose as to whether to back the proposal by the German SPD member, Gerd Walter, to call for an immediate halt to the bombing by the international coalition or

---

47 For parameters of interpretation of both index of agreement and level of absenteeism see table in the Appendix, Section 1.2.

to insist first on the complete withdrawal of Iraqi troops from Kuwait. The outbreak of the war found the group increasingly more divided. In expressing its disagreement with the US and the allies' decision to initiate military operations in the Gulf a faction of the Socialist group, bringing together British, German and Greek MEPs, with the Greens, the European Left Unity and the Left Unity appealed for an immediate ceasefire. It is noteworthy that Labour MEPs distanced themselves from the position taken by their national party, strongly believing that the drastic step of taking military action against Iraq could be justified only when all other attempts at negotiations had failed. As such, the EP was asked to distinguish itself as the only Community institution and the only parliament in Europe to continue supporting a non-military settlement of the crisis (Romeos, 23/1/1991, 162). The Iraqi government was urged to grasp the opportunity offered by the Soviet peace plan and the Council's disregard of the initiative was denounced. By referring to the fact that only four of the twelve member states had received the text of Gorbachev's proposal, the Socialists stressed the importance of coordinating actions between member states (Woltjer, 121-122, Lagorio, 134, Romeos, 135-136, Schinzel, 138 and Sakellariou, 139, 20/2/1991, Sakellariou, Ford, 9, Dury, Collins, 13, 21/2/1991).

Eventually, the defiant attitude of Saddam induced an increasingly larger section of the group to admit that the international community had no alternative but to resort to force. [A note of approval was addressed to the Commission for its efforts to assist refugees and to provide technical support to Egypt, Jordan and Turkey (Crampton interview, 31/1/1996)]. The group pointed out that the West had to acknowledge its responsibility in arming the Arab world by urging the leaders of industrialized countries to initiate a joint policy to limit and control effectively the sale of arms to the Middle East (Sakellariou, 69-70, Cheysson, 11/12/1990, 74-75, Morris, 20/2/1991, 139). The danger was envisaged of the conflict being extended into a general North-South confrontation taking the "insidious and destructive forms of terrorism and a war of religion" (Di Rupo, 23/1/1991, 152).

Following long discussions within the group as well as in the Chamber between belligerents and non-belligerents, a solution was defined by Cot, envisaging a cessation of hostilities as soon as Saddam started to evacuate Kuwait (Cot, 23/1/1991, 126). Furthermore, in order to prevent the widening of the conflict in the region, the Greek Socialist delegation recommended that the Security Council impose a ceasefire and resume negotiations for the liberation of Kuwait. The necessity of peace and stability in the whole region through a durable settlement of the Palestinian, Lebanese and Cypriot questions was emphasized (Romeos, 23/1/1991, 162). Major Socialist concern was "to contain the war and to bring it to a rapid conclusion with minimum casualties" (*OJEC* C 48, 25/2/1991, 115-116).

The Socialists, presumably in order to detect the position of their own members, requested a RCV on the January Joint Resolution tabled in conjunction with the EPP, ED and Rainbow group. Among 138 Socialist members who voted, 90 supported the text, 33 rejected it and 15 abstained. The British Labour members, in particular, were split with 13 voting in favour, 16 voting against and 8 abstaining. The German SPD members also were divided with 14 members endorsing the Joint Resolution, 10 rejecting and 3 abstaining. The Spanish MEPs voted unanimously instead for the January Motion. Consequently, the index of agreement was fairly low, equal to 30.43 percent. With regard to the Motion for a Resolution on the Gulf and the Baltic states, 60 members, including all UK Labour members and over two-thirds of German Socialists (52 MEPs) voted in favour, almost all Spanish and French Socialists members voted against and only one Spanish MEP abstained.

The Community appeared unable to respond to the events in the Gulf due not only to the absence of a defence and security structure, but to the lack of political will to foster the integration process (*OJEC* 3-398, 21/1/1991). Hence, Parliament was encouraged to promote the establishment of firmly based Community institutions to tackle security and defence issues. Concern was expressed at domestic racist reactions against Arabs and Muslims as well as environmental consequences of the conflict. An abstentionist Socialist approach stood out in sharp contrast with the other PG positions and a schism re-emerged at the extraordinary sitting held in Brussels on 31 January. Whilst the group was united on a number of points relating to the crisis, it was unable to paper over the emerging cracks and splits within its ranks over the core issue of strategies. As Chart 1a shows, the trend for the IA during the second stage was very fragmentary and irregular, falling to 50.06 percent, the lowest among all the other groups. In this stage, the Socialists reached even a lower level of absenteeism of 27.74 than in the previous one.

c) Post-War Stage

Following Cot's view that "une guerre juste est inutile si elle n'est pas suivie d'une paix juste",[48] the Socialist Group pleaded that all efforts be made to assist the material reconstruction of the whole region, to find the measures necessary to ensure a long-lasting peace and to recreate the links of trust between Europe and the Arab community (Dury, 1991, 22, *Presse information*, 28/2/1991). Criticism was directed against the Community's approval of the US decision to continue the embargo against Iraq even after its withdrawal from Kuwait (Pagoropoulos, 13/3/1991, 87).

The need for an adequate European defence and security framework was reiterated, this time in conjunction with the proposal of setting up an Arab Development Bank (Cheysson, 13/3/1991, 75). Since the Gulf War showed the obnoxious consequences of the conduct of unscrupulous Western and Soviet entrepreneurs in the arms industry, the Commission should monitor arms exports in the region, promote the reduction of the Iraqi, Syrian and also Israeli armaments and harmonize the penalties for illegal arms dealers (Sakellariou, 13/3/1991, 88-89, Ford, 13/3/1991, 90-91, Randzio-Plath, 13/3/1991, 91-92). The Socialists supported the *Lamassoure Report* regarding the amendment of the 1991 budget so as to provide emergency aid to the Kurds (Tomlinson, 14/5/1991, 81) and applauded the EP for its prompt response to the Council proposal enabling the Commission to implement this humanitarian aid programme without delay. The preference given by the Community to Israel in previous commercial and association agreements should be counterbalanced by developing closer relationships with Arab countries (Belo, 15/5/1991, 142).

In the aftermath of the war, the group seemed to have rediscovered its unity, registering its highest index of agreement, 97.46 percent but with a noticeable increase in absenteeism rising to 56.42 percent, which remained the second lowest if compared to the other groups' records over this stage. The Socialists were unanimous on 6 out of 8 roll-call votes. In the first part of paragraph 8 of Joint Resolution on arms exports in the Gulf region of 18 April 1991, "call[ing] for better coordination of the European arms industry in the EC internal market with a view to reducing surplus capacity and avoiding duplication, particularly in the cost-intensive area of research" only one dissenting voice emerged from a Dutch member (B3-0552, 0555,

---

48 "A just war is worthless if it is not followed by a just peace" (author's translation).

0562, 0564, 0565 and 0660/91). The first part of Amendment 1 to Joint Resolution on the situation of the Kurds (B3-556/91 et al.) was overall opposed by the group, but was endorsed by 7 members including 3 German, one French, one British, one Irish and one Italian MEPs.

In brief, throughout the whole period of the crisis the Socialists' average index of agreement was equal to 73.28 percent, the third lowest outcome among all the parliamentary groups, except for the Independent members. Specifically, the rate of cohesion drastically dropped between the pre-war and war stages by 41.15 percent. However, these figures need to be examined in light of the large size of the group as well as the fairly low absenteeism rate of 33.17 at the RCV sessions to avoid misperceptions over what could appear to be a strong Socialist inclination to factionalism.

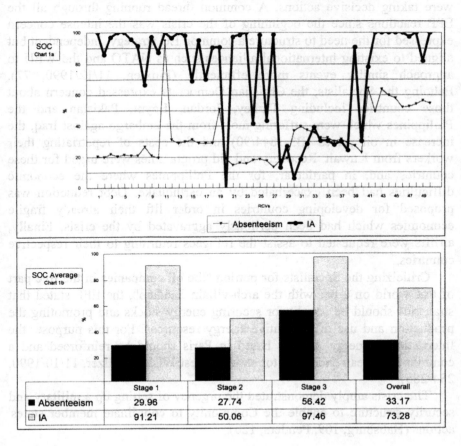

1.2 The European People's Party

a) Pre-War Stage

The European People's Party Group (EPP) categorically demanded an unconditional Iraqi withdrawal from Kuwait, the restoration of the Kuwaiti government and the immediate liberation of all Western hostages as preconditions for opening a dialogue with Saddam on broader issues afflicting the Middle East. The group's profile vis-à-vis the developments in the Gulf mirrored essentially its pro-Atlantic tradition with the endorsement in December 1990 of the UN ultimatum (Pesmazoglou, 11/12/1990, 70). Disappointment was expressed at the passivity of the Community which seemed to be 'looking on' whilst the US and the UN were taking decisive actions. A common thread running through all the EPP reactions since the beginning of the crisis was the intense concern expressed for the need to structure a common EU strategy, independent but aligned to existing international alliances such as NATO and the WEU to approach similar events more efficiently (Pinxten, 11/12/1990, 77). Echoing the Socialists, the Christian Democrats expressed concern about those countries including Turkey, Jordan, Egypt, Pakistan and the Philippines which were suffering most from the embargo against Iraq, the increase in oil prices (B3-1844/90) and the costs of repatriating their workers from Kuwait. Recovery and aid programmes were urged for these countries and, in particular, for the Philippines where the economic difficulties had been exacerbated by an earthquake. Debt reduction was proposed for developing countries in order lift their already fragile economies which had been perilously aggravated by the crisis. Finally, airlifts were requested to assist the refugees returning to their respective countries.

Criticizing the Socialists for putting "the oil companies in the free part of this world on a par with the arch-villain Saddam", the EPP stated that strategies should be sought for securing energy stocks and promoting the production and use of alternative energy resources. For this purpose, the International Energy Agency based in Paris should be reinforced and a common European energy sector should be established (Sälzer, 11/10/1990, 284-285).

The crisis amply demonstrated the urgency of setting up a military and security structure to enable the Community to coordinate member states' actions (Habsburg, 109, Penders, 120).

The Christian Democrats were apprehensive about the risks associated with an open military conflict which might well conflagrate into a "dirty technological war" with devastating consequences for civilians and for the environment as well as serious repercussions in the West-Arab relations.

The EPP members objected, together with the Socialists, to the separate initiatives undertaken by the "Baghdad pilgrims" to release the hostages, as they would render the situation for those remaining more difficult (Habsburg, 108, Penders, 119-120 12/9/1990). In line with the view of José-Maria Aznar, Chairman of Spain's *Partido Popular*, the Spanish Delegation of the EPP voted in favour of the September Joint Resolution, although with certain reservations especially with regard to paragraph 8 which did not fully acknowledge the crucial role played by the United States in the management of the crisis (Robles Piquer, 12/9/1990, 139). The RCV on the September Joint Resolution revealed a high index of agreement within the EPP equal to 95.51 percent with 87 votes in favour, no votes against and 2 abstentions by the Portuguese MEP Luis Filipe Beirôco and the French MEP Jean-Louis Bourlanges.

In November, the general message proposed by the EPP was that although Parliament could not yet opt for peace or war, it had nevertheless the duty to denounce the violence and devastation perpetrated by Saddam (Robles Piquer, 22/11/1990, 249). The average index of agreement within the EPP Group held during this stage on 19 roll-call votes was extremely high, equal to 92.65 percent, showing a very constant trend with the exception of RCVs 17 and 18 which suddenly marked a drastic drop. In addition, the absenteeism rate of the EPP group was fairly low, equal to 38.17.

b) War Stage
In the group's view, Saddam's fanatic and intransigent attitude had finally dispelled hope for a negotiated solution to the crisis in line with the UN objectives, leaving the international community with no other choice but to resort to force. In expressing support for the US-led armed intervention and calling for German contribution, Hans-Gert Poettering, the German CDU Security Policy Spokesman in the EP, stated:

> We Germans cannot stand apart. Germany enjoyed the support of the Western allies for forty years; now the West can rightly demand our support, especially for the future (*The European*, 25/1/1991).

He regretted Germany's decision not to participate militarily due to presumed constitutional restraints which did not exist in the text of the

German constitution as the Federal Constitutional Court ultimately acknowledged (Poettering interview, 25/1/1996).

In January and February 1991, several MEPs attributed the Community's failure to mediate a solution to the crisis to the lack of cohesion between the member states (Cassanmagnago Cerretti, 5, Penders, 9, 30/1/1991, Pesmazoglou, 132-133, Poettering, 135, Reding, 136, Lucas Pires, 137, Oostlander, 138, 20/2/1991). The necessity was stressed for the Community to participate more actively in international issues and to set up a European collective security structure. The EPP restated its backing for the allied military intervention and land attack against Iraq, reiterating, however, the possibility of reopening a dialogue with Iraq when it began to withdraw from Kuwait (Cassanmagnago Cerretti, 5, 30/1/1991, Gaibisso, 130, Poettering, 135, Reding, 136, Merz, 138-139, 20/2/1991). The efforts made by the Soviet President Gorbachev and by Pope John Paul II to facilitate the swift conclusion of the armed conflict were welcomed (Penders, 20/2/1991, 122).

In the second stage, the Christian Democrats suffered a slight reduction in their level of cohesion, keeping, however, a fairly high index of agreement equal to 87.96 percent. Chart 2a displays a fragmented IA trend, dropping to the level of -1.27, with 39 members voting in favour, 33 voting against and 7 abstentions over Motion for a Resolution B3-120/90. After this steep fall, the group found again its cohesiveness, exhibiting a very regular trend in its IA. The level of absenteeism was of lower than in the previous stage, equal to 31.68.

c) Post-War Stage

After praising the United States for the liberation of Kuwait (Pisoni F., 90, Brok, 91, Lucas Pires, 91, Robles Piquer, 92, 13/3/1991), the Christian Democrats felt that the next step was to remedy the ravages of war and embark on the road to peace. In harmony with its political conviction, the EPP contemplated the prospect of founding a society on the Christian Democratic values of solidarity, respect for cultural differences and safeguarding of the environment (PPE document, Dublin, 15-16/5/1990, pars. 6-26-31).

Numerous questions had to be addressed: restoration of peace in Iraq, a homeland for the Palestinians, definitive and internationally guaranteed borders for Israel, acknowledgement of the rights of the Kurds, liberation of Lebanon, assistance in the establishment of democratic régimes in the area and a North-South dialogue (Pisoni F., 13/3/1991, 90). For this purpose, the group as a whole supported the idea of convening an international conference and undertaking bilateral negotiations alongside parliamentary meetings with representatives of the Maghreb, Mashreq and the Gulf states so as finally to reach a long-lasting peace in the region. However, while for some the Middle East questions were to be examined in the wider context of the problems afflicting the Mediterranean basin, for others they would be better tackled separately (Robles Piquer, 13/3/1991, 92). However, to enable the Community to make an impact in the Middle East and "to influence the fate of the world" a genuinely common and coordinated defence should be established under the Western European Union and European Political Cooperation frameworks (Fontaine, 13/3/1991, 83). EPP confirmed its full commitment to the realization of the 'United States of Europe' which would speak in unison, sharing international responsibilities with the United States reviving the traditional Atlantic loyalty and solidarity (Webster, 1994, 284, Robles Piquer, 13/3/1991, 92).

The Christian Democrats condemned the Iraqi setting fire to Kuwaiti oil wells which had caused huge environmental damages without even achieving any military objectives. In addition, the EPP members argued that the European Community and the international community should not tolerate further Saddam's continual violations of fundamental rights towards the Kurdish minority and all opposition groups (Brok, 13/3/1991, 91). In particular, the group succeeded in securing parliamentary endorsement of paragraph 5 of the April Joint Resolution on the Kurds regarding an appeal to the United Nations to prevent authoritarian régimes from committing genocide, if necessary by revising the text of the UN Charter and by elaborating the content of UN Resolution 688 (EPP Report of the activities, 9/1991, 29). The EPP believed that immediate measures were necessary alleviate the sufferings of the Kurds. In May 1991, it was stressed that to ensure the democratic development of this area aid should be granted upon condition of respect for fundamental rights (Lenz, 15/5/1991, 140). The level of cohesion achieved in the RCVs on the Gulf over this final stage was rather high, the highest registered during the whole crisis, with an index reaching 96.77 percent. On 5 of the 8 roll-call votes requested in this post-war stage, the EPP reached full unanimity.

In summary, the overall EPP's index of agreement with respect to the Gulf case was much higher than that achieved by the Socialists, achieving the considerable score of 91.15 percent. The EPP level of absenteeism amounted to 39.69, a figure higher than that attained by its major political opponent, but still slightly below the average.

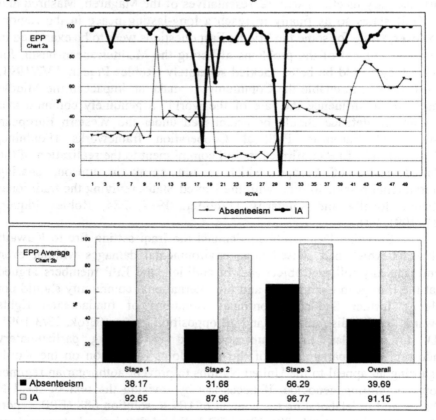

1.3 The Liberal Democratic and Reformist Group

a) Pre-War Stage
The Liberals fully acknowledged the American Presidency's resolute and swift response in the Gulf which had deterred Iraq from attacking Saudi Arabia whilst they reproached the EP's failure to recognize the key role of the United States (Giscard d'Estaing, 12/9/1990, 109-110, 151-152). They criticized the ambiguous 'pseudo-pacifist' expression contained in the September Joint Resolution that "only a diplomatic solution [could] finally settle the crisis". This could be interpreted as Europe's denial to consider military intervention as a possible option, "giving official sanction to a drawn-out waiting game" (Nordmann, 12/9/1990, 155). In their view, no

sufficient emphasis was placed on the need for creating a foreign and security policy structure capable of dealing with emergencies outside the European geographical area such as in the case of the Gulf. The text of the September Resolution did not stress sufficiently the urgency of calling on the Community to get out of the impasse and share international responsibilities with the United States (Amaral, 12/9/1990, 157).

The members of the small Italian Republican Party advocated the sending of Italian and European military contingents to the Gulf, a position that soon after was supported by the whole LDR (La Malfa, 12/9/1990, 121). Despite all the above reservations, the majority of the Liberals eventually decided to endorse the Resolution while the members of the Portuguese Socialist Democratic Party abstained from the vote, as the text had failed in their opinion to address the need to find "a serious and radical solution to the climate of mistrust and confrontation latent in the Mediterranean region and the Persian Gulf" (Amaral, 12/9/1990, 157). The Liberals together with the Greens and the European Right requested a split vote on the September Resolution, yet for diametrically opposite reasons and certainly not for "joining in the ranting and raving of the yobbos of the extreme right" (Nordmann, 12/9/1990, 155). The LDR index of agreement over the final vote on the whole text was of 29.41 percent, with 22 voting in favour, 9 abstaining and 2 Belgian MEPs, Jean Defraigne, François Xavier de Donnea as well as one French MEP Jean-Thomas Nordmann voting against.

Over the following months, the LDR reaffirmed its firm stance against Saddam by also advancing the proposal of establishing international criminal procedures against him (de Donnea, 11/10/1990, 273). The group also expressed disappointment at the separate initiatives for the release of the hostages, regardless of the common agreement to find a collective solution (Nordmann, 251, Veil, 248, 22/11/1990). Finally, the group stressed the need for the Community to grant financial assistance to countries such as Jordan, Egypt and Turkey in order to contain the economic consequences of the crisis (Lacaze, 22/11/1990, 252).

Overall, the LDR shared with the EPP a strict position towards the Iraqi unconditional withdrawal from Kuwait and the release of hostages in support of UN Resolutions and US policy. The group criticized the absence of coordinated Community actions and called for the development of a distinctive and independent foreign policy (Giscard d'Estaing, 12/9/1990, 109, Veil, 22/11/1990, 248-249 and 11/12/1990, 70-71, Capucho, 23/10/1990, 82, Veil, 248-249, Nordmann, 251, 22/11/1990).

As to the means to solve the crisis, the Liberals hoped that diplomatic negotiations and economic sanctions would be sufficient, but did not exclude the resort to arms. They congratulated the Council on its prompt adoption of trade sanctions which had blocked 97 percent of Iraq's revenues coming from oil exports and proposed to impose even a stricter embargo, including a land blockade (Veil, 22/11/1990, 248-249). However, in November 1990, as the situation deteriorated, the LDR Members became increasingly convinced that only military means would force Saddam's hand and stated that the immediate release of the hostages was an absolute precondition for any negotiation regarding the Iraq-Kuwait dispute and all other problems in the Middle East (Nordmann, 22/11/1990, 251).

Echoed by leaders of other PGs, Valéry Giscard d'Estaing stressed that European security policy should be the responsibility of the Community and not just individual member states (*The Guardian*, 13/9/1990). To prevent "the total marginalization of Europe in the next stage of world history" (Palmer, John, 1990, 6), the Community should create a political and security structure.

Between 12 September 1990 and 15 January 1991, the LDR reached the high index of agreement of 76.79 along with a fairly low level of absenteeism of 38.17.

b) War Stage

Although acknowledging that war meant the "defeat of sound sense, reason and diplomacy", the Liberals noted that "it was not possible to find a diplomatic solution to the Gulf crisis and that the only option left was alas to resort to force" (De Clercq, 22/1/1991, 21). As such, the undertaking of US-led military operations against Iraq to prevent the annexation of Kuwait becoming a *fait accompli* was strongly supported. No negotiations should be open with Saddam prior to his complete surrender and full admission of responsibility of the conflict and no ceasefire authorized.

There were, nonetheless, members such as Rafael Calvo Ortega who rejected the idea that war was the only possible option (Ortega, 21/1/1991, 23). The explanation of vote which took place on 23 January triggered a new debate in the House. Simone Veil expressed her earnest opposition to the text of the Joint Resolution which attempted "to compromise all positions by saying simultaneously that the United Nations Resolutions [would] be observed" while agreeing to negotiate "once a start has been made on a total withdrawal from Kuwait", concluding that it would be outrageous if the EP were to vote for such a controversial and equivocal Resolution (Veil, 23/1/1991, 153).

The LDR position, which closely mirrored that adopted by the EPP, was further underpinned at the Enlarged Bureau meeting on 30 January 1991 in Brussels. Liberals advocated the setting up of a European armament agency, placed under the Council of Defence Ministers to regulate and monitor the production and export of arms, the strengthening of the embargo controls and enhancement of EPC actions in the Gulf region. Support was therefore expressed for the realization of a common European foreign policy (de Donnea, 6/2/1991 5, Giscard d'Estaing, 20/2/1991, 122-123). During the second stage of the Gulf issue, the group showed a very irregular trend in their voting behaviour,[49] averaging an high index of agreement of 73.63 percent, and registering a lower level of absenteeism of 31.68 than in the previous stage.

c) Post-War Stage

In the aftermath of the war, the Liberals reiterated the view that the crisis had confirmed the need for a solid European security policy within the UN framework, aimed to "inject a sense of purpose and dynamism into the WEU" (Webster, 1994, 282). The NATO Alliance would remain at the heart of European collective security until a new system, involving all members of the Conference of Security and Cooperation in Europe (CSCE), could be established. The Liberals wished to see the four disjointed foreign policy sectors - EPC, development policy, external relations and security - integrated within the Community system (Ashdown, 19/6/1991, 24 and 26). Hopes were expressed that Europe would "speak with one voice" at least during the peace process. The convening of an international conference on the Israeli-Arab question was once again proposed, together with a symposium on security and cooperation in the Mediterranean (de Donnea, 6/2/1991, 5).

The Liberals refused to support the March compromise text which did not highlight enough the outstanding role played by the US force and the efforts made by the international coalition in the Gulf. In addition, the text failed to demand the United Nations' commitment to regulate arms sales,

---

49 This trend touched the most critical points over Resolution B3-115 of 23 January 1991 proposed by the EDA and Resolution B3-0333 of 21 February 1991 proposed by the Greens.

leading ultimately to the elimination of weapons of mass-destruction in the area (De Montesquiou Fezensac, 13/3/1991, 77).

In April 1991, the group participated in the drafting of the Joint Resolution on the Kurds and the Joint Resolution on arms exports, while in May 1991 it reproached the Community for failing to respect its promise regarding the Middle East peace process (Amaral, 15/5/1991, 140-141).

In the post-war stage, the level of cohesion reached the optimal 100 percent, registering a quite noticeable increase between the second and third stage of the Gulf crisis by 26.37 percent. This flattering outcome is weakened by the extraordinary rate of absenteeism of 76.02 percent. The average degree of cohesion throughout the three-stage crisis touched 79.05 percent, lower than that of the other centre-right groups. The Liberals had a conspicuous level of absenteeism with an average 54.41 percent of its members deserting the RCV sessions on the Gulf.

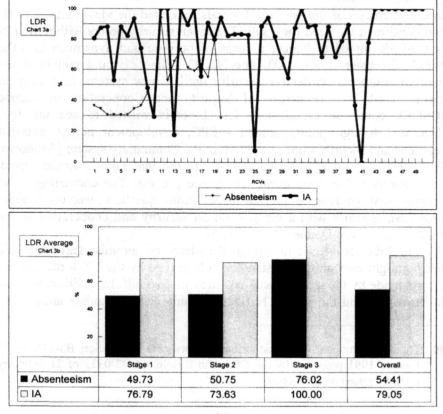

1.4 The European Democratic Group

a) Pre-War Stage

In September 1990, the European Democratic Group (ED) unequivocally expressed its firm condemnation of Saddam's invasion and illegitimate annexation of Kuwait as the nineteenth province of Iraq. This act was regarded as an act of aggression against a sovereign country and a violation of the most basic rules of international law as well as human rights. The group acknowledged the prompt American action in response to the Iraqi threat to invade Saudi Arabia and to expropriate its oil resources, which would affect dangerously the economy of industrialized countries heavily reliant on Saudi oil imports (*The Daily Telegraph*, 13/9/1990). As Sir Christopher Prout, the ED leader, put it "[n]ot for the first time, Europe ow[ed] the United States an immense debt", warning that, if on this occasion the Americans intervened to safeguard out-of-area European interests, in future this might not occur.

The inadequate response by the Twelve to Iraqi aggression was due to the lack of political organization and defence mechanisms (Prout, 12/9/1990, 110-111). Nevertheless, the EC's conduct was defined as exemplary in the field where it could exert its full supranational powers, by quickly enforcing trade sanctions, enacting legislation in order to implement UN Resolutions, providing emergency assistance for refugees and proposing aid plans in favour of countries such as Turkey, Egypt and Jordan. However, as William Francis Newton Dunn pointed out, other countries such as India, Pakistan and Bangladesh, which were also bearing the onerous costs of the crisis, also deserved EC and international attention (Newton Dunn, 12/9/1990, 137-138).

The European Democrats believed that once the expulsion of Iraqis from Kuwait had been completed, the causes of the crisis such as the disparities of wealth in the region as well as the racial tensions should not be forgotten. In addition, Western countries had to face their responsibility for having armed Iraq through the indiscriminate sale of conventional and chemical weapons and take adequate measures. Not surprisingly, the group, consisting almost exclusively of British Conservatives, reflected the UK government's policy line (Rawlings, 12/9/1990, 155). Although naturally preferring a peaceful solution, they remained sceptical about the chances of settling the question diplomatically, considering necessary the use of "additional" steps and notably military means to liberate Kuwait (McMillan-Scott, 12/9/1990, 128-129). The European Democrats took the view that only the 'logic of war' could induce Saddam to comply with the UN Resolutions. In light of the events in the Gulf, a new international order needed to be shaped in which the Community should play its part as a mediator and promoter of international peace (Prag, 12/9/1990, 135-136). Making no attempt to conceal his disappointment with the text of the September Joint Resolution, which he could not but vote against, Derek Prag commented that this showed "how spinelessly" the left-oriented Parliament reacted on defence issues (Prout, 110-111, Jepsen, 121, Prag, 135-136, 12/9/1990).

In early October, the group drafted a Motion for a Resolution,[50] on the "humanitarian consequences of the crisis", urging the Council and the Commission to make all efforts to indistinctly guarantee safe return of all foreign citizens detained in Iraq and to establish an official *ad hoc* intergroup with the task to closely follow its developments (B3-1816/90). Like the EPP, the ED deplored the Socialists' excessively negative remarks about oil companies, criticizing instead the Soviet suppliers for not having complied with their commitments to Yugoslavia and other Eastern European countries (Moorhouse, 11/10/1990, 285).

A substantial degree of group cohesion characterized from the start the ED policy vis-à-vis the Gulf in this stage, as reflected in its RCV record which reached the remarkable index of agreement of 93.68 percent. Moreover, the British Conservatives were the MEPs who most diligently attended RCV sessions over the Gulf in this stage. The level of absenteeism calculated with respect to its 34 members amounted to the low figure of 25.23 percent.

b) War Stage
In January 1991, along with the EPP and LDR, the ED endorsed US-led military operations against Iraq, especially acknowledging valuable British contribution. The group reiterated the view that no negotiation should be carried out with Iraq prior to its complete surrender and full admission of responsibility for the conflict. The group reiterated the view that the European countries should be grateful to the United States for defending

---

50 The ED Motion was replaced by a new text agreed with 8 other parliamentary groups. However, due to the House being inquorate, no Resolutions on the Gulf could be voted.

Western interests by bearing "the brunt of the financial and human cost" (Prout, 21/1/1991, 16).

Yet recognizing the efforts undertaken by President Gorbachev in order to avert a land war, the group asserted that military operations should not be halted without definite Iraqi commitment to the peace plan. Saddam's simple promise of withdrawal could not provide a sufficient guarantee, the only acceptable solution remaining an unconditional and irreversible retreat from Kuwait monitored by the international community (McMillan-Scott, 6, Prout, 10, 30/1/1991, Prag, 20/2/1991, 123-124).

In ED opinion, since Saddam had ignored all peace opportunities, the United Nations had no alternative but to authorize the recourse to force and for the international coalition to implement it in order to free Kuwait. Further delays regarding intervention, in the hope that sanctions would have brought some results, would have meant death and torture for more people, allowing "an evil to flourish unabated" (Jackson, C., 13/3/1991, 77).

The ED joined ranks with the criticisms voiced by the other major PGs at the lack of Community leadership and initiative, underlining the need for the Twelve to reappraise their political priorities and develop a common foreign policy strategy bringing together the European Community, NATO and WEU under the same umbrella (Prout, 10, 30/1/1991).

During the second stage, the ED overall index of agreement was 94.86 percent, reaching in 15 out of 23 cases a unanimity of vote and in only one case an index of agreement as low as 64.29 percent, with one abstention, 23 votes in favour, 4 against the adoption of Amendment 1 to first draft of the January Joint Resolution tabled and later withdrawn by the Socialists and the Rainbow group.

c) Post-War Stage

In March 1991, the ED expressed its appreciation at the courage and proficiency demonstrated by the US-led coalition against the Iraqi enemy in the liberation of Kuwait. The British Conservative MEPs also raised the crucial issue of the Iraqi Parliament's recognition of an independent Kuwait as well as the parliamentary ratification of the treaties of the 1930s and 1960s evoked as one of the reasons for the annexation.

With regard to the conditions to be imposed on Saddam, the group demanded that the Iraqi leader be held responsible for his military aggression, environmental damages as well as crimes against the Kuwaiti population, the Allies and his own people (Rawlings, 13/3/1991, 88). In

95

addition, sanctions should not be lifted until an adequate compensation scheme was drawn up, through, for example, a levy on Iraqi oil revenues (Jackson, C., 13/3/1991, 77-78). As to the wider issues in the region, Patricia Rawlings advocated smaller-scale negotiations, which had proven to be successful between Egypt and Israel, rather than large international conferences. The question of the Kurds was seriously considered by the British Conservatives who tabled a Joint Motion for a Resolution on the subject with the vast majority of MEPs (Rawlings, 13/3/1991, 88).

It was argued that Europe could play a valuable role in supporting the creation of a Middle Eastern Community with the objective of overcoming the differences between Arabs and Israelis as France and Germany had done in 1951 with the establishment of the European Coal and Steel Community (Prag, 21/1/1991, 22). The Community should also draw the attention of the Middle Eastern countries to the advantages of democracy by reminding them that EC loans and assistance would be granted only if human rights were respected and free elections convened (McMillan Scott, 6/2/1991).

The group reiterated throughout the crisis the necessity for Europe to speak with one voice on topical questions of international politics (Webster, 1994, 277) and to strengthen its structures (Elles, James, 25/1/1991). It advocated a modernization of the British nuclear deterrent and the updating of NATO nuclear structures in view of establishing a committed and coordinated European defence sector (Webster, 1994, 277).

The ED showed a quite consistent high level of cohesiveness throughout the crisis, reaching its highest index of agreement, 97.50 percent in the post-war stage. Out of 8 RCVs, the members voted unanimously on 7 occasions with only one dissenting opinion on Amendment 17 of the March Joint Resolution (B3-0398, 0402, 0429, 0450 and 0466/91). Overall, the European Democrats boasted the highest index of agreement and the lowest index of absenteeism in comparison with all groups, by reaching over the whole period of the crisis an exceptionally high figure of 94.83 percent with a low rate of absenteeism of 29.41 percent. These figures demonstrate how the traditional power and efficiency of their whipping system flowed from Westminster to Strasbourg. In this sense, the ED embodied the prototype for the other groups in the European Parliament by carrying the torch of cohesiveness and assiduity.

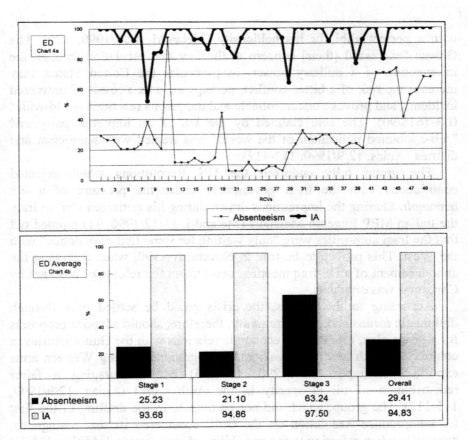

1.5 The Greens

a) Pre-War Stage

The Greens joined the chorus of condemnation at the invasion and annexation of Kuwait perpetrated by Iraq. Their position was conceived in light of their pacifist principles heavily laced with anti-imperialist sentiments, rather than on any grounds of sympathy for the totalitarian régime of the Kuwaiti Royal family (Telkämper, 12/9/1990, 124-125). Furthermore, the unilateral deployment of US troops and equipment in Saudi Arabia was as equally reprehensible as Saddam's enterprise, not least due to the hypocritical attempt to justify it as a measure officially carried out under the auspices of the United Nations. The group also viewed with consternation the prospect of constituting a US-led coalition which would symbolize in the eyes of the majority of Arabs the "alliance of the strong against the weak, the North against the poor South", providing Saddam with a perfect alibi for his bellicosity (Melandri, 12/9/1990, 129). The Greens "expressed [their] concern at the fact that escalation through the intervention of a military power, in particular the United States, may increase the risk of a bitter conflict, perhaps even as a result of unwanted incidents, and provoke uncontrollable and dangerous reactions world-wide" (B3-1618/90). The role claimed by the US of an impartial party and "self-appointed policeman of the world" was treated with scepticism and distrust (Aulas, 12/9/1990, 111-112).

The group fully endorsed the UN Resolutions which rejected negotiations with the Iraqi government under the pressure of a *fait accompli*. Sharing the impressions drawn during his criticized visit to Iraq, the Italian MEP Eugenio Melandri (Melandri, 11/12/1990, 71) pointed out that the Iraqi authorities were "only waiting for some hint of dialogue" with the West. This proved to be true in November 1990, when following the announcement of a US-Iraq meeting, news about the release of hostages by Christmas was divulged.

According to the Greens, the crisis could be settled only through diplomatic means and the Community, therefore, should advance proposals for a peace plan, establishing economic relations with the Gulf countries in conjunction with a wider development programme, halting Western arms exports (Telkämper, 12/9/1990, 124-125) and encouraging a fairer redistribution of oil prosperity in the Arab world (Aulas, 12/9/1990, 111-112). The group, which did not participate in the drafting of the first EP compromise Resolution on the Gulf, considered its text ambiguous, especially when referring to the possibility of introducing "additional" joint measures, tacitly implying military actions (Santos, 152, Piermont, 155, 12/9/1990). Moreover, the Resolution failed to address two fundamental questions, namely the search for alternative energy sources and the violation of frontiers in other parts of the Middle East and the world (Bettini, 12/9/1990, 157).

The group welcomed Council statements and the Commission decision to grant aid to refugees from Kuwait and those countries whose economies were significantly affected by the crisis (Aulas, 12/9/1990, 111). Importance was also placed on the economic and financial difficulties faced by ACP countries, by supporting the Resolution adopted on 25 September 1990 by the ACP-EEC Joint Assembly which envisaged the annulment of the debt incurred by these developing countries vis-à-vis the Community and its member states. The project of setting up a special financial mechanism for the above countries strongly dependent on oil import was also vigorously backed by the group (B3-1821/90). The Gulf crisis and the consequent increase in the price of petroleum products, magnified in the hands of unscrupulous speculators, aroused one of the most crucial quandaries of the contemporary industrial society relating to the limited availability of energy resources and the necessity of introducing energy-saving measures such as speed limits on national and provincial roads as well as looking for alternative and renewable resources such as gas, wind and waste (Bettini, 11/10/1990, 288).

Concern was especially expressed about the human and economic implications of the crisis for those countries whose population represented an important labour force in the region before August 1990. According to the Greens, financial assistance should be granted in order to help those governments facing the losses and the costs of mass-repatriation. As the French MEP and EP member to the Joint Assembly of the Agreement between the African, Caribbean and Pacific States and the European Economic Community (ACP-EEC), Marie-Christine Aulas pointed out, the incidents which occurred in October 1990 in Palestine and Lebanon should remind the international community that the Gulf crisis could not be dissociated from its geo-political context and therefore from the events of the other countries in the region.

For this reason, the group urged the Community to assist the Arab countries in settling their problems rather than exploiting these disputes to its own advantage. An international peace conference was called to ensure that all countries involved, including Israel and Syria, would fulfil the conditions set by all past UN Resolutions (Telkämper, 12/9/1990, 124-125, Aulas, 23/10/1990, 82). The urgency of shaping a coherent EC policy vis-à-vis the Middle East was evident together with the necessity of formulating a new notion of security from the roots entailing the adjustment of the whole defence structure of the European continent (Aglietta, 23/10/1990, 76-77).

In November 1990, the Dutch MEP Herman Verbeek claimed that the reason behind US intervention in the Gulf was primarily that of diverting public attention from increasingly pressing domestic economic problems. As such, the EP had to express its objection to the Community's involvement in military actions and to the American misuse of the United Nations for military purposes (Verbeek, 22/11/1990, 250). Overshadowed by the US, the EC had once again missed the opportunity to assert its own independent common foreign policy, losing the opportunity of being "a force for mediation" between the West and Iraq (Telkämper, 12/9/1990,

124-125, Aulas, 23/10/1990, 82). European 'vassalage' was seemingly confirmed once again in December 1990 when, following the US Administration's decision to receive the Iraqi Foreign Minister, the Community had "pathetically" extended an invitation to Tariq Aziz to stop in Rome on his return journey from the United States (Melandri, 11/12/1990, 71). Throughout the first stage of the crisis, while censuring the Iraqi aggression, the Greens rejected military intervention in the region. Aware of the interconnection between the various conflicts as well as their common economic and social background, the Greens emphasized that the Gulf crisis needed to be seen in a wider context by securing stability and peace in the whole region.

The Greens appeared divided on the question of whether to reject or abstain from voting on the text proposed on 12 September 1990 by the other six PGs. The majority, consisting of 15 MEPs, decided to vote against the Joint Motion, while 7 opted for abstaining and only one member, the German MEP Karl Partsch supported the Resolution, without explicitly or officially providing the grounds for his vote at the plenary.[51] By contrast, the Italian MEP Marco Taradash explained the reason behind his decision to abstain from the vote taken along with the other 6 colleagues, stressing that it would be "pointless to approve or disapprove a report, a document which [had] little effect on the situation" and criticized the EP for failing to convene at the same time as the other national parliaments "to seek to direct policy and the events that were taking place" (Taradash, 12/9/1990, 159).

Overall, in the pre-war stage, the Greens' average index of agreement was the lowest of all the PGs, falling to 50.03 percent, clearly showing that the group was torn over the policy line to adopt with regard to the Gulf issue. They failed to achieve internal cohesion, also being conspicuous by their absence of 50.82 percent.

b) War Stage
During the January plenary session, the Greens, together with some members of the Socialist group and the members of the European Left Unity, preferred to vote for a Motion requesting an immediate ceasefire in

---

51 Aglietta (Italy), Anger (France), Bandrés Molet (Spain), Quistorp (Germany), Staes (Belgium), Taradash (Italy) and Tazdait (France) abstained from the vote of the Joint Motion for a Resolution of 12 September 1990.

the Gulf (Abélès, 1992, 187-188). The group declared itself against military confrontation and in favour of a more sustained embargo, as war would evoke the hatred of the West from the Arab world. Aulas defined as "infamous" UN Resolution 678, for it showed up an absence of awareness and responsibility on the part of its supporters and particularly on the part of the American administration. She strongly criticized the United States for its improper use of the UN agencies for fixing an arbitrary deadline prior to assessing whether previous measures had a chance to reveal their effectiveness. As it soon became clear, this step was "tantamount to opting for war [by] stifling at the same time all diplomatic initiatives". She also reproached the European Community for being a lapdog to the Bush Administration and denounced as "two-faced" the approach of the international community with regard to the Gulf and to other international crises in Timor, Tibet and Cyprus, which revealed that "the implicit motive is far more enlightening than the proclaimed legal one" in the name of international law (Aulas, 21/1/1991, 16).

The Green members supported a further search for a diplomatic solution and a determination to avert war. Alexander Langer regretted that President Gorbachev had eclipsed the EC with his peace plan admitting that he would have preferred to see Jacques Poos, in his capacity of EC President, rather than Mikhail Gorbachev taking this initiative (Philip, Alan, 1991). The EC should take its own initiatives or support other proposals aimed to halt the hostilities. For this reason, the Greens expressed their full backing for the Soviet peace plan, which far from being "a vain piece of diplomatic propaganda" was attempting to reach a diplomatic breakthrough to the crisis. In order to enable Iraqi troops to pull out without the risk of being bombed, a free passage should be afforded. The Greens derided the concept of a 'just war' as medieval and counter-productive in turning Saddam into an Arab hero, while threatening the region's ecology. With reference to the numerous proposals and plan debated over future settlement of the Middle East problems, Langer sharply pointed out that "[f]irst of all (..) [the Community should] do something to bring this war to an end. Otherwise it [would be] useless bothering about the 'post-war period'". Only when the armed conflict was over, should the Community commit itself to favour the convening of an international conference in order to solve the pending problems in the region especially the Palestinian and the Kurdish questions (Langer, 20/2/1991, 124-125).

During the war stage the Greens' overall index of agreement was remarkably high, equal to 92.78 percent, significantly increasing their rate of agreement by 42.75 points between the first and the second stages. This suggests that the Greens went against the grain by passing from a situation of deep internal divide to a situation of high consensus. These figures are even more surprising in the light of the seriousness and intensity of the period and the fact that the Greens included members of almost all EC nationalities who held different views, not least with respect to European integration.

c) Post-War Stage

A couple of days after the end of the hostilities, the Belgian Green MEP Paul Staes made a brief visit to Baghdad where, escaping control and censure, he managed to obtain a more genuine picture of the actual condition of the population, deprived of food and medicine which had been long blocked at the Iraqi border, despite the fact that UN resolutions had exempted these supplies from the blockade, in danger of epidemics due to the shortage of clean water and the impossibility of sterilizing it for lack of fuel and gas and living in the terror of the secret police which still perpetrated atrocities on civilians (*Green Leaves*, 1991, 3).

On 5 March 1991, Co-Chairman Paul Lannoye and Co-vice Chairwoman Solange Fernex met a high clerk of the International Court of Justice in The Hague to convey the wish of the Group to see the question of the legality of the Gulf War brought for judgement. By their symbolic action, since only the States adhering to the Court can officially appeal to the Court, the Greens hoped to bring to public attention the need for a legal clarification of the Gulf case which had set a dangerous precedent for further military interventions by the United States under the aegis of the UN Security Council. The parliamentarians raised questions on the conformity of Resolutions against Iraq and of the military actions undertaken by the allied powers to the principles of the United Nations Charter along with the question of discrimination in the settlement of the Iraqi invasion of Kuwait if compared to the treatment by the Security Council of similar cases in other parts of the region and the world (*Green Leaves*, 1991, 3).

In April 1991, the Greens tabled together with most of the other PGs a Joint Motion for a Resolution on the Kurds' plight. They also contributed to the drafting of another Motion on arms exports for which along with the Rainbow group, they requested 3 roll-call votes. This apparently inconsistent behaviour was explained by Langer, who claimed that although "the only really clear-cut solution would be to impose a general production ban on armaments and to convert the industries concerned", since such a drastic solution could not be adopted in the short-term "even a small amount of disarmament and a small amount of conversion [proposed by the Joint Resolution were] a step in the right direction" (Langer, 18/4/1991, 286-287). For this reason as well as with the aim of halting weapon proliferation and arms races, which favoured black market sales, the Greens had decided to support the joint text with the exception of one part which in their view could be misinterpreted as an open, quasi optional invitation to adhere to this initiative, not as an absolute must and ethical duty (*OJEC* C 129, 122).

In addition, Brigitte Ernst de la Graete emphasized that the joint text called for the non-utilization of Article 223 EEC which hindered all EC control over state aid to arms manufacturers allowing them "to keep alive, by artificial means, businesses that serve no useful purpose and moreover are not economically viable". Overproduction in the arms industry is a strong incentive to sell arms abroad without considering any ethical principle. The European Community legislation should extend the control of arms exports until the achievement of a total ban on arms sale which would gradually lead to a reduction and cessation in the arms production. By giving voice to the opinion unanimously held by her group de la Graete concluded:

> The arms trade [was] a bane because it produc[ed] engines of death and also because it deflect[ed] large sums of money from things that the world badly needed (Ernst de la Graete, 17/4/1991, 142).

In the final stage, the Greens reached a remarkable index of agreement 92.08 percent, though inferior to that reached over the second and most critical period. The group remained significantly united, registering only on 2 occasions a very minimal dissent with respect to RCV on the second part of paragraph 8 of the Joint Resolution on the Gulf crisis and arms exports of 18 April 1991 and only one abstention with respect to the first part of Amendment 1 of the Joint Resolution on the Kurds tabled by all PGs with the exception of the ER group and the Independent members. During all three stages the attitude of the Greens vis-à-vis the Gulf issue remained faithful to their principled pacifism. Concerned about the increasingly fainter distinction between the European Community and NATO competence, the group continued to advocate a Europe without military alliances and free from nuclear, biological and chemical weapons. The

Greens strongly opposed the project of creating a European military superpower and the establishment of a European army (Webster, 1994, 282-283). They were favourable to the forging of an EC common foreign and security policy, though given the principle that security should not be confused with defence, no military purpose should be allowed. Its fundamental objective would instead focus on contributing to the solution of international conflicts through non-violent means (Fernex, 15/5/1991, 155).

Overall, throughout the above three stages, the group reached a satisfactory degree of cohesion of 76.96 percent, especially given the deliberate lack of whipping policy within the group, alongside a percentage of absenteeism of 45.79 at the voting sessions on the Gulf, lower than that of other groups.

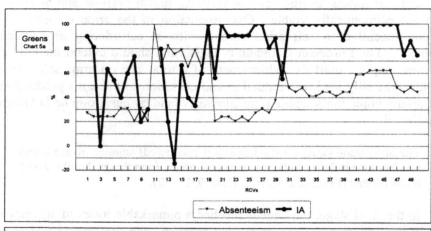

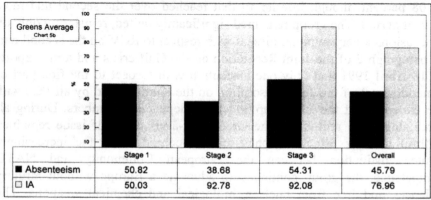

	Stage 1	Stage 2	Stage 3	Overall
■ Absenteeism	50.82	38.68	54.31	45.79
☐ IA	50.03	92.78	92.08	76.96

1.6 The European Unitarian Left

a) Pre-War Stage

As the other PGs in the Europarliamentary arena, the first reaction of the EUL vis-à-vis Kuwait's crisis was of open condemnation, joining the chorus of denunciation for the brutal actions and invasion perpetrated by Iraq (Papayannakis, 12/9/1990, 122). However, with regard to the solutions envisaged, the recourse to military measures was vigorously rejected, the group supporting, instead, the enforcement of the embargo against Iraq and occupied Kuwait as well as parallel negotiations in order to restore peace and order in the region. Emphasis was put on the principle that nothing should be done outside the scope of the United Nations, which should also monitor step by step all developments in the Gulf region (Colajanni, 12/9/1990, 152-153).

In a particularly articulate and perceptive intervention, which received wide acclaim and support within the House, Achille Occhetto, then Secretary-General of the Italian Communist Party *(PCI)* and member of the EUL group argued that the old order characterized by the Western-versus-Eastern blocs had ceased to exist leaving a vacuum which needed to be filled by a new form of world government. In Occhetto's words it should and could ".. be shown that, in the new international circumstances, the will of the international community can make legitimacy and the law prevail" (Occhetto, 12/9/1990, 112). The new world order, better balanced politically and economically should entail "a multipolar concept of power, a global review of trade relations" between the oil producers and the oil consumers, preventing the old bipolarity East-versus-West being replaced by the North-South divide. Europe should accordingly contribute by laying the economic and political foundations for a world democracy where all countries coexist peacefully (Occhetto, 12/9/1990, 113).

The EUL argued that political and diplomatic initiatives should be directed to secure the effective application of the sanctions and therefore the total isolation of Iraq. Through these pressurizing measures, Iraq's economy would be seriously crippled and eventually collapse, forcing Saddam to leave Kuwait. Only after this condition had been fulfilled, would it be possible to look for a solution to the Kuwaiti-Iraqi dispute which had triggered the invasion. In the group's view, the Gulf crisis illustrated the necessity for the active and committed involvement of the Community at international level aimed at opening a dialogue with the

105

Arab world and promoting a peaceful settlement of the major problems affecting the Middle East, such as the crises in Lebanon and Palestine. Closer and more advanced cooperation should be promoted in order to secure economic development and social progress through the setting up of a new Mediterranean policy. However, in order to fulfil this multiple task and to contribute to the creation of a new peaceful world order, the EC was urged to accelerate and complete its unification process (Occhetto, 12/9/1990, 112-113). Despite the many vague and unclear aspects of the September Joint Resolution, the EUL decided to endorse it, for the commitment to a non-military solution given by the Council Presidency and the Commission before the House, for the emphasis put on the role of the United Nations and for the intention of convening an international Middle East conference (Colajanni, 12/9/1990, 152-153). As the Green MEP Melandri pointed out ironically, EUL had voted not for what appeared in the Resolution but for what the Council Presidency had stated with regard to the Gulf crisis, though this was not explicitly included in the actual text (Melandri, 12/9/1990, 157). In agreement with the majority of the other groups, the EUL believed that besides the negative repercussions of the Gulf crisis, speculative movements had indisputably played their part in the rise of oil prices. Actions were therefore encouraged to prevent further damage to the economy of developing countries. The crisis raised the vital question of energy stocks and the necessity of adopting appropriate energy-saving policies at regional level (Porrazzini, 11/10/1990, 286).

The EUL reminded the House that the EC should allocate resources to assist those countries including Bulgaria, Yugoslavia and Romania whose economies had greatly suffered from the embargo against Iraq (EP Debate, 11/10/1990). In November 1990, the group requested the EP to disown Le Pen's journey to Iraq to negotiate the release of French hostages and to condemn "his shabby opportunism" (Pérez Royo, 22/11/1990, 250). The EUL members also protested against the UN and EC refusal to take immediate political steps to solve the Palestinian question, as urged by the EP (Colajanni, 13/3/1991, 79-80).

Referring to the UN deadline for 15 January, the EUL chairman stated that such a date should not be interpreted *strictu sensu* but as a term of reference to put pressure on the Iraqi government. In the unfortunate event that after this date Iraq continued its occupation of Kuwait, the international community should consider the military option "neither [as] automatic nor inevitable". The UN's ability to respond effectively to this crisis would be crucial for its credibility as a mediator in world affairs. The group also supported a more active involvement of the European Community, for instance, in the elaboration of a peace plan, thus finally removing the US monopoly over the conduct of international politics. The Community should make all efforts to promote the establishment of a permanent security structure in the Mediterranean.

The EUL appealed to the international community to pursue a united front in its pro-embargo policy, in its rejection of drastic military solutions and its search for restoring international order through negotiations (Colajanni, 12/12/1990, 71-72). Thus, the group offered its full endorsement to President Mitterand's attempt made within a few hours prior to the lapse of the ultimatum, to solve the crisis without resorting to drastic military means.

The EUL, as the Socialists, considered that the basic conditions for an agreement were Iraqi acceptance to evacuate Kuwait and the effective starting up of troop withdrawal, negotiation over the Iraqi-Kuwait dispute and the organization of an international conference to tackle the pending problems in the area. Disappointment was shown at the Community's failure to submit an independent peace-plan and a call for an extraordinary meeting of the EP Enlarged Bureau was issued to discuss the emergency in view of the UN deadline.

The group rejected absolutely the 'logic of war' which would bring disastrous consequences in terms of loss of human life, delay and perhaps risk of compromising perspectives of peace in the Middle East (PE/GC/08/91). From the outset of the crisis, the prospect of a military confrontation provoked outright opposition from the European Unitarian Left (EUL) which sought a peaceful solution under the UN auspices. All through this stage the official line of the group continued consistently and persistently to be that of rejecting force and violence as the means for settling the conflict, privileging instead peaceful solutions such as a pro-embargo policy and negotiations with the aim of confronting the issue in a wider regional context. Of course, it could be argued that the use of sanctions inevitably implies coercive measures involving sufferings and sometimes the loss of more civilian than military lives. For this reason, in the group's opinion, all efforts would have to be made to spare unnecessary torments to the population by preventing the extension of the embargo to medicine and food products.

The position taken by the European Unity Left was consistent in its search for a peaceful solution and its determination to avert war, boasting throughout this first stage the highest average index of agreement, 94.18

107

percent and with a medium-low level of absenteeism at 38.91 percent of its 28 members.

b) *War Stage*

At the January plenary, the EUL members expressed their regret at the start of the military operations by the US-led coalition against Iraq, affirming that this declaration of war would make Saddam a hero for the Arab world. Italian Communists strongly argued for a ceasefire and for the application of a more sustained embargo. Since the enforcement of a blockade had hitherto proven successful, an extension of the embargo would have further weakened the position of Iraq (Colajanni, 21/1/1991, 17-18). In their view, it was also necessary to open a Middle East conference to prevent the Iraqi leader from using the Palestinian question to attract more Arabs to his side.

Support was given to the Soviet peace plan which, although far from perfect, could be elaborated to stop the horrors of the war. The US decision to reject it was therefore deeply regretted by EUL members (Colajanni, 13/3/1991, 79-80). The group feared that the hatred aroused by the Gulf war in the Arab world would trigger a chain-effect of violence and brutality in the region (Colajanni, 21/1/1991, 17-18). Rage and frustration were conveyed at Europe's silence with respect to the crisis (Napolitano, 20/2/1991, 125-126) as a more elevated moral, political and civilian stance was expected of the Community and Parliament. The European Unitarian Left rejected the speculation that once war had started nothing and nobody could intervene to halt it, meaning that one would have to wait for its 'natural' conclusion (Colajanni, 21/1/1991, 17-18). EUL also criticized the EP and the EC tendency to look ahead to the post-war period, failing to address its responsibilities in order to prevent the spreading of the beyond the UN mandate (Colajanni, 30/1/1991, 7).

During the second stage of the Gulf issue the group's overall index of agreement was equal to 86.83 percent. Out of 23 roll-call votes which took place, 9 displayed a unanimous view, whilst the remaining 14 contained only one or two dissenting voices or abstentions. The greatest dissent within the group occurred in relation to Amendment 2 for the Motion for a Resolution B3-125 of 24 January 1991, when 4 out of 15 members, the Italian MEPs Bontempi, Castellina, De Giovanni and a member of the Spanish United Left Party *(Izquierda Unida)*, Pérez Royo, voted for the adoption of the amendment against the group's opposing line.

c) Post-War Stage

Besides the relief expressed at the end of the conflict and the final liberation of Kuwait, the group naturally welcomed the "tentative signs of a desire" to face the problems in the Middle East and initially the Palestinian Question. It also fully endorsed "every measure, every initiative, no matter who [would] propose it" in order to foster an Arab-Israeli dialogue and to assert the right of the Palestinians to a homeland. The Gulf crisis and war had once more exposed the deficiencies of the UN structure in terms of the means for applying its own Resolutions and its subsequent need for delegating to countries, in particular the United States, the task of enforcing them, with all the risks connected (Colajanni, 13/3/1991, 79-80).

The group blamed the West for its virtually uncontrolled and unlimited supply of arms to the Middle East and in April 1991 in a Joint Motion for a Resolution agreed together with the Socialist, EPP, LDR, ED, Green, Rainbow and LU groups over the urgency of establishing stricter regulations and controls on arms exports. With regard to the humanitarian aid for the Kurds the group was among the signers of the Joint Motion for a Resolution by the Socialist, EPP, LDR, ED, Green, EDA, Rainbow and LU groups passed by the House in April 1991.

During the third stage, no member opposed the official line in the RCVs, with the exception of the first part of Amendment 1 in the Resolution on the Kurds of 18 April 1991, when a Spanish MEP voted against whilst the majority of voting EUL members decided to abstain. On all other roll-call voting sessions with respect to the Gulf in the post-war period, the group expressed unanimity, although it also suffered from a high level of absenteeism. The members of the EUL found themselves in broad agreement over the post-war situation. This raised the index of agreement as compared to the previous stages to 96.43 percent. This figure needs nevertheless to be assessed against the high level of absenteeism of 75.89 percent.

Throughout the whole period, the position of the EUL remained virtually unaltered in its support for economic and political action and its denial of the use of force, retaining an extremely high degree of cohesiveness equivalent to 91.10 percent. The overall rate of absenteeism, although still significant, with 45 percent of the members of the group deserting the Chamber, remained below the average reached by the other groups.

109

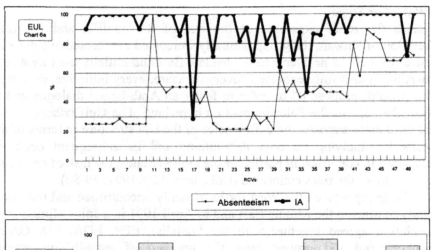

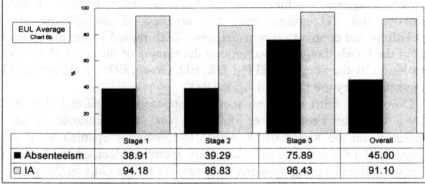

1.7 The European Democratic Alliance

a) Pre-War Stage

In September 1990, the European Democratic (EDA) harshly criticized the use "of a dual vocabulary, of two sets of criteria for judging behaviour (..), of two sets of moral standards": while the Iraqi invasion of Kuwait was unanimously denounced as a breach of international law, similar cases had in the past systematically been ignored, provoking nothing more than timid protests (Perreau de Pinninck, 12/9/1990, 129-130). A distinctive, though complementary position was taken by Greek MEP Nianias, Chairman of the delegation for relations with the Maghreb countries, who focused his attention on the attempted 'Iraqization' of Kuwait aimed at altering the demographic and ideological character of the country, comparing it to the 'Turkization' of Cyprus. Adding his voice to those of other Greek MEPs throughout the EP, he condemned the level of inconsistency shown by the international community when dealing with similar events (Nianias, 22/11/1990, 250). For the Spanish MEP Perreau de Pinninck, more hypocrisy could be seen in the attitude of those countries which had first strengthened the hand of Saddam against Iran by supplying conventional and chemical weapons and which were now accusing it of crimes against humanity (Perreau de Pinninck, 12/9/1990, 129-130).

At the end of September 1990, the Irish MEP Patrick Lane reported on his official visit to the Gulf region to discuss with representatives of the Kuwaiti government in exile, Saudi Arabia, Qatar, and the United Arab Emirates the measures required to face the negative economic effects of the crisis. Many OPEC members, Saudi Arabia in particular, had increased their offer of oil to cover the loss of Iraqi and Kuwaiti production. Against this background, it was undeniable that the increase in oil prices was the result of speculation rather than an effective economic necessity. The international community was asked to find and stop those responsible for this pernicious manoeuvre[52] (Lane, 11/10/1990, 285). In October 1990, the EDA turned its attention to the 'human' aspects of the crisis, expressing anxiety about the fate of the many foreign people forcibly held in Iraq.[53] Sympathy was also addressed to the families of the hostages, urging the Commission to establish a support fund to assist them in tackling at least some practical and financial difficulties. On the refugee issue, emergency aid should be granted to those countries where a vast inward movement of people was taking place and extended to the whole Middle East area and, in general, all the developing countries whose economies were strongly hit by the crisis. The EDA members approved the decision to lift the embargo for medical supplies and products for children in order to alleviate further suffering on the Iraqi people (Musso, 23/10/1990, 78). They maintained the view that every effort should be made to solve the crisis peacefully. In this context, the UN Security Council deadline set for Saddam to retreat from Kuwait was received with considerable reluctance and scepticism (Nianias, 22/11/1990, 250 and 11/12/1990 72).

---

52 With respect to this problem, the EDA Group tabled a Motion for a Resolution B3-1847/90 which was rejected by the House on 12 October 1990 (OJEC 3-394, 325).

53 The Motion for a Resolution B3-1829/90, presented on 11 October 1990 by de la Malène on behalf of EDA, on humanitarian consequences of the Gulf crisis, failed to be included in the Joint Motion for a Resolution tabled by eight parliamentary groups.

111

Worried about drifting towards war and its repercussions in the region, the group reaffirmed the belief that an alternative solution could be reached through the application of a complete anti-Iraq trade embargo, if necessary extended to air transport (de la Malène, 12/9/1990, 114). In the eyes of the EDA, the Gulf experience revealed that the Community was not equipped to face any external challenges and that the process of European integration ought to spillover into the security and defence sector, but should not be created around the wider framework of CSCE (Musso, 23/10/1990, 78).

During the pre-war stage, the attitude of the group reflected the cautious stance of the French government, torn between its traditional *politique arabe* and its solidarity with the allies, and ambitiously trying to reconcile these two opposite approaches. The group, nevertheless, acknowledged and praised the United States and the many Arab States for their efficient and prompt military intervention which had prevented further Iraqi aggression in the region. The EDA remained fairly cohesive in its determination to solve the Gulf crisis, preferably without recourse to military means. All efforts had to be made to ensure an efficient and total trade embargo (de la Malène, 12/9/1990, 114). The average index of agreement within the group was as high as 75.42 percent whilst the level of absenteeism was of 64.11.

b) War Stage
In January 1991, the launching of *Operation Desert Storm* saw an about-turn in the EDA attitude as there had not been the "slightest indication from Iraq in response to the peace efforts". According to de la Malène, support for this military initiative was not "subject to constraint" because he did not believe "in that form of selfishness" which involved being passive and expecting others to take on the difficult tasks. The EDA leader also declared his disbelief in the virtue of pacifism having personally experienced its failure in Europe during 1938-1939. Despite Saddam's attempt to widen the conflict, claiming that it was over oil for the benefit of Israel and the United States, the majority of the group took the view that it was a war for international morality. A tribute was paid to the courage of soldiers risking their lives in the Gulf (de la Malène, 21/1/1991, 18-19).

The French Gaullists insisted on a tougher stance, excluding the possibility of an immediate ceasefire, acknowledging the need for a European collective security policy (Chabert, 126, Nianias, 134, 20/2/1991). The group was not unanimous on this policy. By declaring his preference for a continual embargo to solve the crisis, Lane deplored the

112

decision by the international community to resort to the use of force, rejecting calls for a Community strike force on the grounds that some member states, including Ireland, would wish to retain neutral status (Lane, 20/2/1991, 131). Concerned about the danger that the coalition would overstep the UN mandate and sceptical about the real aims of the war, a few members within the group called for an immediate armistice (Nianias, 20/2/1991, 134). They expressed horror at Saddam's use of foreign citizens and prisoners of war as human shields in Iraqi military targets, resulting in the loss of life of innocent civilians (Lane, 131, Nianias, 134, 20/2/1991). Lane briefly greeted Gorbatchev's peace initiative lamenting, however, that the Ministers of the EEC Troika had been ignored during their visit in Moscow (Lane, 20/2/1991, 131).

During the second stage of the Gulf issue the group's overall index of agreement was equal to 69.64 percent with a level of absenteeism exceeding half of its members, specifically 53.95 percent. It is significant to note that this rate was the lowest recorded by the EDA during the three stages of the crisis.

c) Post-War Stage
In the eyes of the EDA leader, although the Gulf war did not bring peace to the whole Middle East area, it had improved the chances of achieving it, by shaking the foundations of the Iraqi dictatorship and promoting respect for international law. The group turned its attention to the question of human rights, stressing the need for making the international community aware of the torments inflicted on its own people and the Kurdish minority by Saddam as well as the misery suffered by the Palestinians in the territories occupied by Israeli authorities. In addition, if the Iraqi invasion of Kuwait was regarded as a breach of international law, the same principle should be extended to the Israeli occupation of the West Bank and Gaza (de la Malène, 80, Lane, 86, 13/3/1991). The group urgently demanded a settlement of the Palestinian question in order to guarantee a certain stability in the Middle East.

While the majority of the PGs within the EP seemed to find their unity in the aftermath of the conflict, the EDA remained divided over the policies to be adopted with regard to the post-crisis situation with a modest index of agreement equal to 75 percent, curiously enough, even lower than that of the independent members. The EDA members' turnout was also extremely disappointing, the level of absenteeism rising to the staggering level of 82.39 percent. In short, through the whole duration of the crisis, the group registered an average index of agreement of 72.64 percent while the number of members failing to attend the RCV sessions reached 62.36 percent, the highest registered among all groups, except for the Independent members.

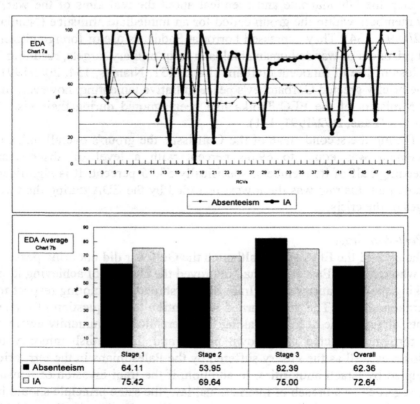

1.8 The European Right

a) Pre-War Stage

Whilst denouncing Saddam for his brutal aggression against Kuwait, the taking of hostages and their placement at strategic sites, the leader of the European Right (ER) Jean-Marie Le Pen contended that the régime existing in the country prior to the Iraqi occupation was certainly not based on respect for humanitarian and democratic principles (Le Pen, 12/9/1990, 114-116). As previously noticed, this view was held by the Greens and the Left, yet with different tones. The French politician stressed the importance of examining the reasons for the invasion which stemmed from Iraq's historical claim over its former province. As such, the conflict, which erupted after long negotiations, should be solved between the countries concerned without external interference, in conformity with the UN principle that problems should preferably be dealt with at regional level. The ER pointed out the inconsistent behaviour of the international community vis-à-vis other cases where territorial state sovereignty had also been breached such as the Turkish invasion of Cyprus, the Israeli occupation of the West Bank and the Syrian invasion of Lebanon. These violations, although generally condemned, had not aroused the same vehement reaction, showing that the nature of Western interests was not based on moral principles but on the thirst and rapacity for oil.

The group vigorously contested the September 1990 Joint Resolution for 'reasons of principle' well beyond the ground that it had not participated in its drafting. The proposed embryonic world government was totally rejected together with "the spurious linkage (..) between the plight of our [European] nationals in the region and condemnation of Iraq" (Martinez, 12/9/1990, 153). In the roll-call survey of 14 voting members, 12 voted against, one abstained (the Belgian MEP Karel Dillen) and only one member, the German MEP Johanna-Christina Grund, voted in favour, albeit with reservations. In her opinion, the text lacked explicit reference to the prospect of using force if Iraqi troops were not evacuated from Kuwait and failed to condemn similar violations of territorial sovereignty in the Gulf and Mediterranean area. Dissociating herself from the ER official line, Grund refused to back the text tabled by the ER group because it did not call for the military deployment of troops in the region and did not urge strongly enough the unconditional release of hostages or support for a total embargo against Iraq (Grund, 12/9/1990, 154). The index of agreement was therefore on this occasion of 71.43 percent.

Over the 10 RCVs on various parts of the September Joint Resolution, the IA of the ER group reached on 2 occasions the optimal figure of 100 percent, on 3 occasions 84.62 percent, decreasing in the other cases respectively to 83.33 percent, 66.67 percent and to 45.45 percent. Consensus was reached with regard to the adoption of that part of paragraph 6 relating to the call addressed to the international community to implement sanctions against Iraq and for making all efforts to promote peaceful solutions and to avert the recourse to force. Paragraph 24 relating to the necessity for the Community to take steps against those countries which did not comply with the trade embargo against Iraq was also unanimously approved by the ER members.

115

The lowest figure referred to paragraph 21 where the EP "recognized the responsibility of the international community in having armed the states of the region and calls on the Community and its member states to consider urgently how to establish an effective common policy to control the export of armaments and of advanced technology with military potential". In October 1990 the group expressed deep concern about incidents in Jerusalem where 20 Palestinian civilians had been killed and several injured by the Israeli police. This new episode of violence exposed the inconsistency of the international community when dealing with infringements of international law which were "condemned with varying degrees of vigour depending on who commit[ted] them".

The Community should abandon its lethargic attitude and undertake the crucial role of mediator in the Middle East disputes, all equally crucial and requiring therefore the same consideration by the international community. Their similarities also demanded that a solution to all these questions should be sought concurrently. Another fundamental issue raised by the group was connected to mass immigration from Muslim countries into the Community which should be halted in order to prevent Europe from "continu[ing] to be at the mercy of the threat of an Islamic fifth column, the infrastructure of a potentially awful terrorist force" (Dillen, 12/9/1990, 162).

In October, the ER unsuccessfully submitted to the House a Motion for a Resolution calling for the release of French and other European nationals detained in Iraq as a first step towards freeing all foreigners wishing to return home. The group believed that increase in oil prices was due to profiteers and that the Community and its member states should take measures to safeguard their citizens who should not become "the defenceless victims of the blackmail and threats of the oil speculators" (Dillen, 11/10/1990, 285-286). The Community was harshly criticized for aligning itself unconditionally with the policy adopted by the American Administration without adequate consideration of the situation (Antony, 23/10/1990, 79).

At the moment of the vote, the ER group, supported by thirteen members, requested a quorum check which confirmed that the MEPs' turnout was insufficient to allow the voting of any of the thirteen Motions for Resolutions tabled by the various groups on the situation in the Gulf. This initiative was considered by many Europarliamentarians to be an obstructive action which contributed to crystallizing the isolation of the ER within the House (von der Vring, 11/10/1990, 309).

In November 1990, the French MEP Bruno Megret informed Parliament that the mission undertaken by the leader of his group had been successful and that many hostages were safely returning home. In his words, this initiative exemplified "the only [sensible] course of political action" carried out to safeguard the "interests of the nations we represent" (Megret, 22/11/1990, 249). Acknowledging Saddam's goodwill gesture in allowing the departure of women, children and other French and European citizens, the ER suggested that the Community would launch a new appeal to the Iraqi government to free the remaining hostages in return for the retreat of the international coalition forces deployed in the Gulf region (B3-2032/90). The trust placed in Saddam by ER members seemed to have been rewarded when in November 1990 the Iraqi government announced its decision to release all foreign citizens still detained. The policy pursued by the group since the outset of what it defined as an 'inter-Arab' conflict was based on negotiation and dialogue, a view held in common with the Greens. Despite the affinities of approach on the Gulf issue, albeit based on different considerations, the Greens and the Extreme Right members did not undertake any joint initiatives, confirming the isolation of the latter in the parliamentary arena (Léhideux, 11/12/1990, 72-73).

The European Right which reaffirmed almost unanimously its anti-interventionist stance, expressed its preference for de-escalation and negotiation, as demonstrated by the mission undertaken by its leader Jean-Marie Le Pen. This position appeared to conflict with its traditional support for French military actions and, in François Heisbourg's words, was "irreconcilable with its inflammatory attitudes on Arab matters and anti-immigration policies" (Heisbourg, 1992, 29). Throughout the pre-war stage, the level of ER cohesion was fairly high, averaging 84.31 percent and the rate of absenteeism reached the slightly below average of 44.62.

b) War Stage
From the extreme right of the parliamentary arena, Le Pen argued that Saddam was not the only one responsible for the war, given Kuwait's provocations, and the fact that the Western powers had supplied Iraq and the Middle East with weaponry. Although disagreeing with European governments' decision to deploy troops in the Gulf, the group fully sympathized with the soldiers sent to fight in an inter-Arab conflict, for Arabs to solve. Their view was that the Community's priority should be to limit the scope and duration of the war (Le Pen, 21/1/1991, 19-20). According to the interpretation given by Heisbourg, Le Pen had elaborated

117

with racial overtones the pro-Iraqi theme that this was exclusively a problem between Arabs, meaning that "this was not something for which non-Arabs deserved to risk their presumedly more precious lives" (Heisbourg, 1992, 21). As such, the ER indicated that the international community should have as its priority to limit the scope and duration of the war (*Financial Times*, 23/1/1991), warning that the member states' troops should be kept in Europe as a deterrent to the "lasting threat from the East". Despite his trust in Gorbachev, Le Pen did not exclude the possibility that the Soviet President could be deposed by a less honourable and therefore more dangerous leader with aggressive intentions towards Western Europe. If such a tragic event occurred, the EC member states would be unable to protect themselves as many of its soldiers were deployed in the Gulf region.

The group persisted in its backing for the continuation of the economic blockade against Iraq and occupied Kuwait, a strategy which had proved successful in the past, as for instance in the case of South Africa (Le Pen, 21/1/1991, 19-20). During the Gulf war stage, the group's overall index of agreement was equal to 75.25 percent. It also had the worst attendance record out of all the EP groups right through this crucial phase with a level of absenteeism of 59.42 percent.

c) Post-War Stage
Deliberately going against the EP's tide and distancing themselves once again from all the other PGs, the members of the European Right opposed any contribution by the European Community for the post-war rebuilding of Iraq and Kuwait. Despite President Bush's rejection of any form of assistance in the region (WEU Report, 1992, 23), the group claimed that the belligerent countries participating in the Gulf War and particularly the United States should bear the costs of the ruin and misery caused as a consequence of their armed intervention (Blot, 16/4/1991, 43). By looking at the prospects for the restoration of Kuwait, the group expressed its hope "that purges [would] not take over from the abuses of the occupying force" and that a more humane and a fairer régime would be established by the ruling al-Sabah Royal family compared to that in force in the pre-Gulf crisis period (Gollnisch, 13/3/1991, 81).

Finally, in Dillen's view, the Community should equip itself with a modern and appropriate defence force. Although in the short-term no other option existed but to continue to cooperate closely with NATO, in the medium and long-term the European Community should be able to face autonomously its security and defence responsibility (Dillen, 15/5/1991, 151).

The ER showed the highest level of conformity in its voting behaviour pattern, assisted by the small number of its members and by the relatively restricted national basis of the group. Some of its MEPs took eccentric and provocative attitudes which attracted the attention of public opinion, members states' governments and third countries.

In the post-war period, the voting behaviour of ER members vis-à-vis the post-crisis policy reached the optimal figure of 100 percent index of agreement, reflecting unanimity within the group, though it is also important to point out the very high level of absenteeism of ER Members at the roll-call voting sessions, equivalent to 84.17 percent. On average, the extreme right members realized during the whole period from September 1990 to April 1991 a very high index of agreement of 82.93 percent with a rate of absenteeism slightly above average, 57.76 percent.

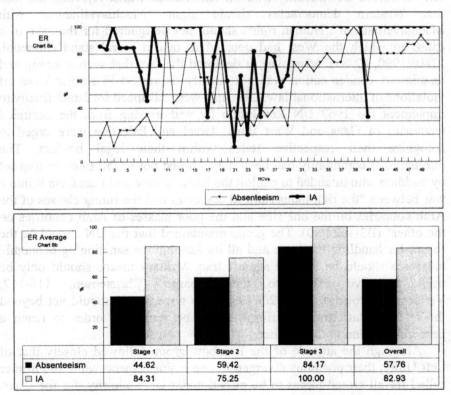

1.9 The Rainbow Group

a) Pre-War Stage

In April 1990, before Kuwait's crisis hit the headlines, the Rainbow group expressed its disapproval of Saddam's totalitarian régime for its violation of human rights, especially against the Kurdish minority, by calling for an immediate ban on the arms trade with Iraq (*OJEC* C 113, 7/5/1990, 144). In September 1990, the group strongly criticized the Community for failing to establish a code of conduct for the export of arms and argued that a conference concerning the reduction of arms trade should be gathered under the aegis of the United Nations, along with the deployment of a permanent UN force in the region (B3-1624/90).

The group joined the voices of indignation condemning the Iraqi aggression that were widespread in the international community, and it fully endorsed UN Security Council Resolutions whilst rejecting the idea that Western democracies should fight "Machiavellianism with Machiavellianism". Human rights should not be ignored for the sake of a cause in which the West had decided to take a moral stand (Simeoni, 23/10/1990, 82-83). Moreover, it deplored the fact that such a strong and unanimous condemnation was not equally expressed in similar cases of violations of international law. Demands were advanced for Israel finally to implement the 1967 UN Resolution by withdrawing from the occupied territories of Gaza and West Bank. Israel and Palestine were urged to recognize their respective states within their legal borders. The international community had been duly warned not to fall into the trap set by Saddam who intended to exploit the Kuwaiti case and transform it into a war between "the rich industrialized countries and the ruling classes of the Arab countries on the one side and the poor masses of Arab countries on the other" (B3-1624/90). The group maintained that the UN should be the forum for handling the issue and all its Resolutions sanctioning economic measures should be applied against Iraq. Military means should only be used to give effect to the embargo (Christensen, 116-117, Vandemeulebroucke, 154, 12/9/1990). No government should act beyond the UN mandate and no efforts should be spared in order to reach a peaceful solution to the conflict.

Although the attitude of the Rainbow group followed closely that of Left Unity, their positions diverged in one major respect: while the former called for all armed forces to be placed under UN authority, for the latter, military action should only be conducted by the United Nations itself to prevent UK and US dominance. The Rainbow group also pointed out the contradictions and the hypocrisies emerging from this crisis. The first entailed the presumed violation of the democratic rights of Kuwait, although it seemed daring to present this country as a genuine example of democracy when only 8 percent of its population had the right to vote. The second concerned the destiny of Western soldiers sent to the Gulf, whose lives were threatened by the same weapons produced and exported by their own countries. The third evoked the different attitudes shown by the Community in other similar circumstances such as the Chinese invasion of Tibet when no significant action had been taken (Ewing, 12/9/1990, 124).

During the long Iran-Iraq war, Saddam's ambition had served the West's purposes of preventing the expansion of Islamic fundamentalism and the subsequent danger of Iranian dominance over the oil reserves in the region (Piermont, 12/9/1990, 130). Therefore no sign of moral disapproval had been shown against Iraq for the brutality of the means employed and no anti-Iraq military coalition had been advocated. On the contrary, the international community supplied Iraq with arms. However, in Kuwait's case, the Iraqi leader's ambition to rule the area was incompatible with Western interests and the international community suddenly felt obliged to denounce the immorality of the action. During the parliamentary session of September 1990, the Rainbow group disapproved the text of the Joint Resolution, for failing to highlight the above-mentioned contradictions and for ignoring the social background of the conflict, notably the deeply unfair allocation of welfare in Arab society (Christensen, 12/9/1991, 116-117). By defining the joint text "a Resolution of hypocrisy", the Rainbow group attempted to amend its contents and clarify some obscure and ambiguous parts, requesting 6 split roll-call votes. The group rejected any military involvement in the Gulf, instead insisting upon the enforcement of the embargo (Vandemeulebroucke, 12/9/1990, 154). Eventually, when it came to the final vote on the whole text, all Rainbow members actually present abstained, with the exception of the Italian MEP Francesco Enrico Speroni from the Lombard League and the German Green MEP Dorothée Piermont who rejected the Resolution. In Speroni's opinion, the text failed to "adopt a determined stance, without doubt, without uncertainty, because by decisive action (..) [which] could also take the form of military action, it [would] be possible to drive the Iraqis out of Kuwait" (Speroni, 12/9/1990, 154). For opposing reasons, Piermont voted against the Resolution because it did not completely exclude the possibility of resorting to the use of force (Piermont, 12/9/1990, 155).

In October, the Rainbow group tabled one Motion for a Resolution on speculation on oil prices and participated in the drafting of the Joint Motion for a Resolution together with 8 other groups on oil prices (B3-1844/90). The failure of the group with respect to the former Motion was compensated by the adoption of the second Joint Motion, revealing once more the necessity of coalition and the limit of manoeuvre and potential power of a small group within the EP. By capturing the essence of the oil price rise, the Irish MEP suggested that "the difficulty [was] not shortage of oil but manipulation of the market by the multinational oil companies" (Blaney, 11/10/1990, 286). As a result, the Rainbow group called for an intervention of governments aimed at freezing the prices.

The position of the group towards the Gulf crisis, which remained unaltered during the pre-war stage, was broadly in support of diplomatic initiatives and rejection of the use of violence which "would just lead to more humiliation and acrimony" between the West and the Arab countries. The accent was also put on the necessity for Europe to promote the gathering of an international Middle East conference which would tackle the most serious issues by promoting economic and social progress in the area (Simeoni, 11/12/1990, 73). During this stage, as with the Greens, the average index of agreement of the Rainbow group on the 19 roll-call votes was rather low, averaging 53.28 percent and the level of absenteeism was slightly below average, equal to 44.59.

b) War Stage
The Rainbow group strongly regretted that the embargo against Iraq had not been given more time in order to reveal its full effects (Ewing). As the Central Intelligence Agency (CIA) had revealed to the US Congress, economic sanctions were producing effective results and, in time, they would not have left any other alternative to the Iraqi dictator but surrender.

Following the start of allied air strikes against Iraq, concern was expressed at the horrific effects of the conflict in terms of human loss, ecological disaster, economic and political repercussions (Ib Christensen). The group hoped that the war would be of a short duration and its damages contained. The scope of the war should be limited to the liberation of Kuwait, without any other ambition of destroying Iraq or putting on trial its leader (Ewing).

In January 1991, the Rainbow group argued that Iraq should be offered the "constant opportunity for a ceasefire" (Ewing, 20, Christensen, 22, 21/1/1991) upon an Iraqi promise to fulfil UN Resolutions and once the retreat had commenced (*OJEC* 3-398, 23/1/1991, 126). The unease over military intervention was reiterated at the February plenary, where the US and UK were criticized for having dismissed the utility of sanctions too readily (Melis, 20/2/1991, 127-128).

The second stage revealed a higher index of agreement in relation to the preceding period, though still counting a fairly high score of 61.18 percent. This was accompanied by a low presence of members at the roll-call voting sessions and, in particular, a percentage of absenteeism equivalent to 50.43.

c) Post-War Stage

In the eyes of the Rainbow group, Europe was impotent when faced with the Gulf crisis since its existence as an international actor "was still on the drawing board" and, therefore, the so-called 'Pax Americana' remained the only feasible solution. However, in the aftermath of the conflict, the Community should play a more active role by providing, for example, humanitarian assistance to refugees. Banning the arms trade as a step for achieving a total disarmament in the region was also highlighted together with the idea of launching a rapid economic development in the Middle East (Simeoni, 13/3/1991, 81-82).

The Rainbow group participated in the negotiation of two compromise resolutions on arms export and on the situation of the Kurds. The Gulf War provided ample demonstration of the need for establishing an effective pan-European security system which should be established within the CSCE framework, without however militarizing the Community. The importance was stressed of democratizing security policy and proceeding with a meticulous revision of the UN in order to provide the organization with the instruments for maintaining world peace (Christensen, 15/5/1991, 151-152). The Rainbow members seemed to have finally found a cohesive position during this final stage, registering a very high level of agreement of 91.67 percent.

In summary, it can be concluded that the position of the Rainbow group with regard to the Gulf crisis was less cohesive than that of all other groups. This can be easily attributed to the fact that the group was established more for technical reasons than as the result of genuine ideological affinity among its members. The Rainbow group achieved the lowest index of agreement of 63.47 percent in comparison with the other groups and a level of absenteeism of 51.88 percent.

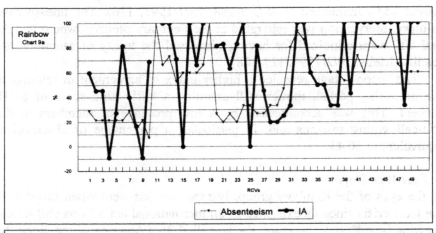

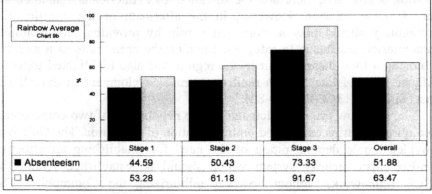

1.10 The Left Unity

a) Pre-War Stage

The Left Unity (LU) group strongly condemned the Iraqi invasion and annexation of Kuwait as well as Saddam's decision to take foreign citizens as hostages. According to the LU the tasks at hand were to induce Iraq to retreat from Kuwait, to free all the hostages and to ban the use of force as an instrument to impose its will over another country (Carvalhas, 12/9/1990, 123-124). The outbreak of the crisis offered the European Community the opportunity to test its own ability to play a role in the international arena, by formulating an independent European viewpoint in order to launch or sustain initiatives for a peaceful settlement of the question (Piquet, 12/9/1990, 116).

The September compromise text certainly contained indisputable principles, notably the resolute denunciation of Iraq's aggression, the demand for a prompt and unconditional retreat from Kuwait and the liberation of all the hostages. Regardless of the above elements and the aspiration cherished by the Left Alliance of seeing the EP taking a distinct, substantial and unanimous position vis-à-vis the Gulf issue, the group could not vote in favour of the Resolution because of its ambivalence and obscurity. In contrast to what paragraph 6 equivocally stated, the Community should, through its Parliament, commit itself to look for a political settlement without resorting to the use of arms. Moreover, the group fiercely criticized the European Community as well as the EP for not daring to reproach the unilateral activities of, for example, the United States which had raised the suspicion that their strategic ambitions in the Gulf region were more important than solving the crisis (Alavanos, 12/9/1990, 153-154).

Against the Machiavellian axiom *the end justifies the means,* the group rejected the resort to force, taking the view that a total embargo against Iraq, except for food and medical supplies, should be sufficient to isolate Saddam and compel him to adopt UN Resolutions (Piquet, 12/9/1990, 116). The group pleaded non-intervention on anti-imperialist grounds. Emphasis was placed on the Community's necessity to allow the Americans to establish a hegemony in the region (Carvalhas, 12/9/1990, 123-124). In order to avert the risks of escalating the conflict, no unilateral military action should be undertaken by the United States or any other country, while the armed forces in the Gulf should be put under the UN authority (Piquet, 12/9/1990, 116). In Carvalhas' words, "[w]ar [should] be banished and give way to new world processes, to a fairer division of resources, to the solution of conflicts by peaceful and political means, to a new economic and world order" (Carvalhas, 12/9/1990, 123-124). The Commission should promote measures in order to improve energy resources in those peripheral countries highly dependent on oil imports and to advance proposals to exploit alternative energy sources. There was a firm and united opposition to the governments' intention to establish austerity measures and increase the price of oil products which would affect workers, in particular. The group manifested concern at the consequences of the conflict for the least favoured countries as well as at the two-faced attitude taken by the rich countries in dealing with international issues on the basis of their own interests (Carvalhas, 12/9/1990, 123-124).

The LU members turned their attention to the economic repercussions of the crisis for developing countries as it emerges in the text of their original Motion for Resolution of 8 October 1990. The Council was urged to establish additional funds for the African, Caribbean and Pacific (ACP) countries in order to assist them in facing an increasingly difficult economic situation. An appeal was also launched for cancelling the debts owed to the European Community and the member states by ACP countries. In order to mitigate the poignant situation of refugees, support was also given to the EC decision to grant humanitarian emergency aid. The dilemma of the thousands of hostages still detained in Iraq was not ignored by the group which joined the parliamentary chorus calling for their unconditional release (B3-1818/90 replaced by B3-1779, 1788, 1808, 1811, 1816, 1818 and 1821/90). Following the reassuring news of Iraqi's decision to free the hostages, further initiatives towards a peaceful settlement of the crisis should be promoted. The Community should open a dialogue with the countries in the Gulf region by sending an *ad hoc* delegation and by convening an international conference to tackle the most urgent problems in the Middle East. The group rejected the idea that, after the expiry of the UN ultimatum, the international community including the EEC should participate in military operations with the objective of restoring Kuwait's sovereignty with the use of force (Ephremidis, 11/12/1990, 73).

When it came to the RCVs on the *Crampton Report* in November 1990 and on Resolution B3-2190 of 12 December 1990, the entire group was absent while, on other occasions, the level of presence was rather low. The data computed on the roll-call votes from September to December 1990 show a high index of agreement of 86.08 percent. The level of absenteeism at the RCV sessions of the LU parliamentarians was very high, 74.81 percent.

b) War Stage
The Left Unity voiced its aversion to war, stressing that it would be possible to restore the independence of Kuwait by tightening sanctions against the Iraqi invader. The European Community should act consistently towards similar cases such as Cyprus and Palestine by proffering more than "pious words".

The LU stressed the importance of maintaining sanctions while it expressed its antiwar sentiment, given that there were no clear economic, political or legal reasons for intervening militarily. In addition, it stressed the fact that it would be impossible to limit the conflict temporarily by containing it to Iraqi territory and there was danger of extending the conflict to the whole Arab world. In January 1991, LU rejected the 'logic of war' by promoting, instead, a peaceful solution through negotiations and calling for a ceasefire. As such, it expressed opposition to the compromise Resolution in favour of armed intervention tabled by the centre-right and requested a roll-call vote for the Joint Motion for a Resolution negotiated and tabled by Socialists, Christian Democrats, European Democrats and Rainbow members.

In February, the LU reaffirmed the principle that the European Community and the Parliament should repudiate a belligerent philosophy and commit themselves instead to a peaceful solution of the problem in the area concerned. The LU fully supported the Soviet plan which represented "the last chance for a peaceful end to the war without slaughter" and reproached the American inflexibility in disregarding the Soviet initiative and its determination to step up a war to destroy Iraq which was aimed at gaining political and economic control in the strategic area of the Middle East. The group renewed its hope that the United Nations would regain the control and settle all the conflicts in the region. Apprehension was expressed about the racist attitudes towards Arab and Muslim immigrants emerging in Europe as a consequence of the crisis (B3-0387/91).

At the plenary session on 20 February, the LU group underlined its criticisms of the joint US/UK led initiatives overstepping UN mandate (Piquet, 128, Ribeiro, 131-132, 20/2/1991). As Heisbourg commented, "anti-war motivations included a mixture of avowedly or embarrassedly pro-Iraqi attitudes in the leadership of the [French] Communists" (Heisbourg, 1992, 29).

The war stage displayed a remarkable level of cohesion within the LU with an IA equal to 95.86 percent. The above outcome becomes even more outstanding in view of the fairly low degree of absenteeism falling to 33.23. The gravity of the events served as a unifying factor for these groups.

c) Post-War Stage

Although welcoming the end of the hostilities in the Gulf, the LU reaffirmed the view that the liberation of Kuwait could be achieved through political and economic means and the ravages of war and the killing of innocent victims made the task of solving the problems of the region more difficult. However, looking to the future, the group expressed the need for the European Community to contribute to the search for peace and stability in the Middle East area. In order to assist this process, the Community should commit itself to implementing reconstruction and aid programmes. The United Nations Organization should safeguard the sovereignty and security of all countries involved through the establishment of a new international order which was not that wished and imposed by the United States but one of "free, independent and sovereign peoples" (Piquet, 13/3/1991, 82).

Along with the other PGs the LU expressed the necessity of achieving a European Union entailing a common foreign and security dimension. A new framework should be independent from the Atlantic Alliance and its US leadership. Its main task should consist of defending the interests of people, contributing to the peaceful solution of international disputes and promoting disarmament (Ephremidis, 15/5/1991, 152).

During the post-war period, the LU registered a peak in the rate of absenteeism of its members reaching 86.61 percent, the highest of all PGs, except for the Independent members. Like the LDR and the ER groups, the LU attained consensus in their voting behaviour vis-à-vis the post-crisis policy, with an index of agreement of 100 percent. The LU registered a steady increase in its level of voting cohesion over the three stages, averaging an IA equivalent to 92.28 percent. This impressive result was, however, overshadowed by the medium average level of absenteeism of 57.57. However, a reading of the percentages relating to either the level of agreement or absenteeism, tend respectively to favour or penalize small groups, providing a more favourable or unfavourable interpretation than that emerging when dealing with larger groups. Indeed, in small groups, each member has a bigger impact in terms of steering up or down the total percentage.

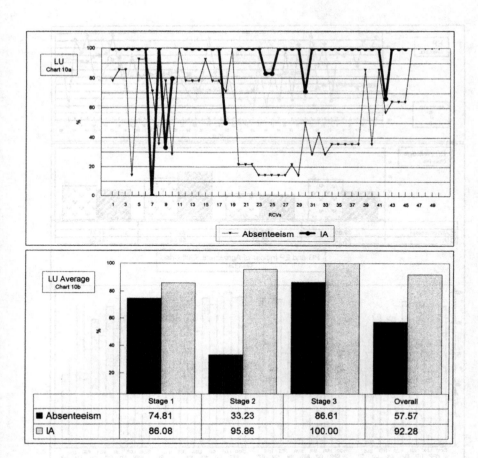

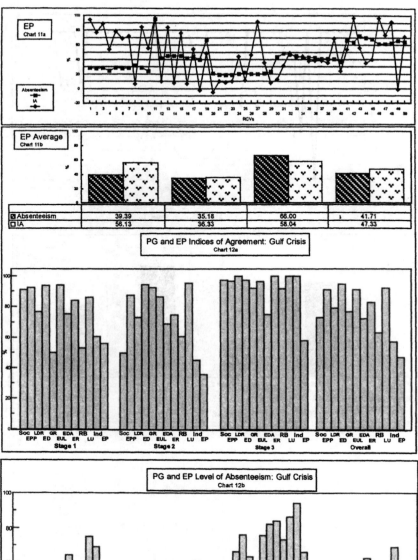
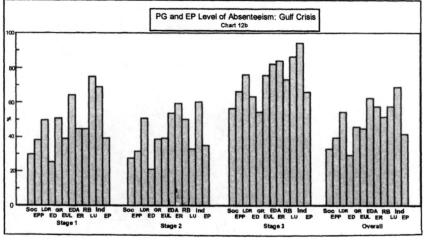

2. Level of Transnationality in Political Groups' Voting Behaviour on the Gulf Crisis

The following section intends to assess whether an effective level of transnationality was reached within the various political groups when voting on the Gulf crisis or whether nationalistic sentiments and preferences prevailed. This inquiry is carried out by computing an index of transnationality on 50 roll-call RCVs (ITv) on the Gulf held by Parliament between September 1990 and May 1991 and is based on the highest voting modality which is assumed to represent the official position of each political group.[54]

The outcome of this analysis shows that the EPP, Socialist, LDR, Greens, Rainbow and LU groups achieved, in decreasing order, a high level of transnationality. This sequence was then followed by the ER, the EUL, the EDA and ended with the ED. It is intuitively clear that due to its almost mono-national constitution, the level of transnationality within the ED group was the lowest. The respective ITv on the Gulf did not correspond proportionally to the index of transnationality based on the composition (ITc) of each group. All PGs reflected slightly lower levels of transnationality according to voting patterns on the Gulf with the exception of the EUL Group which registered a marginal increase. A comparison of the data of both indices of transnationality and agreement for each group can assist in discerning whether heterogeneity in terms of nationality was a factor inhibiting internal cohesion. The results show that there is no evidence of a correlation between group transnationality and its members' ability to achieve a consensus.

During the war stage, the Socialists appeared split between a pro-intervention faction headed by their leader Cot and a non-intervention faction including most British Labour members and the French MEP Cheysson, who cast doubts and publicly played an antiwar profile for the whole duration of the crisis (Gnesotto, 1992, 29). Eventually a third faction prevailed within the Socialist group and within the House in favour of a limited military intervention in the region.

However, this is refuted in the Gulf case by the British Labour MEPs whose position diverged from the interventionist policy dictated by their national headquarters. This decision can be regarded as either a brave or a

---

54 For the method of computing ITc and ITv see Appendix.

foolish step given that the list of the candidates for both European and national elections are drafted by national parties and deselection and ostracism could be the price of dissent. The value of this example is further increased by the fact that, in general, British Labour members regard the decision of opting out from the official view of the party as a particularly serious matter (Bowler and Farrell, 1992, 14).

Despite the evident difficulties arising from such a multicoloured political and cultural landscape, most groups undertook negotiations in order to smooth the edges and achieve a majority within the Parliament over the Gulf. Parliamentarians were continually looking over their shoulder, concerned about the necessity of providing an image of a coherent and solid political forum which might increase the European Parliament's level of influence over the other EC-EU institutions as well as third parties. This case study has shown that although forging a European identity is still far off, steps have been taken in this direction by the European Parliament, where a rather satisfactory average in the level of transnationality of voting, 0.865 was achieved, also if compared to the level of transnationality of its composition of 0.878.

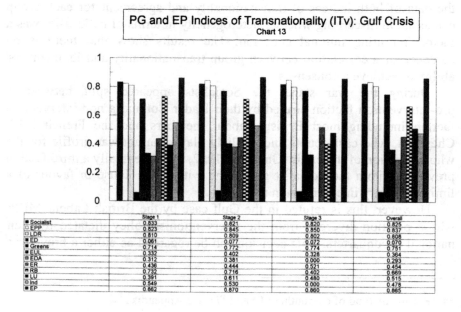

3. MEP National Allegiance versus Political Group Loyalty

A comparison between the indices of agreements for PGs and for national delegations in the European Parliament with respect to the Gulf policies suggests that the national loyalty played a less significant part than the allegiance to the respective PGs, except for the Rainbow group, which however did not have a well-defined political and ideological line. Luxembourg and Spain's delegations registered the highest levels of agreement. The first case does not come as a surprise due to the small size of Luxembourg's delegation. However, national solidarity does not seem to conflict with MEPs' allegiance to their respective groups and generally goes along with their strong Europeanist sentiments. Also in the case of the Spanish MEPs, it can be said that group allegiance was of more concern than national imperatives. In fact, a closer look at the RCVs for the Socialist, EPP, LDR, EUL and Rainbow groups shows that despite the appearances, political allegiance prevailed over that of nationality.

Finally, as has been previously mentioned, most British Labour MEPs, along with the majority of the Socialist group opposed military intervention in the Gulf to the great embarrassment of their own national party. However, in order to assess the magnitude of the factor of nationality, further in-depth research is necessary, based on a comparative analysis of the positions of the national parties and the corresponding political groups in the European Parliament.

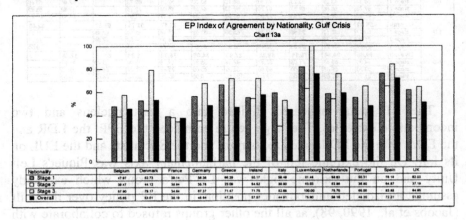

4. Political Groups' Voting Similarity on the Gulf Crisis

The voting similarity percentages between groups, illustrated in Table 3, has been calculated by combining and comparing all 50 roll-call votes taken by Parliament on the Gulf.

Table 3 Political Groups' Voting Similarity on the Gulf Crisis

		SOC	EPP	LDR	ED	GREEN	EUL	EDA	ER	RB	LU	IND
SOC	Overall		69.73	59.13	64.49	51.89	76.39	62.73	52.23	70.62	55.82	49.49
	stage 1		67.53	59.73	71.62	46.17	90.38	72.51	37.69	58.54	60.17	44.30
	stage 2		65.59	61.47	62.87	53.55	62.03	64.86	70.87	87.73	51.20	59.36
	stage 3		86.86	50.97	52.22	59.96	86.23	34.60	36.53	47.10	66.67	21.79
EPP	Overall	69.73		75.80	85.10	32.65	48.52	72.86	52.00	57.07	26.69	64.96
	stage 1	67.53		78.81	83.51	42.83	58.99	80.08	47.22	43.28	32.13	66.16
	stage 2	65.59		77.37	93.27	19.48	31.68	76.05	66.73	66.86	17.78	69.07
	stage 3	86.86		64.11	65.36	47.63	73.39	47.45	24.08	58.22	64.22	42.02
LDR	Overall	59.13	75.80		85.22	38.12	43.63	76.59	50.39	60.18	28.68	76.11
	stage 1	59.73	78.81		84.89	45.50	52.94	70.81	46.50	53.29	25.65	71.05
	stage 2	61.47	77.37		80.79	33.10	38.47	84.55	68.17	61.57	30.31	79.00
	stage 3	50.97	64.11		98.75	35.94	37.50	66.67	12.50	70.83	33.33	80.00
ED	Overall	64.49	85.10	85.22		30.93	43.19	74.22	45.19	59.36	25.76	69.35
	stage 1	71.62	83.51	84.89		38.56	63.79	73.93	41.56	49.53	33.35	67.47
	stage 2	62.87	93.27	80.79		22.79	28.62	76.64	60.27	62.20	18.72	68.86
	stage 3	52.22	65.36	98.75		37.19	38.75	67.92	13.75	72.08	36.67	78.00
GREEN	Overall	51.89	32.65	38.12	30.93		70.95	39.99	53.65	58.00	78.83	37.95
	stage 1	46.17	42.83	45.50	38.56		49.74	48.32	79.77	66.15	65.30	47.44
	stage 2	53.55	19.48	33.10	22.79		86.70	32.35	32.05	51.33	94.77	34.29
	stage 3	59.96	47.63	35.94	37.19		73.44	43.23	51.56	59.90	33.33	22.50
EUL	Overall	76.39	48.52	43.63	43.19	70.95		45.28	44.27	55.24	73.73	34.06
	stage 1	90.38	58.99	52.94	63.79	49.74		65.21	41.26	53.30	63.52	35.91
	stage 2	62.03	31.68	38.47	28.62	86.70		38.18	44.67	64.28	82.19	40.09
	stage 3	86.23	73.39	37.50	38.75	73.44		20.83	50.00	33.33	66.67	0.00
EDA	Overall	62.73	72.86	76.59	74.22	39.99	45.28		52.18	62.87	38.17	74.84
	stage 1	72.51	80.08	70.81	73.93	48.32	65.21		39.41	52.21	41.44	64.15
	stage 2	64.86	76.05	84.55	76.64	32.35	38.18		67.13	65.08	34.94	79.44
	stage 3	34.60	47.45	66.67	67.92	43.23	20.83		41.67	79.17	44.44	90.00
ER	Overall	52.23	52.00	50.39	45.19	53.65	44.27	52.18		62.63	52.71	61.84
	stage 1	37.69	47.22	46.50	41.56	79.77	41.26	39.41		60.73	66.39	55.09
	stage 2	70.87	66.73	68.17	60.27	32.05	44.67	67.13		72.15	34.89	77.27
	stage 3	36.53	24.08	12.50	13.75	51.56	50.00	41.67		41.67	100.00	20.00
RB	Overall	70.62	57.07	60.18	59.36	58.00	55.24	62.87	62.63		57.67	61.16
	stage 1	58.54	43.28	53.29	49.53	66.15	53.30	52.21	60.73		67.98	53.49
	stage 2	87.73	66.86	61.57	62.20	51.33	64.28	65.08	72.15		48.88	65.62
	stage 3	47.10	58.22	70.83	72.08	59.90	33.33	79.17	41.67		66.67	66.67
LU	Overall	55.82	26.69	28.68	25.76	78.83	73.73	38.17	52.71	57.67		32.46
	stage 1	60.17	32.13	25.65	33.35	65.30	63.52	41.44	66.39	67.98		31.27
	stage 2	51.20	17.78	30.31	18.72	94.77	82.19	34.94	34.89	48.88		36.15
	stage 3	66.67	64.22	33.33	36.67	33.33	66.67	44.44	100.00	66.67		0.00
IND	Overall	49.49	64.96	76.11	69.35	37.95	34.06	74.84	61.84	61.16	32.46	
	stage 1	44.30	66.16	71.05	67.47	47.44	35.91	64.15	55.09	53.49	31.27	
	stage 2	59.36	69.07	79.00	68.86	34.29	40.09	79.44	77.27	65.62	36.15	
	stage 3	21.79	42.02	80.00	78.00	22.50	0.00	90.00	20.00	66.67	0.00	

The EP arena appeared divided into a vast nucleus and two incompatible extremes. The large centre embraced the EPP, the LDR and the EDA with the ED located to its right and the Socialists and the EUL on its left. On the extreme left of the parliamentary axis was Piquet's Left Unity and on the extreme right was Le Pen's group which explicitly assumed an isolated and 'outsider position' in the EP policy over the Gulf (Jacobs et al., 1990, 98), as all the other groups refused to collaborate with it. The Greens, not easily placed within any traditional political alignments, could be located in this case on the left wing of the Parliament, showing its strong voting similarity with the LU and EUL groups. The Rainbow group, by contrast, was equidistant from all other groups. A more marked than normal left-right division seemed to emerge within the House as Piquet also confirmed in his interview with the author. The first striking element which emerges from Table 3 with regard to the Socialists is that the EUL, the Greens and the LU voting similarities reached only medium average figures, meaning that they effectively supported Socialist policy as much as the ER. This anomaly could be explained in part by the fact that the prevailing faction within the Socialist group took eventually an interventionist stance approaching to the policy advocated by centre-right groups. Predictably, the group with the highest voting similarity to the Socialist was the EUL with a Voting Similarity Percentage (VSP) equivalent to 76.39, bolstering the Socialist-EUL alliance. The second closest group was the Rainbow group followed by the EPP, marking a fairly high level of similarity which confirms to a certain extent the commitment of the historic alliances between the two 'giants'.

The centre-right groups including EPP, ED, LDR and EDA showed respectively high levels of voting similarity with each other. In particular, the LDR and the ED registered the highest VSP between any of the groups over Gulf policies. It was not surprising to find a low level of similarity between the EPP, ED and LDR on one side and the LU on the other. Their evident policy divergences with the left groups and the Greens could also be seen in their respective VSPs, albeit to a lesser extent in the case of the LDR. According to the figures the ED and LU displayed diametrically opposed policies on the Gulf issue, marking the two very opposite extremes of the EP with the lowest VSP, 25.76. The Greens' high similarity with the LU and EUL groups placed them on the left of the parliamentary spectrum. All three groups firmly maintained their extreme rejection of the war, their position therefore being distant from that of pro-interventionists ED, EPP and LDR groups. The VSP between the Greens and the Socialists was rather disappointing.

The ER group's constant opposition to the parliamentary majority can be shown in its voting behaviour, reflecting similarities with the Rainbow and LU groups, even if throughout the whole crisis, these groups never forged any coalition or drafted a joint text. Tables 4 and 5 show that the extreme right and the extreme left, the latter also including the Green group, remained out of the majority coalitions more often than the other groups.

135

5. Intergroup Cooperation in Shaping the European Parliament's Stance on the Gulf Crisis

A glance behind the parliamentary scenes is essential to unravel the complex process leading to the adoption or rejection of Resolutions. For this purpose, a RCV analysis along with a more general appraisal of the PGs' contribution to the formulation of Resolutions has been undertaken. Between September 1990 and May 1991, the European Parliament adopted 21 Resolutions covering the various political, economic and humanitarian aspects of the Gulf crisis, of which 2 were based on reports of the Political Affairs Committee, 15 were group Resolutions, 3 were individual group Resolutions and one Resolution which was drafted jointly by MEPs acting in a personal capacity. Intergroup coalition emerged unequivocally as the dominant force within the House. Broad coalitions were almost always the rule with respect to the Gulf crisis, with a small and often fragmented opposition embodying in all cases the isolated extreme right and occasionally the Rainbow group, the Greens and the Left Unity. Many small groups aligned themselves with the larger groups and, in some cases, succeeded in obtaining the inclusion of amendments to the texts. The Gulf crisis revealed the highest level of successful cooperation between the Socialists and the EUL group. Clearly, this revealed that the two groups shared the same understanding of the problem and its possible solutions. The 'historic alliance' between the Christian Democrats and the Socialists within the European Parliament, dating back to the 1984 European elections, was also reaffirmed on 10 occasions when the two groups, together with others, drafted compromise texts which found the approval of the House. The presence of either the Socialists or the Christian Democrats was necessary in order to achieve the required simple majority to pass Resolutions. Exceptionally, only in one case did a Joint Resolution, drafted by the EUL, the LU and the Greens, without either of the two largest groups as signatory, reach a majority.

By contrast, as indicated in Table 4, individual political groups failed to gain parliamentary consensus over their respective texts, with the exception of the Socialists and the Christian Democrats.

Table 4 Breakdown of Adopted and Non-Adopted Motions for Resolutions on the Gulf Crisis

Date	Individual Political Groups		Political Groups' Coalitions		Individual MEP / Coalition of MEPs		Committee Reports
	A	NA	A	NA	A	NA	A
Sept 1990	-	5 (V,ERx2,Rainbow, LU)	1 (EPP/ED,S,EDA, LDR,EUL)	-	-	-	-
Oct 1a (12/10/90)	-	6 (S,EPP,EDA,V, EUL,ER)	-	1 (SOC,LDR,LU EUL,EPP,ED,V)	-	1 (all EPP)	-
Oct 1b (12/10/90)	2 (S,EPP)	3 (LDR,Rainbow, EDA)	1 (S,ED,LU,EPP,LDR, V,Rainbow,EUL)	-	-	-	-
Oct 2a (25/10/90)	-	4 (LDR,ED,LU,ER)	1 (S,EUL)	-	-	-	1 A3-261/90 Crampton Report
Nov 1990	-	5 (Vx3,LDR,ER)	2 (1:LDR,EPP,S,EUL, EDA,ED,LU; 2:S,EPP)	-	-	-	1 A3-0321/90 Crampton Report
Dec 1990	1 (S)	9 (LDR,V,EPPx2, ER,ED,Rainbow,LU, EDA)	1 (S,LU,EUL)	-	-	-	-
Jan 1991	-	10 (EDx2, EDAx2, LDR,EPP,EUL,V, LU, ER)	1 (S,Rainbow)	-	1	2	-
Feb 1991	-	5 (Vx3,LDR,ER)	2 (1:S,EUL,EPP,LU, ED,EDA; 2:S,EUL, EPP, LU)	-	-	3 (2:all S)	-
Mar 1991	-	4 (ER,LDR,EDA, Rainbow)	2 (1:S,EPP,ED,EUL, LU,V, 2:V,EUL,LU)	-	-	-	-
Apr 1991	-	9 (LUx2,Sx2,V,EUL, EDA,EPP,ER)	2 (1:S,EPP,ED,LDR, V,LU,EUL, Rainbow, EDA; 2:S,EPP,LDR, V,EUL,LU)	-	-	-	-
May 1991	-	1 (ER)	2 (1:S,LDR,EPP,EUL, V,LU; 2:LDR,EPP,V)	-	-	-	-

A=Adopted
NA=Non-Adopted (Rejected, Fallen and Withdrawn Motions)

In addition, two declarations fell: DE15/90, Stephen Hughes and DE04/91 Kenneth Coates.

137

Table 5   Intergroup Cooperation: Adopted Joint Resolutions on the Gulf Crisis

	S	EPP	LDR	ED	EDA	V	EUL	ER	RB	LU
S	x	10	6	6	4	5	11	0	3	9
EPP	10	x	7	6	4	6	9	0	2	8
LDR	5	7	x	4	3	5	6	0	2	5
ED	6	6	4	x	4	3	6	0	2	5
EDA	4	4	3	4	x	1	4	0	1	3
V	5	6	5	3	1	x	5	0	2	6
EUL	11	9	6	6	4	5	x	0	2	10
ER	0	0	0	0	0	0	0	x	0	0
RB	3	2	2	2	1	2	2	0	x	2
LU	9	8	5	4	3	6	10	0	2	x

Throughout the whole crisis, the House passed only two resolutions drafted individually by the Socialists, respectively in October and December 1990, and only one resolution on the speculative rise of oil prices by the Christian Democrats, on 12 October 1990. Although no evidence can be found to support the following assumption, it seemed that this mutual exchange of favours between the Socialists and the Christian Democrats to support these individual Motions for Resolutions stemmed from the urgency for the EP not to remain silent and look unconcerned about the events in the Gulf in the eyes of the world.

This urgency was felt especially after 11 October when, due to that House being inquorate, no discussion or vote was held on the Gulf crisis. Lastly, it is interesting to notice a timid attempt by individual MEPs to develop cross-boundary initiatives beyond the domain and control of the various parties. This was a direct result of personal relationships of trust and cooperation being built between MEPs, irrespective of their political group affiliation and nationality (Oostlander interview, 1/2/1996). This emerging phenomenon seems to result from the so-called process of socialization.

Chart 14 simplifies roll-call vote analysis of the contribution of political groups to parliamentary activity with respect to the Gulf crisis.

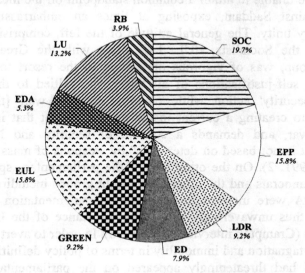

Chart 14 PG Contribution: Gulf Crisis

N.B. ER made no contribution to the EP position on the Gulf

The Socialists contributed more than any other group to forging parliamentary policies towards the Gulf crisis. In particular, the Socialist group endeavoured to bridge the gaps between the left-right blocs, while seeking to overcome its internal divisions. Having said this, the Socialists often succeeded in reaching a majority coalition even without the Christian Democrats. In one case, the Socialists and the Left groups formed a winning coalition against the centre-right front consisting of Christian Democrats, European Democrats and Liberals. The Christian Democrats, albeit to a lesser extent, also made an impact on the EP stance. The extreme right was systematically excluded from taking part in any coalitions. The reluctance of all other groups to be associated with the extreme right-wingers rather than a self-expressed choice by the ER leadership to distinguish itself from the rest of the House explains the marginalization of the far right members as well as their sense of alienation within the EP arena.

This inquiry does not illustrate all 50 RCVs taken on the Gulf crisis, but only those relating to the most controversial texts. At the September

1990 session, all political groups unanimously condemned the Iraqi aggression and the seizure of hostages, while vigorously advocating initiatives for the convening of a Middle East international conference. Yet, the PGs were unable to attain a common standpoint on the measures to be adopted against Saddam, exposing at times an embarrassing lack of parliamentary unity. The general attitude of the left, comprising the vast majority of the Socialists, EUL, LU, along with the Greens and the Rainbow group, was of vigorous opposition to the resort to arms. "By refuting the self-justifications of all those who rallied to the so-called 'collective security' action while claiming to hate war, [the Greens] contributed to creating a current inside the Parliament that is genuinely hostile to war, and demands a concept of security and North-South relations that is not based on deterrence" by weapons of mass destruction (Lannoye, 1991, 2). On the other side of the parliamentary spectrum, the Christian Democrats and the other centre-right groups including the LDR, ED and EDA were inclined to the forceful implementation of the UN resolutions, thus unwaveringly supporting the stance of the UK and US governments (Crampton interview, 31/1/1996). In order to avert the gloomy prospect of stagnation and immobility in terms of policy definition over the Gulf, which had threateningly appeared on the parliamentary horizon, internal EP dynamics drifted, after lengthy debates and negotiations, towards a multiparty strategy. Most groups' chairmen consulted each other, exchanged views on the contents of the text to be submitted and on the strategies to be adopted (Piquet interview, 31/1/1996).

At the conclusion of the September parliamentary debate, after an exhausting marathon of 10 roll-call votes the EP passed a Joint Resolution negotiated between the Socialist, EPP, LDR, ED, EDA, EUL groups and by the *ad hoc* Gulf Delegation, requested once by the European Right and the Socialists individually, 6 times by the Rainbow group as well as once by the LDR and the Rainbow group jointly.[55] A final roll-call vote on the whole resolution was requested by the Greens, the Socialists and the Christian Democrats. Although the Rainbow and the European Right tried to play on the uncertainty of some MEPs who did not fully share the views

---

55 Ten split roll-call votes were held respectively on Recital A, Recital H, Paragraph 6, Paragraph 11 first sentence, paragraph 17 excluding one sentence, paragraph 17, paragraphs 20, 21 and 24. Finally, a roll-call vote took place on the text as a whole.

140

expressed by the dominant groups, their efforts were in vain due to the overwhelming numeric superiority of the coalition. The September Resolution was a grand compromise, inevitably resulting in ambiguity on several aspects. As the parliamentary debates and explanations of vote reveal, the different signatories seemed to contradict each other over the interpretation of the real meaning of the text, which was therefore endorsed on antithetical grounds. However, in a positive light, this might be regarded as an acknowledgement of the dialectic ability of the Parliament in succeeding to reconcile opposing views (Melandri, 12/9/1990, 157).

At the January 1991 session, after six hours of debate, no agreement was reached on a common text on the Gulf crisis, following the rejection of a series of amendments proposed by various PGs. A final draft tabled by the Socialist and Rainbow Groups, calling for the immediate cessation of fighting as soon as there was a declaration of intent by Iraq to evacuate Kuwait, was withdrawn by the authors themselves, Jannis Sakellariou (Socialist, Germany) and Jaak Vandemeulebroucke (Rainbow, Belgium), given that the original content had been deprived of two key points, the condemnation of Iraqi attacks against Israel and the statement that the international community had no quarrel with the Iraqi population and the Arab world (*OJEC* C 48/1991, 29 and Cot, 23/1/1991, 164).

After a week of discussions and a lengthy vote, on 24 January 1991 the EP adopted by 202 in favour, 98 against and 25 abstentions a new text on the conflict in the Gulf, negotiated and tabled by Socialists, Christian Democrats, British Conservatives and Rainbow members. The Joint Resolution incorporated the two disputed references. On this occasion, the significance of inter- and intragroup bargaining was stressed by Cot as the only possible way of forging an EP official stance on the events in the Gulf, the other alternative being parliamentary silence which would be politically inconceivable. It is worth stressing the importance of the adoption of resolutions which, although not a legally binding act, represents a relevant indicator of the way MEPs conceive their function as representatives of the people and which also consists of an exercise for MEPs to take into account the various signals, moods and impressions and turn them into coherent policies. In April, the House adopted by 194 votes in favour and 3 abstentions a Joint Resolution on arms export negotiated by the Socialists, EPP, LDR, ED, Green, Rainbow, EUL and LU (B3-552, 555, 562, 564, 565 and 660).

As clearly displayed in the above tabulations and statistics, no individual political group was in a position to control fully parliamentary

141

voting outcomes. The Socialists greatly influenced the parliamentary policy on the Gulf. However, their strength stemmed not only from a clear numeric superiority, but also from the capacity and willingness to share coalitions with other groups and their acquiescence to compromise. Although owning the largest share of voting power the Socialist group would have not succeeded in determining the voting outcome without the support of other groups. The Christian Democrats participated in tabling many joint resolutions, but failed to create an alternative coalition to that led by the Socialists. Every political group possesses a certain, if different, *a priori* voting capacity naturally linked to its numeric composition which is not always directly proportional to its effective power and influence. In light of the parliamentary debates and RCVs results, it would be inaccurate to assume that the European Parliament reflected a uniform and homogeneous stance on the Gulf. Instead, a variety of political attitudes emerged across the House, requiring repeated multigroup interventions in order to reach at least a slender majority which would enable the House to pass its resolutions. The overall index of agreement of the European Parliament did not touch great peaks, but marked the medium average of 56.13 percent during the first stage, fell to the fairly low level of 36.33 percent in the second stage and rose to the medium figure of 58.04 percent in the final stage, averaging throughout the whole period the medium low percentage of 47.33.

Parliamentarians on all sides showed a distinct lack of cohesion that weighed them down both politically and diplomatically. Yet, despite the fact that it was a unified Parliament that vigorously stressed the need to sustain peace and stability in the region and to deal with the crucial issues in the Middle East once the Gulf War was over, when the moment actually arrived to confront post-war problems, it was disappointing to see that MEPs were reluctant even to participate in the voting, with absenteeism reaching the fairly high level of 66 percent.

Conclusion

The above qualitative and quantitative analyses suggest that the PGs eventually succeeded in uniting their respective members into discernible political entities. In particular the data display a certain cohesion within the individual political groups in relation to the Gulf issue, with indices of agreement between fairly and extremely high values, whilst highlighting deep discrepancies of views within the House as a whole, substantiated by a rather slender level of overall agreement of 47.33 along with a rate of absenteeism that was only just within the medium low boundaries at 41.71. It is indisputable that the war stage was the most grievous and controversial period, accentuating divisions within Parliament, reducing the levels of agreement attained by most PGs in the previous stage and, in particular, breaking up the unity of the Socialists. By contrast, the war stage saw higher indices of agreement for the Left Unity, the Green and the Rainbow groups, united in their firm opposition to military intervention. Overall, absenteeism decreased during this crucial stage, with the exception of the ER and Rainbow groups, reflecting MEPs' concern at the events unfolding in the Gulf.

Throughout the three stages, the voting cohesion was by and large, higher within the Christian Democrats at 91.15 than the Socialists 73.28, counterbalanced, to a certain extent, by the latter's slightly lower level of absenteeism of 33.17 against that of the EPP at 39.69. A comparison of the voting behaviour of the two largest groups suggests that the Socialists were more prone to factionalism than their main political rivals, the Christian Democrats. In decreasing order, ED, LU, EPP and EUL maintained a high rate of cohesion. The ED group reached the highest average level of cohesion, 94.83 percent, consistently maintaining an exceptionally high index of agreement in all three stages. The Left Unity, the European Peoples' Party and the European Unitarian Left then followed with fairly high indices of agreement equal respectively to 92.28, 91.15 and 91.10 percent. The result registered by the ED was not surprising, if one considers that numerically it was a medium-sized group and almost exclusively mono-national with members coming from the British Tory Party, with the exception of 2 Danish Conservative MEPs. By looking at the ED group, one could mistakenly be led to assume that same nationality and affiliation to the same political national party are the imperative factors for securing cohesion within the PGs. Although it is unquestionable that they can contribute to cementing internal cohesion, the major efforts of transnationalization within the EP forum cannot be underestimated. The EPP, for instance, the second largest group in the EP and counting MEPs from all twelve members states, recorded a remarkably high level of agreement and transnationality in its voting. The EPP example proved that it is possible to attain a certain homogeneity and harmony of views in a large transnational context. The Liberals, who also claimed a high level of transnationality, attained a good internal compromise when voting on the

Gulf. Considering that all twelve nationalities were represented within the Socialists group, the level of cohesion was high, with an index equivalent to 73.28 percent, though lower than those of the Christian Democrats, Liberals and the Greens.

Due to their highly transnational configuration, the Socialist, EPP, LDR, Green and Rainbow groups were expected to display a less cohesive approach than the other political groups with a more homogeneous structure. Nevertheless, on the basis of the results achieved, there was no inversely proportional ratio between the degree of transnationality on group composition and the agreement index, indicating that there is no direct link between group heterogeneity and group cohesiveness.

Contrary to the widespread assumption that the political groups lack practice in whipping, it can be argued that the Gulf case revealed *de facto* that there was a certain voting discipline within the groups as the official party line eventually prevailed despite a few dissenting voices. The largest groups, including the Socialists, the Christian Democrats and the Liberals, had their whips, even though these often consisted of "nothing more than a list, prepared by the group secretariats and circulated to members' benches in the hemicycle before voting periods, setting out the recommended group position" (Westlake, 1994a, 238).

Other groups, for example, the Green and the Rainbow groups, officially acknowledged the principle of free voting (Bowler and Farrell, 1993, 14), individualism and egalitarianism. Admission was also *ad hoc* and transversal bridges were allowed and even encouraged between groups. The EDA, a small club-like group dominated by prominent personalities, did not envisage any disciplinary actions against its dissenting members (Ewing, 1989, 19-23).

The centre-right, including the EPP, LDR, ED and EDA groups, scored higher on the rate of cohesion as well as on the rate of participation than the left, embracing the Socialists, EUL, LU, the Green and the Rainbow groups. However, given their chameleonic nature and the consequent difficulty of placing them on the traditional left-right scale, if the Green and Rainbow groups were to be excluded from the left coalition, the balance would move in favour of the left. On the other hand, it is necessary to underline the fact that the poor level of attendance and cohesion by the EDA had a detrimental effect on the average figure for the centre-right parties.

If one compares the levels of cohesion over the three stages, on the whole the results display a small fluctuation in the cases of the ED, EDA,

EPP and EUL. The data also show that the Socialists, Liberals, the Greens varied greatly in their respective IA over the same period. The poor MEP turnout at voting sessions often resulted in a higher level of cohesion, possibly due to the easier management of coalition groups which allowed the achievement of joint strategies.

The *modus operandi* of the political groups with regard to EP policy-definition over the Gulf crisis refutes the allegation that the parliamentary record of debating and voting on the Gulf was dismal. However, whilst the vast majority of the groups succeeded overall in forming a cohesive stance, the EP as a whole failed to achieve a high level of consensus and to present itself as a united political front. In particular, the House was divided in respect of the actions to be taken and whether these should include the use of armed force. The figures also exhibit a high incidence of abstention and absence among MEPs during RCVs on the Gulf. Both appeared as 'neutral' ways of averting the dilemma between personal beliefs, acquiescence to national party and group loyalty.

The appraisal of transnationalization along with the comparison of the indices of agreement of the national delegations and of the political groups vis-à-vis the crisis are not completely gloomy as they show the PGs' attempt to overcome national boundaries and differences, by emphasizing political and ideological affinity. Besides the traditional left-right division which characterizes most national assemblies, other cleavages may be observed in the European Parliament: North versus South and integrationist versus anti-integrationist.

Comparing the voting similarities of the various groups with respect to the Gulf issue, it appeared that, on the one side, the EPP, ED, Liberals and EDA and, on the other, the EUL, LU and the Greens had reached respectively very and fairly high figures creating some kind of bipolarity within the House. The Socialists oscillated between the two blocs, overall tipping the scale and, therefore, the parliamentary voting outcome. The voting records on the Gulf displayed a frequently recurring convergence between the Christian Democrats and the British conservatives. On the other side of the Chamber, the Socialist and EUL group exhibited a high voting similarity. And yet, coalitions gathering Socialists, EUL, EPP and the other centre-right groups were very frequent. Intragroup cohesiveness and intergroup cooperation were based on the necessity of reinforcing the capacity of the parliamentarians, almost devoid of influence over the Council, to participate in policy-making over crucial foreign policy issues. As no majority group exists within the European Parliament, the chairmen of the PGs had to expend all their energy in order to cooperate and unite their forces to shape and/or support the same actions, by voting accordingly at the plenary.

During the past years, a quest for group cohesion and intergroup solidarity has been pursued by suggesting tougher discipline and voting rules aimed at reinforcing political-ideological concepts and party loyalties. Although this book does not focus on what could be referred to as "the conflict of interest between national and European loyalty" and specifically on the different attitudes, if any, between national parties and corresponding EP political groups, it is nevertheless important to detect whether transnationalization was achieved with regard to the Gulf crisis or whether the factor of nationality prevented group cohesion. The case highlighted the fact that the degree to which individual MEPs' liberty was curtailed by their duty to the national party and/or political group varied widely. In the scramble for a consistent parliamentary response, some of the barriers to EP political unity were eventually smashed and tumbled down. As the voting analysis indicates, the expansion of the EP role requires the establishment of European party structure and organization (Attinà, 1990, 574-577). For a correct interpretation of PG level of cohesion, the crucial factor of absenteeism, with its limiting and sometimes paralysing consequences, needs to be considered.

The crisis was not a unifying catalyst between the various parliamentary groups and did not mitigate political and, to a lesser degree, national divergences. The hypothesis that when dealing with foreign policy MEPs tend to show a high level of consensus could not be confirmed since the case presented some crucial defence and military issues which inevitably contributed to decrease parliamentary consensus.

By way of conclusion, it can be said that in harmony with the values of ethics and democracy, it is vital to maintain the multiplicity of political voices which gives a sense of dynamism to the parliamentary forum, but in order to enable the EP to function, it is necessary to keep these diverging tides within the same political river-bed, especially when dealing with serious international crises.

IV The Responses of the European Community and the European Parliament to the Yugoslav Crisis

The aim of this chapter is to provide a brief overview of the main events that occurred in the SFRY from January 1991 until July 1992 and to assess the responses of the European Community and the European Parliament. This serves as the basis for an investigation into the role and voting behaviour of the political groups on the Yugoslav crisis, which is carried out in Chapter V.

With the collapse of communism in Central and Eastern Europe, a new era of harmony, democracy and prosperity seemed to have finally dawned. Yet, regrettably, as the deterrent of the Cold War ceased to exist old and new rivalries began to emerge along with the awakening of latent ethnic feuds. In the aftermath of the Iraqi invasion of Kuwait in August 1990, another challenge loomed on the international political horizon, this time right in the heart of the European continent: the historically explosive area of the Balkans.

1. Brief Historical Background on the Yugoslav Crisis

On 25 June 1991, Croatia and Slovenia officially proclaimed their independence from the SFRY.[56] These decisions did not arise suddenly, but were the result of a long process of reflection starting in 1986, which

---

56 On 27 September 1990, the Slovenian Parliament declared legislation promulgated by Federal authorities no longer applicable to the Republic. Similarly, on 22 December 1990, the Croatian Parliament proclaimed the supremacy of its legislation over Federal law. On 23 December 1990, 88.5 percent of the Slovenian population voted in favour of secession from the Yugoslav Federation. On 19 May 1991, 93.4 percent of the Croatian electorate opted for independence of the Republic (Kritziotis, 1993).

147

stemmed from long-standing political divergences with the newly appointed President of the Serbian League of Communists, Slobodan Milošević. The dramatic events which took place in Kosovo in March 1989 certainly exacerbated a mood of distrust, feeding sentiments of anger towards the Serbs. Feelings of sympathy were instead directed towards the Albanian population, so harshly repressed by the Yugoslav People's Army, *Jugoslovenska narodna armija* (JNA) on Milošević's orders, following their uprising against alleged ethnic discrimination and the envisaged reduction of the autonomy of the province (Bennett, 1995, 11, 142).

The Federal Parliament and government rejected these claims for independence by Slovenia and Croatia seeing them as pure acts of rebellion and interpreting them as veritable declarations of war which required immediate intervention of the Federal Army. Fighting erupted in Slovenia as a result of the JNA's attempt to take control of the Northern border of the Federation, while the Croats failed to comply with the December 1990 pact of mutual assistance agreed with the Slovenes. The reason underpinning this evident betrayal was the accord secretly concluded with Milošević to take a stance of neutrality in the case of a Serb-Slovenian conflict. Violent inter-ethnic clashes followed in the meantime in the Croatian town of Glina where the JNA soon gained ground (Alendar, 1992, 19).

The eruption of the hostilities in Yugoslavia was uncannily reminiscent of the events of 1914 with the reappearance of belligerence between states as well as the reopening of the "Pandora's box of ethnic and religious conflicts" (Simić, 1993, 2). The assassination of the Archduke Franz Ferdinand in Sarajevo by the Serbian nationalist Gavrilo Princip had led to Austria's declaration of war against Serbia. This had forced the various European countries to take a position either in favour of or against Serbia, triggering the outbreak of the Great War. However, as Fred Halliday claims, a full comparison cannot be drawn between the two phenomena since the dimension of the conflict which flared up in 1991 remained circumscribed and rather limited to communal boundaries without affecting major powers and their mutual relationships (Halliday, 1994, 223).

The Yugoslav imbroglio appeared "to have so much in common with the classical Greek tragedy with its element of *ananke*: at each time point, a number of actors are doing what they have been trapped - whether by their own previous actions or those of other actors - into having to do, and as result they sink deeper and deeper into catastrophe" (Wiberg, 1992 cited in Simić, 1993, 2).

The seeds of animosity were sown in the early half of the twentieth century with the creation of the Kingdom of Serbs, Croats and Slovenes, as Yugoslavia was at first named. The Union of 1 December 1918 was not based on equal partnerships between its members, but was largely dominated by the Serbs (Bennett, 1995, 32-33), hence fuelling resentment among the other two communities. In the wake of the Second World War, this situation was partly rectified with the establishment of the SFRY, which provided for a more equitable balance between the Yugoslav population, yet not healing completely ethno-religious divisions nor the rancour and indignation which had arisen since the outbreak of the conflict, when the Serbs killed thousands of Muslims and the Croats conducted an extermination campaign against the Serbs. In addition, it can be argued that the creation and consolidation of Yugoslavia as a state entity had arisen mainly from strategic interests and pressures by the founders of the new international order rather than from the will of the Southern Slavs themselves. Against this background, the post-war Socialist Federation could not survive beyond the death of its founding father, Marshall Josip Broz Tito (14 May 1980). With his departure the promise of stability and unity within the Federation soon faded away (Hancock, 1993, 50). In the absence of a strong and charismatic leader coupled with an increasingly complex economic situation, tensions rose sharply within and between the constituent republics.

In March 1987, as a result of both the high rate of inflation which had reached 100 percent and the heavy foreign debt equivalent to 20 billion US dollars, an upsurge of social discontent spread across the SFRY culminating with a series of protests and strikes. The situation deteriorated further to the extent that in 1988 the total foreign debt amounted to the equivalent of 21 billion US dollars and the level of unemployment exceeded 15 percent, a figure exceptionally high for a country with still a predominantly communist economy. The annual inflation rate, which was running at an already high rate of 250 percent (Altichieri, 27/3/87, 6; Magas, 1993, 190), soared by late 1989 to a staggering 2,000 percent (Bennett, 1995, 118).

With the rise to power of the Serbian Communist leader Slobodan Milošević, the spectre of extreme nationalism had entered the political scene, heightening the concerns and increasing the unrest of the Croatian

149

population. These fears were fuelled by rumours that, in case of the federal structure collapsing, Serbia would seek by all means to reassert its historical claim over the borders with Croatia and Bosnia-Herzegovina.[57] In October 1990, a stern warning signal was given after the declaration of autonomy by Serbs living in Croatia, resulting in clashes between them and the Croatian police. By December, with the electoral victory of Milošević for the Serbian leadership, the situation had spiralled out of control. These events ran almost concurrently with negotiations between the Croatian, Macedonian, Montenegrin, Bosnian, Serbian and Slovenian Republics over the future constitutional structure of the Federation. However, Belgrade rejected all proposals put forward by Slovenia and Croatia for the creation of a confederal system, based on the EC's model.

Both the weakness of the economy and the government's leadership contributed to deepening ethnic cleavages and fomenting conflicts. Certainly, the disastrous economic situation had precipitated the political crisis and endangered the territorial and political integrity of the Yugoslav Federation. Nonetheless, as Christopher Bennett observes, it soon became evident that while economic factors had led "Yugoslavia to the brink of civil war", economic remedies alone would no longer suffice in keeping the country united (Bennett, 1995, 118). Drastic economic measures, including wage-freezes for six months, price liberalization and devaluation of the dinar, converted and bound to the *Deutschmark*, brought immediate and astonishing results so that, by late February 1990 the rate of inflation had dropped below 10 percent. As a result, the architect of this economic miracle, the Federal Prime Minister Ante Marković grew in prestige and the esteem of both the Yugoslav people and the international community. Alas, the initial success achieved in the economic domain did not follow suit on the political front, where strong contrasts persisted and indeed intensified, especially between the Slovenian and Serbian Republics.

Fifteenth May 1991 brought with it a constitutional crisis when the SFRY failed to appoint the Croat Stipe Mesić as Federal President, due to Serbian opposition. This occurrence was unprecedented in the history of the Federation and, more precisely, since the introduction of the rotation system in the early 1970s to emphasize equality between the republics. In the midst of this turmoil, Prime Minister Marković sought to reassure the

---

57 As confirmed at the time by Serbian officials close to Milošević (Benetazzo, 1990, 16).

population by saying that Parliament and government were still functioning and that the Federation was "not spiralling downward towards a military coup, a civil war, or, perhaps most numbingly, perpetual political chaos" (Tanner, 17/5/91). For many Croatian political leaders, the Serbs' objective was to create an atmosphere of disarray, giving a pretext for armed intervention in order to resolve the situation to their own advantage. Concurrently, in the Montenegrin Republic, whose communist leadership was traditionally pro-Serbia, people began to show signs of restlessness concerning the role allotted them by Milošević as political 'cannon fodder' in Serbia's differences with the rest of Yugoslavia. Suddenly, the atavistic loyalty between the two republics seemed to be weakening (Tanner, 17/5/91).

The determinants of the Yugoslav breakdown could be traced to the lack of a stable democratic régime and, above all, to the "amplified expression of a national awakening", which had become the "moving spirit of the [Yugoslav] drama" (Crnobrnja, 1994, xii, 3). Conversely, in line with a "conspiracy theory", the belief was widespread in Yugoslavia that the demise of the Federation was being orchestrated by a few outside countries for the attainment of their own political ambitions. However, as the former ambassador of Yugoslavia to the European Communities, Mihailo Crnobrnja maintains, it is still extremely difficult "to uncover the political mechanics and dynamics of converting a respected, stable and relatively prosperous country into a new Balkan powder-keg" (Crnobrnja, 1994, xiii).

The initial response of the international community was to reject the fragmentation of Yugoslavia, as declared by the American Secretary of State James Baker and by the Ministers of Foreign Affairs meeting in Berlin on 20 June 1991, within the framework of the Conference on Security and Cooperation in Europe (CSCE) (Rémacle, 1992, 34). The United Nations took the safer option of a 'wait-and-see' policy over the recognition of Slovenia and Croatia on the ground that the new independent states would have called for international assistance in order to fight violations of their territorial sovereignty, something that the international community was not prepared to offer at this stage. Meanwhile, on James Baker's proposal, the CSCE had implemented from 9 September 1991 an arms embargo against Yugoslavia, also endorsed by the UN Security Council in its Resolution 713 on 25 September. This international sanctioning policy inevitably attracted criticism, mainly from the Croats, given that the Serbs had inherited the large arsenal of weaponry of the Federation and seized all arms factories to satisfy their demands (Rémacle,

151

1992, 37).[58] Hence, the embargo did not affect the military capacity of the JNA, but accentuated the imbalance in firepower by depriving the Croats[59] and the Bosnians of the means of defending themselves.

By assuming that, after all, the Yugoslav tragedy was an exclusively European problem, as clearly stated by the US administration, the Community felt the responsibility to take the political lead in the handling of the situation (Guicherd, 1992, 159-181; *The Financial Times*, 29-30/6/1991). Luxembourg's Foreign Minister Jacques Poos, who had enthusiastically proclaimed "this is *the hour of Europe*", believed rather optimistically that after the Brioni Agreement the situation was under control (*New York Times*, 29/6/1991). The EC member states rejected the idea of bringing in the United Nations, adopting as 'token gesture' the CSCE in the process. This was not questioned by the United Nations, as confirmed by the Secretary-General Pérez de Cuéllar who stated that "Slovenia [was] not an independent UN member (..), [and therefore] the UN [had] no role in Yugoslavia", unless the EC and CSCE endeavours failed altogether (Steinberg, 1993, cited in Lucarelli, 1995b,4 footnote 10).

With the appointment of the former US Secretary of State Cyrus Vance as Personal Envoy of the UN Secretary-General, the impression was given that the EC would step aside and the UN effectively take over. Vance appeared to have supreme confidence in his powers of persuasion and did not feel the need for the involvement of the European Community. Differences of views and the subsequent lack of coordination sometimes led to friction between the two organizations. As the crisis developed, the international community had to come to terms with the demise of the Yugoslav Federation and the *fait accompli* of the birth of the independent republics. The adoption of Resolution 743 on 21 February 1992 saw the UN Security Council taking a more decisive role. The mobilization of a peacekeeping force was authorized to ensure that sovereignty of the republics was not breached, and to supervise the ceasefire, the withdrawal of the Federal Army and the disbanding of paramilitary forces in four UN protected areas.

---

58 Yugoslavia was a large producer of weaponry and a net exporter. In 1991, even after the outbreak of the war, despite great domestic demand, Yugoslavia managed to increase its export of military equipment with a total sale equivalent to 460 million US dollars (Bennett, 1995, 177, Footnote 16).

59 Since May 1990 the Croatian territorial defence force had been disarmed (Bennett, 1995, 117).

On 29 February and 1 March 1992, a referendum was held on the independence of Bosnia-Herzegovina in which a fairly substantial minority of the Bosnian Serbs (25 percent) also participated, despite Belgrade's pressure to boycott it. The results expressed the determination of the majority of the people in Bosnia-Herzegovina to be independent but also their wish to continue living in a mixed society. However, recognition of Slovenia, Croatia and Bosnia-Herzegovina on the part of the United Nations took place on 7 April 1992, and with it came the deployment of the United Nations Protection Force (UNPROFOR), the second largest contingent ever assembled.

2. The European Community and the Yugoslav Crisis

The Yugoslav débacle seemed an opportunity to establish the Community's place in the post-bipolar world (Crnobrnja, 16/6/92, 1), its leading role in the European continent (Alendar, 1992, 18) and to show "what kind of an international actor the EC could purport to be" (Lodge, 1993, 3). Undoubtedly, the Twelve felt a special responsibility towards Yugoslavia, not least in terms of preventing any conflagration of war throughout the rest of Balkans with serious repercussions in Europe. The Community also felt some degree of loyalty and interest in the light of the then existing trade and cooperation agreement with Yugoslavia. Furthermore, the Twelve were looking for an occasion to test their political cooperation in the field of foreign policy to see whether the intergovernmental formula would be sufficient, in view of the reforms to be introduced in Maastricht. Following the unfortunate experience in the Gulf War, the EC member states were keen to demonstrate in the Yugoslav case, their ability to work jointly, to achieve a common position and to take suitable action vis-à-vis Yugoslavia (Lodge, 1993, 2). The EC role, or rather its 'mission impossible', was to contain the escalation of violence, but in order to fulfil this purpose, the Twelve had first to overcome their own international divisions and eliminate the political and institutional hindrance of the unanimity rule in EPC (Rémacle, 1992, 3).

The EC tried to exert pressure on the Yugoslav central authorities by threatening that if they undertook any military actions, all EC credits and financial assistance would be immediately terminated. In spring 1991, the Community decided to suspend negotiations for the third financial protocol of its existing trade and cooperation agreement with the SFRY and

153

dismissed the possibility of undertaking negotiations for the conclusion of an EEC-Yugoslavia association agreement similar to that concluded with Czechoslovakia, Poland and Hungary, until the Federation had promoted a plan of economic and constitutional reforms, regained a certain political stability, peacefully settled ethnic disputes and taken effective steps towards a visible democratic evolution of the country (Millan, 16/5/91, 269-270).

The Twelve became fully aware of the gravity of the constitutional crisis and the deterioration of the political and economic climate, especially after the visit in April 1991 of the EC Troika to the SFRY in May 1991 by the Commission President Jacques Delors together with the President of the Council Jacques Santer. Yet, the Twelve declared that EC assistance was subject to certain criteria, specifically the rotation of the Federal Presidency, the reopening of dialogue between nationalities, the protection of minorities and the implementation of Marković's economic reforms. In the belief that a united Yugoslavia would be best equipped to become part of the new Europe, EC Foreign Ministers meeting in Dresden on 4 June 1991 stated that the SFRY would only receive financial aid if it complied with principles concerning human and minority rights while also carrying out democratic and economic reforms. In particular, the previously agreed five-year aid package for Yugoslavia of 730 million ECUs, consisting mainly in loans from the European Investment Bank, would be cancelled.

Despite the various warning signals launched over the preceding three years by the Yugoslav authorities requiring the attention of the West, no diplomatic action was undertaken before the declarations of independence by Croatia and Slovenia. The hostilities were foreseeable and were foreseen and it can be argued that the EC pretended to be taken by surprise by the outbreak of violence. Nevertheless, it can also be said that the EC member states did not expect the situation to deteriorate to the point of an armed confrontation leading to the dismantling of the Federation itself.

The initial response of the Community, echoed by the United States, was of support to the economic plan adopted by Marković, whose political economy strategy had already allowed a remarkable reduction of inflation and was geared towards the achievement of a market economy. This policy, in order to succeed, required full commitment and cooperation of all constituent republics to maintain a common currency within a united country. The emerging tendencies of extreme nationalism were undermined and interpreted as natural, but only transient reactions of the people in the post-communist era. In addition, the Community did not acknowledge the

Yugoslav Republics' desire for independence out of the fear that the partitioning of the SFRY may have caused serious repercussions for the geopolitical configuration of Europe, triggering a chain reaction in the Balkans with the result of creating a destabilized area at its doorstep (EP Paper No. 18, 1993, 63). In particular, fear arose that the Yugoslav example would create a precedent emulated by the Soviet Union (Nuttall, 1994, 13). Finally, the Twelve shared the concern of the international community, highlighted in the previous section, that once these republics had been recognized as separate international legal entities, demands for external intervention would become inevitable, a venture that they were unprepared or unwilling to undertake. As early as 28 June 1991, the European Council had the opportunity to deal with the festering situation in Yugoslavia, but failed to formulate a coherent strategy. Particularly susceptible to headlines, the EC Foreign Ministers appeared to have gathered without a clear objective, in order to be seen to be doing something. A decision was reached to dispatch immediately to Yugoslavia the EC Troika[60] with the aim of persuading the parties to resume negotiations on the constitutional and political future of the SFRY. Although a ceasefire was agreed between Slovenian authorities and the JNA, the promise was broken as soon as 2 July, followed by another failed attempt made on 5 July.

Two days later at Brioni, an island town in the south of the Istrian province, the Community's Ministerial Troika brokered an official and long-lasting agreement between the Yugoslav Republics. This entailed the acceptance on the part of Croatia and Slovenia to defer the implementation of their declarations of independence for three months, the enforcement of a ceasefire, the outlining of principles for a peaceful settlement, the establishment of a negotiation procedure and the deployment of EC and CSCE observers in Slovenia and possibly Croatia. An arms embargo was also imposed on Yugoslavia by the European Community. With the Agreement, the Twelve implicitly engaged themselves to proceed with

---

60 Up until 30 June 1991, the EC Troika consisted of the Ministers of Luxembourg, Italy and the Netherlands. From 1 July 1991, when the Netherlands took over the Presidency of the European Community, the European Troika was composed of the Ministers of Foreign Affairs from the Netherlands, Luxembourg and Portugal. From 1 January 1992 to 31 June 1992, it was the turn of Portugal, the Netherlands and Great Britain and from 1 July 1992 to 31 December 1992, it was the turn of Great Britain, Portugal and Denmark.

recognition, irrespective of the outcome of the negotiations: "The success of the Troika at Brioni carried with it the seeds of its own fate" (Nuttall, 14/2/1995). The European Council was rather self-congratulatory with its first important diplomatic negotiation, which represented a big step forward in terms of European foreign policy-making, increasing member states' confidence about the EC capability of becoming a genuine international actor.

However, European solidarity was shortlived. The proposal of deploying lightly armed observers in the SFRY, as suggested by the Secretary-General of the WEU and put forward on the EC platform by France, was opposed by Belgium, Germany and Britain. Slovenian resistance to the attacks perpetrated by the JNA and worldwide political pressures made a ceasefire possible in Slovenia and on 17 July 1991 the dispatch of fifty EC observers, unarmed due to British pressure and financed by national governments.[61]

Once their own safety had been secured and in retaliation for the previous Croatian breach of their secret accord of mutual assistance, the Slovenes did not support the Croats militarily in their fight for independence. The Croats were therefore left with the option of attempting to internationalize the conflict by calling on the guarantee of the UN Charter or fighting on their own.

By late August 1991, the EC member states seemed to be moving slowly from their rigid stance over the future constitutional and political structure of Yugoslavia, according to the wishes of its own people (Statements by the Twelve, 20 and 27/8/1991). The continued unmerciful intervention of the JNA, which appeared to assume the form of a real military aggression, contributed to this change in the Community's policy, solicited by the media and public opinion (Alendar, 1992, 19).

Nevertheless, a full-scale European military intervention was ruled out and the deployment of an interposition force of lightly armed soldiers, backed by Germany and France and overall agreed by the other EC members, was vetoed by Britain until all warring parties had expressed their willingness to accept such intervention and committed themselves to honour the ceasefire, and until the international community, in particular the United Nations, had endorsed EC policy (EP Paper No. 18, 1993,

---

61 The option of financing military operations under the EC budget, subject to unanimous decision of the Council, was introduced later with the ratification of the Maastricht Treaty (Article J 11 (2) TEU).

63-64). Since these conditions were not fully met Britain refused to endorse any proposals to send armed forces to Yugoslavia to the great satisfaction of the Serbian leader who resolutely opposed any form of outside interference.

As Jacques Delors stated, the Community had only three instruments for influencing the course of the events in Yugoslavia: public opinion, the threat to recognize Slovenia and Croatia and economic sanctions. Enforcement was contemplated, albeit with caution and some reservations, especially from the United Kingdom. Failure to attain a settlement through the adoption of these policies would mean having to resort to the coercive option (Salmon, 1992, 248).

On 7 September 1991, under the EC's auspices, a peace conference opened in The Hague, gathering the representatives of all six republics from the Yugoslav Federation and the EC Foreign Ministers with the aim of establishing a permanent dialogue. The idea of convening an international peace conference was considered premature by the Netherlands and the United Kingdom, which preferred to wait until a ceasefire had been sustained. However, France, Germany and Italy insisted on the immediate opening of the discussions in order to prevent any further deterioration of the situation (Lucarelli, 1995a, 8, 10, footnote 12).

Lord Carrington was appointed Chairman of the EC-sponsored international peace conference on Yugoslavia and it was decided that the composition of the chairmanship and the support group would not vary so as to conform to the biannual rotation of the Council Presidency in order to allow stability and continuity to the work of the conference (Nuttall, 1994, 16). Carrington's approach was based on the principle that the Southern Slavs had to find a solution for themselves and that the EC should act as a facilitator rather than an adjudicator wishing to impose its own solution. An Arbitration Commission, chaired by Robert Badinter, was set up as part of the peace conference in order to express a legal opinion on the various positions of the parties to seek an "Arrangement for a General Solution" to the Yugoslav drama, resorting to a 'carrot and stick' strategy which offered rewards to cooperative parties and administered punishments to non-complying sides (Nuttall, 14/2/1995).[62]

---

62 The Arbitration Commission consisted of five Presidents of Constitutional Courts from the EC Member States. Robert Badinter (France), Aldo Corosaniti (Italy), and Roman Herzog (Germany) were selected by the Twelve, while the remaining two were supposed to be appointed by the SFRY. However, as no

On 26 September, three working groups were given the task to draft reports on the above questions while the perspective of secession was still excluded and fiercely denied (EP Paper No. 18, 1993, 65). According to Simon Nuttall, the failure of the Arbitration Commission to achieve the desired outcome was intrinsic in the composition of its members: Western European constitutional lawyers could not work out a possible arrangement in the absence of a proper representation and full endorsement of the parties concerned (Nuttall, 14/2/1995). In the meantime, after long negotiations with Serbia, EC observers were finally sent on 8 September 1991, too late to curb the bloodshed, according to the Croatian leader Franjo Tudjman.

As the end of Brioni deadline approached, fighting intensified, confirming that the Serbs were effectively using this truce as a consolidation exercise to reassert their supremacy over the other factions. The dismal failure of this military-cum-humanitarian operation cast a permanent cloud over this kind of intervention. Undoubtedly, three months were not sufficient either for the EC observers to pursue their missions or for the belligerents themselves to come to a suitable agreement (Nuttall, 14/2/1995). Yet, despite its limitations, the role of the EC observers needs to be reconsidered not least for its important humanitarian contribution (Crnobrnja, 16/6/92, 3). The initiative was a tangible expression of the EC involvement on the ground, with white berets becoming as recognizable as the blue berets, emblem of the United Nations (Nuttall, 14/2/1995).

Eighth October 1991, which marked the historical date for the implementation of the act of independence by Slovenia and Croatia, saw the Twelve still undecided on whether to recognize these republics under international law. Ten days later, a plan was established for a "free association of sovereign and independent republics" where "comprehensive arrangements including supervisory mechanisms for the protection of human rights and special status for certain groups and areas" would be put in place (*Europe*, 15-19/10/1991). The plan was rejected by President Milošević on the ground that it abolished the SFRY itself and represented an act of interference in domestic Yugoslav affairs exceeding "the [Community's] role of provider of 'good offices'" (Alendar, 1992, 20).

---

agreement was reached by the Yugoslavs, the three already appointed chose in their place colleagues from Belgium and Spain (EP Working Paper No. 18, 1993, 76).

As Serbia had proved to be stubborn in its attitude, the Community decided to introduce restrictive measures against Yugoslavia, whilst retaining the option of providing compensation for those republics which had shown their willingness to cooperate in order to reach a solution by peaceful means. On 8 November 1991, the EC Ministers, gathered in Rome, decided to suspend the EEC-SFRY trade and cooperation agreement, to freeze the ECSC-SFRY agreement, to withdraw trade concessions, to restore import quotas on textile products and to exclude Yugoslavia from the Community's General System of Preferences as well as from the PHARE[63] programme. The European Parliament was also urged to endorse these decisions and the UN Security Council was asked to enforce an international oil embargo. As early as 2 December 1991, economic sanctions were lifted for the cooperative parties, while being maintained against Serbia and Montenegro (EP Paper No. 18, 1993, 75).

The EC member states, in the EPC framework, undertook a series of initiatives by organizing diplomatic missions pursued by the Troika of Ministers of Foreign affairs, convening a conference under permanent EC chairmanship, dispatching observers as well as imposing economic sanctions against Yugoslavia. Despite the multiplicity of views the Twelve eventually succeeded in reaching a certain unity, shifting to a more realistic policy which accepted the inevitable demise of the Federation (Nuttall, 1994, 11-12).

By December 1991, the Arbitration Commission acknowledged that the disintegration of the SFRY was irreversible and that its constituent republics had to re-establish mutual relationships by setting up a new association based on the principle of equality between members. With the trumping of his 'ace card' over recognition, Lord Carrington was left with the sole possibility of negotiating the terms and conditions for the independence of the breakaway republics (Nuttall, 14/2/1995). Three main issues needed to be addressed in order to lay the basis for a solid and durable association, notably the minority question, the future institutional framework and the economic relations between the republics. On 17 December, after nine hours of intense discussion throughout the night, the EC Foreign Ministers agreed on the criteria for recognition, entailing guarantees for democracy, human rights and protection of minorities, commitments that borders would be changed only through peaceful means,

---

63   PHARE: Poland/Hungary Assistance for Restructuring Economies.

159

signing of an agreement on the control and non-proliferation of arms as well as support for UN peacekeeping initiatives and the EC peace conference. The final condition, ardently forwarded by Greece anxious at settling the dispute over Macedonia, was to abandon any territorial claim over EC neighbouring countries.

Fifteenth January 1992 was the date fixed for the EC's official recognition of Slovenia and Croatia if the Badinter Commission agreed that they had met the fundamental requisites. Yet, on 19 December 1991, Germany officially announced that it would proceed along the path of recognition. This unilateral decision, effectively to set aside the conditions established by the Badinter Commission, deeply irritated the other EC members. Thus, in a final attempt to placate the anger of its partners and limit the damage to the EC international reputation, Bonn announced that it would undertake open diplomatic relations only after the date officially and collectively agreed.

Meanwhile, Bosnia-Herzegovina, which until then had maintained a low profile and conciliatory attitude, decided to take political steps to prevent the expansion of the conflict. In particular, the Bosnian government had started negotiations with the EC Dutch Presidency for the deployment of European observers in its territory and called for UN intervention from 23 December (Rémacle, 1992, 39-40). In mid-January, the conclusions of the Badinter Report were disclosed, revealing that some of the guidelines drawn by the Community had not been followed, for instance, by Croatia and Bosnia-Herzegovina. Whereas for the former only marginal reservations were forwarded, for the latter,[64] the condition of EC recognition was the convening of an internationally monitored referendum on independence which was to be held on 29 February and 1 March 1992.[65] Yet, it must be acknowledged that, after the official recognition of Slovenia and Croatia, the EC was left with little choice but to consent to the Bosnian outcry for independence. "Recognition made no effective difference to

---

64 The Arbitration Committee found that the Croatian constitution "sometimes [falls] short of the obligations [concerning the status of its minorities], it nonetheless satisfies the requirements of general international law" (Bennett, 1995, Footnote 19, 179).

65 Despite the fact that the Bosnian Serbs attempted to boycott the referendum, the outcome revealed a turnout of 63 percent of the population and an overwhelming majority of people (over 99 percent) in favour of independence including both Bosnian Muslims and Croats (Bennett, 1995, 186; European Parliament, 'The Crisis in the former Yugoslavia', 44).

Bosnia-Hercegovina's status and as Carrington resumed his mediation efforts the Sarajevo government was deemed no more than a 'warring faction' on a par with the [Serb Democratic Party] in a civil war" (Bennett, 1995, 189).

The Bosnian leader Alija Izetbegović felt abandoned when intervention in Bosnia-Herzegovina was ruled out at both EC and international levels, despite the brave and non-violent resistance of the Muslim population to Serbian provocation, in line with the wishes of the international community. This sentiment was replaced by a devastating sense of betrayal when the EC decided to undertake and endorse a policy of *cantonization* within the territory of Bosnia-Herzegovina.

Numerous commentators such as Christopher Bennett, Mihailo Crnobrnja, Simon Nuttall, David Owen and Eric Rémacle have sought to explore the reasons for the blindness or false presumptions on the part of the Community vis-à-vis the Yugoslav débâcle, to uncover the causes of the EC delay and subsequent failure to respond effectively to the emergency in Yugoslavia. The crisis unfolded in concomitance with other major political events, such as the process of the German reunification, the so-called "Revolutions of 1989" in Central and Eastern European countries and finally the outbreak of the Gulf War. It also coincided with a particularly delicate moment in the history of the European Community, approaching the last stage of the Intergovernmental Conference (IGC) convened in Maastricht at the end of 1991 (Lodge, 1993, 2). While engaged in the negotiations on the prospects of establishing a European foreign policy, substantial divergences arose between, on the one hand, the Europeanists and, on the other, the Atlanticists. The former led by the French government, advocated the incorporation of the WEU security mechanism into the European Community structure, whereas the latter, supported by the United Kingdom, preferred to retain NATO as the military and defence structure for Europe. This difference of views re-emerged especially with respect to the Yugoslav case (Nuttall, 1994, 23). The lack of both an existing EC defence structure and an agreement on the definition of a security organization for the future clearly highlighted the fact that the EC was not prepared and not suitably equipped to deal with an armed confrontation.

The Twelve sought to play a mediatory role by at first using diplomatic and economic formulae. Despite the initial strong EC opposition to the use of force, the Community eventually had to come to terms with the fact that some form of "restrained coercive violence" was imperative (Gow and

161

Smith, 1992, 56). In addition, it appeared that the Community did not fully understand the true nature of the dispute and could not empathize with the people with whom it was dealing.

In David Owen's words:

> [L]eaders who had no experience of democracy also displayed a callousness of mind in which the people's view never seemed to come anywhere near the conference table, despite much consulting of assemblies and holding of referenda in circumstances of dubious democratic validity. History points to a tradition in the Balkans of a readiness to solve disputes by the taking up of arms and acceptance of the forceful or even negotiated movement of people as the consequence of war. It points to a culture of violence within a cross-road civilization where three religions, Orthodox Christianity, Islam, Roman Catholicism, have divided communities and on occasions become the marks of identification in a dark and virulent nationalism (Owen, 1995, 2-3).

This view was not shared by others such as Christopher Bennett who "refuse[s] to accept that there was anything inevitable about Yugoslavia's disintegration", rejecting the prejudice "that Balkan peoples are somehow predisposed to violence, or that the international community was powerless to halt the killing" (Bennett, 1995, viii). In retrospect, it can be claimed that a swifter understanding and admission of the gravity of the situation along with prompt financial assistance to support the process of economic and political reforms in the SFRY could have prevented the degeneration into a ruthless civil war.

As Juliet Lodge comments, "[w]ith hindsight, the Europeans were slow to perceive the seriousness of the situation in Yugoslavia even though it had been slowly deteriorating since 1987 and especially throughout 1990" (Lodge, 1993, 3). The EC's tardy, confused and inadequate response to the crisis was vigorously criticized by Crnobrnja: "Instead of 'Waiting for Godot', the EC [should have seized] the opportunity when it presented itself" and should have used the economic and financial tools which were more appropriate to its status (Crnobrnja, 16/6/92, 3).

Nevertheless, as Crnobrnja admits, it would be unfair to attribute the responsibilities for the collapse of Yugoslavia to the European Community or any other outsider, as the burden of blame cannot but rest on the Yugoslavs themselves (Crnobrnja, 16/6/92, 1). Outright condemnation of the Community would be too simplistic as its performance should be seen against the hugely intricate Yugoslav background and the attempt to reconcile the following principles: territorial integrity, self-determination,[66] rights of minorities, non-use of violence and the right to self-defence (Gow and Smith, 1992, 1).

The analysis of the first two years of the crisis revealed that, after a promising start, little progress was achieved on the EC front in terms of foreign policy coordination. The European response to the deteriorating situation in Yugoslavia was reluctant and incoherent, consisting of nothing more than "an aveuglement doublé de *wishful thinkings* sans lendemain" (Rémacle, 1992, 31).[67] The early ambiguity in EC policy with regard to the recognition issue dissolved to be replaced by the widespread confusion and contrasting views among the member states over the issue of military intervention. The problem was not only whether or not to intervene, but rather when, how and which military and defence organizations should be involved and which one should take the lead in coordinating their activities.

The EC "with the blessing of the Conference on Security and Cooperation in Europe (..) and the United Nations Organization (..) had brokered numerous ceasefire agreements, instituted sanctioning measures against the 'aggressors' and staged a series of conferences on the issue" (Nel, 1992). Nonetheless, as violence escalated, the chances for the Community to contribute to a peaceful solution became increasingly poorer. All its attempts to deter the use of force through the adoption of economic sanctions against Serbia and the exclusion of Montenegro and Serbia from the participation in Community aid programmes did not produce the desired effects.

On a positive note, with hindsight it can be said that the Yugoslav war had at least been contained within a relatively small area. The rest of the Balkans had not been consumed by conflict and the spillover into Macedonia had at least been successfully prevented.

---

66 The principle of self-determination, which was conceived by President Wilson in the aftermath of the First World War, was enshrined in the Helsinki CSCE Final Act of 1975, the Charter of Paris for a New Europe of 1990 and the Helsinki CSCE Document of 1992.

67 "Blindness coupled with wishful thinking without a sense of tomorrow" (author's translation).

163

3. The European Parliament and the Yugoslav Crisis

The following overview of the European Parliament's role in the Yugoslav crisis uses the recognition of Slovenia and Croatia on 15 January 1992 as a dividing line. Therefore, the first stage covers from early January 1991 until 14 January 1992 and the second stage, from 15 January 1992 until late July 1992.

a) Pre-Recognition Stage

As early as February 1990 and subsequently in October 1990, long before the outbreak of war in the territory of the SFRY, the European Parliament expressed concern at the discriminatory policy undertaken by the Serbian authorities against the Albanian population in Kosovo (*OJEC* C 68/1990, 138 and *OJEC* C 284/1990, 129). In November 1990, the French MEP Yvan Blot, on behalf of the Technical Group of European Right, also endeavoured to draw the attention of the House to the growing peril of a civil confrontation, highlighting the forceful intimidating actions carried out by the Serbian Communist government (B3-1862/90).

In the following month, other MEPs such as Paraskevas Avgerinos (Socialist, Greece), Nereo Laroni (Socialist, Italy) and Doris Pack (EPP, Germany) spoke of their fears for the direct consequences and possible repercussions of the crisis in the Balkans, the Mediterranean region and ultimately in the European continent, urging the EP Foreign Affairs Committee to draft a report on the existing situation in Yugoslavia (B3-1941/90).

In January 1991, Parliament pointed out that the Yugoslav Federation was "in the midst of its most serious crisis since the Second World War. The country, which [was] bogged down in ethnic and political rivalries [was] plagued at the same time by economic and social difficulties. The Yugoslav model [was] under threat. The process of disintegration [was] moving ever faster and little by little the federation seem[ed] to be moving towards a confederation, so irreconcilable [were] the positions of the six republics" (PE 146.209). Against this background, in February 1991 the European Parliament sent to Belgrade and Kosovo its Delegation for Relations with Yugoslavia in order to evaluate the country's political and economic developments.[68] In Belgrade the MEPs received a briefing by EC

---

68 The delegation, chaired by Paraskevas Avgerinos (Socialist, Greece), consisted

164

ambassadors who expressed their fears about the peril of a disintegration of the Federation into two or three separate units: Slovenia, Croatia and the remainder of the country. The Delegation also held the tenth interparliamentary meeting with the Yugoslav Federal Assembly,[69] talked with representatives from the Serbian, Croatian, Slovenian and Montenegrin Assemblies,[70] contacted Serbian intellectuals and exchanged views with Federal Prime Minister Marković. In Kosovo the MEPs engaged in talks with representatives of political parties, independent trade unions and other organizations such as the Committee for the Protection of Human Rights, the Kosovo Academy of Sciences and Arts and finally met the Serbian Governor of Kosovo Moncilo Trajković. The visit gave the MEPs "the opportunity to hear at first hand the views of all the most important political forces at work in Yugoslavia". As their report sharply highlighted, "the country [was] indeed in turmoil" and there was the danger of the eruption of violence and of civil war (EP Report 10-15/2/1991).

Clearly, "politics as such [appeared to be] subordinated to ..ethnic loyalties" and members of all Assemblies seemed convinced that "the group to which they belonged was in the right and was suffering from discrimination within Yugoslavia and misunderstanding outside". The Federal government, in particular, expressed its desperate need for EC assistance to pursue its objective "to Europeanize Yugoslavia rather than Balkanize Europe" (EP Report 10-15/2/1991). The report concluded that Parliament should not obstruct the signing of the third financial protocol offering aid to support Yugoslav economic development and should consider the possibility of establishing in future an EEC-Yugoslavia association agreement, similar to those agreed with certain Central and Eastern European countries such as Czechoslovakia, Poland and Hungary.

---

of Pavlos Sarlis (Christian Democrat, Greece), Doris Pack (EPP, Germany), Nereo Laroni (Socialist, Italy), Brian Simpson (Socialist, UK), Christopher Beazely (ED, UK) as well as Cesare De Piccoli and Giorgio Rossetti (EUL, Italy). Beazeley, Laroni and Rossetti were only present on the first two days of the mission.

69 This four-hour long exchange was the first between the two parliaments since 1989.

70 The Yugoslav delegation, chaired by a Serbian MP Simović, consisted of members from both chambers of the Federal Assembly and included a Croatian member from the Croatian Democratic Union, a representative from Bosnia-Herzegovina who was a member of the Party for Islamic Democratic Action and an Albanian member of the Federal Chamber from Kosovo.

In conducting relations with the Federation and its constituent republics, the Community should continue to pressure for guarantees on human rights (EP Report 10-15/2/1991).

In its Resolution of 21 February 1991, the European Parliament urged in vain the Serbian government to halt its repressive policy aimed at destroying Albanian identity and culture in Kosovo. Moreover, it insisted against the opinion of its Delegation that the guarantee for human and minority rights was an absolute precondition for negotiating financial aid with the Federation (*OJEC* C 72/1991, 131).

In the following month, the EP Delegation made a two-day visit to Yugoslavia to consult the then recently elected members of the Serbian, Slovenian, Croatian and Montenegrin Legislative Assemblies and representatives of the Federal government. During these consultations, the Europarliamentarians stressed several issues: the need to promote a series of institutional reforms both within the individual republics and at federal level in order to carry forward the passage from a socialist to a pluralist and market economy; the preference of maintaining the territorial unity of Yugoslavia, which had represented, at least to the Western establishment, a workable model of peace and security in the Balkans and in Europe; the acceptance of the existing borders of Europe, in accordance with the principles enunciated at the Helsinki Conference; the protection of human and minority rights by all governments; the opening of a more intense and systematic dialogue between the republics and the Federal government and the need for the emergence of new political groups, thus promoting the process of transformation of the country from a single- to a multiparty system, from a society based on expediency to a society based on the rule of law, from the veneration of the state to the elevation of individual identity (Sarlis, 14/3/91, 215-216).

Most of these principles were eventually set out in a Joint Resolution which was signed by all EP political groups, with the exception of the European Right and the Rainbow Groups, and adopted by the House on 15 March 1991. The vast majority of Members in the European Parliament expressed their unwillingness to approve the Commission's decision to continue the negotiations for the third financial protocol unless the Yugoslav government confirmed its commitment to respect the pluralism of cultural identities and introduced the necessary reforms for an economic transition to a social market economy (Pack 221-222; von Alemann, 222, 14/3/91). Parliament blocked an aid plan for the equivalent amount of one billion US dollars, warning effectively that negotiations on the third financial protocol of the EEC-Yugoslavia cooperation agreement should be postponed until the settlement of the crisis and the achievement of some progress over the implementation of the economic reforms planned by Prime Minister Marković.

By this time, the House was fully aware of the serious institutional, political and economic crisis which was "shaking the foundations of the .. Federation with the risk of rendering it ungovernable and bringing about its dissolution" (*OJEC* C 106/1991, 168). The EP's view appeared slightly ahead of that of EC governments in recognizing the likely demise of the Yugoslav Federation and accepting the right of the republics and autonomous provinces to decide over their political future in a peaceful and democratic way "and on the basis of recognized external and internal borders" (*OJEC* C 106/1991, 169).

In May 1991, following the constitutional crisis caused by Serbia's veto over the nomination of the Federal President, the European Parliament warned "the Yugoslav Government that a seizure of power by or with assistance from the army would bring about the immediate end of all assistance or preferential treatment accorded by the Community". While reiterating the EC "preference" for maintaining a single, federal Yugoslavia, as wished for by Serbia and Montenegro, the EP acknowledged the right to self-determination of the constituent republics and autonomous provinces of Yugoslavia. As such, Parliament emphasized that "full respect for multi-party democracy and regard for the freely expressed will of all peoples [was], to the European Community, a fundamental principle that [could] not be sacrificed to any opportunistic consideration" (*OJEC* C 158/91, 242-243). Words of appreciation and encouragement were addressed to the Federal Presidency for its efforts to find a peaceful solution to the country's difficulties. Parliament stressed that "the European Community, the United Nations and the CSCE should be prepared to assist in any way in maintaining the peace within Yugoslavia if so requested by the legitimate Federal authorities" (*OJEC* C 158/1991, 242-243). The House voiced its deepening concern about the growing tensions in Yugoslavia, calling for the intervention of the CSCE.

The Joint Resolution, drafted by all political groups with the exception of the European Right and the Left Unity, placed respectively on the extreme right and extreme left wings of the European Parliament, notably warned the parties that their recourse to military means would bring about an immediate cessation of all Community's aid or preferential treatment (*OJEC* C 158/1991). Criticism was focused on the delays of the EP

167

delegation in charge of following the Yugoslav crisis to gather promptly. This was regarded as "an example of the laziness, the slowness and the complicity of [the European Parliament] or at least of some political bodies within it" (Aglietta, 12/5/1992, 71-72).

In June 1991, ambassador Crnobrnja spoke before the House about the grave economic situation of his country, stressing the importance of the implementation of the third financial protocol of the EEC-SFRY cooperation agreement, the PHARE programme and transport negotiations (Crnobrnja, 20/6/1991). The European Parliament criticized the inability of the EC member states to act jointly on foreign issues as well as the tendency to align themselves with external powers, rather than work autonomously (Buffotot, 1994, 208-209). This problem was addressed in the Resolution on the prospects for a European Security Policy of 10 June 1991, based on a Report drafted by the German Christian Democrat MEP Poettering, on behalf of the Defence Subcommittee of the Political Affairs Committee (A3-107/91).

On 27 June 1991, following the news of the clashes between the JNA and the Slovenes, the EP Political Affairs Committee issued a statement whereby it called for an immediate cessation of the fighting, requesting a CSCE meeting and urging the Community to act as a mediator between the parties in order to find a peaceful solution (EPP Report, 7/1990-7/1991, 30).

A few days later, the House fiercely condemned the violence perpetrated by the JNA in Slovenia and called on the Yugoslav authorities to secure an immediate withdrawal of the troops. It "recognize[d] the democratic legitimacy of the Presidents, Parliaments and Governments of Slovenia and Croatia, elected in free, peaceful and democratic elections in April 1990". It also welcomed the decision by the Slovenian and Croatian governments to suspend the implementation of their declarations of the independence with the objective of seeking a suitable political and institutional solution which would take into consideration human rights, minority rights as well as the respect for internal and international borders (*OJEC* C 240/1991, 137-138).

Although no urgent meeting was convened at plenary level during the summer recess, the activities of the Parliament did not cease altogether. Oostlander, in his capacity of rapporteur for the EP Political Affairs Committee made a visit to Yugoslavia in July 1991 (EPP Report, 7/1990-7/1991, 30). Two extraordinary meetings of the Political Affairs Committee took place in August, chaired by the Italian MEP Maria Luisa

Cassanmagnago Cerretti. These resulted in declarations condemning the Serbian military attacks perpetrated under the federal flag and blaming Milošević for his obstinacy and unwillingness to cooperate to find a peaceful solution (Déclaration, 12/8/1991; Avgerinos, 10/9/1991, 84). The Community was also invited to seek a negotiated solution, whilst the Committee declared its readiness to consult directly with parties (Commission politique du PE, 12/8/1991). At the end of the meeting held on 30 August, it was decided that the EP President would invite the Yugoslav Federal Parliament and the Parliaments of the republics to Strasbourg in order to open a dialogue and to seek possible solutions to the crisis (EP Document C/JN/46/91). All the parties, with the exception of Montenegro, replied to the EP invitation and discussions took place on 12 and 13 September. They also signed a joint statement whereby they expressed their hope that the EC peace conference could lead to an agreement, based on the principles of self-determination, rights of minorities and democracy (Info Memo 141, 13/9/1991).

At the September session, the House restated its condemnation of the ferocious actions of the Federal Army and the paramilitary elements fighting in Croatia. It also called for the participation of a democratically elected representation from Kosovo and Vojvodina Parliaments in the peace conference. Moreover, EP forwarded the proposal to set up "a regional and possibly institutional grouping on a strictly voluntary basis". Solidarity was expressed for the protests of soldiers' mothers and hopes were articulated for a more direct involvement of political parties, churches and social organizations to foster the peace process (*OJEC* C 267/1991).

From 25 September 1991, a few MEPs participated in the 'European peace caravan', sponsored by the Helsinki Citizens' Assembly and organized by the Peace Association along with the Italian branch of the Cultural association ARCI.[71] The caravan consisted of two convoys which left from Trieste and from Skopje respectively and crossed most of the territory of Yugoslavia to finally converge in Sarajevo. The journey came to a close with a final demonstration, speeches, songs in many languages and "a long human chain (..) linking the Catholic cathedral, the Orthodox cathedral, the mosque and the synagogue". This experience convinced

---

71 The Members of the European Parliament who participated in the initiative were Castellina, De Piccoli and Rossetti (EUL, Italy), Cramon Daiber (Greens, Germany), Langer and Melandri (Greens, Italy) along with Formigoni (EPP, Italy). van den Brink (Socialist, Netherlands) was also supposed to take part.

Alexander Langer that the European Community should encourage similar initiatives "which play an important role in spheres where governments cannot intervene so easily" (*Langer Report*, PE 153.297, 10/1991).

On 9 October, Mesić denounced before the European Parliament the brutal war raging in his country and the impotence of the Federal government and Parliament. Whilst denying that the conflict had erupted as the inevitable consequence of ethnic clashes, he accused the JNA of carrying out a military *coup* with the purpose of preserving its privileges and blamed the Serbian leader, Slobodan Milošević, of pursuing an expansionistic policy aimed at creating a Greater Serbia. Mesić finally appealed for the taking of clear and definitive measures in order to halt the carnage, to be achieved by first distinguishing the victims from the aggressor (*The Week*, PE 155.623, 29). The House admitted that the Yugoslav break-up had become irreversible, and that the Community should acknowledge the questions of independence of Croatia and Slovenia. However, Parliament pointed out that the Community should undertake relationships with the breakaway republics only if they provided sufficient guarantees for human and minority rights (*OJEC* C 280/1991, 127). The EP condemned the JNA's role in the Serb-Croatian conflict, rejecting its claims of fighting to maintain the unity of the country and safeguard Serbian minorities (De Piccoli, 9/10/1991, 167). Finally, it expressed its reservations at the sending of an armed force to the area, believing that "only a peace-keeping force should be deployed, and then only with the agreement of all parties involved and once a ceasefire ha[d] been firmly agreed" (*OJEC* C 280/1991, 127). On 25 October, the EP President urged the Serbian authorities to cease bombing the Croatian town of Dubrovnik, reiterating that it had become evident that the JNA was no longer representative of the Yugoslav Federation, but had fallen in the hands of Serbian command (Info Memo 173, 25/10/1991).

The EP recognized the right of the Yugoslav people to self-determination, whilst pointing out that this principle had to be implemented along with full respect of human and minorities rights, not excluding the possibility of a subsequent change in internal borders, provided it was done peacefully and with the agreement of the parties concerned. As to the steps to be taken, Parliament supported, under the assent procedure, the Council's decision to freeze the cooperation agreement between the EEC and Yugoslavia because of the latter's continued use of force. It also implemented restrictive measures against Yugoslavia, with the exception of those republics which responded positively to the EC's peace efforts. Concerned about the negative repercussions on the economy of some regions in Greece and North-Eastern Italy arising from the enforcement of embargo against Yugoslavia, Parliament supported the decision to grant them assistance (*The Week*, 18-22/11/1991, 28; *OJEC* C 280/1991, 127). The EP supported the combined deployment of United Nations and European Community peacekeeping troops in Yugoslavia, on condition that the ceasefire would last.

On 20 December 1991, the Enlarged Bureau of the EP convened especially to discuss the decision taken four days earlier to establish a timetable for the official recognition of Slovenia and Croatia with the EC President, the Dutch Foreign Minister Hans van den Broek, as well as Commissioners Matutes and Andriessen. This led to the setting up of a crisis unit, consisting of the EP President, the Chairman of the Political Affairs Committee and the Head of the EC-Yugoslavia Delegation. The EP Political Affairs Committee called for an emergency meeting of the CSCE Foreign Ministers and asked the Community to exert its 'good offices' to assist the Yugoslav republics to find a peaceful solution.

Seen through the eyes of the German Socialist MEP Jannis Sakellariou, within the EP only a very small minority was truly aware of the tragedy unfolding in Yugoslavia, while the majority, approximately 80 percent of the MEPs, had only a vague knowledge of the drama, receiving information only from media coverage. Finally, there was a faction which, nourished by anti-Serb propaganda, tended to demonize Milošević's government (Sakellariou interview, 1996).

The above overview of the EP's stance during the months preceding the recognition shows that there was a clear desire within the House to look for a peaceful solution to the Yugoslav crisis. Faced with an increasingly grave situation, the EP felt obliged "to shoulder anew its responsibilities towards the peoples who [were] the victims of a bloody war which (..) caused so much loss and destruction" (De Piccoli, 9/10/91, 167). The events unfolding in Yugoslavia were discussed at length both at Committee and plenary level. The perception shared by many Europarliamentarians of an imminent tragedy looming over the Balkans was, nevertheless, overlooked by the Community, which failed to recognize the signals of alarm. Moreover, the House did not limit itself to issuing general declamatory statements on Yugoslavia, but it strove to take an active part in the handling of the crisis. At first, it supported the economic and constitutional reforms in the SFRY aimed at preserving the unity of the country, but it

171

realized soon that the will of the Yugoslav people, their desire for independence could not be ignored. It therefore opened a dialogue with the parties by sending delegations and participating in several meetings and arranging a joint interparliamentary session in Strasbourg attended by both the Yugoslav Federal Parliament and the Assemblies of the republics. The European Parliament backed diplomatic channels, the provision of humanitarian aid for refugees and the deployment of peacekeeping forces if agreed by the parties involved. Despite these efforts, the EP was unable to 'get down to the business' of forging a European foreign policy towards the crisis.

b) Post-Recognition Stage
Although the first parliamentary session of 1992 was dominated by the election of a new President and did not consecrate any space for a debate, the EP passed a Joint Resolution which acknowledged the *fait accompli* of the recognition of Slovenia and Croatia, insisting that the rights of all ethnic groups should be respected and the international commitments previously made by the Yugoslav Federation should be maintained by the newly-born independent states. In addition, the Resolution backed the recognition of other republics complying with the EC guidelines and urged the convening of a referendum in Bosnia-Herzegovina. The EP called again for the cessation of fighting and endorsed the deployment of European forces to join the UN peacekeeping contingent in the unfortunate event of the hostilities continuing (*OJEC* C 39/1992, 130).

During the Question Time on European Political Cooperation held on 15 January, the Portuguese Socialist MEP Maria Belo asked the EC President João de Deus Pinheiro to provide Parliament with an insight concerning the *rationale* and criteria followed by the Council over the decision to recognize Slovenia and Croatia, whilst denying such a status to other republics. For this purpose, she requested that the contents of the Badinter Report be communicated to the Parliament, obtaining the reply that "this was not a decision taken by the Council. It was a decision taken at national level on which the twelve Member States [had] agreed". As to Belo's second request for the European Parliament to be informed about the contents of the Badinter Report, Deus Pinheiro answered that "unless the Foreign Ministers agree to divulge the contents of that report, the presidency should not do so of its own accord". This once again evidenced the deficiencies of the mechanisms of European Political Cooperation, in this case at the expense of the European Parliament which was denied the right to obtain important information other than through newspaper leaks (Belo; Deus Pinheiro, 15/1/1992, 70).

Between 28 February and 3 March 1992, an *ad hoc* parliamentary delegation led by Avgerinos was sent to Bosnia-Herzegovina with the task of monitoring the referendum on independence. The Members of the European Parliament met political leaders, representatives of the Bosnian government and the President and Vice-President of the Chamber of Communes and Citizens which constituted the Bosnian parliamentary assembly. During a subsequent visit to Belgrade, the delegation had the opportunity to consult the Greek and French ambassadors as well as the Commission representative. The referendum was held under acceptable conditions, despite some minor technical irregularities and amidst a climate of growing tension which escalated into the killing of a Serb in the Muslim quarter. Members of the delegation tried to use all their political contacts in order to arrest clashes and, in particular, the Dutch MEP Arie Oostlander undertook a visit to the barricades to negotiate freedom of passage for the observers and civilians who wanted to leave Sarajevo. Eventually, the delegation returned safely to Brussels, albeit after twenty-four hours' delay to their schedule, together with approximately one hundred people (*Avgerinos Report*, March 1992).

On 9 April 1992, the European Parliament passed by RCV, as requested by the EPP, a Motion for a Resolution tabled by the Christian Democrats themselves. The text endorsed "the recognition of Bosnia-Herzegovina by the European Community and its Members States". It also "called EPC, Council and Commission to do their utmost to:

-have the existing border recognized (..) and guarantee the integrity of Bosnia-Herzegovina
-extend the mandate of the UN forces, so that they [could] also be deployed to avert war in Bosnia-Herzegovina
-safeguard the republics' political cohesion
-safeguard the rights of minorities in the republic" (*OJEC* C125/1992, 220).

In its Joint Resolution of 14 May 1992, the EP expressively referred to reports by human rights organizations including Amnesty International and Helsinki Watch on civilians held in concentration camps in Serbia, Vojvodina and Croatia. Parliament stipulated that it would consider the Yugoslav Republic of Serbia and Montenegro as a new state, only if it

173

complied with the same general guidelines previously applied to the other republics on recognition, concerning the protection of minorities, the "disavowal of territorial claims against other republics" and the full restoration of the autonomy of Kosovo and Vojvodina (*OJEC* C 150/1992, 234-235).

In June, Parliament adopted a Resolution based on a Report on Relations between the Community and the Republics of the former Yugoslavia, tabled by the Dutch Christian Democrat MEP Arie Oostlander on behalf of the Committee on Foreign Affairs and Security. This represented the most comprehensive parliamentary document regarding Yugoslavia. Unlike the resolutions drafted by the political groups, the above text provided more detailed and complete insight into the historical background and included a more accurate political analysis (Silvestro interview, 1996). It dealt specifically with a host of issues such as the question of recognition of the republics, the rights of minorities, human rights, borders within Yugoslav territory, the armed forces, observers and peacekeeping troops, regulation of relations between parties in the fields of the economy, internal trade, transport, the environment, the legal system and foreign policy.

At the following session, Parliament called "for initiatives to establish and maintain safe zones and humanitarian corridors as soon as possible, thus (..) preventing further displacements and (..) establishing favourable conditions for the return of the temporary refugees to the Republic of Bosnia-Herzegovina and the Republic of Croatia" (*OJEC* C 241/1992, 145). The House condemned the summary executions of Croatian citizens in Belgrade and the outrages perpetrated by the JNA regarded as a clear breach of international law and urged the Community to warn the Serbian authorities that stricter sanctions would be imposed unless this practice of illegal trials and death sentences was put to an end (*OJEC* C 241/1992, 147).

Within the parliamentary forum a welter of disparate opinions which extolled the virtues of political, humanitarian and military options emerged, often transformed into nothing more than a sense of impotence. Nevertheless, the EP inability to exert its political clout over the Council in relation to policy-making on Yugoslavia can be ascribed to the lack of necessary political and institutional instruments (Imbeni interview, 7/2/1996). Until the Parliament acquires such means, as the Italian Communist MEP Luigi Colajanni emphasized, it will remain "a voice in the desert". In the case of former Yugoslavia, the European Parliament could

174

not determine any political orientation, but only raise its protests louder (Colajanni interview, 31/1/1996).

The European Parliament undertook consultations with EC institutions, member states' national governments and national parliaments. Exchanges of information also took place with the United Nations, the Congress and government of the United States, WEU, NATO and embassies at parliamentary and occasionally at PG levels (Alavanos, Rocard, Bergamaschi, D'Alimonte written interviews, 7-9/1995). Non-governmental organizations, voluntary groups and the Bosnian government itself lobbied the European Parliament, raising the question of the value of this instrument as an expression of democracy. The phenomenon was regarded by the leader of the Left Unity Réné-Emile Piquet as unacceptable and unbearable: "Le lobbying est dans tous les bureaux, tous les couloirs, toutes les réunions. L'interlocuteur s'installe sans même donner la possibilité aux deputés de juger l'opportunité de la rencontre" (Piquet interview, 31/1/1996).[72] It is not feasible for the House to function on the basis of external pressures, especially when the source remains unknown. Lobbying certainly raises problems about the quality of democracy and the fulfilment of MEPs' obligations towards their institution, the political party to which they belong as well as to their electorate. More appropriately, Piquet felt that the EP could develop exchanges with other international organizations and countries in order to obtain information. It could appoint interparliamentary delegations with the task of listening to its interlocutors in addition to just conveying the official EP opinion.

Conclusion

The inability of the international community to promote a peaceful solution to the Yugoslav crisis during 1991-1992 dented the euphoria following the fall of the Iron Curtain, diminishing and denigrating "the spirit of integration and cooperation which prevailed in international institutions" in search of a new identity in the post-Cold War era (Gow, 1992, 1).

---

72 "Lobbying is carried out in all offices, all corridors, all meetings. The interlocutors place themselves [in the European Parliament] without even giving MEPs the possibility of deciding for themselves whether or not they were willing to meet" (author's translation).

The European preventive and reactive strategies for dealing with the civil wars raging in former Yugoslavia did not flatter the Twelve. In Nuttall's words, "It is a truth universally acknowledged that the [Community] (..) did not pass the Yugoslav test with flying colours"; indeed it shamefully failed in all the attempts undertaken with the instruments at its disposal in the SEA framework (Nuttall, 1994, 13). Notwithstanding the clear opposition expressed by the Slovenian and Croatian governments, opposition parties, and people, the Council was persistent in its anachronistic position of support for a federal state, which was interpreted as an indirect way of taking the Serbian side. However, this position was later reassessed in the light of Milošević's intransigence and refusal to reach any political compromise with the other republics, and of the brutality of the actions perpetrated by the Serbs under the flag of the JNA.

The Twelve were not united over the policy of recognition - with Germany pushing for it to come into effect immediately - nor over "the wisdom of intervening without strong military support - whether for humanitarian relief purposes or as a threat to impel a ceasefire and the end of all hostilities" (Lodge, 1993, 3). Such divergences risked jeopardizing the equilibrium of the Community and the relations between its member states on the eve of the Maastricht summit (Alendar, 1992, 20).

Institutional inadequacies within the existing EPC framework prevented the member states from coordinating with one another and promptly defining a common strategy, whilst the absence of a European security framework precluded the realization of such a strategy. In the circumstances, the Community did just about as well as it could have been expected, appearing once again as an economic giant and a political dwarf. This can explain the dominantly economic, as opposed to political, approach with respect to the crisis. However, it must be also borne in mind that economic instruments were used for political purposes and as a way of implementing EPC policies.

As in the Gulf case, the Yugoslav crisis triggered a debate on the prospect for the Community ever to become an international actor. Some maintained that the crisis represented "an indictment of the whole concept of European unity, a powerful refutation of the arguments for a single foreign policy with majority voting, let alone a United States of Europe". Others argued that the experience served as a lever for bolstering the demands for a common foreign and security policy for the United States of Europe (Owen, 1995, 3; Lodge 1993, 2).

176

As to the EP's response to the events unfolding in Yugoslavia, the House turned its attention to the unrest of the Albanian population in the Serbian province of Kosovo, even before other EC institutions and member states did so. Yet, parliament's warning call remained unheard and it was unable to persuade the Community to address promptly and efficiently the Yugoslav emergency.

MEPs from all political orientations and nationalities agreed that the EC member states' diplomacies had failed vis-à-vis Yugoslavia, while acknowledging that the Community had no effective powers to engage in the management of the crisis (Rocard, 22/7/1995). Throughout the 1991-1992 period, the European Parliament adopted political resolutions in which its Members hid behind the screen of rhetorical expressions where it condemned, reproved, reaffirmed, urged, called upon, demanded and supported actions and policies of the parties concerned. Already in November 1990, and subsequently from March 1991 up to July 1992, Parliament concerned itself at nearly every sitting with the developments of the situation in Yugoslavia, not least in view of the latter's geographical proximity to the Community and its strategic importance for the security of the whole continent. Following the often inconclusive missions and visits carried out by delegations or individual MEPs in Yugoslavia, public declamation appeared to be the only instrument at the disposal of Parliament: an open admission that it was powerless to determine or influence a concrete outcome. And yet, its role was useful in terms of publicising issues and mobilizing public opinion.

The European Parliament, although initially not favourable to the fragmentation of the SFRY, took a more flexible stance over the constitutional future of the Yugoslav Republics. While expressing its "preference" for one Yugoslavia, Parliament stressed that this could not be used as a pretext for military intervention. In addition, it recommended the creation of a regional organization based on the EC's model, albeit on a voluntary basis, explicitly recognizing the right of self-determination of each of the six republics and the two autonomous provinces of Kosovo and Vojvodina.

Visitors from Slovenia, Croatia and Kosovo were invited to address the House whereby they requested EC and EP missions to investigate the situation and called for the Community and its members states to intervene. The European Parliament consistently supported all peaceful initiatives, political negotiations and humanitarian actions whilst rejecting the resort to violence. Although it initially sought to maintain an impartial stance among the parties, as the conflict escalated, Parliament acknowledged, ahead of the EC Foreign Ministers, that the Serbs were the principal aggressors, cautiously showing a sympathetic attitude towards the breakaway republics. In summary, it has to be acknowledged that the EC and EP's failure to address the crisis was also due to the fact that "[t]he goals set were too high and the situation in Yugoslavia too complex" (Crnobrnja, 16/6/1992, 1).

Time will assist political analysts in lifting the veil of mist which still surrounds the Yugoslav crisis and lead to a better understanding of the EC's reaction. Yet, it cannot be denied that the commitment made fifty years ago by the then Six, in a surge of idealism, to create a new way of life and to prevent, by all means, the conflagration of another conflict on the European continent has not been fulfilled, just as the idea that Europe would never again experience the physical devastation and moral ravages of war has turned out to be a myth.

V The Role of the Political Groups in Forging the European Parliament's Stance on the Yugoslav Crisis

This chapter aims firstly to identify the attitudes of the EP political groups towards the Yugoslav crisis during its pre- and post-recognition stages. Secondly, it attempts to evaluate the respective levels of transnationality of the individual groups as well as the voting similarities and cooperation between the PGs in relation to the crisis. This aspect is particularly important considering that no majority group exists in the Europarliamentary spectrum.

Table 6a   List of EP Roll-Call Votes on the Yugoslav Crisis
Pre-Recognition Stage

Stage	Date	Resolution	Recital / Paragraph	OJ	Page
Pre-Rec	15-Mar-91	Joint Resolution, B3-395, 397, def, 399, 403, 431, 482	Paragraph 2	C106	165
	15-Mar-91		Paragraph 8		165
	16-May-91	Joint Resolution, B3-745, 779, 786, 794, 806, 807, 822, 826		C158	281
	11-Sep-91	Joint Resolution, B3-1325, 1360, 1371, 1372, 1374, 1375, 1383, 1390, 1407	Amendment 1	C267	115
			Paragraph 19, Part 2		116
			Whole		116-117
	10-Oct-91	Joint Resolution, B3-1587, 1608, 1614, 1615, 1623	Paragraph 6	C280	157-158
			Amendment 3		157
	22-Nov-91	Joint Resolution, B3-1882, 1886, 1888, 1890, 1894, 1895, 1896	Whole	C326	293

Table 6b   List of EP Roll-Call Votes on the Yugoslav Crisis Post-Recognition Stage

Stage	Date	Resolution	Recital / Paragraph	OJ	Page
Post-Rec	12-Mar-92	Joint Resolution, B3-405, 406, 407, 408, 409, 410, 411 & 413	Paragraph 11	C94	316-317
			Paragraph 12		317
			Paragraph 13		317-318
			Paragraph 23, Part 2		318
	09-Apr-92	Resolution B3-0532	Whole	C125	251-252
	11-Jun-92	Joint Resolution, Oostlander Report A3-0208	Paragraph 7	C176	209
			Amendment 8		209-210
			Amendment 17		210-211
			Paragraph 33		210
			Whole		211
	09-Jul-92	Joint Resolution, B3-0973 & 1049	Whole	C241	190-191

1. The Political Groups' Positions vis-à-vis the Yugoslav Crisis

1.1 The Socialist Group

a) Pre-Recognition Stage

As early as February 1991, the Socialists within the European Parliament addressed their attention to the events unfolding in the Socialist Federal Republic of Yugoslavia, particularly in the Serbian province of Kosovo. They urged the Yugoslav government to stop its discriminatory policies and flagrant violations of human rights perpetrated against the Albanian population, if it intended to continue and develop further its relations with the Community (Desmond, 21/2/1991, 271).

In the following month, the Socialists expressed concern at the constitutional crisis faced by the SFRY by stressing that the Yugoslav people should be left free to find their own solution. Only in this way could peace in the Balkans and security in Europe be achieved. However, they expressed consternation at the idea that in order to promote democracy "every manifestation of nationalist identity and every separatist movement" should be recognized and supported (Avgerinos, 14/3/1991, 218-219).

Although the reaction of the Yugoslav people was understandable, considering their troubled history and long years of repression, the Greek MEP Paraskevas Avgerinos argued that "high-flown expectations [would] not solve their problems".[73] The focus should be, instead, on the reorganization of their society with the objective of building a solid system of parliamentary democracy. This meant, first of all, restoring economic order, depoliticizing public administration, establishing a new institutional framework as well as promoting respect for human and minority rights and only then calling for free and democratic federal elections. The whole state apparatus had to be dismantled and replaced by a completely new constitutional, political and economic structure with the consensus of all the Yugoslav republics.

---

73 The Greek MEPs showed great concern at the events unfolding in former Yugoslavia, by participating assiduously at the debates and often by taking the floor. This high level of participation in conjunction with an extraordinary level of absenteeism amongst the members of the other nationalities resulted in a Greek dominance at the EP debates, which is reflected in the larger space devoted to them in this chapter.

The Socialists fiercely believed that the survival of the SFRY depended on the establishment of democracy and the fortification of its key institutions. For this purpose, the European Community had to support, both politically and financially, the reform proposed by the Prime Minister Ante Marković (Avgerinos, 14/3/1991, 218-219). As the Italian MEP Nereo Laroni emphasized, "after the glorious season when the walls [between Western and Eastern Europe] came down, another seem[ed] to be looming, insidious and widespread: a season in which every difference becomes a pretext for clashes, conflict and imbalance" (Laroni, 14/3/1991, 221). He also contended that Europe had remained deaf to the foreboding signals and persistent requests for assistance launched by the Yugoslav leaders and failed to deter the resort to arms by persuading the parties to solve their disputes diplomatically and peacefully. Furthermore, the Community should open the door to a united Yugoslavia and discourage separatist trends which would leave the problems of minorities unresolved (Laroni, 14/3/1991, 221). Also, it should endorse a negotiated solution, halt arms export to the area and support the suspension of economic relationships with Yugoslavia until the parties had opened a dialogue over possible formulas of government (Woltjer, 9/7/1991, 68-69). This view was not shared by the French Socialist MEP and former Foreign Minister, Claude Cheysson, who stressed that it was not through economic sanctions, but via economic benefits that the Yugoslav people would establish a common future and identify peaceful answers to the right of self-determination (Cheysson, 9/7/1991. 82-83). The Labour MEP Stan Newens also pointed out that, although this right could not be denied to the Yugoslav people, "at a time when economic integration [was] in the logic of history, small independent republics [were] not viable and could lead to instability and war" (Newens, 9/7/1991, 84).

On 28 June 1991, the Socialists condemned the violence perpetrated by the JNA in Slovenia. In Jean-Pierre Cot's words, "however provocative the unilateral declaration of independence of Slovenia and Croatia might be, nothing could justify the use of military force. (..). It is not sufficient for the federal government to call for a cessation to hostilities as if it were an innocent bystander: it should command the army to withdraw its forces from the streets". Any attempts to mediate in order to solve the crisis were to be undertaken with willingness to listen and take into consideration the needs and wishes of all parties without any "preconceived idea of what is the most desirable outcome from a West European perspective" and without seeking to use political and economic muscle to impose a solution which is unacceptable to the peoples of Yugoslavia" (Cot's statement, 28/6/1991).

In September 1991, the Socialists admitted that neither the Community nor the European Parliament had succeeded in achieving a common standpoint on the measures to be taken in Yugoslavia. While the Community was trying to convince the parties involved in the crisis to agree to sit together at the negotiating table, some among the member states such as Germany were taking opposite steps, threatening to recognize "the fragments of Yugoslavia". The view was reiterated that "[u]nilateral, unforced, *de facto* recognition of one or some republics at this time would lead, at best, to annihilation of the substantial minorities living in that republic, and at worst to conflict not only inside the country but along its external frontiers as well" (Avgerinos, 10/9/1991, 84). There was a general fear that the process of recognition of the breakaway republics might trigger a chain reaction whereby each group would proclaim itself as an independent nation. However, as the time passed, the group became increasingly divided over the issue of the recognition of Slovenia and Croatia. According to Newens, with hindsight, Germany and Austria should not have pushed for recognition before the republics concerned had provided sufficient guarantees for the safety and welfare of their minorities. He also noted that during the Cold War the West widely supported Tito's régime and the maintenance of the political *status quo*, but with the fall of the Iron Curtain Yugoslavia had lost its strategic geopolitical position. This had diminished the interest of the West to grant sufficient economic aid, precipitating the Yugoslav crisis (Newens interview, 26/3/1997).

In the Socialist eyes, "outsiders clearly had no moral right to dictate the state, inter-state or supra-state structures (..) in Yugoslavia, even though it [was] in our backyard". However, as an official Gareth Williams remarked, "they [the Socialists] would appear to be lagging hopelessly behind events, and incapable of a meaningful policy, if [they failed] to adopt [an] approach (..) which recognize[d] the reality.. that while the Yugoslav crisis [was] not a simple one, it [was] not one in which blame [was] to be equally apportioned to all parties" (Williams, 1991). Conversely, according to Sakellariou, the entire responsibility for the deterioration of the situation could not be attributed to the Serbs, despite their blatant violations of the most basic principles of international law (Sakellariou interview, 31/1/1996).

In October 1991, the group endorsed the Council's policy, stressing that it was "not within the competence of the European Community to send troops to Yugoslavia or anywhere else". Only in exceptional circumstances could the member states be encouraged to intervene in the region as a buffer force, notably if a genuine mandate existed, a ceasefire held and upon consensus of the warring parties (Sakellariou, 9/10/1991, 165-166). Following his meetings with Yugoslav leaders, the Chairman of the EP Delegation Avgerinos claimed that the fervour demonstrated by extreme nationalists augured badly for peace in the country (Avgerinos, 9/10/1991, 168).

In November 1991, the group raised the issue relating to the status of the EEC observers, requesting that Parliament be regularly informed about their activities. The Socialists welcomed the long advocated decision of the Council of Ministers to impose an arms embargo, compensated by granting humanitarian assistance directed to alleviate people's suffering, especially in the republics which had demonstrated their willingness to find a diplomatic solution (Sakellariou, 20/11/1991, 155). During the first stage of the Yugoslav crisis, between January 1991 and January 1992, the approach of most Socialists could be described as prudent and impartial with the parties involved in the conflict. Yet internal tensions arose within the group especially on the key issue of the recognition of Slovenia and Croatia. A majority of German MEPs supported the policy adopted by the *Sozialdemokratische Partei Deutschlands (SPD)* aimed at accelerating the process while other Socialist MEPs maintained a more cautious approach, believing that the fragmentation of Yugoslavia would worsen the problems in the area (Newens interview, 26/3/1997). The view that all German MPs and MEPs had embraced a pro-recognition policy was contested by Jannis Sakellariou. To provide an example, he stated that in Autumn 1991 during a meeting of the Working Group on Foreign Policy of the German *Bundestag* in which he participated as the Spokesman of the Socialist MEPs, one third of the members opposed the immediate recognition of Slovenia and Croatia (Sakellariou interview, 31/1/1996).

Once the independence of the new republics was recognized, the Socialists regained a certain unity over the economic and diplomatic measures to be adopted in order to halt the fighting. Stress was once again put on the actual ruling out of violence and the pledge of fully respecting human and minority rights, in accordance with the principle that peace is an absolute requirement for democracy (van den Brink, 9/10/1991, 173-174). In the light of Gorbachev's formula, envisaging the framing of a union of sovereign states, speedy recognition of the independence of the new

184

republics was advocated as "perhaps .. by being separated, (..) they may be united" (Baget Bozzo, 9/10/1991, 174).

As to the intervention of the army in the area, the Socialists opposed the use of force until the grenade attack in Sarajevo, after which the majority of them started to consider it as a viable option. A small part, instead, among whom was Sakellariou, remained steadfastly against the use of the military option even after this attack (Sakellariou interview, 31/1/1996). Over this stage, despite the divisions emerged during the debates, it is interesting to notice an extremely high index of agreement of 91.56 percent on the RCVs taken over the crisis yet with a fairly high level of absenteeism of 63.21.[74]

b) Post-Recognition Stage
In March 1992, Sakellariou welcomed the outcome of the referendum held on 29 February 1992 in Bosnia-Herzegovina, but stressed that the EC's official recognition of the republic should only occur following a conference concerning the possible implications arising from its independence (Sakellariou, 11/3/1992, 91). For Avgerinos the Community had foolishly rushed to recognize the independence of the breakaway republics prior to settling an appropriate institutional structure to safeguard the rights of minorities. The Yugoslav drama was feared to be only in its first act and that worse was to follow (Avgerinos, 12/5/1992, 73).

As for the case of Macedonia, independence should be endorsed only after a revision of its constitution with respect to "its aggressive provisions" towards Greece (Sakellariou, 11/3/1992, 91). The British Labour MEP Brian Simpson pointed out that the international community had two options, either to ignore the events in Yugoslavia or to continue promoting peace in the area by imposing sanctions, carrying out UN peacekeeping operations and recognizing or derecognizing the new republics (Simpson, 12/5/1992, 75-76).

According to Avgerinos, "the European Parliament [could] not condemn to starvation a people [who were] paying the price of [their] historical contrasts and the irresponsibility of [their] leaders in blood" by sanctions which did not affect the leaders but rather the population. The EP should demand the lifting of the embargo for all republics. As regards Bosnia, external pressures should be averted as it could lead to the sparking

---

74 The average index of agreement is computed on all 9 RCVs of the first stage.

of a civil war. The Community should not interfere but remain close to the republics as a "trustworthy reference-point" and an impartial arbiter (Avgerinos, 11/3/1992, 94). Laroni pointed out that as events were irreversible it was pointless to reproach the Community's policy in Yugoslavia, but lessons should be drawn and further mistakes prevented. The Community should ensure that the Helsinki principles were fully honoured in the independent Republic of Bosnia (Avgerinos, 11/3/1992, 94).

At the May 1992 session, the majority of the group stressed that although all the warring parties involved in the Serb-Bosnian conflict were to be blamed, it had become clear that the Serbian government was pursuing the ambitious design of creating a Greater Serbia, using for this purpose the federal army. Following the failure of the European Community in its negotiating role, the Socialist group was concerned about the further escalation of violence and the destiny of the EEC observers (Woltjer, 12/5/1992, 70).

According to the group, the inability of the European Community to act efficiently in Yugoslavia was due to the absence of authority in the field of foreign policy and security and the shortage of the necessary instruments to carry out peacekeeping operations. Criticism was levelled at the Portuguese Presidency of the Council, as well as at the previous Italian and Luxembourg Presidencies for the way the Community had handled the Yugoslav emergency. Slovenia and Croatia had been recognized only following the threat by the German government that it would proceed alone, with or without the other EC partners. Yet some amongst the Socialists felt that the guidelines for the recognition of the independence of the Yugoslav republics drawn by the Badinter Report were virtually ignored (Sakellariou, 12/5/1992, 77).

The Socialists stressed the necessity for the European Community to act with great caution and undertake initiatives to assist the hundreds of refugees fleeing from the troubled areas (Woltjer, 12/5/1992, 70, Medina Ortega, 12/5/1992, 76). The group supported the *Oostlander Report*,[75] on the ground that changes in the internal frontiers of Yugoslavia were regarded as intolerable and the recourse to violence and the aggressive policy by the Serbian government were strongly attacked. The group tabled

---

75 Two Greek MEPs, Panayotis Roumeliotis and Konstantinos Tsimas, rejected the report whilst the Belgian MEP van Hemeldonck and the German MEP von der Vring abstained from the vote.

some amendments expressing support for UN Resolution 757 calling for a total embargo including oil as a last attempt to halt the massacre prior to taking up arms.

It objected to the amendment introduced by Oostlander on behalf of the EPP group which urged selective WEU air and naval strikes directed against specific targets as any decision to undertake military intervention in former Yugoslavia should be taken neither by the Community nor the WEU nor the CSCE but only the UN Security Council (Woltjer, 9/6/1992, 54).

By contrast, for Avgerinos peace could not be achieved in the region "unless the borders [were] changed and populations [were] exchanged". He then expressed his firm opposition to the military option proposed in the amendment submitted by Oostlander, concluding that "Peace [could not be] made through warfare" (Avgerinos, 9/6/1992, 58). On 7 July 1992, the Socialist group reiterated its view that Croatia should not be included in the PHARE programme because of its still very unclear role in the conflict in Bosnia-Herzegovina (Woltjer, 7/7/1992, 103).

Overall, the Socialist group's position towards the situation in Yugoslavia, and particularly Bosnia, became clearer after some degree of initial confusion and contradiction. Notwithstanding some resistance from a few quarters led by Avgerinos, the group's policy was anchored on the support of sanctions and selectively targeted military operations to be accompanied by humanitarian missions under the aegis of the UN.

The second stage showed a decreasing level of cohesion with an IA of 84.93 percent combined with a negligible increase in the level of absenteeism of 61.01. With respect to the last Joint Motion for a Resolution (taken into consideration within this research) which was passed by the House on 9 July 1992, the group was split down the middle with 37 Socialist MEPs voting in favour, 40 against and 3 abstentions (B3-0973 and 1049/92). Among the MEPs opposing the text were 14 from the British Labour Party, 8 Spanish, 6 German, 6 Greek, 3 Belgian, 2 French and one Portuguese. Among the supporters of the Motion for a Resolution were 8 German, 6 French, 6 Spanish, 6 British, 4 Dutch, 3 Portuguese, 2 Belgian, one Irish and one Luxembourg MEPs.

The overall cohesion coefficient[76] reached 87.91 percent which, although not reflecting full consensus, still indicated a fairly high cohesion,

---

76 The overall index of agreement has been calculated on all 20 Roll-Call Votes on Yugoslavia between January 1991 and July 1992.

given the large numeric size of the group and the high level of participation at the roll-call votes. If compared to the other EP groups, the Socialists registered a fairly high index of absenteeism of 62 percent. It is arguable whether the high index derived directly from the ability of the group to enforce discipline among its members, although a correlation certainly exists. According to the Socialist internal rules, dissent from the official view of the group is condoned only for serious political reasons. In other words, MEPs can vote freely recurring to the so-called conscience clause only exceptionally, when for instance, a vote bears significant national implications (Ladrech and Brown-Pappamikail, 1995, 269).

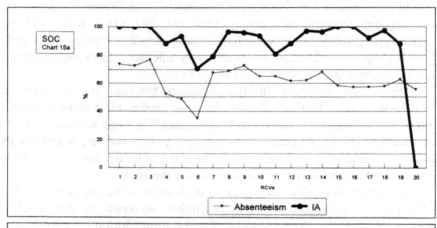

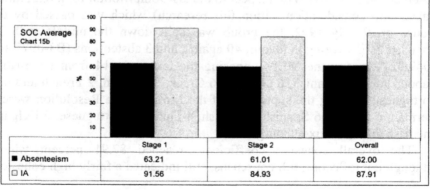

1.2 The European People's Party

a) Pre-Recognition Stage

During the February 1991 session, the European People's Party drafted a Motion for a Resolution on the crisis and human rights violations in Kosovo. During the debate on topical and urgent matters the German MEP Doris Pack stressed that over the previous two years and in particular since February 1989, Kosovo had been in a state of emergency characterized by a repressive and discriminatory policy carried out by the Serbian authorities with the closure of Albanian schools, the dismissal of its teachers and the ban of the only independent trade union for the whole Albanian workforce. An appeal was addressed to the Community not to abandon these people to their fate, but to consider the question as a European rather than a purely internal matter (Pack, 21/2/1991, 270-271, B3-279/91).

In the EPP's view, a precondition to the conclusion of the third financial protocol of the EEC-Yugoslavia cooperation agreement should be for the conflicting parties to resume negotiations[77] (Sarlis, 14/3/1991, 215-216, B3-197/91). In addition, the leader of the Albanian minority in Kosovo should be admitted to the negotiations. Despite their decision to depart from the Yugoslav federation, the Slovenes and the Croats did not exclude the possibility of a political compromise and the Bosnians and the Albanians had shown themselves to be open to seeking a non-violent solution while the Serbs were the only ones who did not show any inclination to "seek the peaceful route of dialogue", continuing their repressive measures in Kosovo (Pack, 14/3/1991, 221-222).

Although a signatory of the Joint Motion for a Resolution of 15 March 1991 (B3-0395, 0397/fin, 0399, 0403, 0431 and 0482/91), the EPP did not want to be associated with the EC policy supporting the territorial integrity of the SFRY. Consequently, the Christian Democrats strongly opposed the adoption of such policy, rejecting the inclusion of Paragraph 2 of the text of the EP Resolution and requested a roll-call vote. Out of the 22 members participating in the RCV 20 voted against and only 2, the Greek MEPs Sarlis and Stavrou voted in favour. Considering that Sarlis and Pack were the drafters on behalf of the EPP, Sarlis may have felt somehow compelled to support the general line of the Parliament, even though this meant going

---

77 The EEC-Yugoslavia Agreement was directed to promoting cooperation in the field of industry, environment, telecommunication and transport infrastructures.

189

against the official position of his group. Neither the attendance register nor the record of the RCV for 15 March 1991 makes mention of Pack being present. In May 1991, the Christian Democrats stressed that a long-lasting peace could only be achieved in Yugoslavia if people's rights to self-determination were respected (Habsburg, 16/5/1991, 266-267).

The EPP was the first group to send a small delegation, consisting of Habsburg, Pack, Oostlander and Sarlis, to Slovenia and Croatia between 29 June and 1 July 1991 and to propose the dispatch of an official parliamentary delegation to Yugoslavia. At the July 1991 session, following four consecutive visits since January 1991, Pack stressed that the SFRY, as conceived by Tito, had long ceased to exist, regardless of the efforts made by Slovenia and Croatia to maintain a loose federal formula within a programme of political, institutional and economic reforms. In her opinion, the Slovenian and Croatian attempts had been wrecked due to the lack of effective and genuine support on the part of the federal government which, despite the change of its political summit from the appointed Marković to the democratically-elected Mesic, remained strictly under the control of the Serbian government (Pack, 9/7/1991, 69).

The group believed, in accordance with the principles of the Helsinki Final Act and the CSCE Paris Charter of 21 November 1990 acknowledging the people's right to self-determination, that all EC member states should accept the independence of Slovenia and Croatia, fiercely supported by their respective parliaments and people. No change in the existing frontiers or in the language and cultural configuration of the various republics would be admissible (B3-1223/91). The Community should not grant funds to Yugoslavia, as it would only strengthen the Serbian aggressor and the Council should take into greater account the opinion of Parliament which should also act as mediator in the negotiations between the Yugoslav parties during the three months' moratorium (Pack, 9/7/1991, 69, Oostlander, 9/7/1991, 78-79). The adoption of the principle of self-determination by the Slovenes and Croats should be fulfilled in accordance with other democratic principles and responsibilities towards all the ethnic groups (Oostlander, 10/9/1991, 89-90). The German Liberal MEP von Alemann denounced the incoherent behaviour of the German Christian Democrats at national and European level. While in the *Bundestag* they had urged vehemently for such recognition, pointing the finger at the Serbs for their aggression against Slovenia and reproaching Foreign Minister Genscher for not having recognized early enough the independence of the secessionist republics, at the EP level they did not even propose the inclusion of this request in the text of the September resolution (von Alemann, 10/9/1991, 85).

In October 1991, the Christian Democrats pleaded for an immediate ceasefire with a clear condemnation of any violation of this agreement from either Serbian or Croatian parties (Sarlis, 9/10/1991, 168). In the following month, they emphasized that the Community should have enforced sanctions much earlier, as argued by Parliament since December 1990, so as to express condemnation of the human rights violations against the Albanians in Kosovo. A distinctive view, yet in line with the group, was taken by Habsburg who compared the arrival of Serbs in Vukovar with the Nazi occupation of Vienna during the Second World War and believed that the conflicts in former Yugoslavia were not civil wars, but "national struggle[s] by people who have been oppressed" and wish to free themselves from the Serbian domination (Habsburg, 20/11/1991, 159-160).

From the beginning, the EPP supported the recognition of the new republics which had democratically chosen their independence and elected their own parliaments. In Habsburg's words, *"Ceterum autem censeo Croatiam et Sloveniam esse recognoscendam"* (Habsburg, 9/10/1991, 165).[78] The Christian Democrats also stressed the importance of apportioning war-guilt, hence implying that the Serbs were unquestionably to blame for the conflict. This allegation was supported by the fact that the fighting had been taking place especially in the areas where Serbian guerrillas had infiltrated, supported by the Federal Army and effectively consisting of Serbian troops. Finally, the group condemned the sluggish EC's response to the Yugoslav crisis highlighting the need to realize that the "Council speaks only for the Governments, not for the people of Europe" (Habsburg, 9/10/1991, 165).

Unlike the Socialists, the Christian Democrats within the European Parliament clearly appeared from the beginning to be on the side of the Slovenes and Croats, sustaining their quest for independence. They also considered the Serbian government accountable for the deterioration of the events in former Yugoslavia. During the first stage, the Christian Democrats registered a very high index of agreement of 86.27 yet combined with a high level of absenteeism of 72.68.

---

78 "After all, I do believe that Croatia and Slovenia should be recognized" (author's translation).

b) Post-Recognition Stage

After the official recognition of Slovenia and Croatia and following the positive outcome of the referendum on Bosnian independence, the Christian Democrats argued that the Community should accept the will of the Bosnian people and endorse the legal international personality of the republic, whilst ensuring the continuation of peaceful negotiations between the various ethnic groups (Oostlander, 11/3/1992, 89-90).

The group emphasized that it was necessary to enforce a total oil embargo both by air and by land against Serbia (Howell, 12/5/1992, 76-77) and undertake military actions against the Serbian aggressors, by deploying UN and WEU forces, in order to contain the slaughter and to stop the action of ethnic cleansing (Habsburg, 9/4/1992, 273-274, Pack, 12/5/1992, 75). The government of Bosnia-Herzegovina was praised for its efforts to maintain cooperation between the various parts of the population and for its commitment to the search of a peaceful solution. Sympathy was expressed for the population of Sarajevo besieged by the JNA army as well as the people of several villages in Bosnia, victims of Serbian bombardments (Oostlander, 9/4/1992, 274). In addition, it was felt that the new Serbia and Montenegro were to be recognized only if, like the other republics, it followed the guidelines set by the Badinter Commission (Pack, 12/5/1992, 75). Habsburg denounced the partiality and the bias of the press agency Tanjug which provided only pro-Serbian propaganda and retained monopoly over newsbroadcasts (Habsburg, 12/5/1992, 73-74).

There was concern about the possible involvement of Croats in the alleged plan to divide the lands in the Bosnian Republic and regain disputed territories inhabited by its population. This seemed therefore to justify the intervention of the Serbian forces in the above area, in order to protect Bosnian Serbs (Robles Piquer, 12/5/1992, 76).

The necessity of a forceful action by the international community was elaborated further in June by Oostlander in his Report on *Relations between the European Community and the Republics of the former Yugoslavia,* where he stressed that "the course of peaceful means [had] been followed at great length", but despite some progress, reached through negotiations under the leadership of Lord Carrington and through the imposition of sanctions, the situation was doomed to deteriorate. For this reason, the EPP should call for a limited intervention by air and sea forces to pinpoint limited military targets, to neutralize the air space and to ensure that the Yugoslav Navy cease shelling the villages and towns along the Dalmatian coast (Oostlander, 9/6/1992, 52-53).

As to the plan of resettlement, Habsburg defined it as a "barbarity from the Second World War" that had to be fiercely resisted. A statute regarding the rights of ethnic groups should be drawn up, the implementation of which should be secured by the European Community (Habsburg, 9/6/1992, 58-59). The British Conservative MEP Edward McMillan-Scott, whose group, the ED, had joined the EPP since May 1992, advocated a military operation within the framework of the WEU or the CSCE and with the consent of the United Nations to secure Bosnian air space as well as the Adriatic sea (McMillan-Scott, 9/6/1992, 54-55).

A minority view was instead taken by the British Conservative MEP Derek Prag who disapproved of the *Oostlander Report* and accused the Community of having "got itself hooked on the principle of self-determination" without properly defining the criteria according to which people were entitled to such a claim. The main fault of the Report was to assume that the existence of a multi-ethnic state was a positive solution, without regard for the wishes of the population involved. The principle of non violation of the internal frontiers was criticized in view of the fact that those borders had been imposed by a dictator who had ignored the fact that over 2.5 million Serbs had remained outside Serbia, and so compelling them to become a minority "in what had been their own South-Slav, Yugoslav country". For this reason, a political settlement involving a change of borders could not be rejected and the Community should appoint several commissions each of them with the respective task of studying possible modifications of borders, monitoring human rights and defining the rights of minorities (Prag, 9/6/1992, 59-60).

In July 1992, the majority of the Christian Democrats opposed the granting of economic assistance and the extension of the PHARE programme to Croatia, due to the absence of accurate information about its actual involvement in the conflict in Bosnia-Herzegovina. Doubts were raised over the effective existence of a Serb-Croatian political agreement envisaging the partition of Bosnia-Herzegovina between them. Furthermore, uncertainty still remained on whether the Republic of Croatia had fulfilled the necessary requirements on human as well as minority rights (Moorhouse, 7/7/1992, 103-104).

The dissenting voices within the EPP group included Pack and Habsburg who pointed out that given the difficult situation in Croatia arising from the arrival of 650,000 refugees from Bosnia and Slavonia and in view of the fact that Croatia had proved to be more favourable to refugees than the EC member states, the Community could not deny them some kind of assistance (Pack and Habsburg, 7/7/1992, 105). To face this emergency, Oostlander proposed to establish an alternative programme in accordance with the terms suggested by the UN High Commission, while confirming the group's condemnation of the policy of cantonizing Bosnia-Herzegovina. Finally, Oostlander pointed out the inconsistency of the Community's policy, which had visibly neglected the case of Macedonia (Oostlander, 7/7/1992, 105).

During the second stage, the EPP group maintained and even reinforced its anti-Serbian stance. Since all other means had failed to produce any results, the Christian Democrats were favourable to the idea of a targeted military intervention to halt the hostilities in the area. The adhesion of the ED members to the EPP in May 1992, did not determine any substantial alteration in the level of group congruity[79] over the Yugoslav crisis so that the IA of RCVs registered only a negligible fall to 85.08 percent.

Throughout the whole period under examination, the EPP achieved the very high average index of agreement of 85.62 percent. This figure, marginally lower than that registered by the Socialists, represented the sixth highest outcome among parliamentary groups. However, this level of cohesion needs to be seen in light of the high rates of absenteeism of 72.68 percent in the first stage and 70.06 in the second stage, averaging 71.24 percent.

---

79 For the last six votes, specifically from 15 to 20, the ED group was incorporated into the EPP.

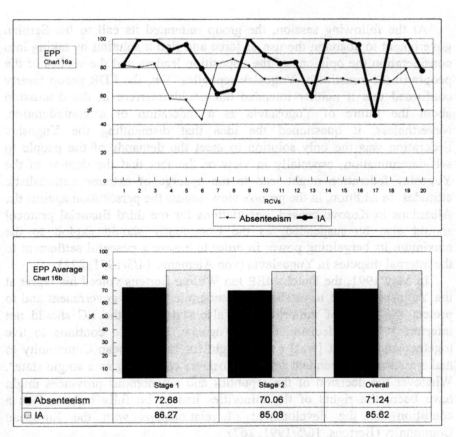

1.3 The Liberal Democratic and Reformist Group

a) Pre-Recognition Stage

In February 1991, the Liberals turned their attention towards the incidents in Kosovo, drafting a Motion for a Resolution B3-302/91 which eventually became part of a joint text adopted by the House. At the debate in the plenary, the group raised the question relating to the repression of the Albanian population in Kosovo and urged the Federal Yugoslav and the Serbian authorities to comply with the basic principles of human and minority rights. "Our claim is to make Parliament realize that something must be done and that in the light of our experiences in Western Europe, we have to use our influence to see that repression of this kind no longer takes place in Yugoslavia" (von Alemann, 21/2/1991, 270).

At the following session, the group reiterated its call to the Serbian government to abandon the use of force and find a solution by taking into consideration the opinions of the opposition leaders and the wishes of the people in the constituent Yugoslav republics. Yet, the LDR group clearly confirmed that it neither intended nor could interfere in the discussion about the future of Yugoslavia as a federation or a confederation. Nevertheless, it questioned the idea that dismantling the Yugoslav Federation was the only solution to meet the demands of the people to self-determination, especially in view of the fact that the demise of the Yugoslav federation might lead to the upsurge of extreme nationalistic attitudes. In addition, in the group's view, unless the persecution against the Albanians in Kosovo ceased, negotiations for the third financial protocol should also be suspended, as the Community should exploit to the maximum its bargaining power in order to ensure a peaceful settlement to the internal disputes in Yugoslavia (von Alemann, 14/3/1991, 222).

In May 1991, the Dutch MEP Jan Willem Bertens voiced his regret at the Yugoslav failure to establish a democratic form of government and to protect the rights of minorities. He also stated that the EC should not interfere with the decision of the Yugoslav people to continue to live together and that "it [was] (..) not right for the European Community to make assistance dependent upon Yugoslavia continuing as a single state". Whatever the decision of the republics and autonomous provinces might have been, the rights of the minorities had to be fully honoured as a condition for the development of relationships with the European Community (Bertens, 16/5/1991, 267).

The group identified three priorities for Community action. First, it argued that the EC would not accept the force of arms as a possible solution to the emerging problems in Europe and that those countries perpetrating violence should be excluded from EC financial assistance as well as prevented from establishing and maintaining privileged economic relationships. Second, it posited that the Community should promote a process of democratization by ensuring that all the negotiating parties were democratically elected, that the final decision would receive proper democratic endorsement and that the aspirations of Slovenes and Croats would be taken into account. Third, the group shared the Community's preference for the preservation of the Yugoslav federation, yet democratically orientated, as it was European credo that "in the modern world, some responsibilities are better shouldered by large groupings than by fragmented states" (Giscard d'Estaing, 9/7/1991, 69-70). The EC institutions should therefore continue to promote peace and democracy in the Balkans, as elsewhere.

The group, in line with the policy adopted by the Federation of Liberal and Democratic Parties at the Poitiers Congress a few weeks earlier, called for the establishment of a European army capable of carrying out peacekeeping operations as well as humanitarian actions in cases such as the Yugoslav conflict. Faced with the escalation of violence, the group stressed that the Community should recognize the international legal personality of Slovenia and Croatia, condemn Milošević's aggression and impose an embargo exclusively on Serbia and call for a ceasefire to be monitored by an international police force (von Alemann, 10/9/1991, 85, Lamassoure, 9/10/1991, 166-167). The LDR deprecated the Community's double standard of denying the deployment of a buffer force in Yugoslavia, on the request of the victim of the aggression while considering this option on the request of the assailant (Lamassoure, 20/11/1991, 156).

In summary, like the EPP, the Liberals advocated the recognition of independence of Slovenia and Croatia in line with the wishes of their people. They also condemned Serbian pugnacity, recommending the imposition of economic sanctions, the resumption of aid to the parties that were behaving cooperatively and the intervention of an international peacekeeping force (Lamassoure, 20/11/1991, 156). During the first stage, among all the political groups the Liberals registered the lowest index of agreement of 77.32 combined with a high percentage of absentees equal to 71.88 percent of the component members.

b) Post-Recognition Stage
Following the recognition of Slovenia and Croatia, the Liberals expressed concern at the escalation of violence in Croatia and at the prospect of further widening of the fighting in Bosnia (Bertens, 11/3/1992, 91-92). The siege of Sarajevo seemed to dash forever hopes of a peaceful settlement, replaced by public outcries for a military intervention and for an ultimatum to the Serbs, especially after the official independence of Bosnia-Herzegovina in April 1992. In the LDR view, military steps should be carried out under the auspices of the UN, CSCE and WEU in order to deter the continued JNA attacks on the Croatian and Muslim population, to protect Sarajevo airport and to secure the delivery of humanitarian supplies (von Alemann, 9/4/1992, 274, De Clercq, 71, Bertens, 74, 12/5/1992). The Liberal group supported the *Oostlander Report* as well as the amendment

197

relating to selective military operations if the sanctions failed to bring an immediate ceasefire.

In addition, the group strongly believed that the same guidelines set up by the Badinter Committee for recognition should be applied to all the individual republics in former Yugoslavia, including the new Serbia and Montenegro. Strong opposition was expressed to its automatic recognition and its taking over the role once played by the SFRY within the UN and CSCE (von Alemann, 59, Bertens, 55-56, 9/6/1992). As to the case of Macedonia, given that it had fulfilled the Badinter's requirement of providing sufficient guarantees for the rights of minorities, the Community should not delay further its recognition, especially after the Macedonian government's reassurance concerning the absence of any dispute over Greek territory (Bertens, 11/3/1992, 91-92). MEP von Alemann argued that the EP should approve the proposal by the Commission to grant technical assistance to Slovenia and Croatia and that allegations concerning a Serb-Croatian agreement for the partitioning of the territory of Bosnia-Herzegovina should be substantiated prior to taking the arbitrary decision of denying Croatia assistance (von Alemann, 7/7/1992, 104).

Overall, the Liberal group shared the view that the European Community should undertake military operations in order to halt the bloodshed in Bosnia-Herzegovina. The second stage marked a substantial increase in the group's cohesion with an extremely high figure of 92.77 percent but with a further increase in the level of absenteeism of its members up to 73.94. This rise in the level of consistency may well be due to this factor of absenteeism and to the departure from the group of its leader Giscard d'Estaing together with other French MEPs who decided to join the EPP group.

On the whole, the Liberals reached a very high IA of 85.82 percent coupled with, however, a non-flattering percentage of absenteeism of 73.01. However, among the LDR members von Alemann was particularly concerned about the Yugoslav issues, acting on a few occasions as a 'free-agent' by signing on her own behalf and participating in the drafting of the text of Joint Resolutions together with other groups.

198

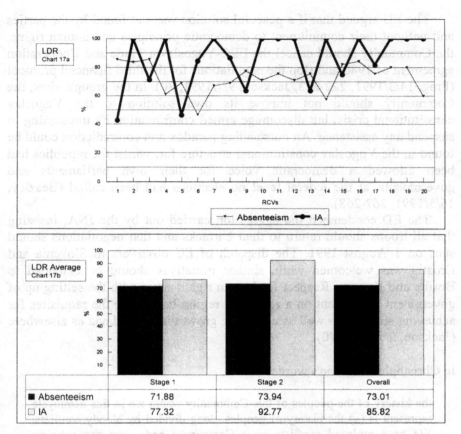

1.4 The European Democratic Group

a) Pre-Recognition Stage

The European Democrats supported the initiatives of Prime Minister Marković, a Croat and moderate, to re-establish economic order in the SFRY. They believed that the Community should not favour the break-up of the Federal Republic of Yugoslavia into six separate republics "based on extreme, intolerant nationalism" and therefore backed the attempts of Borislav Jović's presidency to prevent the disintegration by the means of negotiation. In the group's view, the Community had an interest in seeing a "strong, prosperous and democratic Yugoslavia.. at the heart of the Balkans" (Prag, 14/3/1991, 222-223). In addition, they accused Serbian leaders of promoting "the worst kind of nationalism" and expansionism directed at creating a greater Serbia.

The ED argued that if a peaceful solution was not found by the parties and without their commitment to democratic principles and human rights, the Community should cancel the EEC-Yugoslavia Trade and Cooperation agreement of 1980 and stop the negotiations for the third financial protocol (Prag, 14/3/1991, 222-223, Jackson, 9/7/1991, 70). In the group's view, the Community should not impose its own solution to the Yugoslav constitutional crisis, but discourage armed confrontation by threatening to suspend any assistance. An outstanding paradox and contradiction could be found in the Yugoslav constitutional structure for, whilst the republics had been allowed a democratic voice for their own parliaments and governments, at the federal level no elections had been called (Beazley, 16/5/1991, 267-268).

The ED condemned the aggression carried out by the JNA, insisting that all troops should return to their barracks and that negotiations should start on 1 August 1991. The dispatch of EC observers to Slovenia and Croatia was welcomed while similar initiatives should be extended to Bosnia and Kosovo. Respect for human rights along with the setting up of government by consent on a region by region basis were the requisites for achieving stability as well as economic growth in Yugoslavia as elsewhere (Jackson, 9/7/1991, 70).

In Christopher Jackson's words:

> the history of the peoples of this Community whom we in this hemicycle represent is (..) the history of peoples.. long divided by bloody conflicts. We have replaced conflicts by a Community and .. we can pass on something of our experience, not only of building a Community, but the spirit of bringing peace and prosperity out of war, to [the people .. of Yugoslavia (Jackson, 9/7/1991, 70).

Similarly, the republics of the Yugoslav Federation could also overcome their legacy of enmities finally prosper together in peace (Jackson, 10/9/1991, 85).

By September 1991, the ED group acknowledged that Yugoslavia as a state no longer existed, calling for the EC recognition of the new republics. The group clearly blamed the Serbs for the escalation of the fighting. The ED also disapproved the suggestion of imposing a generalized embargo in the area which would "be like denying David stones for his catapult against Goliath", stressing that sanctions should be enforced against Serbia (Spencer, 9/10/1991, 165). Yet the group welcomed the Commission's decision to provide aid to the population through non-governmental organizations, in particular the Red Cross, demonstrating that the quarrel was not with Serbs as such, but with their dissolute and ruthless government (Prout, 10/9/1991, 93-94).

The British Conservatives supported the text of the compromise resolution and proposed the inclusion of Paragraph 6, which foresaw that if a ceasefire and separation of forces had not proven effective the Community should begin to move towards recognition of Croatia and Slovenia in order to enable the UN Security Council to act without breaching Article 2 paragraph 7 of the UN Charter which prohibits any interference in the internal affairs of a state. In addition, in accordance with Article 42, where diplomatic and economic measures prove inadequate, the Security Council could authorize military action by air, sea or land in order to restore international peace (Jackson, 9/10/1991, 168-169). The group stressed that "the Southern Slavs cannot wait while [the EC member states] argue over the creation of a European defence identity" (Spencer, 9/10/1991, 165).

Following the Kurdish plight in the aftermath of the Gulf War, a new phase in international relations had been opened, where limits to sovereignty seemed to be being imposed by the international community. Given that the USA was no longer prepared to fulfil the role of 'policeman' of the world as in the Gulf War, the Community, although not ready to take over this responsibility, should at least undertake humanitarian actions in order to assist the Albanians in Kosovo (Jackson, 20/11/1991, 156) and the Macedonians (The Week, 20/11/1991, 28).

Along with the Christian Democrats and the Liberals, the British and Danish Conservatives MEPs soon identified the Serbs as the aggressors and accused them of a breach of the basic principles of international law. After having initially supported the maintenance of the unity of the Yugoslav Federation, the group shifted to the side of the breakaway republics, endorsing their international recognition in accordance with people's right to self-determination. Throughout the first stage, the European Democrats boasted a remarkable internal congruity, reaching an index of agreement of 91.05, but registering a fairly high level of absenteeism, 63.73 percent.

b) Post-Recognition Stage
The position of the group cannot be fully assessed over the second stage given that from 1 May 1992 the European Democrats joined the European People's Party group as affiliated members. In fact, the plenary session of

March 1992 was the last occasion that the ED, as a distinctive group, expressed its opinion over the crisis in former Yugoslavia. Support was given to humanitarian actions promoted by the Commission and the Council, while praising the work carried out as well as the courage demonstrated by the EC observers. "It is through discussion, through negotiation, through the good offices of the European Community, through the United Nations and indeed, through other agencies that (..) a solution" to the autonomous aspirations of the various republics could be found. Recognition had to be achieved in due course only if the conditions guaranteeing the rights of each member of the population were fulfilled (McMillan Scott, 11/3/1992, 92).

A distinctive line was taken by Derek Prag who argued in favour of the possibility of changes in the Yugoslav internal borders along ethnic lines, although these changes ought to be realized peacefully and by negotiation and not on the basis of the conquest of territory by force (Prag, 10/9/1991, 90-91, 11/3/1992, 94). In his opinion, the Community bore the responsibility for having spurred Croatia to declare independence which led inevitably to the outbreak of war. Prag urged the Community to discourage the rise of extreme nationalistic positions and promote cooperation leading to a customs union between the republics (Prag, 11/3/1992, 94).

In the 5 RCVs of the second stage in which the ED participated as a distinct political group in the European Parliament, total unanimity was displayed but along with a high rate of absenteeism of 79.41 percent. Out of 14 roll-call votes, unanimity was reached on 10 occasions.[80] Overall, throughout the whole period between January 1991 and July 1992, the ED reached an extremely high index of agreement of 94.25 overshadowed by a fairly high level of absenteeism of 69.33.

---

80 In the remaining three cases, one member abstained and in one case, specifically on amendment 1 of the Joint Resolution of 11 September 1991, MEP Edward Kellett-Bowman went against the group's official position.

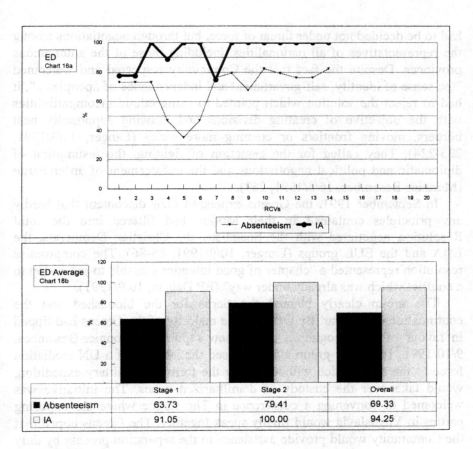

1.5 The Greens

a) Pre-Recognition Stage

In March 1991, largely drawing on his personal experience as a member of the German minority in the Italian region of South Tyrol/Alto Adige, Alexander Langer expressed the Greens' dismay at the Yugoslav situation. The fulfilment of the autonomous aspirations of the Southern Slavs did not represent a viable solution to the fundamental problems afflicting the country which, would inevitably re-emerge within the six or eight sovereign republics (Langer, 14/3/1991, 223-224). The events, which followed with the fragmentation of the SFRY and the outbreak of a vicious civil confrontation, proved the accuracy of this prediction.

The group supported a process of democratic reform in the SFRY aimed at protecting the rights of all ethnic groups. The future of the country had to be decided not under threat of force, but through negotiations among the representatives of all nationalities, including those of the autonomous provinces. Despite the fact that the Community respected and welcomed "the sense of identity, self-government and independence of ..peoples ..", it had to reject the solution which pointed to using ethnic incompatibilities with the objective of creating divisions and drawing supposedly neat borders, moving frontiers or creating more states (Langer, 14/3/1991, 223-224). They called for the cessation of fighting, the resumption of diplomatic and political negotiations and the enforcement of an embargo (Monnier-Besombes, 16/5/1991, 269).

In September 1991, the Greens expressed their discontent that hardly any principles contained in their Motion had filtered into the Joint Resolution negotiated with the Socialists, the Christian Democrats, the EDA and the EUL groups (Langer, 10/9/1991, 85-86). The compromise resolution represented a "chapter of good intentions unable to put a stop to a conflict which was already under way" (EP Debate, 10/9/1991).

The group clearly blamed the Serbs for the bloodshed and the continuation of the war. By October, the majority of the Greens had tipped in favour of the recognition of the new republics (Monnier-Besombes, 9/10/1991, 167). The group also proposed the sending of a UN mediation force to the area, which without taking the form of a military expedition, would take over the custody of demilitarized zones. The initiative was welcomed of convening a conference in The Hague where the opposing parties in Yugoslavia would finally speak together. The Greens hoped that the Community would provide assistance to the separation process by duly monitoring that fundamental rights were not infringed (Langer, 9/10/1991, 169-170).

At the November session, incredulity and shame were expressed with regard to the 'wait-and-see' approach taken by the Community towards the events unfolding in Croatia. Reference was made to the analogous case of Kosovo when the EC had also remained silent vis-à-vis the martyrdom of the Albanian people (Taradash, 20/11/1991, 157).

Although the Greens initially endorsed the maintenance of the territorial and political integrity of Yugoslavia, they shifted in favour of recognition of the new republics because of Milošević's brutal policy. The group therefore advocated the dispatch of a buffer force to the area. The option of dividing the country along ethnic lines was also ruled out as being against the principle of peaceful coexistence on which the European Community was first conceived and founded. The first stage of the crisis found the Greens relatively cohesive in their voting behaviour, with a very high IA of 83.41 percent but with a fairly high rate of absenteeism of 63.51 percent.

b) Post-Recognition Stage
During the March 1992 session, the Greens reiterated their opposition to the ethnic division into cantons of Bosnia-Herzegovina. In addition, they expressed their support for the recognition of Macedonia as this would not bring any dangerous implications for the territorial integrity of Greece (Langer, 11/3/1992, 93).

Langer put forward the view that "virtually nothing ha[d] been done to support the peacekeeping forces in Yugoslavia" and that the Community had failed to back Bosnia-Herzegovina and Macedonia. He entreated the CSCE forces to intervene in order to halt the hostilities, whilst granting EC assistance to refugees and Serbian deserters seeking asylum (Langer, 12/5/1992, 74).

At the June 1992 session, Langer conveyed to the House the common position reached between 30 May and 1 June by peace groups from all parts of former Yugoslavia,[81] aimed at ending the armed confrontation The sanctions imposed on Serbia and Montenegro were a clear condemnation of the aggression perpetrated in Bosnia-Herzegovina, but they alone would neither halt the war in Croatia and Bosnia-Herzegovina nor prevent the spreading of war in other neighbouring areas such as Macedonia, Montenegro, Serbia, Vojvodina, Kosovo and Sandrak. The international community was called on to recognize the Republic of Macedonia and to allow the Albanian representatives lawfully elected in Kosovo on 24 May 1992 to sit as legitimate partners at the negotiating table. Furthermore, the Serbs had to be persuaded to undertake negotiations to solve the crisis. Only upon a final settlement should the embargo be lifted. After imposing a definitive ceasefire, the international community had to secure peace by placing the affected zones under military supervision (Langer, 9/6/1992, 56).

During the second stage the Greens felt that combined diplomatic, economic and restricted military means should be employed in order to stop

---

81 Between 30 May and 1 June 1992, peace groups from Croatia, Serbia, Kosovo, Slovenia, Macedonia, Bosnia-Herzegovina, Capodistria and Dalmatia gathered together at the invitation of Austrian university students and the Serb-Croatian initiative and discussion group to draw up a common position.

the massacre in Bosnia. There was stern opposition to any form of ethnic cleansing while unwavering support was given to plans to assist refugees. The second stage registered a small increase in the index of agreement up to 85.97 along with a rising degree of MEP participation in the RCVs reflecting medium average percentage of absenteeism of 52.53.

Throughout the whole period, the Greens achieved a very high level of cohesion at 84.82 percent with the lowest rate of absenteeism among the political groups, 57.47. As such, David Bowler and Shaun Farrell's overall criticism of the Greens as being "unwilling or unable to adequately pool their strategies and resources as a group" cannot be extended to the 1991-1992 Yugoslav crisis, showing, instead, a fairly cohesive voting behaviour and a less accentuated level of absenteeism compared to the other political groups (Bowler and Farrell, 1992, 134).

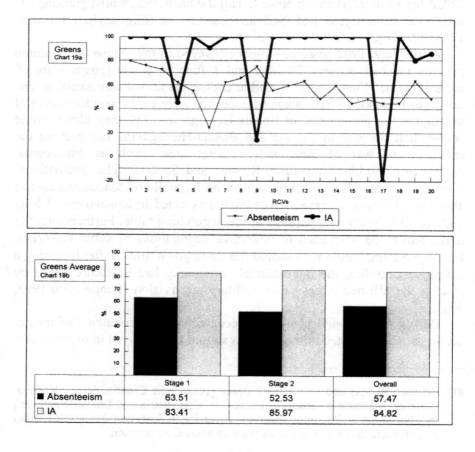

1.6 The European Unitarian Left

a) Pre-Recognition Stage

In March 1991, the European Unitarian Left was especially concerned about the critical developments of the situation in Yugoslavia which was seen as a Community problem that could alter the geopolitical balances of the Balkan region and especially affect neighbouring countries such as Austria, Italy, Germany and Greece. The group stressed that in order to defeat the emerging forms of authoritarianism, the EC member states had to work together for achieving a democratic and multi-ethnic European Union, of which the Yugoslav federation could become a part in the future (De Piccoli, 14/3/1991, 216). The EUL was in favour of the territorial integrity of the Yugoslav state, although it stressed the necessity to promote institutional reforms with the aim of safeguarding the autonomy of every region, granting a certain degree of independence to each republic and respect for human rights and all the ethnic groups. The Community should also adopt the third financial protocol with Yugoslavia and verify whether an association agreement could be concluded, provided that the crisis was resolved and that fundamental rights were fully respected (De Piccoli, 14/3/1991, 216).

In May 1991, the group claimed that "the Council should take action to safeguard the integrity of the Yugoslav state". The Italian MEP Trivelli pointed out that the agreements between the Italian government and the Yugoslav federation, finally sealed by the Osimo Treaty of 1975, should remain in force. Peaceful solutions should be promoted and civil wars should be prevented at any costs by trying to achieve an understanding between the various ethnic enclaves (Trivelli, 16/5/1991, 268).

By July 1991, the EUL had tipped towards a more flexible stance over the future of Yugoslavia. The group congratulated the Community Troika consisting of Foreign Ministers from Luxembourg, the Netherlands and Portugal on their success achieved at Brioni. The European Unitarian Left condemned the ferocity of the JNA attacks against Slovenes and Croats. It argued that the European Community should not propose the preservation of the Yugoslav state, nor regard its disintegration as inevitable. A revision of the constitutional positions of Yugoslavia should be undertaken, yet the Community should not be allowed to dictate the terms. Negotiations should be carried out by taking into consideration the right of self-determination of the Yugoslav people as well as the rights of the minorities (Napolitano, 9/7/1991, 76). However, the group rejected the creation of homogeneous national microstates based on the banishment or repression of minorities. In the words of the Italian MEP Rossetti,"[i]t would be anachronistic to consider the creation of states on a purely ethnic basis" (Rossetti, 10/9/1991, 86-87).

The President of the Council should address the Southern Slavs with a televised message inviting them to desist from aggressive nationalistic attitudes and to seek peaceful ways of coexistence. As the Italian MEP Giorgio Napolitano pointed out, the conflict in former Yugoslavia represented "a test (...) of the European Community's ability to act in situations of acute crisis in [Europe] and .. a test of how far it [was] possible to transform the existing Central and Eastern European structures, without causing savage disintegration" (Napolitano, 9/7/1991, 76).

Once they had achieved their independence, the various republics of former Yugoslavia should encourage forms of voluntary association of economic and institutional nature. In October 1991, the EUL expressed concern at the proliferation of "war mentality between the parties" which, by appealing to the most fanatical nationalistic attitudes, would precipitate political and religious confrontation. By contrast, the group advocated negotiation without laying down time limits (De Piccoli, 9/10/1991, 167). However, if the appeals for a ceasefire were to remain unheard, steps should be taken at the CSCE and UN levels to dispatch a peacekeeping force to the area in order to prevent the spreading of the fighting to other cities and to the Republic of Bosnia-Herzegovina. Support should be given to the enforcement of a strict embargo on arms sales, the UN embargo on petroleum products and the suspension of the cooperation agreements as well as the compensatory measures for the cooperative republics (De Piccoli, 20/11/1991, 157).

The EUL was initially in favour of preserving the Federation, albeit introducing institutional reforms and a certain degree of autonomy for the republics. However, over the summer 1991 its official view shifted towards pro-recognition and the deployment of peacekeeping forces. Over the first stage, the members of the European Unitarian Left boasted a remarkable degree of congruity of 95.06 with one of the lowest, though still high rate of absenteeism of 71.03 percent.

b) Post-Recognition Stage
In March 1992, the European Unitarian Left expressed concern about the situation in the territory of former Yugoslavia (De Piccoli, 11/3/1992, 92). The group acknowledged the decision of the people in Bosnia-Herzegovina

to seek independence. However, it insisted that prior to proceeding to the official recognition of the new republic, the Community should prevent the partitioning of Bosnia-Herzegovina into cantons and encourage peaceful cohabitation of the various ethnic groups. The EUL also urged the Community to give "a new and strong impetus" to the Peace Conference which, in conjunction with the actions carried out by the UN peacekeeping forces, should pave the way for the settlement of the crisis. Finally, the necessity was stressed for the Community to undertake negotiations for establishing cooperation agreements with the new republics (De Piccoli, 11/3/1992, 92, Trivelli, 9/4/1992, 274).

On 12 May 1992, the European Unitary Left stressed that the Community had to search for a solution to the crisis by ensuring the inviolability of borders and respect for minorities. The group criticized the EC political leaders who seemed to follow the events in Yugoslavia "just like newspaper readers rather than as responsible political forces" (Papayannakis, 12/5/1992, 71). The group also endorsed the *Stavrou Report*[82] which proposed the suspension of extending the PHARE programme to Croatia until the rights of the Serbian as well as the Italian minorities were fully recognized (Rossetti, 7/7/1992, 104).

Throughout the second stage, the EUL placed emphasis on the survival of a multi-ethnic society in Bosnia-Herzegovina where the rights of all groups should be duly respected. The stage saw a marginal decline in the levelof group cohesion to 89.09 and with a higher percentage of absenteeism 80.25 percent. Between January 1991 and July 1992, the group reached an extremely high index of agreement of 91.78 percent yet accompanied by a high rate of absenteeism of 76.10.

---

82 The *Stavrou Report* amended the Commission proposal of extending economic aid to Slovenia and Croatia.

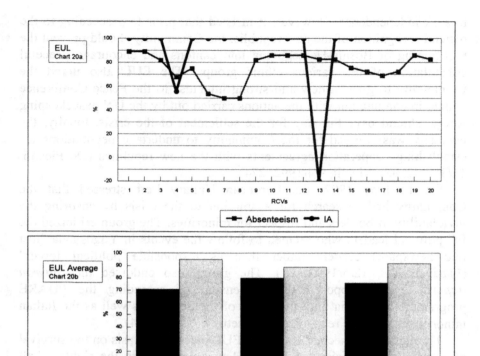

1.7 The European Democratic Alliance

a) Pre-Recognition Stage

As early as March 1991, the European Democratic Alliance expressed the view that the Community should not interfere in Yugoslav internal affairs, but should press for its political viability by financially assisting the country's economic development and promoting a process of democratization. Only by achieving these two objectives, rather than "through interference, dissension and outbreaks of nationalist unrest" would the Balkan states be able to reach stability (Nianias, 14/3/1991, 225-226).

In July, the EDA stressed the importance of taking into account the wishes of the Slovenian and Croatian populations especially as their demand for independence was "broad-based, peaceful and democratic" (de la Malène, 9/7/1991, 76-77).

At the September session, the group supported diplomatic and political measures while encouraging the dispatch of a large peacekeeping force to secure the rights of the minorities. The threat of non-cooperation was also envisaged as an ultimate deterrent to the continuance of the conflict and the consequent violations of fundamental rights (Alliot-Marie, 10/9/1991, 87). Criticism was directed at the Twelve for exercising contradictory national policies that prevented the achievement of a common stance. With reference to the referendum held in Macedonia, the Greek MEP Dimitrios Nianias pointed out the irregularities surrounding the voting procedure and the atmosphere of intimidation which prevailed. In addition, the creation of another independent state joining "the ring of states hostile to Serbia" would deteriorate further the situation in the territory of former Yugoslavia. Finally, the Greek MEP denied the legal or ethnological existence of a Macedonian nation, defining it as nothing but "a distortion of history". There was no Macedonian national or cultural identity as its population consisted of a mixture of Slavs, Serbs, Bulgarians, Greeks and Albanians (Nianias, 10/9/1991, 91). This is a very contentious point since the Macedonians believe that they have a separate identity.

Overall, the group discouraged the formation of a multitude of small countries in the Balkans on the grounds that they were not economically self-sufficient and would inevitably fight for resources (Nianias, 9/10/1991, 170). As such, the only wise policy for the Community was to promote dialogue between the parties in order to achieve peace and unity.

The group supported the Council's decision to enforce sanctions on Yugoslavia, while introducing compensatory measures for the Slovenian and Croatian Republics which had proved to be willing to cooperate for the attainment of a peaceful solution to the crisis. In addition, the EC firm opposition concerning the abolition or the change of borders was shared by the EDA members (Nianias, 20/11/1991, 157).

The policy espoused by the European Democratic Alliance in relation to the Yugoslav crisis was in line with the position taken by Lord Carrington and the Community as a whole and could be simply summarized in a three-word slogan: peace, unity and democracy. Over the first stage, the EDA displayed a very high index of agreement of 88.89 percent accompanied by the highest rate of absenteeism of 83.84 percent.

211

b) Post-Recognition Stage

At the May 1992 session following the statements by Council and Commission on the situation in Bosnia-Herzegovina, the group stressed that its policy was not addressed against Serbs but against Belgrade's government. The Council's decision to set a deadline of 18 May for the JNA to leave the territory of Bosnia-Herzegovina was strongly endorsed (de la Malène, 12/5/1992, 72). Nianias pointed out that his prophetic statement that the creation of mini-states in the territory of former Yugoslavia would lead to civil war had unfortunately proved to be right. He also voiced his uncertainty about the full and parallel implementation of two opposing principles, maintenance of the existing borders and empowerment of minorities (Nianias, 12/5/1992, 74-75).

In June 1992, the group rejected the adoption of the amendment introduced by Oostlander to his own Report concerning a military option. Doubts were once again raised by the Greeks concerning the recognition of Macedonia, as its constitution incorporated the principle of self-determination, which held within the ambition of reuniting neighbouring regions even those belonging to other states. This was interpreted by Greece as a veiled threat of war. In addition, by naming the republic as 'Macedonia', the communist leader Kiro Gligorov sought to find further legitimation for his expansionist design. The Community had by all means to avert the spread of the conflict and prevent American military intervention in the region (Nianias, 9/6/1992, 56-57). The European Democratic Alliance perceived the Serbian government as responsible for the bloodshed in Bosnia, though remaining against the military alternative in the belief that the crisis would not be solved by bullets.

The second stage saw a small decrease in the voting cohesion of the group which reached 81.82, compensated however by a lower level of absenteeism which dipped slightly to 79.65 percent. Over the whole period, the average index of agreement was 85.00 percent while the rate of absenteeism was a marked 81.54 percent.

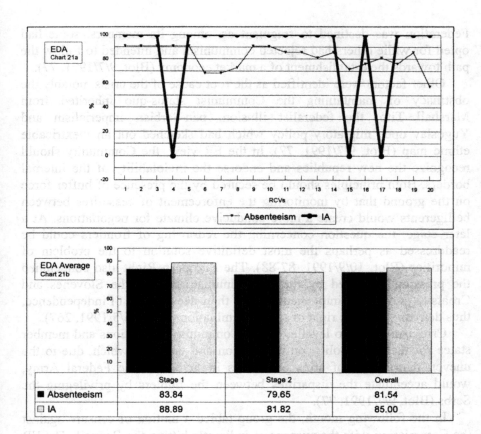

1.8 The European Right

a) Pre-Recognition Stage

As early as March 1991, the ER supported the quest for independence of the Yugoslav republics, distancing itself from the other political groups. The group drafted various Motions for Resolutions urging the international community to recognize the will of the Slovenian, Croatian and Macedonian peoples to become independent partners (Blot, 14/3/1991, 218) and to ease their journey from communism to democracy.

The group attributed the main causes of the flare-up of the civil wars in former Yugoslavia to the paradoxical and unthinkable coexistence of communist and democratic régimes (Blot, 10/9/1991, 87). It was inconceivable, for instance, for the Croatian government to promote the principle of a market economy "when federal laws still carr[ied] the stamp of the communist totalitarian regime" (Blot, 16/5/1991, 267). The Yugoslav

Federation was destined to fragment as, among its members, some had opted for while others had rejected communism and intended to follow the path towards the establishment of a market economy (Blot, 9/7/1991, 77).

Other factors were identified as the root cause of the crisis, notably the obstinacy of maintaining the Communist status-quo inherited from Marshall Tito, the federalist illusion, pan-Serbian imperialism and Yugoslav open migratory policy which had sketched out an inextricable ethnic map (Blot, 9/7/1991, 77). In the ER view, the Community should recognize the new republics and endorse the inviolability of the internal borders. Both principles should be secured by the presence of buffer force on the ground that by monitoring the enforcement of ceasefires between belligerents would create a more conducive climate for negotiations. At a later stage, the question concerning the redrawing of frontiers could be readdressed as perhaps the most definitive solution to the problem of minorities (Blot, 10/9/1991, 87-88). The European Right also condemned the pressure exercised by the US Administration on the Slovenes and Croats to prevent the implementation of their declarations of independence, thus denying them the right of self-determination (Blot, 16/5/1991, 267).

Criticism was also levelled at the Community institutions and member states for their idle policy on recognition and embargo which, due to the uneven distribution of arms provisions in favour of the Federal Army, would accentuate the disparities between the fighters by privileging the Serbs (Blot, 9/7/1991, 77).

In the following month, the group tabled a motion of censure against the Commission with the purpose of indirectly hitting the Council. The ER reiterated its opposition to the proposal of enforcing an arms embargo in the region as it would only accentuate the imbalance between the parties to the benefit of the Serbs. In view of their geographical proximity to the troubled area, the Community should be closely involved in the settlement of the war (Blot, 9/10/1991, 164-165). It also condemned the two-faced approach taken by the Community with regard to the Gulf and the Yugoslav crises (Antony, 20/11/1991, 158).

The European Right deplored the fact that the Community had failed to prevent the Serbs from attacking Slovenia, Croatia and then Bosnia-Herzegovina. It also blamed the EC's unreasonable policy of discouraging the Slovenian and Croatian quest for independence, because it would inevitably lead to chaos in the Balkans. Criticism was levelled at the weak response of the Community to the Serbs, especially at the inability or perhaps unwillingness of the EC member states' governments to identify the guilty party in the war. The ER most definitely leaned in favour of the internationalization of the conflict and therefore the deployment of a considerable military contingent in order to oppose the creation of a Greater Serbia and to prevent the Communist Serbian army from committing further ravages (Blot, 22 November 1991, 346). During this stage, the position of the ER group towards the Yugoslav crisis was unanimous, as the analysis of the RCVs also confirms, but its level of absenteeism was also high, equal to 76.39.

b) Post-Recognition Stage
In the group's view, the tragic events occurring in the territory of former Yugoslavia revealed the reality of "an artificial state with several nationalities locked into a straitjacket, in which some [sought] to dominate others, some [sought] freedom, autonomy and independence and others [used] force imperialistically in order to stifle this quest for freedom". In addition, the Yugoslav crisis revealed the inability and inactivity of the European Community which failed immediately to recognize the independence of the Slovenian and Croatian republics and to take strict and firm measures against the Serbs. Furthermore, the US Administration should be blamed for having played "the centralist card in Yugoslavia" for reasons of selfish commercial interests (Dillen, 11/3/1992, 93-94).

In the group's opinion, the Twelve could halt the war in Yugoslavia by taking joint actions against Milošević's imperialistic ambitions (Dillen, 9/6/1992, 59). A decisive military intervention was therefore advocated to put an end to the genocide carried out against the Muslim population. The ER members firmly believed that the French and the British naval and air forces alone could defeat the Serbian artillery in a short period of time. However, for this to happen, the sovereign states within Europe had to come to an agreement (Antony, 9/6/1992, 57).

In both stages, the group reached unanimity in its voting stance. This exceptional result, eased by the homogeneous composition of the group, needs to seen in the context of the high rate of absenteeism that oscillated between 76.39 and 81.17 percent over the two stages, resulting in an average rate of 79.02 percent.

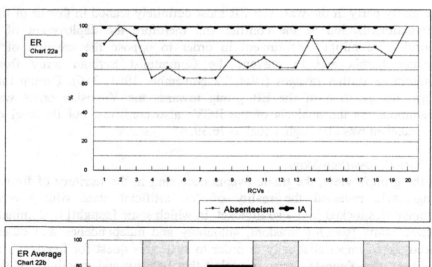
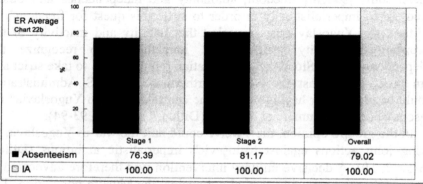

1.9 The Rainbow Group

a) Pre-Recognition Stage

As early as February 1991, prior to the flare-up of the armed confrontation in former Yugoslavia, the Rainbow group drafted a Motion for a Resolution on the crisis in Kosovo.[83] The Serbian policy of imposing its own language and culture on the Albanian minority was strongly condemned. The group highlighted the necessity of suspending trade negotiations until the Federal government had provided explicit guarantees safeguarding human and minority rights. The group went further in stating that any future association agreement with the SFRY or financial assistance from the

---

83 Motion for a Resolution tabled by MEPs Jaak Vandemeulebroucke and Winifred Ewing.

European Investment Bank had to be subject to an official commitment from the Yugoslav government to respect human rights and pluralism (Simeoni, 14/3/1991, 216-217). The same preconditions had to be fulfilled if the Yugoslav government wished to join the Council of Europe (Vandemeulebroucke, 21/2/1991, 270).

The group challenged the view shared by the majority of the European Parliamentarians, that nationalist movements were the cause of conflicts in Yugoslavia. Therefore, it refused to sign the text of the March 1991 Joint Resolution which entailed "the commitment not to reinforce ethnic or nationalist differences which are irreconcilable with a European approach".

During the topical and urgent debate held on 16 May 1991, the group expressed its concern with the developments of the Yugoslav crisis, which had already "cost many human lives and the effects of which [were] unpredictable, [and] liable to fester at the gates of the Community". It condemned the policy espoused by the Council and Commission supporting the territorial unity of Yugoslav federation as a precondition for the country's membership of the Community. This policy was used as a coercive instrument by the reactionary forces in Yugoslavia. In rejecting paragraph 7 of the compromise resolution, the group insisted that "states [should not be seen] as sacred at the expense of democracy, which cannot exist without respect for the rights of individuals and peoples" (Simeoni, 16/5/1991, 268).

The Community should adopt a positive stance in the negotiations over the Yugoslav constitutional future starting on 1 August and be open to all options from that of a federal system, to a confederation, an association of states or simply of independent states. The Community had neither the authority nor the right to decide over the destiny of Yugoslav people, but they themselves had to decide whether they were prepared to live together. The group insisted that the July 1991 resolution make reference to the principle of self-determination, warning that, otherwise, it would not endorse the text (Vandemeulebroucke, 9/7/1991, 75-76). At the September session, it stressed that the JNA was clearly acting as the Serbian government's military force. This intervention was regarded as exceeding the official task of protecting the external border of the Federation and therefore "equivalent to a military coup". The country's internal frontiers were also considered as not "immutable", although any change had to be achieved by peaceful means (Barrera i Costa, 10/9/1991, 87). The group denounced the EC's stubborn attitude of insisting upon the preservation of the unity of the Yugoslav Federation which supported "the Serbian dominance" (Vandemeulebroucke, 9/7/1991, 75-76, 9/10/1991, 166). The Rainbow MEPs reproached the EC-EPC for its inability to distinguish between the aggressor and the victim. It also censured the choice of extending the arms embargo in the area, as it would inevitably penalize the Slovenes and the Croats more than the Serbs (Vandemeulebroucke, 9/10/1991, 166, Christensen, Ib, 20/11/1991, 176-177). The group envisaged the military option under the auspices of the WEU, UN or CSCE and only upon the consent of all warring parties (Christensen, Ib, 20/11/1991, 176-177, 22/11/1991, 346).

For the Rainbow group, the Serbian government was undoubtedly responsible for the flare-up of the conflict. The international community ought to help the republics in question to withstand Milošević's aggression first of all by seeking a solution through diplomatic channels. The Rainbow MEPs presented a united front during the RCVs of the pre-recognition stage, including, of course, the amendment proposed by them to the Joint Resolution of September 1991. However, members' absenteeism reached the high level of 74.81 percent.

b) Post-Recognition Stage
During the March 1992 sitting, the Rainbow group expressed anxiety at the threat of the Serbian government not to withdraw the JNA from the territory of Bosnia-Herzegovina, irrespective of any request from the Bosnian government. In the group's view, the Community should impose severe economic sanctions, insist on the removal of the JNA from Croatia and Bosnia as well as demand guarantees for the rights of Romanians in Kosovo and ensuring that no policy of settlements and annexation was carried out. The Spanish MEP Barrera i Costa endorsed the French President Mitterand's proposal for a "loose European Confederation where the Community would be associated with European countries" which had not yet fulfilled the requirements for full membership (Barrera i Costa, 11/3/1992, 93).

In May 1992, the group praised the EC observers for their courageous actions aimed at assisting the civilians and ensuring that ceasefires were upheld. There was disappointment at the response of the international community to the Yugoslav crisis, which had differed enormously from that directed to Saddam Hussein, following his invasion of Kuwait (Canavarro, 12/5/1992, 72).

In the group's opinion, the European Community had limited itself to undertake a so-called 'preventive diplomacy' by organizing a peace conference, without making real pressures on Yugoslavia for instance by suspending it from participating in the CSCE proceedings, by sending UN intervention troops with the task of compelling the Serbs to withdraw from the new republics, by disarming the local militias and so bringing the war to an end. The group strongly underlined the point that the Community should deny the official recognition of the new entity consisting of Serbia and Montenegro until peace was restored and the principles of inviolability of internal frontiers, respect for democracy, human rights and rights of minorities had been entirely fulfilled (Canavarro, 12/5/1992, 72).

During the post-recognition stage, the Rainbow group sanctioned the use of diplomatic and economic means, envisaging UN military intervention solely as a last ditch effort to halt the conflict. The group's level of unanimous voting dropped drastically to 59 percent, displaying, however, a slight decrease in the rate of absenteeism of its members to 63.03 percent. Overall, the average index of agreement was of 74.95 percent accompanied by a percentage of absenteeism of 68.33.

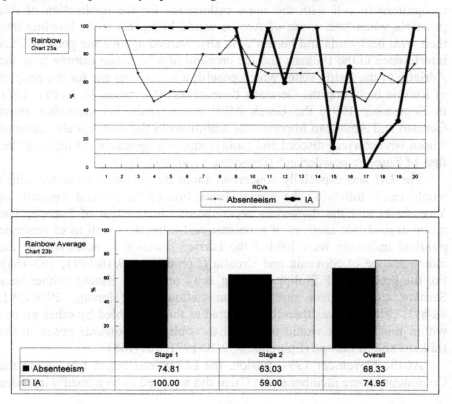

1.10 The Left Unity

a) Pre-Recognition Stage
During the March 1991 parliamentary debate, the spokesperson for the Left Unity, the Greek MEP Vassilis Ephremidis expressed the view that, considering the destabilizing repercussions in the Balkans and, generally, in the whole of Europe that the Yugoslav crisis might have caused, the Community had rightly taken a cautious and impartial attitude. Its actions had to be directed towards the economic sphere by granting financial assistance to the Yugoslav federation and towards the institutional political structure by favouring the necessary reforms aimed at averting the break-up of the Yugoslav state (Ephremidis, 14/3/1991, 226-227).

While acknowledging the right of the Yugoslav people to self-determination, the Greek MEP Dimitrios Dessylas warned against the internal and external repercussions of the fragmentation of the Yugoslav state by challenging those countries which so ardently supported recognition to call with the same enthusiasm for the application of this principle when "the winds of Aeolus would bring this tactic howling into their own backyards and homes". He also warned against the peril of USA interference in the Balkans and the creation of a "German Europe from the Adriatic to the Baltic states which pose[d] a serious danger for the peoples of Europe including the Germans themselves" (Dessylas, 10/7/1991, 167). In September 1991, the Greek MEP stated again his suspicion about German and American imperialistic ambitions in the area. He also accused "those who sow[ed] discord and [sold] arms to Yugoslavia" of lighting "the fuse of Europe's powderkeg" (Dessylas, 11/9/1991, 162).

The LU was especially concerned about the vacuum and chaos which would result following the formal dissolution of the Federal Republic of Yugoslavia and the dangerous repercussions in the rest of Europe. The group argued that motives of economic self-interest as well as of strategic political influence were behind the hurried decision to acknowledge the independence of Slovenia and Croatia (Ephremidis, 9/10/1991, 167-168). For the French MEP Philippe Herzog, the Community should neither back Serbian expansionism nor Croatian nationalism (Herzog, 10/9/1991, 88-89). Criticism was therefore directed at the text tabled by other groups within the EP as it would not fulfil the obligation towards peace in the Balkans and in Europe (Ephremidis, 9/10/1991, 167-168).

At the November 1991 session, the LU voiced regret that within the Community some member states ("that did not need to be named") intended to exploit the disintegration of the Socialist Federal Republic of Yugoslavia and the proliferation of small republics in order to gain influence in the area. It then expressed opposition to the policy of sanctions which inevitably would affect the civilian population without solving the crisis. Finally, it called for an effective involvement of the United Nations in the search for a peaceful solution (Ephremidis, 20/11/1991, 157-158). As to the strategies to be adopted to solve the crisis, the group realistically envisaged the possibility of having to resort to the use of arms, stressing that in such event the CSCE along with the UN should take the lead in the management of the military operations (Herzog, 10/9/1991, 88-89).

As confirmed by the leader of the Left Unity Réné-Emile Piquet during the course of an interview, the official line of the group was against immediate recognition of Slovenia and particularly of Croatia. These strong reservations were founded on the realization that a policy backing the independence of the constituent republics from the Federation was not the most positive approach in the quest for a suitable and peaceful solution. The recognition of the secessionist republics by Germany, soon followed by the other EC member states, made the Yugoslav problem intractable. Recognition meant that the battles fought in former Yugoslavia were no longer civil but interstate wars. As to measures to be taken, the Community should bring its contribution to the negotiation of a peaceful solution without having to resort to arms (Piquet interview, 1996). Over the first stage, although the Left Unity's index of agreement over the RCVs on Yugoslavia was rather high, at 80 percent, the rate of absenteeism was also very high at 82.54.

b) Post-Recognition Stage
At the March 1992 session, the group urged the Community to grant all possible humanitarian assistance to the republics of former Yugoslavia and to advocate political solutions. It also stressed that with hindsight the question of recognition should have been fully discussed first and foremost by the parties so that the outbreak of violence could have been prevented (Alavanos, 11/3/1992, 95). The Community had to avoid repeating in the case of Bosnia-Herzegovina the same mistake made with respect to Croatia, viz recognizing the independence of the republic (Ephremidis, 11/3/1992, 95). Finally, as to the case of the Republic of Macedonia, Ephremidis, who shared the concern of many Greek MEPs, confirmed that the opposition of Greece was motivated by the fear of possible territorial claims towards its

221

own province by its namesake in former Yugoslavia (Ephremidis, 11/3/1992, 95, 12/5/1992, 75, 9/6/1992, 57-58).

The brief contribution of Alavanos to the May debate consisted in addressing some questions to the Portuguese Presidency requesting more detailed information about Council's decisions over the Yugoslav crisis. Specifically, if and when unilateral actions had to be taken by the Community regarding the Republic of Macedonia and which measures had to be adopted in order to protect minorities in the above republic (Alavanos, 12/5/1992, 73).

In May 1992, the group defined the EC's behaviour vis-à-vis Yugoslavia as "the policy of Pontius Pilatus". It also criticized the view that the Serbs were the only party responsible for the conflict and the fact that the Community had recognized states which did not fulfil all conditions. (Ephremidis, 12/5/1992, 75).

With regard to the *Oostlander Report*, the LU group put forward strong reservations over the need of greater military involvement by the Community. The crisis had to be settled under the aegis of the United Nations by insisting on compliance with the principle of inviolability of the national borders set after the Second World War and respect for minorities (Ephremidis, 9/6/1992, 57-58). A more extreme view was expressed by Dessylas, according to whom the only solution to the Yugoslav conflict required that the people fight for peace and social development by expelling imperialist adventurers such as the USA, NATO, EEC, WEU, "the NATO-ized CSCE and the Americanized UN". People had to reject war, racism, nationalism, dictatorship, forceful modification of borders as well as violation of minority rights (Dessylas, 9/6/1992, 59).

At the July 1992 session, LU opposed the proposal to extend the PHARE programme to Croatia in view of its coresponsibility for the bloodshed in Bosnia-Herzegovina. The group also deplored the fact that both the European Parliament and the Community had ignored the worrying developments that led to further fragmentation in the territory of former Yugoslavia (Alavanos, 7/7/1992, 104-105).

Overall, the impact of the Left Unity group on the definition of the EP's stance on the conflict was modest, often with an adversary position. Its contribution consisted mainly in the introduction of amendments (Alavanos written interview, 7/1995). The cohesion figures marginally improved over the second stage with an increased rate of cohesion of 83.64 percent accompanied by a higher MEP participation, producing a level of absenteeism of 78.32 percent. Overall, the index of agreement showed a very high average figure of 82 percent along with a rate of absenteeism of 80.22 percent. There was an especially high level of absenteeism among the French MEPs who were not so keen to participate to the debates over Yugoslavia as their Greek colleagues.

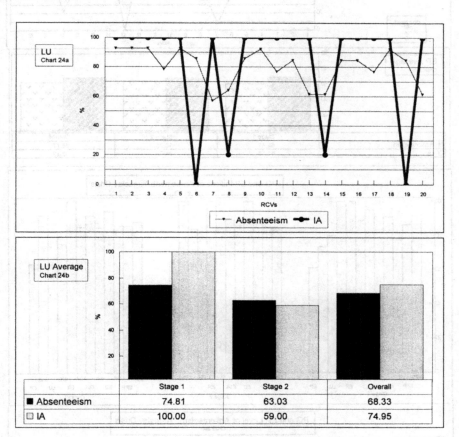

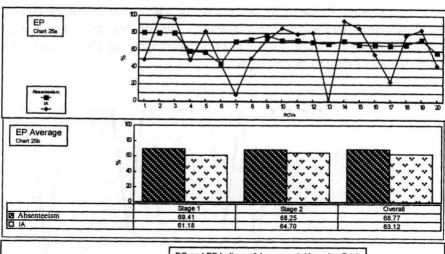

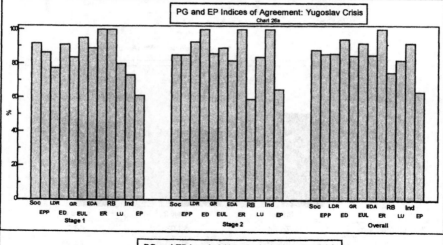

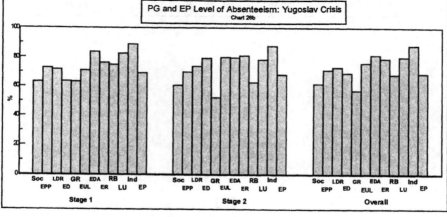

2. Level of Transnationality in Political Groups' Voting Behaviour on the Yugoslav Crisis

The creation of the EP political groups not along national lines but according to political affiliation was designed by the founding fathers of the European Community in order to overcome the rigidity of national divisions and eventually achieve a supranational dimension. The following section aims to assess if, despite the MEPs' natural inclination to bring with them their individual national identities to the EP, this experiment has succeeded and if and to what extent nationality remained one of the major factors determining group voting outcome in relation to the Yugoslav crisis. Concomitantly, an attempt is made to establish whether heterogeneity can be considered a factor deterring the achievement of a high level of cohesion. The indices of transnationality of the various PGs on Yugoslavia have been calculated on 20 RCVs.

Chart 27 shows that the level of transnationality in voting within the various political groups was fairly high with the exception of the ED, ER, EUL. The highest degree of transnationality of 0.819 was registered within the Christian Democrats, immediately followed by the Liberals with 0.817 and the Socialist group with 0.807. When considering the rate of transnationality in relation to MEP voting behaviour, the actual composition of each political group and, more specifically, the number of effective nationalities contained within it, needs to be considered. As expected, the larger groups showed a much higher degree of transnationality when compared to the smaller groups, except for the LDR and Green groups. The national element remained strongly present among most Greek MEPs with regard to the thorny question of the recognition of the former Yugoslav Republic of Macedonia (or the Republic of Skopje as they preferred to call it). A comparison of the tables on PGs' indices of transnationality on the RCVs (ITv-s) on Yugoslavia and on PGs' composition (ITc-s)[84] shows that the former was less than the latter for most PGs, albeit to a different degree. Conversely, an opposite trend was registered by the EUL which appeared to be more cohesive and more multinational in its RCV on Yugoslavia than in its configuration. By way

---

84 For the Itv-s on the individual RCVs see Appendix. For the Itc-s of the various PGs, see Tables 1a-1f in Chapter I.

225

of conclusion, the data prove that no direct relationship existed between the heterogeneity of the EP political groups and their level of cohesion.

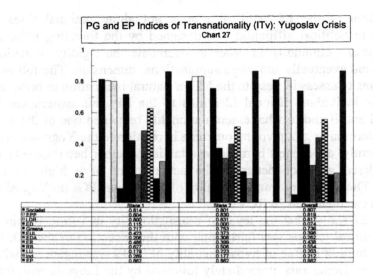

3. MEP National Allegiance Versus Political Group Loyalty

By comparing the results of the indices of agreement of PGs and of national delegations in the European Parliament with respect to the Yugoslav crisis, it can be concluded that group allegiance was higher than national solidarity when voting on Yugoslavia, except for the Rainbow group which, as previously stated, spanned a rather wide ideological spectrum. The delegations from Luxembourg, Great Britain, Greece and Spain displayed high levels of agreement. Cohesion within a delegation as small as the one from Luxembourg is not difficult to understand. However, national solidarity does not seem to conflict with MEPs' allegiance to their respective groups and generally goes along with their strong Europeanist sentiments. Also in the case of the Spanish MEPs, it can be said that group allegiance was more of a concern than national imperatives. In fact, a closer look at the RCVs for the Socialist, EPP, LDR, EUL and Rainbow groups shows that despite the appearances, political allegiance prevailed over nationality.

In the case of the Greek delegation, the high level of solidarity resulted from the perceived threat that an expansionistic policy lay behind the recognition of the Republic of Macedonia, a name also borne by one of

Greece's provinces, and the ambition of reuniting Macedonian people. However, it was only in a few RCVs that Greek MEPs formed a cohesive front, disregarding the positions of their respective groups. Overall, they endorsed the official line of their groups.

The high level of cohesion of the British delegation was the result of the very high level of absenteeism of British MEPs within the EPP group with no members turning up to the RCV session between votes 1 and 14. It is interesting to note that after the merger with the ED group in the last 5 votes, the group had some representatives at the voting sessions that fully agreed with the official policy of the EPP group. However, the British Labour delegation which regularly attended the voting sessions, also followed the preferences indicated by the Socialist group with only one exception, in vote 6, when the British contingent was split with 16 members abstaining and 13 voting in favour, in line with the official group standpoint.

In the case of the Greens, the British members turned up on three occasions only, but did support the group majority while in the case of the Rainbow group, the British MEP only bothered to turn up on one occasion, abstaining from the vote and failing to support the voting preference of the group majority.

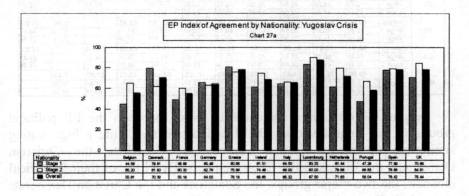

4. Political Groups' Voting Similarity on the Yugoslav Crisis

The purpose of this section is to gauge the distance between the EP political groups over their respective twenty roll-call votes on the 1991-1992 Yugoslav crisis. Table 7 illustrates the voting similarity percentages (VSPs) reached by the PGs in the two stages of the crisis as well as during the whole period.

Table 7 Political Groups' Voting Similarity on the Yugoslav Crisis

		SOC	EPP	LDR	ED	GREEN	EUL	EDA	ER	RB	LU	IND
SOC	Overall		80.58	68.65	75.41	62.48	87.33	81.44	25.13	52.16	68.91	69.96
	stage 1		80.03	59.49	74.95	61.67	84.61	91.40	3.72	42.92	79.29	77.58
	stage 2		81.03	76.14	76.24	63.14	89.55	73.28	42.25	58.04	60.42	66.49
EPP	Overall	80.58		80.37	82.32	67.03	74.41	80.94	33.74	64.25	50.81	70.93
	stage 1	80.03		63.85	77.19	58.68	68.31	73.79	24.22	52.97	60.92	71.33
	stage 2	81.03		93.88	91.55	73.86	79.41	86.78	41.35	71.43	42.54	70.75
LDR	Overall	68.65	80.37		70.99	75.57	64.24	77.12	45.33	67.24	43.50	74.42
	stage 1	59.49	63.85		56.89	78.91	47.79	61.74	49.30	60.56	51.70	78.84
	stage 2	76.14	93.88		96.36	72.84	77.71	89.70	42.16	71.50	36.80	72.42
ED	Overall	75.41	82.32	70.99		71.62	87.48	81.85	23.40	62.34	43.91	54.58
	stage 1	74.95	77.19	56.89		55.85	87.19	71.76	25.52	41.87	63.86	49.17
	stage 2	76.24	91.55	96.36		100.00	88.00	100.00	20.00	91.00	8.00	60.00
GREEN	Overall	62.48	67.03	75.57	71.62		57.00	69.40	28.79	77.48	45.45	65.73
	stage 1	61.67	58.68	78.91	55.85		49.21	64.65	46.02	68.18	71.31	65.76
	stage 2	63.14	73.86	72.84	100.00		63.38	73.29	15.00	83.40	24.29	65.71
EUL	Overall	87.33	74.41	64.24	87.48	57.00		79.22	26.17	46.34	66.44	57.92
	stage 1	84.61	68.31	47.79	87.19	49.21		84.57	13.89	30.16	75.43	53.33
	stage 2	89.55	79.41	77.71	88.00	63.38		74.85	36.00	56.65	59.09	60.00
EDA	Overall	81.44	80.94	77.12	81.85	69.40	79.22		25.93	66.79	51.67	65.63
	stage 1	91.40	73.79	61.74	71.76	64.65	84.57		6.25	50.00	73.33	73.33
	stage 2	73.28	86.78	89.70	100.00	73.29	74.85		41.67	77.47	33.94	62.12
ER	Overall	25.13	33.74	45.33	23.40	28.79	26.17	25.93		42.68	48.89	42.22
	stage 1	3.72	24.22	49.30	25.52	46.02	13.89	6.25		57.14	23.75	26.67
	stage 2	42.25	41.35	42.16	20.00	15.00	36.00	41.67		32.55	69.00	50.00
RB	Overall	52.16	64.25	67.24	62.34	77.48	46.34	66.79	42.68		35.54	57.99
	stage 1	42.92	52.97	60.56	41.87	68.18	30.16	50.00	57.14		44.29	46.67
	stage 2	58.04	71.43	71.50	91.00	83.40	56.65	77.47	32.55		29.98	63.14
LU	Overall	68.91	50.81	43.50	43.91	45.45	66.44	51.67	48.89	35.54		47.92
	stage 1	79.29	60.92	51.70	63.86	71.31	75.43	73.33	23.75	44.29		55.33
	stage 2	60.42	42.54	36.80	8.00	24.29	59.09	33.94	69.00	29.98		44.55
IND	Overall	69.96	70.93	74.42	54.58	65.73	57.92	65.63	42.22	57.99	47.92	
	stage 1	77.58	71.33	78.84	49.17	65.76	53.33	73.33	26.67	46.67	55.33	
	stage 2	66.49	70.75	72.42	60.00	65.71	60.00	62.12	50.00	63.14	44.55	

Despite the obvious divergences of views between the EP political groups in the Yugoslav case, the data indicate that quite a high voting similarity percentage resulted between the Socialists, the Christian Democrats, the EUL and the EDA members. By virtue of their 'historical alliance', the two major groups, the Socialists and the Christian Democrats showed similar voting behaviour. The highest VSP of 87.48 percent was, however, achieved somewhat surprisingly between the ED and the EUL groups, while the lowest of 23.40 percent was registered between the ED and the ER groups. Voting behaviour analysis has also confirmed that the Left Unity, albeit closer to the Socialists and the EUL, remained distant from the other groups.

Throughout the whole period, the ER seemed ostracized from the rest of the PGs. Yet, its spurned participation in the drafting of joint resolutions did not discourage its members from going it alone with their endeavours to formulate policies over Yugoslavia. The Rainbow members appeared virtually equidistant from their colleagues in five of the other EP political groups, their voting gap increasing in relation to both the extreme wings, the European Right and the Left Unity. A comparison of the VSPs between the various groups conclusively refutes the existence of a neat left-right cleavage in the chamber with regard to the Yugoslav issue. A certain voting discipline was imposed within the various groups as the official party line generally prevailed despite a few defecting members. The above statistics also revealed that the bigger the group, the greater its chances to act as a political magnet to the other groups, irrespective of their ideological colours.

5. Intergroup Cooperation in Shaping the European Parliament's Stance on the Yugoslav Crisis

This inquiry does not illustrate all 20 RCVs taken on the Yugoslav case, but only the most controversial.[85] The first RCV was held by the EP on 15 March 1991 and concerned paragraph 2 of the Joint Resolution on the situation in Yugoslavia (B3-0395, 0397/fin, 0399, 0403, 0431 and 0482), stating that the EP "reaffirm[ed] (..) the position frequently expressed by Parliament and the Council and more recently by EPC in favour of 'the unity and territorial integrity of Yugoslavia'". The Joint Motion, tabled by the Socialists, the Christian Democrats, the Liberals, the Greens, the European Unitarian Left and the European Democratic Alliance, found overwhelming consensus in the House, except for the aforementioned paragraph which was opposed by the EPP.

The crisis was discussed only very briefly during the May 1991 session where all groups, with the exception of the Left Unity, presented their own individual texts of Motions for Resolutions. However, on 16 May, a joint text, which was tabled by the Socialist, the EPP, the LDR, the ED, the Green, the EUL, the EDA and the Rainbow groups, was endorsed by the House by 101 votes in favour and only 2 against. The EPP managed to

---

85 Full details of all RCVs are illustrated in the Appendix.

229

secure the inclusion of a new Recital expressing concern "at the constitutional crisis which had been caused by the refusal of the Serbian representatives to elect to the Presidency the Croatian member of the Praesidium pursuant to the principles of the Constitution" (*OJEC* C 158/1991, 141).

The Rainbow group requested a split vote on paragraph 7 which read "[the European Parliament], while reiterating the preference of the European Community and the international community more generally for the maintenance of one federal Yugoslavia, insists that this cannot and must not be seen as a willingness to countenance the suppression of democracy and human rights". The efforts of the Rainbow group were in vain, as the paragraph was adopted and included in the text of the Joint Resolution.

In September 1991, the Socialists, EPP, EUL and EDA groups tabled a Joint Motion for a Resolution on the Situation in Yugoslavia, which was adopted by the House by roll-call vote, as requested by the Liberals.[86] As a result, the majority of LDR members abstained from the vote while 2 MEPs Defraigne and Holzfuss voted against. The Greens also abstained from the vote with the exception of the Italian MEP Falqui who supported the Joint Motion. As expected, due to the role of opposition often taken by the ER, the text of whole resolution was unanimously rejected by the group, whilst being passed by the House with 208 votes in favour, 10 against and 70 abstentions. An amendment presented by the Rainbow group, urging the international recognition of the breakaway republics in case of continued attacks by the JNA, was rejected by 157 votes against, 46 in favour and 8 abstentions. The amendment was taken by a roll-call vote at the request of the Christian Democrats. The second part of paragraph 19 was also subject to a roll-call vote following the request of the Rainbow group and finally approved by 196 votes out of 215. All 7 Rainbow members present at the sitting along with the Irish MEP Patrick Cooney rejected the inclusion of the paragraph. Among those abstaining from the vote were all 4 ER members present, 3 British Labour MEPs, Peter Crampton, Brian Simpson and Alex Smith, and 4 Liberals, the Dutch MEP Gijs de Vries, the Spanish MEP Carles-Alfred Gasòliba i Böhm, the French MEP Jeannou Lacaze and the Danish MEP Tove Nielsen. On 22 November 1991, the whole text of

---

86 Joint Resolution B3-1325, 1360, 1371, 1372 and 1390 of 11 September 1991 tabled by Socialists, EPP, EUL, EDA and Prag.

the Joint Motion for a Resolution was adopted by RCV, as requested by the EPP, after a long voting marathon imposed by the Greens.[87]

On 12 March 1992, the House passed a Joint Resolution on the situation in former Yugoslavia especially focusing on the Bosnian crisis, after having scrutinized the different parts of the text.[88] As requested by the EUL paragraphs 11, 12, 13 and second part of paragraph 23 were voted by roll-call vote.[89] While the first three paragraphs were approved respectively by an overwhelming majority, the last was rejected by a slim majority of 83 out of 165 with 7 abstentions from all ER members attending the vote as well as the German Christian Democrat MEP Bernhard Sälzer, the Italian Communist MEP Pasqualina Napoletano and a German Independent. The first three aforementioned paragraphs were the object of many disputes, especially by Greek members. In the first case, the Greek contingent was split down the middle with 5 EPP members in favour and 6, including 2 Socialists, 2 EPP, one Rainbow and one LU members, against. In the second case, among the Greek members attending the vote only 2 EPP members voted in favour while the remaining 9, including 4 Socialists, 3 EPP and 2 LU members, voted against. Amongst the Greek MEPs,

---

87 The Greens requested a split vote on Recitals A,B, Recitals C,D and Paragraph 1, Paragraph 2, Paragraph 3, Paragraphs 4-5, Paragraphs 6-8, Paragraphs 9-10 and Paragraphs 11-12.

88 On 12 March 1992, EP approved the Joint Resolution B3-405, 406, 407, 408, 409, 410, 411 and 413/92 tabled by the Socialist, the EPP, the LDR, ED, EUL, Green, EDA and Rainbow groups after going through a series of votes on amendments, Recital D, paragraph 14 which was subject to a split vote requested by the Greens, paragraph 21, paragraph 23 which was also subject to a split vote on three parts. Finally, paragraphs 11, 12, 15, 23 (2nd part) were adopted by a RCV requested by the EUL group.

89 11. [The European Parliament] takes note of the request from the former Yugoslav 'Republic of Macedonia' for diplomatic recognition on the basis of the referendum of 8 September 1991, the views of the 'Badinter' Commission on this request, and the Council decision of 16 December 1991 on the guidelines for recognition.
12. Urges that any change in the constitutional status of Macedonia must be accompanied by unequivocal undertakings by the Macedonian Government and Parliament that they will not seek any territorial changes in the frontiers of their republic.
15. Believes, however, that it is totally unacceptable for political disagreements between Member States to be pursued by economic means: welcomes the condemnation of popular initiatives of this sort by the authorities of the Member States concerned.

paragraph 13 was supported by 2 members from the EPP and rejected by 9, specifically 4 Socialists, 3 EPP and 2 LU members.

On 9 April 1992, the House passed a Motion for a Resolution on the crisis in Kosovo tabled by the LDR group, after having accepted two amendments and after a split vote on Paragraphs 3 and 4, as requested by the Socialists (*OJEC* C 125/1992). At the same sitting, the Christian Democrats tabled a Motion for a Resolution on the situation in Bosnia-Herzegovina, requesting that it be put to a roll-call vote. After the introduction of three amendments, the text was adopted by the House, with 145 members voting for, 3 against and with just one abstention.

On 11 June, after the drafting of three versions, Parliament finally adopted the *Oostlander Report* which concerned relations between the European Community and the republics of former Yugoslavia. This was passed by RCV at the request of Socialists and Christian Democrats with 129 votes in favour, 3 against and 8 abstentions (*Oostlander Report, OJEC* C 176/198). Coalitions were created across the parliamentary spectrum between the Socialists, Christian Democrats, Liberals, Italian Communists and French Gaullists. At the margins of the parliamentary debate there were the European Right as well as, yet to a lesser degree, the Left Unity and the Rainbow group whilst the Greens appeared generally distant from the other party groups. As expected, the larger groups continued to dominate the votes in the Parliament.

It must be remembered that throughout the period in question, the Socialists and the Christian Democrats held respectively 180 and between 128-162 seats in the Chamber while, for instance, the European Unitarian Left and the European Right held only 29 and 14. Hence, it is not surprising that the internal proceeding of each group varied accordingly. Both Socialist and Christian Democrat MEPs had the possibility of an extreme specialization while the members of the smaller groups, such as the EUL and ER, had to share more competencies and their coverage could not be so meticulous and exhaustive. As a result, their chances of making an impact on the EP's stance were greatly diminished. Despite the evident shortcomings of the smaller groups, exceptional circumstances need to be considered. An example was provided by the Greens, and in particular by Langer who revealed a genuine commitment to promote peace initiatives in Yugoslavia. As his voice remained unheard beyond the parliamentary walls, the Yugoslav tragedy acquired the dimension of a personal battle which unfortunately ended with his untimely death.

The Yugoslav case confirmed MEPs' tendency to acquire a certain expertise in a particular field often through their membership to a specific committee. By proving the quality of their interventions and affirming their competence, these MEPs become influential amongst their colleagues and their opinions are generally followed and adopted as the official group position. The Socialists and the EPP cooperated to gain the majorities required to forge a parliamentary stance on the Yugoslav crisis with the result that the political centre was bound to vote together. Yet, the European Parliament did not fully succeed in speaking with one voice on the issue, reaching a fairly high IA for the whole period of 63.12 percent. Certainly, this does not represent an outstanding figure, but when considering the multiplicity of the political groups within the parliamentary spectrum, it is reasonable to claim that the EP's cohesion was nevertheless fairly impressive. If compared to the Gulf crisis, the Yugoslav case showed some progress with regard to the level of parliamentary cohesion. This positive outcome was, however, overshadowed by the higher level of absenteeism which touched the average percentage of 68.77.

The high absenteeism at the RCV sessions suggests that, even more in the Yugoslav case, a sense of scepticism and frustration prevailed within the House due to the incapacity of the European Parliament to make any impact in the formation of EC/EU foreign policy, lacking effective powers over the Council. Throughout the two stages of the crisis, the EP tended to secure a multigroup coalition without relying on the participation of the ER, confirming the latter's marginalization within the Chamber. With extreme nationalism being the central issue in Yugoslavia, the fact that the far right was associated with a fervently nationalistic outlook may have had a significant bearing on this matter. In fact such a connection could be altogether unjustified as the policies advocated by the ER, whilst being to a certain extent nationalistic, were based on the respect of principles of democracy, ethnic tolerance and the right of people's self-determination. Such exclusion is striking as the same policies envisaging both recognition and limited military intervention were ultimately adopted by the Chamber. As clearly substantiated by the following tabulations of statistics, the Christian Democrats seemed to be most active and influential in moulding the EP's stance on Yugoslavia. However, the presence of the two largest groups, the Socialist and the EPP was a constant factor in the adoption of parliamentary joint resolutions. The data show just one exception, the July 1992 text which was tabled only by EPP, EDA, Rainbow groups and von Alemann in her own name (*OJEC* C 241/1992, 145-146; 134). As Woltjer

233

confirmed, the call for an EC-CSCE selective air and naval intervention could certainly not gain the agreement of the Socialists who "were definitely not a party to it" (Woltjer, 9/7/1992, 243) and any decision on military intervention should be urgently and exclusively taken within the UN Security Council (Woltjer, 9/6/1992, 54).

Table 8   Breakdown of Adopted and Non-Adopted Motions for Resolutions on the Yugoslav Crisis

Date	Individual Political Groups		Political Groups' Coalitions		Individual/ Coalition of MEPs		Committee Reports
	A	NA	A	NA	A	NA	A
Feb 1991	-	1 (ER)	1 (S,LDR,V,EPP,ED, RB)	-	-	-	-
Mar 1991	-	3 (ER, RB,EUL)	1 (LDR,V,S,EPP,ED, EUL,EDA)	-	-	-	-
Apr 1991	-	1 (V)	-	-	-	-	-
May 1991	-	1 (ER)	1 (EPP,LDR,ED,S,V, EUL,RB,EDA)	-	-	-	-
June 1991	-	-	-	-	-	-	-
July 1991	-	3 (ER,EDA,RB)	1 (ED,S,EPP,LDR,V EUL,LU)	-	-	1 B3-1106 (Fini, Rauti, Mazzone, Muscardini)	-
Aug 1991						1 B3-1258 (Guidolin)	
Sept 1991	-	7 (EPP,LDR,V, RB,ED,ER,LU)	1 (EPP,EPP,EUL,S, EDA)	-	-	-	-
Oct 1991	1 (S)	5 (S,EPP,ED. ER,LU) *	-	1 (ED,EPP, RB,LDR,V, EUL)	-	-	-
Nov 1991	-	3 (LDR, V,ER)	1 (S,EPP,EUL,ED + von Alemann)	-	-	2 B3-1716 Coates & B3-1745 Muscardini	1 A3-0323 Cassanmagnago-Cerretti Report (Political Affairs Committee) on EP assent to denunciation of the EC-Yugoslav agreement
Dec 1991	-	-	-	-	-	-	-
Jan 1992	-	1 (ER)	1 (S,EPP,ED,LDR,V, EDA,EUL,RB)	-	-	-	-
Feb 1992	-	-	-	-	-	-	-
Mar 1992	-	1 (ER)	1 (EPP,LDR,S,EDA, V,EUL,RB)	-	-	-	-
Apr 1992	2 (LDR,EPP)	1 (RB)	-	-	-	-	-
May 1992	-	2 (ER,V)	1 (EPP,RB,S,LDR, EDA,EUL)	-	-	-	-
June 1992	-	-	-	-	-	-	1 A3-0208 Oostlander Report Committee on Foreign Affairs
July 1992	1 (EPP)	-	1 (EPP,EDA,RB + von Alemann)	-	-	-	1 A3-0232 Stavrou Report Committee on External Economic Relations

A=Adopted
NA=Non-Adopted (Rejected, Fallen and Withdrawn Motions for Resolutions)

* EPP and ED originally tabled as part of a Motion for a Joint Resolution which was rejected, and subsequently tabled as individual Motions for Resolutions which fell.

235

Table 9   Intergroup Cooperation: Adopted Joint Resolutions on the Yugoslav Crisis

	S	EPP	LDR	ED	EDA	V	EUL	ER	RB	LU
S	x	9	7	6	6	6	8	0	5	1
EPP	9	x	7	6	7	6	8	0	6	1
LDR	7	7	x	5	5	6	6	0	5	1
ED	6	6	5	x	3	5	5	0	3	1
EDA	6	7	5	3	x	4	6	0	5	0
V	6	6	6	5	4	x	5	0	4	1
EUL	8	8	6	5	6	5	x	0	4	1
ER	0	0	0	0	0	0	0	x	0	0
RB	5	6	5	3	5	4	4	0	x	0
LU	1	1	1	1	0	1	1	0	0	x

Between January 1991 and July 1992, the EP adopted 16 resolutions, of which 10 were drafted by political groups, 4 from individual political groups (2 from the EPP, one from the Socialists and one from the LDR) and 2 from committees. As Woltjer emphasized, the Socialists regretted that a Joint Resolution had not been produced by all political groups on the topic raised by Oostlander. This did not mean, however, that the Socialists did not share the view that both the Community and the EC member states' governments had to face the emergency stemming from the increasing flow of refugees from Bosnia as well as other corners of Yugoslavia. Among the adopted resolutions, 10 consisted of Motions negotiated and drafted jointly by political groups and 4 were Motions drafted by individual PGs: one by the Socialists, 2 by the Christian Democrats and one by the Liberals. For instance, in October 1991 the Joint Motion for a Resolution tabled by EPP, RB, EUL and Greens failed to reach a consensus so that the individual groups tried, to no avail, to get their respective Motions passed. Eventually only the Motion for a Resolution tabled by the Socialists succeeded and that by electronic vote.

The European Right performed the function of an opposition within the parliamentary arena. A similar critical role was also occasionally exerted by the Rainbow group which played 'devil's advocate', to quote an example in the joint text of 16 May 1991 when, despite being one of the drafters of the Joint Motion, the group requested a split vote on paragraph 7.

No Motions for Resolutions were passed from texts tabled by MEPs in their own name and hence without the official support of, their respective groups, showing that the groups and their network were dominant. The case provides examples of close intergroup cooperation: the 'historic alliance' between the Christian Democrats and the Socialists proved successful on 9 occasions when, along with various other groups, Joint Motions for Resolutions were adopted. The EUL and Christian Democrats as well as the EUL and the Socialists both cooperated on 8 occasions. Similarly, the LDR collaborated with the Socialists and the EPP respectively on 7 occasions. The data illustrate equally numerous cases between the EDA and the Christian Democrats, whilst registering only 6 alliances with the Socialists.

Apart from the ER, the other group which seemed lacking in its involvement in parliamentary coalition was the group at the opposite extreme of the Chamber, the Left Unity. Only once, and specifically in July 1991, was the LU involved in drafting a joint text together with the Socialists, the Christian Democrats, the Liberals, European Democrats, the Greens and the European Unitarian Left.

In the Yugoslav case, the level of consensus within the Europarliamentary forum was higher than that achieved during the Gulf crisis (Piquet interview, 31/1/1996). The intensity of the control by political groups in parliamentary activity with respect to the Yugoslav crisis is mapped in Chart 28.

Chart 28 PG Contribution: Yugoslav Crisis

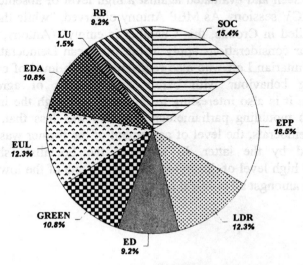

N.B. ER made no contribution to the EP position on Yugoslavia

237

The level of activity did not always reflect the degree of control over the formulation of the EP policies over Yugoslavia, as, for instance, the ER was rather prolific in tabling and forwarding Motions, albeit unsuccessfully, to the House. As the voting analysis demonstrates, no exclusive line-up arose on the Europarliamentary horizon during the Yugoslav crisis, coalitions being generally spread over the parliamentary arena. The voting records display a frequently recurring convergence between the Christian Democrats and the British Conservatives, which eventually led to the affiliation of the ED group to the EPP group in May 1992. On the other side of the Chamber, the Socialist and EUL groups revealed a similar political approach, confirmed by their voting behaviour, which seemed to presage the eventual joining of the EUL to the Socialist group in January 1993.

The Christian Democrats dominated the parliamentary debate and the policy-definition on the Yugoslav crisis. This could be attributed to the British Conservatives' adhesion to the EPP group in the Strasbourg Parliamentary arena. This hypothesis can, however, be dismissed as the merger only occurred officially in May 1992 and could not have perceptibly determined the shaping of any policy.

The European Right reached unanimity in its voting behaviour pattern, assisted both by the modest number of its members and by the relatively narrow national basis of the group. However, this exceptional outcome needs to be seen and evaluated against a high level of absenteeism during the above RCV sessions. As MEP Antony observed, "while the cemeteries are being filled in Croatia, this Chamber is empty" (Antony, 20/11/1991, 158). Similar considerations apply to the European Democrats and to the European Unitarian Left who also registered a high level of conformity in their voting behaviour with barely lower levels of agreement and absenteeism. It is also interesting to note that, although the impact of the Socialists in moulding parliamentary policies was less than that of the Christian Democrats, the level of agreement of the former was higher than that reached by the latter. In addition, the Socialists showed their traditionally high level of discipline, registering one of the lowest levels of absenteeism amongst all political groups.

Conclusion

EP political groups exhibited a fairly high index of agreement with regard to the Yugoslav crisis, all exceeding 80.00, with the exception of the Rainbow group. The rank ordering the political groups with regard to these indices from the most to the least cohesive was: the European Right, the European Democrats, the European Unitarian Left, the Socialist, the LDR, the EPP, the EDA, the Greens, the Left Unity, with the Rainbow group taking up the rear with an index of agreement even lower than that achieved by the Independent MEPs. The Socialists were ahead of their main rivals, the Christian Democrats, although both achieved impressive levels of congruity, especially when considering their heterogeneous composition, resulting from the various nationalities and parties represented within the political groups. After the Socialists and only just ahead of the EPP were the Liberals whose cohesion improved substantially between the first and the second stages of the crisis.

In particular, a comparison of the levels of cohesion attained during the pre- and post-recognition stages reveals no fluctuation in the case of the European Right, virtually no fluctuation for the EPP, marginal shifts towards cohesion for the Left Unity, the Greens, the ED and a tangible rise for the Liberals of 15.45 from 77.32 to 92.77. An increasing level of fluctuation away from cohesion was instead recorded in the case of the EUL, the Socialists and the EDA. Over the post-recognition stage, the Rainbow group saw its unity broken, registering the most substantial loss of cohesion amongst the political groups, by 41 percent from 100 to 59.

Up to January 1992, the Chamber showed a scarcely lower rate of agreement, although this remained higher than the 60 percent threshold, still indisputably higher than the figures registered throughout the three stages of the Gulf case. The centre-right consisting of the EPP, LDR, ED and EDA groups scored higher on the rate of agreement than the left comprising the Socialists, EUL, LU, the Greens and the controversial Rainbow group. However, by omitting the last two groups from the alignment, the balance shifted slightly in favour of the left. When considering attendance, however, the left wing of the House could claim a higher figure, due mainly to the Socialists and the Greens. Despite this, there was still a very high level of absenteeism at the RCV sessions on the 1991-1992 Yugoslav events. While the data illustrated that the House reached a not-displeasing level of cohesion, attendance was alarmingly

239

poor with just over 31 percent of members actually "bothering to turn up to the voting sessions".

Fitzmaurice's remarks of 1975 still apply in relation to the Yugoslav case, albeit to a much lesser extent:

> If any group gives the appearance of a party group in a national parliament then it is the Socialists. (...) outright opposition to the point of voting against the party line in a roll-call vote is rare in the Socialist group. (...) the Christian Democrats and the Liberals appear a great deal less cohesive than the Socialists (Fitzmaurice, 1975, 164-166).

Overall, the data reveal that, at least when votes were taken on the Yugoslav crisis, the various PGs within the European Parliament acted as proper groups. As a result, the allegation that there is an absence of an adequate group dimension within the parliamentary spectrum proves therefore to be inaccurate. Furthermore, it is possible to argue that, while differences still exist within EP political groups, these disparities also surfaced within political groups at national parliamentary level, for instance within the Spanish or Italian legislative Assemblies on the basis of the region of provenance of the individual members (Written interview of a Spanish EPP official, 7/1996). The problem of cohesion in the PGs needs therefore to be kept in the context of the difficulty of maintaining agreement in any parliamentary group.

In relation to the political distance between PGs' cultures, the case revealed that the European Parliament was far from adversarial as no clear demarcation arose between the two wings of the parliamentary arena. The leaders of the various PGs strove to cooperate and combine their forces to mould and/or back policies, ultimately succeeding in hammering out compromise positions. It was felt that political alignments were required in order to enable the House to function: "where Yugoslavia is concerned (..) Parliament must all times speak with a united voice" (Avgerinos, 16/5/1991, 268-269).

More specifically, efforts at achieving intragroup cohesion and intergroup coalition proved necessary for Parliament to improve its chances of influencing the Council and therefore contributing to foreign policy-making. Within the Socialist group there was no cohesion over the recognition of Slovenia and Croatia and over the necessity of military measures to be adopted in Yugoslavia. This lack of internal cohesion among the Socialists made them more than ever aware of the necessity of finding a compromise with other PGs (Crampton interview, 31/1/1996). The Christian Democrats retained slightly greater power than the Socialists because of their willingness to enter into coalition with almost all other groups. Naturally, the case showed a greater proliferation of coalitions between the EPP and the Socialists to which the majority of the remaining groups, the EUL, the LDR, the EDA, the ED, the Greens and the Rainbow, also participated. Although the PGs had slowly tended to coalesce over the recent years, the Socialists and the Christian Democrats remained by far the most influential groups within the EP spectrum.

And yet, as Christopher Bennett argues, although politicians may continue to "pontificate" about the values of justice, peace and democracy, their endeavours "rarely imping[e] on foreign policy where ethical considerations come a poor second to narrowly defined national interests" (Bennett, 1995, 174). Furthermore, the above study has shown that during the Yugoslav crisis group cohesion was rather high with regard to the voting outcome, however with an effective MEP presence lacking on the floor. This can be seen as a measure of the disenchantment of members with the institution they represented.

Conclusion

This concluding chapter aims to draw together the various strands of the previous discussion by briefly reviewing the Gulf and Yugoslav crises, the stances of the European Community and the European Parliament, summarizing and comparing the results attained in the intra- and intergroup analysis on both events and evaluating the competence of the European Parliament in foreign affairs. In the light of the above, the central hypotheses about the emergence of a supranational Parliament and cohesive and transnational political groups at European level are assessed. Finally, future developments are briefly addressed.

1.   The Gulf and the Yugoslav Crises

Parallels can be drawn between the Gulf and the Yugoslav cases: subsequent to the invasion of Kuwait, the international community led by the United States launched a campaign depicting Iraq as an 'outlaw' state and demonizing its leader Saddam Hussein as a cruel dictator who had proved himself capable of using biological and chemical weapons during the war with Iran and against the Kurds. He was also deemed responsible for violations of human rights against his own people. A similar campaign, albeit on a smaller scale, was launched against Serbia's President Slobodan Milošević for pursuing an expansionistic policy aimed at creating a Greater Serbia, for his repressive policy aimed at destroying Albanian identity and culture in Kosovo, and for his aggression against Slovenia and Croatia which led, in the second case, to bloodshed.

In the Gulf crisis, Saddam had violated the territory of one pro-Western oil producing Arab country, and had his army lined up along the border of another, Saudi Arabia. The potential effect on the world economy and the power base within the Middle East was a threat that had to be checked promptly and efficiently, at least in the eyes of the West, so as not to destabilize the international order. Tanks bearing the Iraqi colours made an easily recognizable enemy and public opinion generally confirmed this. In the Yugoslav case, where world economic interests were not at stake,

242

where neighbour turned against neighbour and where human rights violations were taking place within what initially seemed to be a delicate domestic crisis, it was far more difficult to distinguish the good from the bad and to pinpoint a discernible enemy The situation was far more confusing, both practically and morally and there was less to be gained from 'getting involved', ultimately causing it to drag on.

Furthermore, it is interesting to note that while Saddam and Milošević were considered responsible for the Gulf and Yugoslav crises respectively and for crimes against humanity, as a result of the atrocities they had perpetrated, neither of them was apprehended and put on trial. Indeed, they even persevered in their discriminatory and violent policies: the Kurdish and Albanian dramas continue to resurface to public attention, making the headlines, and still await a definite solution. Finally, the increasing international dimension of public opinion highlighted the need to render foreign policy more democratic and more transparent.

2. The Response of the European Community to the Gulf and Yugoslav Crises

The Gulf and the Yugoslav crises have shown the failure of the European Community to act as a real international player, revealing the difficulty of overcoming national divisions and undertaking common actions. Overall, the nation states remained the principal international actors, just as the realist tradition would predict.

The Twelve meeting within the framework of European Political Cooperation showed their inability to reconcile their different interests and objectives and to formulate a common policy. The consensus requirement inevitably hampered a swift and smooth decisional process. Both cases clearly evidenced the shortcomings of the intergovernmental structure of EPC, highlighting the need for a European foreign policy *latu sensu*, which would incorporate both economic and political aspects, and the need to set up a military structure which would enable the European Community (now the European Union) to participate actively and efficiently in the management of international crises. And yet, the Community was able to mobilize resources in trade and aid, as well as to impose sanctions, showing that when given the will, it could find the means to act promptly and efficiently. The multiplicity of actors and the variety of the role played in the various economic, diplomatic and military *fora* made it difficult to discern the identity of the interlocutor, raising once more Henry Kissinger's question: "When I want to speak to Europe, who do I phone?"

In the crucible of the Gulf and Yugoslav Wars, the issue of the definition of a common foreign policy became acute. The two examples pointed to the need for reform in order to provide the Community with the instruments to face its international responsibilities and to act not only as an economic, but also as a political power. Undoubtedly, the crises acted as catalyst for the adoption of the Second Pillar of the Maastricht Treaty, which for the first time encompassed foreign policy and defence. Both the Gulf and Yugoslav crises served the purpose of contributing to cast doubts on "whether collective action [by the EC member states] can be sustained over time without a further leap into federalist obligations and structures" (Hill, 1994, 123).

The European Union seems increasingly aware that it has to view its international responsibility as a combination of self-interest and moral imperative. Christopher Hill has detected six principal ways that involvement in international politics could be expanded: first, as a "replacement for the USSR in the global balance of power"; second, as a "regional pacifier" and therefore a magnet and model for Central and Eastern European countries; third, as a "global intervenor" in international crises; fourth, as "mediator of conflict"; fifth, as "bridge between rich and poor" and sixth, as "joint supervisor of the world economy" (Hill, 1994, 110-112). To these another element can be added, namely the EU as a champion of human rights and democracy, a role fervently emphasized and often taken by the European Parliament. Whether the European Union will be able to fulfil these tasks remains a key question for the future.

3. The Response of the European Parliament to the Gulf and Yugoslav Crises

It is interesting to look at the similarities and differences of the parliamentary attitudes towards the Gulf and Yugoslav crises bearing in mind the difficulty of this exercise due to the multiplicity of the factors involved and the different nature of the cases. The EP response to the Gulf case was slow to arrive, partly because the House did not convene until September 1990. Conversely, in the Yugoslav case, Parliament attempted to act as an opinion former by bringing the successive events unfolding in the SFRY to the attention of the other EC institutions and the world before the

Slovenian and Croatian declarations of independence and the outbreak of the hostilities. In both cases, the EP issued general declarations. It unanimously condemned the Iraqi occupation of Kuwait which was regarded as an act of aggression and of violation of international law. The dissolution of Kuwait as an independent state and its incorporation in Iraq as its nineteenth province was never taken into consideration as an acceptable solution since it resulted from a unilateral decision of Iraq's government which was not supported by the Kuwaiti population. By contrast, in the Yugoslav case, the European Parliament discussed at length the demise of the SFRY and the question of recognition of the secessionist republics, since these decisions had been taken with wide support of the governments and parliaments of Slovenia and Croatia as well as their people. The dispatch of the Yugoslav army to Slovenia and Croatia was at first seen as a legitimate act to re-establish order on the command of the federal authorities, but when it became apparent that behind this operation were hidden Serbian expansionistic ambitions, the EP strongly called for the JNA's withdrawal and advocated the recognition of these republics.

The European Parliament's stance on both cases was vague and ambiguous, as it resulted from a precarious equilibrium between forces pulling in different directions, showing that its policies were based on the art of compromise and resulting from a process of accommodation among different groups. The European Parliament was a vociferous participant in lobbying with respect to both cases and was itself subject to lobbying by the various parties, but it did not succeed in raising its international stature.

In both cases, the EP appeared to be united in its defence for human and minority rights, the granting of aid to refugees and compensation to countries hit most severely by the crises. Diplomacy and the application of sanctions were also unanimously advocated. Support was shown for the positions of the Council and Commission, while the House was reluctantly and belatedly acquiescent in the Community's decision to endorse military intervention in the Gulf, albeit with strong opposition from the left. In the Yugoslav case, the EP called for the sending of observers and of peacekeeping forces. In July 1992, it urged the deployment of UN naval forces to halt the bombing in the Adriatic coast without however envisaging full military intervention in the region. By way of summary, it can be argued that the EP did not succeed in expressing a firm and unanimous position on the above international events.

The voting records on the Gulf and Yugoslav crises displayed a frequently recurring convergence between the Christian Democrats and the

British conservatives, which led to the affiliation of the ED group to the EPP group in May 1992. On the other side of the Chamber, the Socialist and EUL groups revealed a similar political approach, confirmed by a high VSP, which, it can be argued with hindsight, seemed to prelude the eventual joining of the EUL into the Socialist Group in January 1993.

4. The Political Groups' Positions vis-à-vis the Gulf and Yugoslav Crises

The following section summarizes and compares the specific results of RCV analysis undertaken on the Gulf and Yugoslav cases with respect to their levels of absenteeism, their indices of agreements and transnationality as well as their levels of voting similarities. Since these findings relate to two cases and to a limited number of roll-call votes, they do not pretend to offer a fully comprehensive assessment, but provide a snapshot of the overall state of cohesion of the PGs. In addition, it must be borne in mind that the use of percentages, which is inevitable for this kind of survey, has a disproportionate effect on the various groups, depending on their size. For instance, in a group of 10, only a few members are sufficient to alter drastically the total levels of absenteeism, cohesion and similarity since each MEP has a magnitude of 10 percent. Conversely, in a large group, say of 100 MEPs, the magnitude of the impact of one member is much smaller, equivalent to only 1 percent.

4.1 Political Groups' Levels of Absenteeism

The Socialist group registered a much higher level of absenteeism in the Yugoslav case than in the Gulf case, going from 33.17 to 62 percent. An even higher level prevailed within the EPP, from 39.69 in the Gulf case to 71.24 percent in the Yugoslav case. The most striking increase in the level of absenteeism was registered by the ED Group which went from 29.41 in the Gulf crisis to the significantly higher percentage of 69.33 in the Yugoslav crisis. In both cases the EDA Group registered the highest level of absenteeism among all PGs, reaching 62.36 and 81.54 percent in the Gulf and Yugoslav cases respectively. This record of absenteeism was beaten only by the independent members who reached 69.11 in the Gulf case and 88.33 percent in the Yugoslav case.

246

A general negative trend can be observed in the levels of absenteeism of the political groups which almost doubled during the RCVs on Yugoslavia. Indeed, without considering the Independent groups, the highest rates of absenteeism, 62.36 and 57.57 reached by the EDA and the LU in the Gulf case corresponded almost to the lowest rates of absenteeism, 57.47 and 62.00 reached by the Greens and the Socialists respectively in the Yugoslav case.

Deserting the House could be seen as a strategy for the MEPs to elude the embarrassment of having to disclose dissent with their respective group and to avoid the dilemma between political conscience, acquiescence to the national party and group loyalty. However, the difficulty which arises from any evaluation of the level of absenteeism is that such a consideration is highly speculative, since unless explicitly stated by MEPs, there is no evidence to prove a direct correlation between absenteeism and opposition to the group line. The Yugoslav crisis, even more than the Gulf crisis, exposed a higher level of MEP absenteeism. This result may suggest that the latter, was more important for the EP with a higher rate of attendance while the Yugoslav case was more peripheral, with a lower attendance.

It must be remembered, however, that absenteeism is not confined uniquely to the two foreign policy cases, where it can be argued the EP did not possess decisional powers. It represents, instead, a common negative approach and self-destructive *modus vivendi* of Europarliamentarians. MEPs' negligence in carrying out the duties inherent to their office offends their electorate and does little to foster belief in the House as a proper institution. Absenteeism represents a lack of conformity with disciplinary measures and lack of respect by MEPs for their group and for the parliamentary institution they represent. And yet, some attenuating elements need to be considered. The problem of poor turnout in the Chamber may be linked to the geographical dispersion of the EP's working place and the frequency of the travel required to and from MEPs' constituencies. In addition, on many occasions, MEPs were not present at the plenary sessions because they were attending political group and committee meetings.

Absenteeism may also result from a pragmatic approach, for instance, where agreement had already been reached on a certain policy among the various groups, such that there was no need for all members to attend the voting session in order to ensure its adoption. This is especially true in the case of the two largest groups. Conversely, the members of smaller groups may sometimes be discouraged from participating, since even if all group members were to turn up and vote *en bloc*, their effort would make no difference to the overall parliamentary outcome. The so-called 'effect of hopelessness' pervaded the European Parliament and frustration prevailed among the members, who grew disenchanted by their inability to influence EC/EU foreign policy-making.[90] In addition, as Martin Westlake argues, absenteeism is partly connected to the phenomenon of 'loss leaders' on group electoral lists. These represent famous national politicians who lead their parties' lists, knowing that they will not participate in the EP's life (Westlake, 1994a, 207).

Anecdotes flourish within the House on diligent MEPs who end up at the bottom of their parties' lists or are even excluded as they neglected national party headquarters, whilst negligent MEPs who privilege their domestic party contacts, have better chances of re-election (Westlake, 1994a, Note 3, 213). Poor attendance can also be considered a measure of how little confidence members place in the institution in that it represents a reflection of people's lack of understanding and appreciation of MEPs' actual functions. Lastly, besides the fact that this phenomenon is particularly detrimental for the European Parliament's image and working, it also produces a distorting effect on measurement of both the indices of agreement, transnationality and intergroup similarities. It would be interesting to see whether a more active whipping system would decrease the level of absenteeism within the groups. However, this is a speculative issue with no basis for substantiation.

4.2 Political Groups' Indices of Agreement

The statistical data calculated on 50 and 20 RCVs respectively demonstrate that the Socialist group was far more in agreement over the Yugoslav crisis than the Gulf crisis, since it reached the index of agreement of 87.91 in the former and 73.28 in the latter. The opposite can be said for the EPP, which attained the index of agreement of 91.15 in the Gulf case, and registered the slightly lower figure of 85.62 in the Yugoslav case. Similar to the Socialists, the Liberals saw an improvement in their degree of cohesion with regard to the Yugoslav case, with its IA rising by 6.77 points from

---

90 This expression was originally used by Petr Kopecký (1996, 10) with regard to the first Czech Parliament.

79.05 to 85.82. In both cases, the ED exhibited a very high level of cohesion, albeit with an almost imperceptible decrease from 94.83 to 94.25. The Greens, who were particularly active in the Yugoslav case, also saw an increase in their index of agreement of 7.86 points from 76.96 to 84.82 percent. The EDA's level of cohesion improved by 12.36 points from 72.64 in the Gulf case to 85 in the Yugoslav case. The EUL reasserted its traditional solidarity by recording a minimal rise in its IA, from 91.10 to 91.78, respectively in the Gulf and Yugoslav cases.

The ER boasted the optimal index of agreement of 100 percent in the Yugoslav case, substantially improving from the previous IA of 82.93 registered in the Gulf. The Rainbow Group also signalled a growth of 11.48, from 63.47 in the Gulf case to 74.95 in the Yugoslav Case. By contrast, the LU did not follow this positive trend, marking a 10.28 fall in its IA between 92.28 in the Gulf and 82 percent in the Yugoslav cases. In brief, the political groups in the European Parliament generally succeeded in reaching a comfortable majority internally with respect to the cases in question.

Overall, the PGs from the most centralized, including the EPP, ED and the Communist groups, where the option exists for the leaders to resort to disciplinary measures in order to ensure cohesion, to the more liberal, including the LDR, EDA, Greens and Rainbow groups, where power remains diffuse, all registered fairly high indices of agreement. As such, the cases did not confirm the hypothesis that a strong whipping system is necessarily required to achieve a high level of cohesion.

4.3 Political Groups' Indices of Transnationality

A comparison of the indices of transnationality in PG voting behaviour on the Gulf and Yugoslav cases reveals that the highest ITv was registered by the EPP in both cases, while the second highest index was claimed by the Socialists and the Liberals in the Gulf and Yugoslav crises, respectively. The ER saw a negligible decline in its ITv, from 0.454 in the Gulf case to 0.438 in the Yugoslav case. As a reflection of its almost mononational composition, the ED registered in both cases the lowest index of transnationality, rising slightly from 0.070 to 0.074. It was followed in the Gulf case by the EDA with an IT of 0.293 case and in the Yugoslav case by the LU with an IT of 0.203. Overall, seven of the EP political groups

249

registered lower levels of transnationality in the Yugoslav than in the Gulf cases with the exception of the LDR, ED and EUL.

The ED and EUL examples suggest that the lower the indices of transnationality with respect to group composition (ITc), the higher the levels of congruity within the groups. However, the EPP demonstrated that even a big and multinational group can reach a high level of internal cohesion. In summary, cleavages within the EP did not often appear along national, but rather along group affiliation or ideological lines. Similarly, within the groups, divisions did not often occur along national lines. There is no clear evidence that a correlation exists between group heterogeneity and cohesion. The capability of aggregating interests within political groups is not in any way proportional to the number of nationalities within the groups. Therefore, the two cases revealed that heterogeneity does not represent an obstacle to group cohesion.

Overall, the Yugoslav case displayed a lower level of transnationality with respect to voting. However, with the exception of most Greek MEPs over the Macedonia question and, to a lesser degree, the majority of the German MEPs over the recognition of Slovenia and Croatia, the views and voting patterns of Europarliamentarians did not reflect purely national priorities and concerns. When looking at the difference between the ITv-s for the cases, only two groups in particular stood out. These were the LU group where the ITv fell from 0.515 to 0.203 and the Rainbow Group where it also fell, albeit to a lesser degree, from 0.669 to 0.554.

4.4 MEP National Allegiance versus Political Group Loyalty

A glance at the European Parliament shows that the level of cohesion within the various PGs was much higher than the level of cohesion amongst the various nationalities in the Chamber as a whole, for both the Gulf and Yugoslav cases. As such, it can be argued that the variable of 'nationality' had less of an impact than the allegiance to the respective PGs. However, an exception can be found in the Rainbow group, which never asserted for itself a clear ideological line nor aimed at being elevated to the rank of a truly European political group, and was formed only for technical reasons.

The MEPs from Luxembourg and Spain registered a high level of cohesion. However, in the first case, this outcome is not surprising due to the small number of Luxembourg's members. In the second case, the high level of agreement amongst Spanish MEPs may lead to a deceptive interpretation that group allegiance was of less concern than national imperatives. Indeed, a closer inspection of RCVs for the Socialist, EPP, LDR, EUL and Rainbow groups for both the Gulf and Yugoslav cases reveals that the loyalty of Spanish MEPs to their group was higher than their national allegiance. It may be therefore concluded that the high index of agreement amongst the Spanish MEPs was rather coincidental. Furthermore, as a delegation, they averaged higher figures than their respective groups as a whole and generally helped to keep cohesion high.

Another example which deserves mention is that of the Greek members who appeared more cohesive in the Yugoslav than in the Gulf case. This increased level of solidarity was mostly due to the commonly perceived danger to Greece's territorial sovereignty which stemmed from an alleged expansionistic policy of the neighbouring Republic of Macedonia. However, just in a few RCVs Greek MEPs disregarded their respective group standpoint, bound together in their national solidarity. Indeed, on the majority of the 20 RCVs, Greek Socialist, EPP and LU members still supported the official line of their groups.

With regard to the issue of military intervention in the Gulf, British Socialist MEPs found themselves in a quandary, torn between their loyalty to national party and to political group. And yet, contrary to the spontaneous tendency of 'going native', MEPs increasingly adopted 'Europeanist' views in parliamentary debate, to the embarrassment of their own national government (Tranholm-Mikkelsen, 1991, 14). The British delegation registered an increase in its level of cohesion in the Yugoslav case, yet this outcome was due to the extremely high level of absenteeism.

In both cases, the assumption that MEPs are naturally inclined to conform to national policies and follow the guidelines dictated by their national party headquarters did not prove to be accurate. The findings prove that only on rare occasions, MEPs distanced themselves from the rest of their group on the basis of national 'egoism' or concern. Overall, political groups succeeded in reaching a level of cohesion by surmounting those obstacles set by distinct national traditions, when only a few years ago this claim would have been considered utopian. In John Fitzmaurice's words, "[this conclusion] is what one would expect if the political groups are to acquire any significance" (Fitzmaurice, 1975, 170).

4.5 Political Groups' Voting Similarities

The RCV analysis on the Gulf and Yugoslav cases revealed a high level of voting similarity between the various groups to the extent that left-right divisions did not seem very pronounced in the European Parliament. The overall trend of all political groups' voting similarity was higher in the latter case than in the former, except for the ER and Rainbow Groups. The Left Unity and the European Right registered the lowest voting similarity in the Gulf and the Yugoslav cases, respectively. Surprisingly, the ER highest voting similarity percentage in the Gulf Case was found with Rainbow, followed by the Independent members and the Greens. This similarity between extreme left- and right-wingers, ideologically hard to reconcile, can however be explained in the light of the role of opposition that both the ER and the Rainbow groups, and to a lesser extent the Greens, often sought to take on within the European Parliament. However, while the ER was ostracized from coalition-building, the other two groups acted as a counterbalance within the coalition by putting forward constructive criticisms and securing, on some occasions, the adoption of amendments to the texts of joint resolutions.

5. Intergroup Cooperation within the European Parliament

By looking at the European Parliament's attitude towards the Gulf and Yugoslav crises, this study reveals an increasing trend in terms of parliamentary cohesion, and therefore of institutional efficiency and stability, with an overall index of agreement of 47.33 in the first case and of 63.12 in the second. Overall, the voting surveys indicate in both cases that the European Parliament was far from adversarial and that it required cooperation among its political groups, given that none of them enjoyed a majority in the House. The RCVs did not display a clear demarcation between the two wings of the parliamentary arena. By contrast, a careful reading of the parliamentary debates makes it clear that no consensus was reached between the various groups. On one side, the extreme left (LU, EUL) voted with the Greens and Rainbow groups against military intervention in the Gulf and Yugoslavia. On the other side, the centre-right (EPP, ED, EDA) supported the resort to armed force and, in the middle, the Socialists were split between the two camps. Unexpectedly, the ER, led by the French leader Le Pen, traditionally inclined to a pro-military position, took instead an anti-interventionist policy in the Gulf case. The inconsistency between the results that emerged in the quantitative analysis of RCVs and those that emerged in the qualitative analysis of parliamentary debates and resolutions may be ascribed to several factors. The first is due to the extraordinary level of absenteeism at the RCV sessions which meant that members often declined the opportunity to support, reject or abstain from voting and there is no certain way to establish how the absent members would have voted had they turned up. The second is that only a small proportion of resolutions was actually subject to RCVs, especially in the Yugoslav case, and often RCVs were carried out not only for whole resolutions, but also for amendments of individual recitals, paragraphs or sentences of resolutions. Finally, the possibility cannot be excluded that MEPs might have changed their minds over a certain policy in the light of new elements that emerged during the debate, or might have agreed to support its adoption following considerable modifications to the text.

Both analyses reveal that long debating and voting sessions were necessary between the various groups in order to enable Parliament to adopt resolutions. As expected, the two largest groups, the Socialists and the Christian Democrats, remained the most influential in terms of forging the official EP policies on the two crises. However, whilst in the Gulf case, the Socialists seemed to dominate parliamentary debate, in the Yugoslav case, the pendulum appeared to swing slightly in favour of the Christian Democrats. The traditional gap which separates the parties on the left from those on the centre-right was narrowed. This blurring of group differences can be seen in the gradual broadening of the range of coalition alternatives or as a consolidation of the *oligopoly* of the two main blocs: the Socialists and Christian Democrats. The groups tended to support those texts tabled by themselves in conjunction with others and to oppose those motions which were not drafted by themselves. And yet, the European Parliament's policy with respect to both crises resulted from a strategy of interbloc compromise and alliances between most political groups which participated in the tabling of texts of joint motions for resolutions. Overall, the PGs did not appear ideologically streamlined, but showed a certain propensity to cooperate and to settle on a common, although often general position. They contributed with roughly proportional degrees of influence, to the drafting of joint motions for resolutions and thus the definition of the EP policies on both cases.

A 'splendid isolation' on purist ideological positions seemed out of the question even in the case of the ER which did not deliberately choose to alienate itself, but rather seemed to be ostracized by the rest of the PGs. This search for a compromise appeared as a sign of political maturity and responsibility on the part of the PGs.

However, it is arguable whether the political groups effectively reached a common outlook or if they camouflaged their opinions behind vague expressions. The texts often contained rather general and rhetorical statements based on compassionate feelings, in line with both Christian Democrat and Socialist beliefs. Furthermore, it can be claimed that since no immediate political effect stems from EP declarations and resolutions, the members felt more available and more naturally inclined to accommodate others' partisan and territorial concerns. In addition, it must be borne in mind that, on some occasions, the PGs formulated general texts, whilst having different objectives and different policy interpretations. Indeed, most PGs tended to search for wide agreement, aware that texts drafted by them individually, although more ideologically coherent, would not get through the House and thus cause a lapse in the ability of the EP to impress its views on the Council.

Yet, as the findings indicate, divergences of opinions emerged within the House, highlighting a variety of attitudes amongst the various PGs as well as less accentuated internal deviations within individual political groups. Whilst the latter succeeded in mobilizing their respective members into a reasonably united front, the EP did not reach an overwhelming consensus and failed to present itself as a strong, even a discernible political entity. This lack of intra-institutional cohesiveness may be seen as a reflection of the emergence of transnational political groups and may result from a process of politicization and party development at European level. The findings suggest that, only after a long and excruciating process, broad policies were forged between the various political views represented in the parliamentary spectrum. The following conclusion by Martin Westlake did not prove to be fully valid in either the Gulf or Yugoslav cases.

> The European Parliament has a potential vested interest in intra-institutional solidarity in a way that occurs only occasionally in other parliaments, generally when their powers are perceived to be under threat (Westlake, 1994a, 8).

Fulvio Attinà's assumption that the EP is inclined to agree on foreign issues since its declarations do not entail immediate and direct domestic consequences could not be proved. This was mainly due to the fact that in both cases vital interests were at stake and crucial decisions were to be debated in the Chamber, especially over military involvement. In fact, Luciano Bardi's observation that parliamentary consensus decreases when defence implications arise was accurate.

Despite a margin of improvement in the Yugoslav case, both crises confirmed that Parliament is neither a monolithic bloc nor "a unity obtained by a single, united thrust", but an institution resulting from a variety of forces (Rose, 1946, 46 cited in Bale, 1996, 1).[91]

The research has revealed the eagerness of the PGs to express their own distinctive views, thus satisfying the need for democracy and pluralism. The image of political groups as "molecules of the parliament", where "atoms are [identified with] individual members", accurately reflects the polychromatic configuration of the EP spectrum (Hagevi, 1996, 1). A corollary to this is the question of whether Parliament can tolerate the discrepancies arising from the aggregation of such multifarious views which undermine its credibility as an institution and still be able to claim more powers.

It is maintained that if the EP intends to gain more influence in the development of foreign policy and play a propelling role in this sector, it should become more cohesive rather than engage itself in a hopeless ideological struggle between its groups. Speaking with one voice seems the only strategy for the European Parliament to become a strong institution capable of upstaging the Council over decisions on foreign affairs, whilst fulfilling the ambition to raise its international profile. As John Fitzmaurice claims, "disunity makes the opinions of the parliament easier to ignore" (Fitzmaurice, 1975, 163). The "lure of power politics" (Johansson, 1997, 215) demands that institutional imperatives prevail, meaning that political groups have to de-emphasize their differences and follow the ebbs and the flows of the parliamentary mainstream.

The ancient Greek axiom envisaging politics as "the art of the attainable and compromise" still proves to be cogent and remains valid within the macrocosm of contemporary politics as well as with regard to the microcosm of the European Parliament. Yet, this quest for unity and efficiency could undermine the principle of democracy which certainly constitutes the foundations of any parliamentary construction and could

---

91   Richard Rose's reflection was originally addressed to British political parties.

deprive the EP of its essence as a forum for discussion where all distinct views and opposing interests are represented.

In summary, it may be argued that the controversies arising from the 'efficiency-versus-democracy' debate have not found an easy and smooth solution. Nevertheless, it may be comforting to think that any adverse effects which may arise from the prevalence of one factor over the other will be only transitory until such a time as when the EP establishes its full authority and a perfect balance is finally reached between these two exigencies.

6. The European Parliament and Foreign Affairs

Despite the progress achieved with the institutional reforms introduced by the 1986 Single European Act, the 1992 Treaty on European Union and the 1997 Treaty of Amsterdam, the EP's catalogue of powers remains limited in the field of foreign affairs. It consists of the right of assent on most international treaties, including accession and association agreements, as well as the right of consultation "on the main aspects and basic choices of the common foreign and security policy" (Article J.7 TEU). Its competence extends to a veto power over the ratification of the treaties and to consultation on CFSP issues, if it is agreed that they fall within the definition of the article, which is rather loose and therefore subject to interpretation. Finally, the EP has no supervisory role over the Council of Ministers and the European Council, the main institutions which deal with foreign policy issues.

In light of this, many MEPs have become gradually disenchanted at their own vain efforts to influence change. A sense of incompleteness, unevenness and disappointment pervades the European Parliament with regard to the progress towards further integration and the realization of a European foreign policy. To the great frustration of many of its members, the EP is not yet in a position to act as an effective international player.

On a brighter note, it must be said that despite its limitations, the EP is considered by third countries' statesmen and politicians as an institution that should be addressed. Over the years, it has increasingly become a target for a wider number of lobbyists, suggesting that its international profile is likely to rise in the future.

There is no reason to be too pessimistic with regard to possible reforms. The history of the European Parliament has shown that this institution over the years has been very successful in fighting for more influence in the decisionmaking process. A silent revolution - and regional integration is nothing else - needs time (Schmuck, 1991, 43).

The cases brought to light once more the peripheral nature of parliamentary involvement in foreign policy and the need for more powers in this area. A premise to this book is that the EP's role in foreign affairs cannot be dismissed as irrelevant, since it is representative of public opinion. However, only by accruing its power will the EP be able to gain in international status and become the preferred platform for debate and deliberation. This will certainly capture the interest of its own members, resulting in a higher turnout at EP sessions and a closer involvement and participation in parliamentary and group activities. Recognized in their role of active politicians who can make a real impact on the international agenda, MEPs will feel the necessity to prove themselves in the eyes of their electorate beyond the obvious declamatory calls for peace, freedom and democracy.

The EP's grand design to foster a federal Europe with an autonomous European foreign policy is slowly, but steadily taking shape. With the increasing public interest in foreign policy, the European Parliament seems sure to be central to any development that might occur in this direction. According to Juliet Lodge, one way forward would be for the European Parliament and the political groups to develop a 'foreign policy memory' so that changes in the European Parliament's composition after each election would not result "in contradictory policy statements or partial institutional amnesia" (Lodge, 1988, 132).

7. Towards a Supranational European Parliament and European Political Parties?

Since its inception and particularly after gaining full legitimacy from its direct election in 1979, the European Parliament has claimed to be a promoter of European integration. Despite this, Parliament reveals some inherent contradictions which prevent it from effectively proceeding along the path of Europeanization.

257

The first relates to the adoption of different electoral systems in each member state. The lack of uniform criteria to determine eligibility for voting means that member states still take decisions individually as whether to allow Community citizens to vote in their country or to restrict this to their own nationals. Another contradiction inherent to the European Parliament is the recourse to national quotas which represents, as Martin Holland points out, "an anathema to the notion of a supranational election". By accepting these national boundaries, the perception is reinforced that EP elections represent more a kind of national election than a supranational one (Holland, 1993, 145-146). Paradoxically, MEPs' legitimacy is not EU-wide, but geographically tied to the individual member states (Abélès, 1992, 184). A truly federal integrated Europe has to adopt an electoral system that reflects the characteristics of the European electorate, reinforces the links between citizens and their representatives and revive the concept of European identity against the prevailing intergovernmental approach reinforced through the adoption of national quotas (Holland, 1993, 102).

The establishment of a list of candidates to the Euro-elections according to nationality is incompatible with the supranational objective and federal orientation of the European Parliament. When a common electoral system is adopted the necessity for fixing national quotas will disappear and group lists will then become effectively supranational. Only recently did British Prime Minister Tony Blair agree to introduce a proportional system in Euro-elections. The adoption of a uniform procedure, which was unimaginable just a few years ago, is likely to become a reality at the next EP elections. This could be a first step towards making these groups less dependent on and less vulnerable to their respective national parties. It also could ease the development of genuine European parties which will draw up their own lists of candidates as well as the switching of MEPs' allegiances from national parties to political groups. As Maurizio Cotta argues:

> ..if one looks at the history of parliamentary institutions their powers weren't given free, they have been slowly conquered by new political [é]lites that could oppose a stronger legitimation to the old élites. This suggests that the empirical test of institutional build up at the supranational level will be the formation of a European political [é]lite (Cotta, 1984, 124, cited in Westlake, 1994a, 7).

Both cases illustrate that forging transnational parliamentary groups remains an outstanding and ambitious experiment which has not yet fully succeeded. It is daring to assert that a new European political élite in the making has emerged in the EP. In Fulvio Attinà's words:

> [t]he EP political groups still have not gone beyond the organizational threshold of decisional centralization on how to amalgamate [the] demands and expectations of the interests they represent into coherent supranational programmes (Attinà, 1990, 576).

Nevertheless, they have embarked on a transnationalization process on the way to becoming real European parties. The PGs enrich political dialogue and serve as catalysts for integration. According to Sicco Mansholt, former President of the Commission, "[i]f there is a hope for Europe, it is from them that it will come" (Mansholt, 1974, cited in Barón Crespo, 1989, 39). This view is fully shared by Cotta who concludes by warning that:

> ..unless an institutional embryo of a European system develops, all the opportunities that might materialise...will not be exploited in the direction of further supranational integration but may even produce a setback in the process and promote a renationalisation (Cotta, 1984, 123, cited in Westlake, 1994a, 9).

In future, they may well work at cross-purposes with governmental leaders in their home countries or when dealing with the Council, which possesses the formal authority to issue foreign policy decisions. The destiny of political groups is inextricably linked to the future of the European Parliament, subject to the development of the powers of the institution itself. Indeed, increasing the functions of the PGs within the EP will serve no purpose whilst the EP remains a secondary institution. Only by giving full consideration to the European Parliament as a whole will the nature and extent of the influence of its constituent political groups and their role in policy-making become more meaningful.

The EP provides a laboratory where, following a process of political alchemy, interactions take place between actors of various national origins and political traditions with the aim of overcoming partisan and individualistic impulses and transcending national boundaries. The ultimate test to prove that a truly supranational parliamentary institution and genuine federal parties have emerged is to assess whether in cases of conflict between the European and national views, the former effectively prevails.

On the basis of the findings that emerged in the quantitative and qualitative analysis on the two cases, this book claims that although the process of elimination of the old nationalistic barriers is still far from being completed, some embryonic supranational elements can be detected within the European Parliament. Indeed, a slow but steady process has started within the European Parliament whereby perceived national interests and identities expressed by the various MEPs are gradually overcome within the political groups, which seem on the way to becoming effective and cohesive parties at European level

Finally, the research argues that it is possible to pursue a holistic approach and forge joint policies and supranational solutions within the parliamentary laboratory even on questions of international politics. The inquiry seems to suggest a certain degree of optimism. Undeniably, on the parliamentary front at the level of political groups, a Europeanization process seems to have started, confirming Graham T Allison's observation that "[w]here you stand depends on where you sit" (Allison, 1971, 176).

This book concludes that it is becoming obsolete to think about these groups as pursuing essentially national interests, and to deny that a process of erosion of national boundaries is under way. Despite their flaws, political groups play a decisive role in the dynamics of the European Parliament and have a great potential with regard to the definition of European politics. The PGs are becoming more cohesive and transnational while the intensity and frequency of contact between MEPs is increasing and their prospects of turning into genuinely integrated "parties at the European level" is growing. It is undeniable that a kernel of transnationality runs through the political groups and is spreading within the EP.

While many, and especially the realists, will disagree with this interpretation, it is only through continuing debate and analysis of this kind that it will be possible to unravel whether a real phenomenon of Europeanization will affirm itself within the political groups and the European Parliament.

8. Future Developments

The 1992 Maastricht Treaty failed to lay the foundations for a fully-fledged European foreign policy, exposing member states' hesitation or even reluctance to accept further political unification. Subsequently, the most recent Intergovernmental Conference, culminating in the signing of the 1997 Amsterdam Treaty, did not solve the conundrum relating to the inability of the Union to play a significant role on the international stage, due to its well-known institutional deficiencies, on the one hand, and the unwillingness of the member states to relinquish some of their traditional sovereignty prerogatives, on the other. In this context, the basic question concerning the identity and purpose of the Union will have to be addressed. Only by solving these fundamental issues, will the European Union be able to confront the internal and external challenges looming on the political and economic horizon. As Susan Strange aptly suggests, the paradox of power seeking domestic politicians voluntarily pooling aspects of national sovereignty within the European Union (Strange, 1994, 11) requires the supervision of the European Parliament, which professes to have a supranational and European vocation. It is very difficult to eliminate raw national interests to create *ex novo* European interests and it will take time to overcome the most difficult obstacle to the establishment of a supranational European Union, namely the psychological dimension of nationalism.

> The unification of Europe, like all peaceful revolutions, takes time - time to persuade people, time to change men's minds, time to adjust to the need for major transformations (Monnet, 1978, 432).

As Fred Halliday comments:

> There is no doubt that any (..) evolution will involve uncertainties and disappointments: a world in which the state is no longer conveniently taken to represent the totality, and in which 'nation-state', 'sovereignty' and 'national interest' are no longer secure landmarks, will be harder to chart (Halliday, 1994, 93).

On the eve of the twenty-first century, the ideal of forging a European identity seems to have found resolute supporters as well as fierce adversaries in the various member states. And yet, only by cultivating the concept of European identity, will a revival of nationalism within the territory of the Union be deterred. Furthermore, through the definition of a common European foreign policy, the European Union will be able respond effectively and coherently to external challenges. The evolution of transnational political groups will help the fostering of the European unification process, the European Parliament being the ideal political forum where all distinct views can be expressed, debated and acted upon.

Epilogue

Suggestions for Further Research

Some areas have been touched upon briefly in the book that could lead to further research, such as the relationships between EP political groups and national parties of the various member states. It would be interesting to look at the relationships between the European Parliament and the individual member states' parliaments and governments in order to assess the extent of their inward and outward influence as well as the leverage of the national parties on EP political groups with regard to the Gulf and Yugoslav crises. Such an investigation would provide a complementary outlook on the results achieved by this book.

Since the focus of this research has been introspective of the dynamics within the political groups and the European Parliament rather than on their impact on other EU institutions, another aspect which may warrant a more in-depth investigation is the study of the effect (if any) of the EP's policies on the decisions of the Council, in these two cases. The preceding chapters may, arguably, highlight the need to investigate in greater depth the complex and varied relationship between the EP including its political groups and foreign policy. This may be done for events that have occurred in the Gulf and the Balkans beyond the periods allotted within this book, for issues of a nature more diverse and far less dramatic than international military conflicts, and with respect to the political evolution of the European Union since 1992.

In addition, this book does not assess whether and to what extent PGs are actively pursuing European integration *per se*. However, as the expansive integration dynamic predicts, it is undeniable that the unintended consequences of their actions may have an impact on the construction of supranational policy and the deepening of integration. As such the EP, along with its political groups, may function as a "midwife for the integration process" (Tranholm-Mikkelsen, 1991, 6).

The application of integration theory as a tool to understand the behaviour of MEPs at PG and EP level also deserves attention and may open up a whole new area of research. However, according to other

263

authors, an explanation of the reasons why MEPs gather in transnational party groups together with the structure of their interests, incentives and institutional constraints can be found in theories of comparative politics (Hix, 1994). Finally, the activities and the evolution of the political groups and the European Parliament deserve to be explored more in-depth both empirically and theoretically. It is hoped that this book has already in part redressed this omission in the academic literature and has built a platform on which further investigations can be taken forward.

Appendix

1 Formulae employed

1.1 Index of Agreement (IA)

The roll-call analysis is carried out by using the same index of agreement (IA) proposed by Fulvio Attinà and based on a variant of Stuart Rice's formula. While Rice's index gauges only positive and negative votes, displaying scores from 0 to 100, Attinà's index takes into consideration "the relation exist[ing] between the three modalities of votes - in favour, against and abstention - cast by the members of a Group; more exactly it is the percentage measure of the relations between (a) the difference between the highest numbering modality and the sum of the other two modalities in a vote by the MEPs of a Group and (b) the total number of votes cast by the Group":

$$IA = \frac{\text{highest modality - sum of the other two modalities}}{\text{total number of votes}} \times 100$$

Whilst admitting that abstention represents a neutral position, undoubtedly it increases the voting power of the opposition and, as such, may be regarded as non-compliance with the official group line. For the purpose of this inquiry, the number of abstainers, provided that they are not the majority of the group, is added to the modality that represents those members not following the official party line. Similar considerations could be extended to absentees who resort to this strategy to conceal opposition to their group's stance. However, since absences occur for a multiplicity of reasons, more evidence would be required to justify such an indictment and, therefore, absences are removed from the equation. The index is equal to 100 when all the members of a PG vote unanimously, while it is 99 and 1 when the agreement decreases but still more than half of the deputies express the same vote respectively. '0' (zero) indicates a split in half of the votes in two modalities while in three modalities one of these corresponds to the sum of the other two. The index assumes a negative value when the

265

highest voting modality is less than half of the total number of group votes, reaching -33 when the group voting is equally divided between the three options.

1.2 Voting Similarity Percentage (VSP)

The voting affinity between groups is assessed by employing Stuart Rice's 'index of voting likeness' (Rice, 1928), referred to in this book as Voting Similarity Percentage (VSP).

VSP (IVL) = 100 - (A-B) where:

A= percentage of party group A voting pro on resolution x
B= percentage of party group B voting pro on resolution x
(A-B)= absolute value of A-B

The overall VSP has been calculated by adding the VSP on individual votes on the Gulf crisis and the situation in former Yugoslavia respectively and dividing the sum by the number of votes. The VSP ranges between 0 percent which indicates the maximum disagreement and 100 percent complete identity in voting behaviour. Average VSPs are calculated by computing the sum of the VSPs on individual votes and then dividing the sum by the number of votes (Hurwitz, 1983).

266

The following table can serve as a guide to reading percentages of IA,[92] level of absenteeism and VSP:

Table 10 Key for Index of Agreement and Level of Absenteeism

90 - 100	extremely high
80 - 89.99	very high
70 - 79.99	high
60 - 69.99	fairly high
50 - 59.99	medium average (slightly above average)
40 - 49.99	medium low (slightly below average)
30 - 39.99	fairly low
20 - 29.99	low
10 - 19.99	very low
0 - 9.99	extremely low

1.3 Indices of Transnationality on PG Composition (Itc) and Voting Behaviour (ITv)

Two formulae based on Douglas Rae's index of fractionalization indices are used to compute groups' degree of transnationality on PG composition and on PG voting behaviour with regard to the Gulf and Yugoslav crises (Rae, 1967).

$$IT = 1 - (\sum_{i=1}^{n} SC_i^2)$$

As regards the degree of transnationality of PG composition, 'SC' indicates the respective share of members from the various countries within a group, whilst 'n' refers to the number of countries concerned. As regards the degree of transnationality of the PG voting behaviour, 'SC' represents the share of members who voted according to the PG official policy line (which was assumed to be the highest modality of vote for each group) and 'n' is the number of nationalities present in each political group.

---

92 For an evaluation of negative percentages with regard to IAs, see Section 1.1 above.

267

Table 11   Chairmen/Women of the Political Groups between June 1990 and June 1991

Political Group	Chairmen / women
Socialist	Jean-Pierre Cot
EPP	Egon Klepsch 1992 Léo Tindemans
LDR	Valéry Giscard d'Estaing (till November 1991) Yves Galland (from December 1991)
ED	Christopher Prout
Greens[93]	Alexander Langer Chairman, Maria Santos[94] Co-Chairwoman from 15/3/1990 to 31/10/90 Adelaide Aglietta Chairwoman Paul Lannoye Co-Chairman from 1/11/1990 to 31/5/1991 Paul Lannoye, Chairman Adelaide Aglietta, Co-Chairwoman from 1/6/1991 till 31/11/1991 Adelaide Aglietta, Chairwoman Paul Lannoye, Co-Chairman from 1/12/1992
EUL	Luigi Colajanni
EDA	Christian de la Malène
ER	Jean-Marie Le Pen
RB	Jaak Vandemeulebroucke Birgit Bjørnvig
LU	Réné-Emile Piquet

Source: Lists of Members of the European Parliament between 11 June 1990 and 11 June 1991

---

93   As Martin Westlake notes, "[The] originally patrician principle of rotating leadership [has been] adopted by the Greens and the Rainbow Group". See Westlake, 1994a, Note 3, p. 25.

94   Maria Santos joined the Socialist group on 22 July 1991.

268

Chart 29a EP Composition by Political Group: June 1991

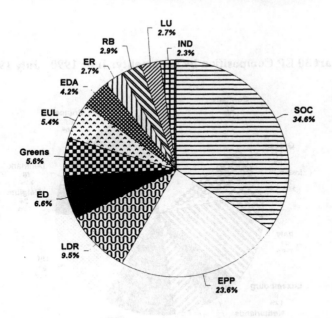

Chart 29b EP Composition by Political Group: July 1992

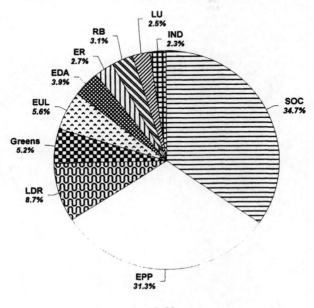

269

Chart 30 EP Composition by Nationality: June 1990 - July 1992

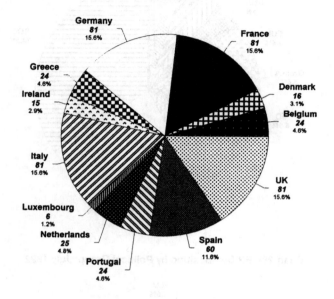

Table 12 Adopted Joint Resolutions according to PG Contribution on the Gulf Crisis

	Socialist	EPP	LDR	ED	GREEN	EUL	EDA	ER	RB	LU
Sept 1990	1 B3-1602	1 B3-1600	1 B3-1604	1 B3-1600	-	1 B3-1623	1 B3-1603	-	-	-
Oct 1990 (1b)	1 B3-1844 IPG B3-1843	1 B3-1844 IPG B3-1846	1 B3-1844	1 B3-1844	1 B3-1844	1 B3-1844	-	-	1 B3-1844	1 B3-1844
Oct 1990 (2a)	1 B3-1889	-	-	-	-	1 B3-1881	-	-	-	-
Nov 1990	2 B3-2027 B3-2023	2 B3-2017 B3-2023	1 B3-2009	-	-	1 B3-2043	1 B3-2062	-	-	1 B3-2083
Dec 1990	1 B3-2188 IPG B3-2190	-	-	-	-	1 B3-2189	-	-	-	1 B3-2232
Jan 1991	1 B3-0127	-	-	-	-	-	-	-	1 B3-0123	-
Feb 1991	2 B3-0359 & B3-0382 B3-0388	2 B3-0311 B3-0392	-	1 B3-0334	-	2 B3-0341 B3-0389	1 B3-0338	-	-	2 B3-0343 & B3-0347 B3-0387
Mar 1991	1 B3-0398	1 B3 0402	-	1 B3-0426	2 B3-0477 B3-0466	2 B3-0429 B3-0458	-	-	-	2 B3-0450 B3-0470
Apr 1991	2 B3-0552 B3-0624	2 B3-0562 B3-0618	2 B3-0619 B3-0660	1 B3-0556	2 B3-0555 B3-0560	2 B3-0564 B3-0623	1 B3-0621	-	1 B3-0622	2 B3-0565 B3-0620
May 1991	1 B3-0811	2 B3-0746 B3-0751	2 B3-0740 B3-0741 & B3-0744	-	2 B3-0777 B3-0798	1 B3-0765	-	-	-	1 B3-0755
Total	13	11	7	5	7	12	4	0	3	10

IPG= Individual Political Groups' Resolutions.

Table 13 Individual PG Non-Adopted Motions for Resolutions on the Gulf Crisis

	Socialist	EPP	LDR	ED	Green	EUL	EDA	ER	RB	LU
September 1990	-	-	-	-	F B3-1618	-	-	W B3-1601 F B3-1622	F B3-1624	F B3-1656
October 1990 (1a) Gulf/Kuwait	F B3-1770	F B3-1809	-	-	F B3-1799	F B3-1800	F B3-1829	F B3-1772	-	-
October 1990 (1b) Oil price	-	-	R B3-1845	-	-	-	R B3-1847	-	R B3 1842	-
October 1990 (2) International issues	-	-	F B3-1890	F B3-1883	-	-	-	F B3-1882	-	F B3-1894
November 1990	-	-	R B3-2060	-	F B3-2051 W B3-2067 W B3-2072	-	-	F B3-2032	-	-
December 1990	-	R B3-2185 R B3-2196	R B3-2182	R B3-2187	F B3-2184	-	F B3-2197	F B3-2186	F B3-2194	W B3-2191
January 1991	-	R B3-0109	R B3-0108	W B3-0070 R B3-0111	R B3-0116	R B3-0113	F B3-0081 R B3-0115	R B3-0119	-	R B3-0117
February 1991	-	-	F B3-0088	-	W B3-0085 R B3-0333 F B3-0391	-	-	R B3-0101	-	-
March 1991	-	-	F B3-0428	-	-	-	F B3-0448	R B3-0393	F B3-0465	-
April 1991	W B3-0558 F B3-0589	W B3-0570	-	-	F B3-0655	W B3-0561	F B3-0569	F B3-0597	-	F B3-0587 W B3-0559
May 1991	-	-	-	-	-	-	-	F B3-0804	-	-
Total	3	5	7	4	11	3	7	11	4	6

Table 14 Adopted Joint Resolutions according to PG Contribution on the Yugoslav Crisis

	Socialist	EPP	LDR	ED	Green	EUL	EDA	ER	RB	LU
February 1991	1	1 B3-0379	1 B3-0302	1	1	-	-	-	1 B3-0336	-
March 1991	1 B3-0399	1 B3-0403	1 B3-0395	1 B3-0431	1 B3-0397	1 B3-0482	1	-	-	-
April 1991	-	-	-	-	-	-	-	-	-	-
May 1991	1 B3-0822	1 B3-0745	1 B3-0779	1 B3-0786	1 B3-0826	1 B3-0806	1 B3-0794	-	1 B3-0807	-
June 1991	-	-	-	-	-	-	-	-	-	-
July 1991	1 B3-1216	1 B3-1223	1 B3-1222	1 B3-1119	1 B3-1220	1 B3-1217	-	-	-	1 B3-1218
September 1991	1 B3-1372	1 B3-1390 & B3-1325	-	-	-	1 B3-1371	1 B3-1360	-	-	-
October 1991	IPG B3-1604	-	-	-	-	-	-	-	-	-
November 1991	1 B3-1882	1 B3-1886	*	1 B3-1896	-	1 B3-1890	-	-	-	-
December 1991	-	-	-	-	-	-	-	-	-	-
Jan 1992	1 B3-0037	1 B3-0047	1 B3-0045	1 B3-0049	1 B3-0042	1 B3-0037	1 B3-0040	-	1 B3-0038	-
Feb 1992	-	-	-	-	-	-	-	-	-	-
March 1992	1 B3-0407	1 B3-0405	1 B3-0410	-	1 B3-0413	1 B3-04092	1 B3-0408	-	1 B3-0406	-
April 1992	-	IPG B3-0532	IPG B3-0528	-	-	-	-	-	-	-
May 1992	1 B3-0679	1 B3-0675	1 B3-0682	-	-	1 B3-0681	1 B3-0680	-	1 B3-0677	-
June 1992	-	-	-	-	-	-	-	-	-	-
July 1992	-	1 B3-0973 & B3-1049	**	-	-	-	1 B3-0973 & B3-1049	-	1 B3-0973 & B3-1049	-
Total	9	10	7	6	6	8	7	0	6	1

IPG= Individual Political Groups' Resolutions
* The November 1991 Joint Resolution was cosigned by von Alemann on her own behalf
** The July 1992 Joint Resolution was cosigned by von Alemann on her own behalf

Table 15 Individual PG Non-Adopted Motions for Resolutions on the Yugoslav Crisis

	Socialist	EPP	LDR	ED	Greens	EUL	EDA	ER	RB	LU
February 1991	-	-	-	-	-	-	-	F B3-0297	-	-
March 1991	-	-	-	-	-	F B3-0400	-	R B3-0394	F B3-0396	-
April 1991	-	-	-	-	F B3-0654	-	-	-	-	-
May 1991	-	-	-	-	-	-	-	F B3-0782	-	-
June 1991	-	-	-	-	-	-	-	-	-	-
July 1991	-	-	-	-	-	-	F B3-1219	F B3-1137	F B3-1221	-
August 1991	-	-	-	-	-	-	-	-	-	-
September 1991	-	W B3-1324 W B3-1391	F B3-1383	F B3-1329	F B3-1374	-	-	F B3-1375	F B3-1373	F B3-1407
October 1991	W B3-1567	R B3-1587	F B3-1614	R B3-1580	F B3-1623	F B3-1615	-	R B3-1578	F B3-1608	F B3-1626
November 1991	-	-	F B3-1888	-	F B3-1894	-	-	F B3-1895	-	-
December 1991	-	-	-	-	-	-	-	-	-	-
January 1992	-	-	-	-	-	-	-	F B3-0043	-	-
February 1992	-	-	-	-	-	-	-	-	-	-
March 1992	-	-	-	-	-	-	-	F B3-0411	-	-
April 1992	-	-	-	-	-	-	-	-	F B3-0459	-
May 1992	-	-	-	-	F B3-0683	-	-	F B3-0678	-	-
June 1992	-	-	-	-	-	-	-	-	-	-
July 1992	-	-	-	-	-	-	-	-	-	-
Total	1	3	3	2	5	2	1	10	5	2

Table 16 Socialist Group Voting Trends: Gulf Crisis

	Mode +	Mode -	Mode 0	Absent /	Members	% Absent	% Mode +	IA	ITv
Stage 1,Vote 1	143	0	0	37	180	20.56	100.00	100.00	0.837
2	134	7	3	36	180	20.00	93.06	86.11	0.854
3	138	0	2	40	180	22.22	98.57	97.14	0.846
4	143	0	0	37	180	20.56	100.00	100.00	0.833
5	141	0	0	39	180	21.67	100.00	100.00	0.834
6	139	3	0	38	180	21.11	97.89	95.77	0.833
7	136	4	2	38	180	21.11	95.77	91.55	0.847
8	7	110	15	48	180	26.67	5.30	66.67	0.824
9	140	1	1	38	180	21.11	98.59	97.18	0.832
10	136	0	9	35	180	19.44	93.79	87.59	0.849
11	9	0	0	171	180	95.00	100.00	100.00	0.790
12	2	121	0	56	179	31.28	1.63	96.75	0.826
13	127	0	0	52	179	29.05	100.00	100.00	0.832
14	124	1	0	54	179	30.17	99.20	98.40	0.834
15	104	19	0	56	179	31.28	84.55	69.11	0.853
16	124	1	2	52	179	29.05	97.64	95.28	0.827
17	108	19	0	52	179	29.05	85.04	70.08	0.852
18	121	0	6	52	179	29.05	95.28	90.55	0.841
19	84	1	3	91	179	50.84	95.45	90.91	0.778
Stage 2,Vote 20	71	28	46	34	179	18.99	48.97	-2.07	0.831
21	2	151	0	26	179	14.53	1.31	97.39	0.828
22	1	149	0	29	179	16.20	0.67	98.67	0.828
23	0	151	0	28	179	15.64	0.00	100.00	0.828
24	36	104	7	32	179	17.88	24.49	41.50	0.846
25	1	145	0	33	179	18.44	0.68	98.63	0.822
26	34	106	8	31	179	17.32	22.97	43.24	0.839
27	0	154	1	24	179	13.41	0.00	98.71	0.838
28	83	28	36	32	179	17.88	56.46	12.93	0.818
29	92	36	17	34	179	18.99	63.45	26.90	0.840
30	60	52	1	66	179	36.87	53.10	6.19	0.701
31	36	64	8	71	179	39.66	33.33	18.52	0.813
32	33	72	7	67	179	37.43	29.46	28.57	0.812
33	31	80	4	64	179	35.75	26.96	39.13	0.820
34	24	79	18	58	179	32.40	19.83	30.58	0.823
35	36	79	6	58	179	32.40	29.75	30.58	0.825
36	38	80	7	54	179	30.17	30.40	28.00	0.817
37	37	80	6	56	179	31.28	30.08	30.08	0.827
38	40	79	8	52	179	29.05	31.50	24.41	0.827
39	1	124	5	49	179	27.37	0.77	90.77	0.831
40	90	33	15	41	179	22.91	65.22	30.43	0.829
41	3	57	4	115	179	64.25	4.69	78.13	0.833
42	91	0	0	88	179	49.16	100.00	100.00	0.806
Stage 3,Vote 43	0	65	0	114	179	63.69	0.00	100.00	0.818
44	0	72	0	107	179	59.78	0.00	100.00	0.817
45	0	75	0	104	179	58.10	0.00	100.00	0.818
46	86	0	0	93	179	51.96	100.00	100.00	0.811
47	84	1	0	94	179	52.51	98.82	97.65	0.810
48	82	0	0	97	179	54.19	100.00	100.00	0.811
49	7	71	0	101	179	56.42	8.97	82.05	0.836
50	81	0	0	98	179	54.75	100.00	100.00	0.840

Ave's	Absent	Mode+	IA	ITv
Stage 1	29.96	86.41	91.21	0.833
Stage 2	27.74	29.31	50.06	0.821
Stage 3	56.42	50.97	97.46	0.820
Overall	33.17	54.47	73.28	0.825

Table 17 EPP Group Voting Trends: Gulf Crisis

	Mode +	Mode -	Mode 0	Absent /	Members	% Absent	% Mode +	IA	ITv
Stage 1,Vote 1	87	0	1	33	121	27.27	98.86	97.73	0.850
2	88	0	0	33	121	27.27	100.00	100.00	0.845
3	86	0	0	35	121	28.93	100.00	100.00	0.846
4	83	2	4	32	121	26.45	93.26	86.52	0.823
5	86	0	0	35	121	28.93	100.00	100.00	0.847
6	89	0	0	32	121	26.45	100.00	100.00	0.844
7	88	0	0	33	121	27.27	100.00	100.00	0.842
8	79	0	0	42	121	34.71	100.00	100.00	0.840
9	90	0	0	31	121	25.62	100.00	100.00	0.843
10	87	0	2	32	121	26.45	97.75	95.51	0.842
11	9	0	0	113	122	92.62	100.00	100.00	0.642
12	75	0	0	47	122	38.52	100.00	100.00	0.815
13	68	1	0	53	122	43.44	98.55	97.10	0.830
14	1	72	0	49	122	40.16	1.37	97.26	0.822
15	73	0	0	49	122	40.16	100.00	100.00	0.817
16	2	75	0	45	122	36.89	2.60	94.81	0.839
17	60	8	2	52	122	42.62	85.71	71.43	0.811
18	4	26	45	47	122	38.52	5.33	20.00	0.830
19	0	33	0	89	122	72.95	0.00	100.00	0.801
Stage 2,Vote 20	84	16	3	19	122	15.57	81.55	63.11	0.816
21	101	1	3	17	122	13.93	96.19	92.38	0.841
22	103	1	3	15	122	12.30	96.26	92.52	0.840
23	101	1	4	16	122	13.11	95.28	90.57	0.844
24	1	103	0	18	122	14.75	0.96	98.08	0.842
25	100	1	5	16	122	13.11	94.34	88.68	0.837
26	1	106	0	15	122	12.30	0.93	98.13	0.842
27	0	101	2	19	122	15.57	0.00	96.12	0.837
28	103	3	1	15	122	12.30	96.26	92.52	0.845
29	83	16	2	21	122	17.21	82.18	64.36	0.826
30	39	33	7	43	122	35.25	49.37	-1.27	0.832
31	0	60	1	61	122	50.00	0.00	96.72	0.858
32	0	66	1	55	122	45.08	0.00	97.01	0.853
33	0	64	1	57	122	46.72	0.00	96.92	0.848
34	0	67	1	54	122	44.26	0.00	97.06	0.855
35	0	69	1	52	122	42.62	0.00	97.14	0.853
36	0	68	1	53	122	43.44	0.00	97.10	0.849
37	0	71	1	50	122	40.98	0.00	97.22	0.852
38	0	72	1	49	122	40.16	0.00	97.26	0.855
39	5	69	2	46	122	37.70	6.58	81.58	0.831
40	75	1	3	43	122	35.25	94.94	89.87	0.853
41	0	52	0	70	122	57.38	0.00	100.00	0.854
42	37	0	0	85	122	69.67	100.00	100.00	0.865
Stage 3,Vote 43	2	27	0	93	122	76.23	6.90	86.21	0.831
44	1	30	0	91	122	74.59	3.23	93.55	0.860
45	1	35	0	86	122	70.49	2.78	94.44	0.844
46	49	0	0	73	122	59.84	100.00	100.00	0.855
47	50	0	0	72	122	59.02	100.00	100.00	0.866
48	49	0	0	73	122	59.84	100.00	100.00	0.851
49	42	0	0	80	122	65.57	100.00	100.00	0.840
50	43	0	0	79	122	64.75	100.00	100.00	0.851

Ave's	Absent	Mode+	IA	ITv
Stage 1	38.17	78.08	92.65	0.823
Stage 2	31.68	38.91	87.96	0.845
Stage 3	66.29	64.11	96.77	0.850
Overall	39.69	57.82	91.15	0.837

Table 18	LDR Group Voting Trends: Gulf Crisis							
	Mode +	Mode -	Mode 0	Absent /	Members	% Absent	% Mode +	IA	ITv
Stage 1,Vote 1	28	1	2	18	49	36.73	90.32	80.65	0.819
2	30	0	2	17	49	34.69	93.75	87.50	0.836
3	32	0	2	15	49	30.61	94.12	88.24	0.844
4	3	26	5	15	49	30.61	8.82	52.94	0.793
5	32	0	2	15	49	30.61	94.12	88.24	0.844
6	31	0	3	15	49	30.61	91.18	82.35	0.841
7	31	0	1	17	49	34.69	96.88	93.75	0.841
8	27	1	3	18	49	36.73	87.10	74.19	0.829
9	20	4	3	22	49	44.90	74.07	48.15	0.875
10	22	3	9	15	49	30.61	64.71	29.41	0.818
11	3	0	0	46	49	93.88	100.00	100.00	0.667
12	23	0	0	26	49	53.06	100.00	100.00	0.798
13	10	6	1	32	49	65.31	58.82	17.65	0.740
14	0	13	0	36	49	73.47	0.00	100.00	0.817
15	18	1	0	30	49	61.22	94.74	89.47	0.827
16	0	20	0	29	49	59.18	0.00	100.00	0.800
17	4	14	0	31	49	63.27	22.22	55.56	0.806
18	0	21	1	27	49	55.10	0.00	90.91	0.807
19	9	1	0	39	49	79.59	90.00	80.00	0.790
Stage 2,Vote 20	0	34	1	14	49	28.57	0.00	94.29	0.844
21	31	1	2	15	49	30.61	91.18	82.35	0.826
22	33	2	1	13	49	26.53	91.67	83.33	0.836
23	33	0	3	13	49	26.53	91.67	83.33	0.858
24	1	32	2	14	49	28.57	2.86	82.86	0.844
25	14	9	3	23	49	46.94	53.85	7.69	0.765
26	1	33	1	14	49	28.57	2.86	88.57	0.843
27	0	34	1	14	49	28.57	0.00	94.29	0.820
28	30	1	2	16	49	32.65	90.91	81.82	0.840
29	1	26	4	18	49	36.73	3.23	67.74	0.828
30	17	5	0	27	49	55.10	77.27	54.55	0.817
31	1	15	0	33	49	67.35	6.25	87.50	0.818
32	0	17	0	32	49	65.31	0.00	100.00	0.830
33	1	16	0	32	49	65.31	5.88	88.24	0.813
34	1	17	0	31	49	63.27	5.56	88.89	0.824
35	3	16	0	30	49	61.22	15.79	68.42	0.805
36	1	16	0	32	49	65.31	5.88	88.24	0.781
37	2	16	1	30	49	61.22	10.53	68.42	0.773
38	2	17	0	30	49	61.22	10.53	78.95	0.789
39	18	1	0	30	49	61.22	94.74	89.47	0.790
40	2	13	4	30	49	61.22	10.53	36.84	0.722
41	2	4	2	41	49	83.67	25.00	0.00	0.750
42	8	0	1	40	49	81.63	88.89	77.78	0.781
Stage 3,Vote 43	10	0	0	39	49	79.59	100.00	100.00	0.780
44	11	0	0	38	49	77.55	100.00	100.00	0.826
45	11	0	0	38	49	77.55	100.00	100.00	0.826
46	14	0	0	35	49	71.43	100.00	100.00	0.816
47	13	0	0	36	49	73.47	100.00	100.00	0.793
48	13	0	0	36	49	73.47	100.00	100.00	0.817
49	11	0	0	38	49	77.55	100.00	100.00	0.777
50	11	0	0	38	49	77.55	100.00	100.00	0.777

Ave's	Absent	Mode+	IA	ITv
Stage 1	49.73	66.36	76.79	0.810
Stage 2	50.75	34.13	73.63	0.809
Stage 3	76.02	100.00	100.00	0.802
Overall	54.41	56.92	79.05	0.808

Table 19 ED Group Voting Trends: Gulf Crisis

	Mode +	Mode -	Mode 0	Absent /	Members	% Absent	% Mode +	IA	ITv
Stage 1, Vote 1	24	0	0	10	34	29.41	100.00	100.00	0.080
2	25	0	0	9	34	26.47	100.00	100.00	0.077
3	25	0	0	9	34	26.47	100.00	100.00	0.077
4	1	26	0	7	34	20.59	3.70	92.59	0.074
5	27	0	0	7	34	20.59	100.00	100.00	0.071
6	26	1	0	7	34	20.59	96.30	92.59	0.074
7	26	0	0	8	34	23.53	100.00	100.00	0.074
8	3	16	2	13	34	38.24	14.29	52.38	0.000
9	23	2	0	9	34	26.47	92.00	84.00	0.083
10	25	2	0	7	34	20.59	92.59	85.19	0.077
11	2	0	0	32	34	94.12	100.00	100.00	0.000
12	30	0	0	4	34	11.76	100.00	100.00	0.064
13	30	0	0	4	34	11.76	100.00	100.00	0.064
14	0	30	0	4	34	11.76	0.00	100.00	0.064
15	28	1	0	5	34	14.71	96.55	93.10	0.069
16	1	29	0	4	34	11.76	3.33	93.33	0.067
17	28	2	0	4	34	11.76	93.33	86.67	0.069
18	0	29	0	5	34	14.71	0.00	100.00	0.067
19	19	0	0	15	34	44.12	100.00	100.00	0.000
Stage 2, Vote 20	1	30	1	2	34	5.88	3.13	87.50	0.064
21	29	1	2	2	34	5.88	90.63	81.25	0.067
22	31	1	0	2	34	5.88	96.88	93.75	0.062
23	30	0	0	4	34	11.76	100.00	100.00	0.064
24	0	32	0	2	34	5.88	0.00	100.00	0.061
25	32	0	0	2	34	5.88	100.00	100.00	0.061
26	0	31	0	3	34	8.82	0.00	100.00	0.121
27	0	31	0	3	34	8.82	0.00	100.00	0.062
28	31	1	0	2	34	5.88	96.88	93.75	0.121
29	23	4	1	6	34	17.65	82.14	64.29	0.159
30	26	0	0	8	34	23.53	100.00	100.00	0.142
31	0	23	0	11	34	32.35	0.00	100.00	0.083
32	0	25	0	9	34	26.47	0.00	100.00	0.077
33	0	25	0	9	34	26.47	0.00	100.00	0.077
34	0	24	0	10	34	29.41	0.00	100.00	0.080
35	1	23	0	10	34	29.41	4.17	91.67	0.083
36	0	26	0	8	34	23.53	0.00	100.00	0.074
37	0	27	0	7	34	20.59	0.00	100.00	0.071
38	0	26	0	8	34	23.53	0.00	100.00	0.074
39	2	23	1	8	34	23.53	7.69	76.92	0.083
40	26	0	1	7	34	20.59	96.30	92.59	0.074
41	0	16	0	18	34	52.94	0.00	100.00	0.000
42	10	0	0	24	34	70.59	100.00	100.00	0.000
Stage 3, Vote 43	9	1	0	24	34	70.59	90.00	80.00	0.198
44	10	0	0	24	34	70.59	100.00	100.00	0.180
45	9	0	0	25	34	73.53	100.00	100.00	0.198
46	20	0	0	14	34	41.18	100.00	100.00	0.000
47	15	0	0	19	34	55.88	100.00	100.00	0.000
48	14	0	0	20	34	58.82	100.00	100.00	0.000
49	11	0	0	23	34	67.65	100.00	100.00	0.000
50	11	0	0	23	34	67.65	100.00	100.00	0.000

Ave's	Absent	Mode+	IA	ITv
Stage 1	25.23	73.27	93.68	0.061
Stage 2	21.10	38.17	94.86	0.077
Stage 3	63.24	98.75	97.50	0.072
Overall	29.41	61.20	94.83	0.070

	Mode +	Mode -	Mode 0	Absent /	Members	% Absent	% Mode +	IA	ITv
Table 20 Green Group Voting Trends: Gulf Crisis									
Stage 1,Vote 1	20	0	1	8	29	27.59	95.24	90.48	0.810
2	20	2	0	7	29	24.14	90.91	81.82	0.810
3	11	9	2	7	29	24.14	50.00	0.00	0.793
4	18	1	3	7	29	24.14	81.82	63.64	0.809
5	3	17	2	7	29	24.14	13.64	54.55	0.789
6	3	14	3	9	29	31.03	15.00	40.00	0.735
7	2	2	16	9	29	31.03	10.00	60.00	0.805
8	0	20	3	6	29	20.69	0.00	73.91	0.805
9	12	1	7	9	29	31.03	60.00	20.00	0.819
10	1	15	7	6	29	20.69	4.35	30.43	0.800
11	0	0	0	29	29	100.00			
12	0	9	1	19	29	65.52	0.00	80.00	0.617
13	0	2	3	24	29	82.76	0.00	20.00	0.667
14	2	2	3	22	29	75.86	28.57	-14.29	0.667
15	1	5	0	23	29	79.31	16.67	66.67	0.720
16	7	1	2	19	29	65.52	70.00	40.00	0.449
17	1	1	4	23	29	79.31	16.67	33.33	0.625
18	2	8	0	19	29	65.52	20.00	60.00	0.625
19	0	0	2	27	29	93.10	0.00	100.00	0.500
Stage 2,Vote 20	1	18	4	6	29	20.69	4.35	56.52	0.765
21	0	22	0	7	29	24.14	0.00	100.00	0.769
22	1	21	0	7	29	24.14	4.55	90.91	0.748
23	0	22	1	6	29	20.69	0.00	91.30	0.769
24	21	0	1	7	29	24.14	95.45	90.91	0.794
25	0	22	1	6	29	20.69	0.00	91.30	0.769
26	21	0	0	8	29	27.59	100.00	100.00	0.771
27	0	20	0	9	29	31.03	0.00	100.00	0.775
28	1	19	1	8	29	27.59	4.76	80.95	0.770
29	0	17	1	11	29	37.93	0.00	88.89	0.768
30	7	0	2	20	29	68.97	77.78	55.56	0.694
31	15	0	0	14	29	48.28	100.00	100.00	0.773
32	16	0	0	13	29	44.83	100.00	100.00	0.789
33	15	0	0	14	29	48.28	100.00	100.00	0.773
34	17	0	0	12	29	41.38	100.00	100.00	0.782
35	17	0	0	12	29	41.38	100.00	100.00	0.782
36	16	0	0	13	29	44.83	100.00	100.00	0.789
37	16	0	0	13	29	44.83	100.00	100.00	0.789
38	17	0	0	12	29	41.38	100.00	100.00	0.782
39	0	15	1	13	29	44.83	0.00	87.50	0.800
40	0	16	0	13	29	44.83	0.00	100.00	0.789
41	12	0	0	17	29	58.62	100.00	100.00	0.764
42	12	0	0	17	29	58.62	100.00	100.00	0.750
Stage 3,Vote 43	0	11	0	18	29	62.07	0.00	100.00	0.744
44	11	0	0	18	29	62.07	100.00	100.00	0.744
45	0	0	11	18	29	62.07	0.00	100.00	0.760
46	11	0	0	18	29	62.07	100.00	100.00	0.777
47	0	15	0	14	29	48.28	0.00	100.00	0.809
48	14	2	0	13	29	44.83	87.50	75.00	0.786
49	0	14	1	14	29	48.28	0.00	86.67	0.776
50	0	14	2	13	29	44.83	0.00	75.00	0.796

Ave's	Absent	Mode+	IA	ITv
Stage 1	50.82	31.83	50.03	0.714
Stage 2	38.68	55.95	92.78	0.772
Stage 3	54.31	35.94	92.08	0.774
Overall	45.79	43.82	76.96	0.751

Table 21 EUL Group Voting Trends: Gulf Crisis

	Mode +	Mode -	Mode 0	Absent /	Members	% Absent	% Mode +	IA	ITv
Stage 1,Vote 1	20	0	1	7	28	25.00	95.24	90.48	0.265
2	21	0	0	7	28	25.00	100.00	100.00	0.322
3	21	0	0	7	28	25.00	100.00	100.00	0.322
4	21	0	0	7	28	25.00	100.00	100.00	0.322
5	21	0	0	7	28	25.00	100.00	100.00	0.322
6	0	20	0	8	28	28.57	0.00	100.00	0.335
7	21	0	0	7	28	25.00	100.00	100.00	0.322
8	0	21	0	7	28	25.00	0.00	100.00	0.322
9	20	1	0	7	28	25.00	95.24	90.48	0.335
10	21	0	0	7	28	25.00	100.00	100.00	0.322
11	0	0	0	28	28	100.00			
12	0	13	0	15	28	53.57	0.00	100.00	0.272
13	15	0	0	13	28	46.43	100.00	100.00	0.338
14	14	0	0	14	28	50.00	100.00	100.00	0.357
15	13	1	0	14	28	50.00	92.86	85.71	0.379
16	14	0	0	14	28	50.00	100.00	100.00	0.357
17	9	5	0	14	28	50.00	64.29	28.57	0.370
18	17	0	0	11	28	39.29	100.00	100.00	0.381
19	15	0	0	13	28	46.43	100.00	100.00	0.338
Stage 2,Vote 20	18	1	2	7	28	25.00	85.71	71.43	0.346
21	0	22	0	6	28	21.43	0.00	100.00	0.310
22	0	22	0	6	28	21.43	0.00	100.00	0.368
23	0	22	0	6	28	21.43	0.00	100.00	0.368
24	20	1	1	6	28	21.43	90.91	81.82	0.335
25	0	21	1	6	28	21.43	0.00	90.91	0.322
26	16	2	1	9	28	32.14	84.21	68.42	0.375
27	0	21	0	7	28	25.00	0.00	100.00	0.381
28	1	18	1	8	28	28.57	5.00	80.00	0.426
29	1	21	0	6	28	21.43	4.55	90.91	0.381
30	9	1	1	17	28	60.71	81.82	63.64	0.346
31	15	0	0	13	28	46.43	100.00	100.00	0.436
32	2	11	0	15	28	53.57	15.38	69.23	0.430
33	15	1	0	12	28	42.86	93.75	87.50	0.507
34	4	11	0	13	28	46.43	26.67	46.67	0.545
35	14	1	0	13	28	46.43	93.33	86.67	0.459
36	13	1	0	14	28	50.00	92.86	85.71	0.379
37	15	0	0	13	28	46.43	100.00	100.00	0.436
38	14	1	0	13	28	46.43	93.33	86.67	0.459
39	0	15	0	13	28	46.43	0.00	100.00	0.436
40	1	15	0	12	28	42.86	6.25	87.50	0.436
41	6	0	0	22	28	78.57	100.00	100.00	0.278
42	12	0	0	16	28	57.14	100.00	100.00	0.486
Stage 3,Vote 43	0	3	0	25	28	89.29	0.00	100.00	0.000
44	0	4	0	24	28	85.71	0.00	100.00	0.375
45	0	5	0	23	28	82.14	0.00	100.00	0.000
46	9	0	0	19	28	67.86	100.00	100.00	0.444
47	9	0	0	19	28	67.86	100.00	100.00	0.444
48	9	0	0	19	28	67.86	100.00	100.00	0.444
49	0	1	6	21	28	75.00	0.00	71.43	0.444
50	0	0	8	20	28	71.43	0.00	100.00	0.469

Ave's	Absent	Mode+	IA	ITv
Stage 1	38.91	80.42	94.18	0.332
Stage 2	39.29	51.03	86.83	0.402
Stage 3	75.89	37.50	96.43	0.328
Overall	45.00	59.62	91.10	0.364

Table 22	EDA Group Voting Trends: Gulf Crisis							
	Mode +	Mode -	Mode 0	Absent /	Members	% Absent	% Mode +	IA	ITv
Stage 1,Vote 1	11	0	0	11	22	50.00	100.00	100.00	0.397
2	11	0	0	11	22	50.00	100.00	100.00	0.397
3	11	0	0	11	22	50.00	100.00	100.00	0.397
4	2	9	1	10	22	45.45	16.67	50.00	0.198
5	7	0	0	15	22	68.18	100.00	100.00	0.000
6	11	0	0	11	22	50.00	100.00	100.00	0.000
7	11	0	0	11	22	50.00	100.00	100.00	0.000
8	9	1	0	12	22	54.55	90.00	80.00	0.346
9	11	0	0	11	22	50.00	100.00	100.00	0.397
10	9	0	1	12	22	54.55	90.00	80.00	0.444
11	0	0	0	22	22	100.00			
12	2	4	0	16	22	72.73	33.33	33.33	0.375
13	3	1	0	18	22	81.82	75.00	50.00	0.444
14	3	4	0	15	22	68.18	42.86	14.29	0.000
15	7	0	0	15	22	68.18	100.00	100.00	0.612
16	3	1	0	18	22	81.82	75.00	50.00	0.444
17	6	0	0	16	22	72.73	100.00	100.00	0.611
18	5	0	5	12	22	54.55	50.00	0.00	0.560
19	0	0	1	21	22	95.45	0.00	100.00	0.000
Stage 2,Vote 20	1	11	0	10	22	45.45	8.33	83.33	0.463
21	7	5	0	10	22	45.45	58.33	16.67	0.000
22	11	1	0	10	22	45.45	91.67	83.33	0.463
23	10	2	0	10	22	45.45	83.33	66.67	0.420
24	1	11	0	10	22	45.45	8.33	83.33	0.463
25	10	1	0	11	22	50.00	90.91	81.82	0.420
26	2	9	0	11	22	50.00	18.18	63.64	0.346
27	0	12	0	10	22	45.45	0.00	100.00	0.444
28	10	2	0	10	22	45.45	83.33	66.67	0.420
29	4	7	0	11	22	50.00	36.36	27.27	0.245
30	0	7	1	14	22	63.64	0.00	75.00	0.490
31	1	7	0	14	22	63.64	12.50	75.00	0.490
32	1	8	0	13	22	59.09	11.11	77.78	0.500
33	1	8	0	13	22	59.09	11.11	77.78	0.500
34	1	8	0	13	22	59.09	11.11	77.78	0.500
35	1	9	0	12	22	54.55	10.00	80.00	0.494
36	1	9	0	12	22	54.55	10.00	80.00	0.494
37	1	9	0	12	22	54.55	10.00	80.00	0.494
38	1	9	0	12	22	54.55	10.00	80.00	0.494
39	11	2	0	9	22	40.91	84.62	69.23	0.397
40	5	8	0	9	22	40.91	38.46	23.08	0.219
41	2	1	0	19	22	86.36	66.67	33.33	0.000
42	4	0	0	18	22	81.82	100.00	100.00	0.000
Stage 3,Vote 43	2	1	0	19	22	86.36	66.67	33.33	0.000
44	5	0	1	16	22	72.73	83.33	66.67	0.000
45	5	0	1	16	22	72.73	83.33	66.67	0.000
46	4	0	0	18	22	81.82	100.00	100.00	0.000
47	0	1	2	19	22	86.36	0.00	33.33	0.000
48	0	1	0	21	22	95.45	0.00	100.00	0.000
49	4	0	0	18	22	81.82	100.00	100.00	0.000
50	4	0	0	18	22	81.82	100.00	100.00	0.000

Ave's	Absent	Mode+	IA	ITv
Stage 1	64.11	76.27	75.42	0.312
Stage 2	53.95	37.15	69.64	0.381
Stage 3	82.39	66.67	75.00	0.000
Overall	62.36	56.34	72.64	0.293

Table 23 ER Group Voting Trends: Gulf Crisis

	Mode +	Mode -	Mode 0	Absent /	Members	% Absent	% Mode +	IA	ITv
Stage 1,Vote 1	13	0	1	3	17	17.65	92.86	85.71	0.556
2	0	1	11	5	17	29.41	0.00	83.33	0.463
3	15	0	0	2	17	11.76	100.00	100.00	0.524
4	12	1	0	4	17	23.53	92.31	84.62	0.444
5	1	12	0	4	17	23.53	7.69	84.62	0.444
6	1	12	0	4	17	23.53	7.69	84.62	0.444
7	0	2	10	5	17	29.41	0.00	66.67	0.480
8	1	2	8	6	17	35.29	9.09	45.45	0.469
9	13	0	0	4	17	23.53	100.00	100.00	0.521
10	1	12	1	3	17	17.65	7.14	71.43	0.375
11	0	0	0	16	16	100.00			
12	0	9	0	7	16	43.75	0.00	100.00	0.568
13	0	8	0	8	16	50.00	0.00	100.00	0.625
14	0	3	0	13	16	81.25	0.00	100.00	0.444
15	0	2	0	14	16	87.50	0.00	100.00	0.000
16	0	6	0	10	16	62.50	0.00	100.00	0.444
17	1	4	1	10	16	62.50	16.67	33.33	0.375
18	0	8	1	7	16	43.75	0.00	77.78	0.219
19	0	3	0	13	16	81.25	0.00	100.00	0.444
Stage 2,Vote 20	8	0	2	5	15	33.33	80.00	60.00	0.531
21	0	4	5	6	15	40.00	0.00	11.11	0.320
22	1	9	1	4	15	26.67	9.09	63.64	0.568
23	1	6	3	5	15	33.33	10.00	20.00	0.278
24	0	10	1	4	15	26.67	0.00	81.82	0.580
25	0	6	3	6	15	40.00	0.00	33.33	0.278
26	0	9	1	5	15	33.33	0.00	80.00	0.568
27	8	0	1	6	15	40.00	88.89	77.78	0.469
28	7	0	2	6	15	40.00	77.78	55.56	0.449
29	2	0	9	4	15	26.67	18.18	63.64	0.568
30	0	4	0	11	15	73.33	0.00	100.00	0.375
31	0	5	0	10	15	66.67	0.00	100.00	0.640
32	0	4	0	11	15	73.33	0.00	100.00	0.375
33	0	5	0	10	15	66.67	0.00	100.00	0.640
34	0	4	0	11	15	73.33	0.00	100.00	0.625
35	0	3	0	12	15	80.00	0.00	100.00	0.444
36	0	4	0	11	15	73.33	0.00	100.00	0.625
37	0	4	0	11	15	73.33	0.00	100.00	0.625
38	0	1	0	14	15	93.33	0.00	100.00	0.000
39	0	0	0	15	15	100.00			
40	0	1	0	14	15	93.33	0.00	100.00	0.000
41	1	4	1	9	15	60.00	16.67	33.33	0.375
42	0	0	0	15	15	100.00			
Stage 3,Vote 43	0	3	0	12	15	80.00	0.00	100.00	0.667
44	0	0	3	12	15	80.00	0.00	100.00	0.667
45	3	0	0	12	15	80.00	100.00	100.00	0.667
46	0	0	3	12	15	80.00	0.00	100.00	0.667
47	0	2	0	13	15	86.67	0.00	100.00	0.500
48	0	2	0	13	15	86.67	0.00	100.00	0.500
49	0	1	0	14	15	93.33	0.00	100.00	0.000
50	0	2	0	13	15	86.67	0.00	100.00	0.500

Ave's	Absent	Mode+	IA	ITv
Stage 1	44.62	24.08	84.31	0.436
Stage 2	59.42	14.31	75.25	0.444
Stage 3	84.17	12.50	100.00	0.521
Overall	57.76	17.75	82.93	0.454

Table 24	Rainbow Group Voting Trends: Gulf Crisis							
	Mode +	Mode -	Mode 0	Absent /	Members	% Absent	% Mode +	IA	ITv
Stage 1,Vote 1	8	0	2	4	14	28.57	80.00	60.00	0.656
2	1	8	2	3	14	21.43	9.09	45.45	0.688
3	8	1	2	3	14	21.43	72.73	45.45	0.750
4	4	2	5	3	14	21.43	36.36	-9.09	0.800
5	7	2	2	3	14	21.43	63.64	27.27	0.571
6	10	0	1	3	14	21.43	90.91	81.82	0.760
7	1	7	2	4	14	28.57	10.00	40.00	0.612
8	3	7	2	2	14	14.29	25.00	16.67	0.612
9	5	4	2	3	14	21.43	45.45	-9.09	0.720
10	0	2	11	1	14	7.14	0.00	69.23	0.793
11	0	0	0	14	14	100.00			
12	0	5	0	10	15	66.67	0.00	100.00	0.800
13	4	0	0	11	15	73.33	100.00	100.00	0.750
14	6	1	0	8	15	53.33	85.71	71.43	0.833
15	3	3	0	9	15	60.00	50.00	0.00	0.667
16	6	0	0	9	15	60.00	100.00	100.00	0.833
17	1	5	0	9	15	60.00	16.67	66.67	0.800
18	0	0	5	10	15	66.67	0.00	100.00	0.800
19	0	0	0	15	15	100.00			
Stage 2,Vote 20	10	1	0	4	15	26.67	90.91	81.82	0.780
21	0	11	1	3	15	20.00	0.00	83.33	0.860
22	0	9	2	4	15	26.67	0.00	63.64	0.815
23	0	11	1	3	15	20.00	0.00	83.33	0.860
24	0	0	10	5	15	33.33	0.00	100.00	0.780
25	1	5	4	5	15	33.33	10.00	0.00	0.800
26	1	0	10	4	15	26.67	9.09	81.82	0.780
27	0	8	3	4	15	26.67	0.00	45.45	0.875
28	6	4	0	5	15	33.33	60.00	20.00	0.833
29	6	3	1	5	15	33.33	60.00	20.00	0.833
30	5	3	0	7	15	46.67	62.50	25.00	0.800
31	1	0	2	12	15	80.00	33.33	33.33	0.500
32	0	0	1	14	15	93.33	0.00	100.00	0.000
33	0	0	2	13	15	86.67	0.00	100.00	0.500
34	1	0	4	10	15	66.67	20.00	60.00	0.750
35	1	0	3	11	15	73.33	25.00	50.00	0.667
36	1	0	3	11	15	73.33	25.00	50.00	0.667
37	2	0	4	9	15	60.00	33.33	33.33	0.750
38	2	0	4	9	15	60.00	33.33	33.33	0.750
39	0	7	0	8	15	53.33	0.00	100.00	0.735
40	5	0	2	8	15	53.33	71.43	42.86	0.720
41	4	0	0	11	15	73.33	100.00	100.00	0.750
42	6	0	0	9	15	60.00	100.00	100.00	0.667
Stage 3,Vote 43	0	0	2	13	15	86.67	0.00	100.00	0.000
44	3	0	0	12	15	80.00	100.00	100.00	0.000
45	3	0	0	12	15	80.00	100.00	100.00	0.000
46	1	0	0	14	15	93.33	100.00	100.00	0.000
47	0	5	0	10	15	66.67	0.00	100.00	0.800
48	4	2	0	9	15	60.00	66.67	33.33	0.750
49	6	0	0	9	15	60.00	100.00	100.00	0.833
50	6	0	0	9	15	60.00	100.00	100.00	0.833

Ave's	Absent	Mode+	IA	ITv
Stage 1	44.59	46.21	53.28	0.732
Stage 2	50.43	31.91	61.18	0.716
Stage 3	73.33	70.83	91.67	0.402
Overall	51.88	43.46	63.47	0.669

Table 25 LU Group Voting Trends: Gulf Crisis

	Mode +	Mode -	Mode 0	Absent /	Members	% Absent	% Mode +	IA	ITv
Stage 1,Vote 1	3	0	0	11	14	78.57	100.00	100.00	0.444
2	0	0	2	12	14	85.71	0.00	100.00	0.500
3	2	0	0	12	14	85.71	100.00	100.00	0.000
4	12	0	0	2	14	14.29	100.00	100.00	0.694
5	0	0	1	13	14	92.86	0.00	100.00	0.000
6	0	1	0	13	14	92.86	0.00	100.00	0.000
7	0	2	2	10	14	71.43	0.00	0.00	0.500
8	0	9	0	5	14	35.71	0.00	100.00	0.617
9	1	0	2	11	14	78.57	33.33	33.33	0.500
10	0	1	9	4	14	28.57	0.00	80.00	0.716
11	0	0	0	14	14	100.00			
12	0	3	0	11	14	78.57	0.00	100.00	0.444
13	3	0	0	11	14	78.57	100.00	100.00	0.444
14	3	0	0	11	14	78.57	100.00	100.00	0.444
15	0	1	0	13	14	92.86	0.00	100.00	0.000
16	3	0	0	11	14	78.57	100.00	100.00	0.444
17	3	0	0	11	14	78.57	100.00	100.00	0.444
18	3	1	0	10	14	71.43	75.00	50.00	0.444
19	0	0	0	14	14	100.00			
Stage 2,Vote 20	0	11	0	3	14	21.43	0.00	100.00	0.711
21	0	11	0	3	14	21.43	0.00	100.00	0.678
22	0	11	0	3	14	21.43	0.00	100.00	0.711
23	0	12	0	2	14	14.29	0.00	100.00	0.694
24	11	0	1	2	14	14.29	91.67	83.33	0.678
25	1	11	0	2	14	14.29	8.33	83.33	0.694
26	12	0	0	2	14	14.29	100.00	100.00	0.694
27	0	12	0	2	14	14.29	0.00	100.00	0.694
28	0	11	0	3	14	21.43	0.00	100.00	0.678
29	0	12	0	2	14	14.29	0.00	100.00	0.722
30	0	6	1	7	14	50.00	0.00	71.43	0.500
31	10	0	0	4	14	28.57	100.00	100.00	0.660
32	8	0	0	6	14	42.86	100.00	100.00	0.719
33	10	0	0	4	14	28.57	100.00	100.00	0.660
34	9	0	0	5	14	35.71	100.00	100.00	0.691
35	9	0	0	5	14	35.71	100.00	100.00	0.691
36	9	0	0	5	14	35.71	100.00	100.00	0.691
37	9	0	0	5	14	35.71	100.00	100.00	0.691
38	9	0	0	5	14	35.71	100.00	100.00	0.691
39	0	2	0	12	14	85.71	0.00	100.00	0.000
40	0	9	0	5	14	35.71	0.00	100.00	0.617
41	2	0	0	12	14	85.71	100.00	100.00	0.000
42	5	0	1	8	14	57.14	83.33	66.67	0.480
Stage 3,Vote 43	0	0	5	9	14	64.29	0.00	100.00	0.480
44	0	0	5	9	14	64.29	0.00	100.00	0.480
45	5	0	0	9	14	64.29	100.00	100.00	0.480
46	0	0	0	14	14	100.00			
47	0	0	0	14	14	100.00			
48	0	0	0	14	14	100.00			
49	0	0	0	14	14	100.00			
50	0	0	0	14	14	100.00			

Ave's	Absent	Mode+	IA	ITv
Stage 1	74.81	47.55	86.08	0.391
Stage 2	33.23	51.45	95.86	0.611
Stage 3	86.61	33.33	100.00	0.480
Overall	57.57	48.64	92.28	0.515

Table 26 Independent Members' Voting Trends: Gulf Crisis

	Mode +	Mode -	Mode 0	Absent /	Members	% Absent	% Mode +	IA	ITv
Stage 1,Vote 1	3	1	1	5	10	50.00	60.00	20.00	0.667
2	1	3	2	4	10	40.00	16.67	0.00	0.667
3	1	2	1	6	10	60.00	25.00	0.00	0.500
4	1	3	1	5	10	50.00	20.00	20.00	0.667
5	4	0	1	5	10	50.00	80.00	60.00	0.750
6	4	0	0	6	10	60.00	100.00	100.00	0.750
7	1	2	0	7	10	70.00	33.33	33.33	0.500
8	3	1	0	6	10	60.00	75.00	50.00	0.667
9	3	0	0	7	10	70.00	100.00	100.00	0.667
10	3	2	0	5	10	50.00	60.00	20.00	0.667
11	0	0	0	10	10	100.00			
12	2	1	0	7	10	70.00	66.67	33.33	0.500
13	0	1	0	9	10	90.00	0.00	100.00	0.000
14	0	2	0	8	10	80.00	0.00	100.00	0.500
15	2	0	0	8	10	80.00	100.00	100.00	0.500
16	0	3	0	7	10	70.00	0.00	100.00	0.667
17	1	0	0	9	10	90.00	100.00	100.00	0.000
18	0	3	0	7	10	70.00	0.00	100.00	0.667
19	0	0	0	10	10	100.00			
Stage 2,Vote 20	1	2	4	4	11	36.36	14.29	14.29	0.625
21	4	1	1	5	11	45.45	66.67	33.33	0.625
22	4	2	0	5	11	45.45	66.67	33.33	0.625
23	2	4	0	5	11	45.45	33.33	33.33	0.625
24	0	5	1	5	11	45.45	0.00	66.67	0.720
25	3	3	0	5	11	45.45	50.00	0.00	0.667
26	1	7	0	3	11	27.27	12.50	75.00	0.776
27	0	5	2	4	11	36.36	0.00	42.86	0.800
28	6	1	1	3	11	27.27	75.00	50.00	0.722
29	1	3	2	5	11	45.45	16.67	0.00	0.667
30	1	2	1	7	11	63.64	25.00	0.00	0.500
31	0	2	1	8	11	72.73	0.00	33.33	0.500
32	0	2	1	8	11	72.73	0.00	33.33	0.500
33	0	2	1	8	11	72.73	0.00	33.33	0.500
34	0	2	1	8	11	72.73	0.00	33.33	0.500
35	0	3	0	8	11	72.73	0.00	100.00	0.667
36	0	1	1	9	11	81.82	0.00	0.00	0.000
37	0	3	0	8	11	72.73	0.00	100.00	0.667
38	0	2	0	9	11	81.82	0.00	100.00	0.500
39	2	1	0	8	11	72.73	66.67	33.33	0.500
40	0	2	1	8	11	72.73	0.00	33.33	0.500
41	1	0	0	10	11	90.91	100.00	100.00	0.000
42	0	0	1	10	11	90.91	0.00	100.00	0.000
Stage 3,Vote 43	1	0	0	10	11	90.91	100.00	100.00	0.000
44	1	0	0	10	11	90.91	100.00	100.00	0.000
45	0	0	0	11	11	100.00			
46	0	0	0	11	11	100.00			
47	0	0	0	11	11	100.00			
48	0	1	0	10	11	90.91	0.00	100.00	0.000
49	1	0	0	10	11	90.91	100.00	100.00	0.000
50	1	0	0	10	11	90.91	100.00	100.00	0.000

Ave's	Absent	Mode+	IA	ITv
Stage 1	68.95	49.22	60.98	0.549
Stage 2	60.47	22.90	45.60	0.530
Stage 3	94.32	80.00	100.00	0.000
Overall	69.11	39.19	57.46	0.478

Table 27 European Parliament Voting Trends: Gulf Crisis

	Mode +	Mode -	Mode 0	Absent /	Members	% Absent	% Mode +	IA	ITv
Stage 1,Vote 1	360	2	9	147	518	28.38	97.04	94.07	0.876
2	331	21	22	144	518	27.80	88.50	77.01	0.876
3	350	12	9	147	518	28.38	94.34	88.68	0.877
4	300	70	19	129	518	24.90	77.12	54.24	0.876
5	329	31	8	150	518	28.96	89.40	78.80	0.871
6	314	51	7	146	518	28.19	84.41	68.82	0.869
7	317	19	33	149	518	28.76	85.91	71.82	0.871
8	132	188	33	165	518	31.85	37.39	6.52	0.860
9	338	13	15	152	518	29.34	92.35	84.70	0.871
10	305	37	49	127	518	24.52	78.01	56.01	0.868
11	23	0	0	495	518	95.56	100.00	100.00	0.832
12	134	165	1	218	518	42.08	44.67	10.00	0.865
13	260	19	4	235	518	45.37	91.87	83.75	0.862
14	153	128	3	234	518	45.17	53.87	7.75	0.864
15	249	33	0	236	518	45.56	88.30	76.60	0.877
16	160	136	4	218	518	42.08	53.33	6.67	0.861
17	222	58	7	231	518	44.59	77.35	54.70	0.864
18	152	96	63	207	518	39.96	48.87	-2.25	0.863
19	127	38	6	347	518	66.99	74.27	48.54	0.779
Stage 2,Vote 20	195	152	63	108	518	20.85	47.56	-4.88	0.864
21	174	230	14	100	518	19.31	41.63	10.05	0.873
22	185	228	7	98	518	18.92	44.05	8.57	0.868
23	177	231	12	98	518	18.92	42.14	10.00	0.870
24	91	298	24	105	518	20.27	22.03	44.31	0.871
25	162	224	17	115	518	22.20	40.20	11.17	0.866
26	89	303	21	105	518	20.27	21.55	46.73	0.874
27	8	398	10	102	518	19.69	1.92	91.35	0.878
28	278	88	44	108	518	20.85	67.80	35.61	0.876
29	213	145	37	123	518	23.75	53.92	7.85	0.870
30	164	113	14	227	518	43.82	56.36	12.71	0.826
31	79	176	12	251	518	48.46	29.59	31.84	0.868
32	60	205	10	243	518	46.91	21.82	49.09	0.876
33	73	201	8	236	518	45.56	25.89	42.55	0.868
34	57	212	24	225	518	43.44	19.45	44.71	0.880
35	82	203	10	223	518	43.05	27.80	37.63	0.874
36	79	205	12	222	518	42.86	26.69	38.51	0.872
37	82	210	12	214	518	41.31	26.97	38.16	0.872
38	85	207	13	213	518	41.12	27.87	35.74	0.876
39	39	259	9	211	518	40.73	12.70	68.73	0.867
40	204	98	26	190	518	36.68	62.20	24.39	0.870
41	33	134	7	344	518	66.41	18.97	54.02	0.865
42	185	0	3	330	518	63.71	98.40	96.81	0.875
Stage 3,Vote 43	24	111	7	376	518	72.59	16.90	56.34	0.870
44	42	106	9	361	518	69.69	26.75	35.03	0.858
45	37	115	12	354	518	68.34	22.56	40.24	0.858
46	194	0	3	321	518	61.97	98.48	96.95	0.859
47	171	24	2	321	518	61.97	86.80	73.60	0.853
48	185	8	0	325	518	62.74	95.85	91.71	0.862
49	82	87	7	342	518	66.02	46.59	-1.14	0.853
50	157	16	10	335	518	64.67	85.79	71.58	0.867

Ave's	Absent	Mode+	IA	ITv
Stage 1	39.39	76.68	56.13	0.862
Stage 2	35.18	36.41	36.33	0.870
Stage 3	66.00	59.97	58.04	0.860
Overall	41.71	55.48	47.33	0.865

Table 28 Socialist Group Voting Trends: Yugoslav Crisis

	Mode +	Mode -	Mode 0	Absent /	Members	% Absent	% Mode +	IA	ITv
Stage 1, Vote 1	47	0	0	132	179	73.74	100.00	100.00	0.784
2	49	0	0	130	179	72.63	100.00	100.00	0.789
3	41	0	0	138	179	77.09	100.00	100.00	0.849
4	1	80	4	94	179	52.51	1.18	88.24	0.820
5	89	0	3	87	179	48.60	96.74	93.48	0.810
6	99	0	17	63	179	35.20	85.34	70.69	0.851
7	5	52	1	121	179	67.60	8.62	79.31	0.813
8	0	55	1	123	179	68.72	0.00	96.43	0.818
9	48	1	0	131	180	72.78	97.96	95.92	0.790
Stage 2, Vote 10	61	2	0	117	180	65.00	96.83	93.65	0.785
11	57	6	0	117	180	65.00	90.48	80.95	0.798
12	65	4	0	111	180	61.67	94.20	88.41	0.780
13	1	67	0	112	180	62.22	1.47	97.06	0.796
14	56	0	1	123	180	68.33	98.25	96.49	0.809
15	75	0	0	105	180	58.33	100.00	100.00	0.823
16	0	77	0	103	180	57.22	0.00	100.00	0.823
17	2	74	1	103	180	57.22	2.60	92.21	0.802
18	75	1	0	104	180	57.78	98.68	97.37	0.821
19	63	2	2	113	180	62.78	94.03	88.06	0.794
20	37	40	3	100	180	55.56	46.25	0.00	0.784

Ave's	Absent	Mode+	IA	ITv
Stage 1	63.21	65.54	91.56	0.814
Stage 2	61.01	65.71	84.93	0.801
Overall	62.00	65.63	87.91	0.807

Table 29 EPP Group Voting Trends: Yugoslav Crisis

	Mode +	Mode -	Mode 0	Absent /	Members	% Absent	% Mode +	IA	ITv
Stage 1, Vote 1	2	20	0	100	122	81.97	9.09	81.82	0.770
2	24	0	0	98	122	80.33	100.00	100.00	0.799
3	21	0	0	101	122	82.79	100.00	100.00	0.880
4	2	49	0	71	122	58.20	3.92	92.16	0.823
5	51	1	0	70	122	57.38	98.08	96.15	0.806
6	62	0	7	53	122	43.44	89.86	79.71	0.812
7	17	1	3	101	122	82.79	80.95	61.90	0.761
8	1	14	2	105	122	86.07	5.88	64.71	0.827
9	23	0	0	99	122	81.15	100.00	100.00	0.764
Stage 2, Vote 10	34	2	0	92	128	71.88	94.44	88.89	0.860
11	32	3	0	93	128	72.66	91.43	82.86	0.838
12	34	3	0	91	128	71.09	91.89	83.78	0.834
13	32	7	1	88	128	68.75	80.00	60.00	0.826
14	35	0	0	93	128	72.66	100.00	100.00	0.877
15	45	0	0	117	162	72.22	100.00	100.00	0.838
16	1	48	0	113	162	69.75	2.04	95.92	0.832
17	33	12	0	117	162	72.22	73.33	46.67	0.803
18	48	0	0	114	162	70.37	100.00	100.00	0.831
19	34	0	0	128	162	79.01	100.00	100.00	0.792
20	72	8	1	81	162	50.00	88.89	77.78	0.801

Ave's	Absent	Mode+	IA	ITv
Stage 1	72.68	65.31	86.27	0.804
Stage 2	70.06	83.82	85.08	0.830
Overall	71.24	75.49	85.62	0.819

Table 30 LDR Group Voting Trends: Yugoslav Crisis

	Mode +	Mode -	Mode 0	Absent /	Members	% Absent	% Mode +	IA	ITv
Stage 1,Vote 1	5	2	0	42	49	85.71	71.43	42.86	0.800
2	8	0	0	41	49	83.67	100.00	100.00	0.813
3	6	1	0	42	49	85.71	85.71	71.43	0.778
4	19	0	0	30	49	61.22	100.00	100.00	0.848
5	11	0	4	34	49	69.39	73.33	46.67	0.810
6	0	2	24	23	49	46.94	0.00	84.62	0.819
7	16	0	0	33	49	67.35	100.00	100.00	0.781
8	1	14	0	34	49	69.39	6.67	86.67	0.786
9	9	2	0	38	49	77.55	81.82	63.64	0.765
Stage 2,Vote 10	13	0	0	32	45	71.11	100.00	100.00	0.817
11	11	0	0	34	45	75.56	100.00	100.00	0.843
12	13	0	0	32	45	71.11	100.00	100.00	0.840
13	9	2	0	34	45	75.56	81.82	63.64	0.840
14	19	0	0	26	45	57.78	100.00	100.00	0.842
15	7	0	1	37	45	82.22	87.50	75.00	0.776
16	0	0	7	38	45	84.44	0.00	100.00	0.816
17	10	0	1	34	45	75.56	90.91	81.82	0.840
18	9	0	0	36	45	80.00	100.00	100.00	0.840
19	9	0	0	36	45	80.00	100.00	100.00	0.840
20	18	0	0	27	45	60.00	100.00	100.00	0.852

Ave's	Absent	Mode+	IA	ITv
Stage 1	71.88	68.77	77.32	0.800
Stage 2	73.94	87.29	92.77	0.831
Overall	73.01	78.96	85.82	0.817

Table 31 ED Group Voting Trends: Yugoslav Crisis

	Mode +	Mode -	Mode 0	Absent /	Members	% Absent	% Mode +	IA	ITv
Stage 1,Vote 1	8	0	1	25	34	73.53	88.89	77.78	0.219
2	8	0	1	25	34	73.53	88.89	77.78	0.219
3	9	0	0	25	34	73.53	100.00	100.00	0.000
4	1	17	0	16	34	47.06	5.56	88.89	0.111
5	22	0	0	12	34	35.29	100.00	100.00	0.087
6	18	0	0	16	34	47.06	100.00	100.00	0.105
7	7	0	1	26	34	76.47	87.50	75.00	0.000
8	7	0	0	27	34	79.41	100.00	100.00	0.000
9	11	0	0	23	34	67.65	100.00	100.00	0.298
Stage 2,Vote 10	6	0	0	28	34	82.35	100.00	100.00	0.000
11	7	0	0	27	34	79.41	100.00	100.00	0.000
12	8	0	0	26	34	76.47	100.00	100.00	0.000
13	8	0	0	26	34	76.47	100.00	100.00	0.000
14	6	0	0	28	34	82.35	100.00	100.00	0.000
15									
16									
17									
18									
19									
20									

Ave's	Absent	Mode+	IA	ITv
Stage 1	63.73	85.65	91.05	0.115
Stage 2	79.41	100.00	100.00	0.000
Overall	69.33	90.77	94.25	0.074

Table 32 Green Group Voting Trends: Yugoslav Crisis

	Mode +	Mode -	Mode 0	Absent /	Members	% Absent	% Mode +	IA	ITv
Stage 1,Vote 1	6	0	0	23	29	79.31	100.00	100.00	0.611
2	7	0	0	22	29	75.86	100.00	100.00	0.612
3	8	0	0	21	29	72.41	100.00	100.00	0.781
4	8	0	3	18	29	62.07	72.73	45.45	0.625
5	13	0	0	16	29	55.17	100.00	100.00	0.757
6	1	0	21	7	29	24.14	4.55	90.91	0.753
7	11	0	0	18	29	62.07	100.00	100.00	0.760
8	0	10	0	19	29	65.52	0.00	100.00	0.800
9	0	4	3	21	28	75.00	0.00	14.29	0.750
Stage 2,Vote 10	12	0	0	15	27	55.56	100.00	100.00	0.778
11	11	0	0	16	27	59.26	100.00	100.00	0.793
12	10	0	0	17	27	62.96	100.00	100.00	0.760
13	14	0	0	13	27	48.15	100.00	100.00	0.816
14	11	0	0	16	27	59.26	100.00	100.00	0.711
15	15	0	0	12	27	44.44	100.00	100.00	0.756
16	14	0	0	13	27	48.15	100.00	100.00	0.735
17	6	5	4	12	27	44.44	40.00	-20.00	0.722
18	0	15	0	12	27	44.44	0.00	100.00	0.756
19	9	0	1	17	27	62.96	90.00	80.00	0.765
Stage 1,Vote 1	13	0	1	13	27	48.15	92.86	85.71	0.686

Ave's	Absent	Mode+	IA	ITv
Stage 1	63.51	64.14	83.41	0.717
Stage 2	52.53	83.90	85.97	0.753
Overall	57.47	75.01	84.82	0.736

Table 33 EUL Group Voting Trends: Yugoslav Crisis

	Mode +	Mode -	Mode 0	Absent /	Members	% Absent	% Mode +	IA	ITv
Stage 1,Vote 1	3	0	0	25	28	89.29	100.00	100.00	0.444
2	3	0	0	25	28	89.29	100.00	100.00	0.444
3	5	0	0	23	28	82.14	100.00	100.00	0.320
4	1	7	1	19	28	67.86	11.11	55.56	0.490
5	7	0	0	21	28	75.00	100.00	100.00	0.490
6	13	0	0	15	28	53.57	100.00	100.00	0.260
7	0	14	0	14	28	50.00	0.00	100.00	0.439
8	14	0	0	14	28	50.00	100.00	100.00	0.439
9	5	0	0	23	28	82.14	100.00	100.00	0.480
Stage 2,Vote 10	4	0	0	25	29	86.21	100.00	100.00	0.375
11	4	0	0	25	29	86.21	100.00	100.00	0.375
12	4	0	0	25	29	86.21	100.00	100.00	0.375
13	2	2	1	24	29	82.76	40.00	-20.00	0.500
14	5	0	0	24	29	82.76	100.00	100.00	0.320
15	7	0	0	22	29	75.86	100.00	100.00	0.245
16	0	0	8	21	29	72.41	0.00	100.00	0.375
17	0	9	0	20	29	68.97	0.00	100.00	0.346
18	8	0	0	21	29	72.41	100.00	100.00	0.375
19	4	0	0	25	29	86.21	100.00	100.00	0.500
20	0	5	0	24	29	82.76	0.00	100.00	0.320

Ave's	Absent	Mode+	IA	ITv
Stage 1	71.03	79.01	95.06	0.423
Stage 2	80.25	67.27	89.09	0.373
Overall	76.10	72.56	91.78	0.396

Table 34 EDA Group Voting Trends: Yugoslav Crisis

	Mode +	Mode -	Mode 0	Absent /	Members	% Absent	% Mode +	IA	ITv
Stage 1,Vote 1	2	0	0	20	22	90.91	100.00	100.00	0.000
2	2	0	0	20	22	90.91	100.00	100.00	0.000
3	2	0	0	20	22	90.91	100.00	100.00	0.500
4	1	1	0	20	22	90.91	50.00	0.00	0.000
5	2	0	0	20	22	90.91	100.00	100.00	0.000
6	7	0	0	15	22	68.18	100.00	100.00	0.408
7	0	7	0	15	22	68.18	0.00	100.00	0.449
8	0	6	0	16	22	72.73	0.00	100.00	0.500
9	2	0	0	20	22	90.91	100.00	100.00	0.000
Stage 2,Vote 10	2	0	0	19	21	90.48	100.00	100.00	0.000
11	3	0	0	18	21	85.71	100.00	100.00	0.000
12	3	0	0	18	21	85.71	100.00	100.00	0.000
13	4	0	0	17	21	80.95	100.00	100.00	0.000
14	3	0	0	18	21	85.71	100.00	100.00	0.444
15	2	3	1	15	21	71.43	33.33	0.00	0.000
16	0	5	0	16	21	76.19	0.00	100.00	0.640
17	2	2	0	17	21	80.95	50.00	0.00	0.500
18	5	0	0	16	21	76.19	100.00	100.00	0.640
19	3	0	0	18	21	85.71	100.00	100.00	0.667
20	9	0	0	12	21	57.14	100.00	100.00	0.494

Ave's	Absent	Mode+	IA	ITv
Stage 1	83.84	72.22	88.89	0.206
Stage 2	79.65	80.30	81.82	0.308
Overall	81.54	76.67	85.00	0.262

Table 35 ER Group Voting Trends: Yugoslav Crisis

	Mode +	Mode -	Mode 0	Absent /	Members	% Absent	% Mode +	IA	ITv
Stage 1,Vote 1	0	0	2	14	16	87.50	0.00	100.00	0.500
2	0	0	0	16	16	100.00			
3	0	1	0	13	14	92.86	0.00	100.00	0.000
4	5	0	0	9	14	64.29	100.00	100.00	0.560
5	0	0	4	10	14	71.43	0.00	100.00	0.625
6	0	5	0	9	14	64.29	0.00	100.00	0.640
7	5	0	0	9	14	64.29	100.00	100.00	0.560
8	5	0	0	9	14	64.29	100.00	100.00	0.560
9	0	3	0	11	14	78.57	0.00	100.00	0.444
Stage 2,Vote 10	0	0	4	10	14	71.43	0.00	100.00	0.000
11	0	0	3	11	14	78.57	0.00	100.00	0.444
12	0	0	4	10	14	71.43	0.00	100.00	0.375
13	0	0	4	10	14	71.43	0.00	100.00	0.375
14	1	0	0	13	14	92.86	100.00	100.00	0.000
15	0	0	4	10	14	71.43	0.00	100.00	0.625
16	0	2	0	12	14	85.71	0.00	100.00	0.500
17	2	0	0	12	14	85.71	100.00	100.00	0.500
18	2	0	0	12	14	85.71	100.00	100.00	0.500
19	0	0	3	11	14	78.57	0.00	100.00	0.667
20	0	0	0	14	14	100.00			

Ave's	Absent	Mode+	IA	ITv
Stage 1	76.39	37.50	100.00	0.486
Stage 2	81.17	30.00	100.00	0.399
Overall	79.02	33.33	100.00	0.438

Table 36   Rainbow Group Voting Trends: Yugoslav Crisis

	Mode +	Mode -	Mode 0	Absent /	Members	% Absent	% Mode +	IA	ITv
Stage 1,Vote 1	0	0	0	15	15	100.00			
2	0	0	0	15	15	100.00			
3	5	0	0	10	15	66.67	100.00	100.00	0.720
4	8	0	0	7	15	46.67	100.00	100.00	0.781
5	0	7	0	8	15	53.33	0.00	100.00	0.816
6	7	0	0	8	15	53.33	100.00	100.00	0.735
7	3	0	0	12	15	80.00	100.00	100.00	0.667
8	0	3	0	12	15	80.00	0.00	100.00	0.667
9	0	1	0	14	15	93.33	0.00	100.00	0.000
Stage 2,Vote 10	3	1	0	11	15	73.33	75.00	50.00	0.000
11	5	0	0	10	15	66.67	100.00	100.00	0.560
12	4	0	1	10	15	66.67	80.00	60.00	0.375
13	5	0	0	10	15	66.67	100.00	100.00	0.560
14	5	0	0	10	15	66.67	100.00	100.00	0.800
15	4	0	3	8	15	53.33	57.14	14.29	0.750
16	6	0	1	8	15	53.33	85.71	71.43	0.667
17	4	4	0	7	15	46.67	50.00	0.00	0.375
18	2	3	0	10	15	66.67	40.00	20.00	0.000
19	4	0	2	9	15	60.00	66.67	33.33	0.750
20	4	0	0	11	15	73.33	100.00	100.00	0.750

Ave's	Absent	Mode+	IA	ITv
Stage 1	74.81	57.14	100.00	0.627
Stage 2	63.03	77.68	59.00	0.508
Overall	68.33	69.70	74.95	0.554

Table 37   LU Group Voting Trends: Yugoslav Crisis

	Mode +	Mode -	Mode 0	Absent /	Members	% Absent	% Mode +	IA	ITv
Stage 1,Vote 1	1	0	0	13	14	92.86	100.00	100.00	0.000
2	1	0	0	13	14	92.86	100.00	100.00	0.000
3	1	0	0	13	14	92.86	100.00	100.00	0.000
4	0	3	0	11	14	78.57	0.00	100.00	0.444
5	1	0	0	13	14	92.86	100.00	100.00	0.000
6	1	1	0	12	14	85.71	50.00	0.00	0.000
7	0	6	0	8	14	57.14	0.00	100.00	0.722
8	2	3	0	9	14	64.29	40.00	20.00	0.444
9	0	2	0	12	14	85.71	0.00	100.00	0.000
Stage 2,Vote 10	0	1	0	12	13	92.31	0.00	100.00	0.000
11	0	3	0	10	13	76.92	0.00	100.00	0.444
12	0	2	0	11	13	84.62	0.00	100.00	0.000
13	0	5	0	8	13	61.54	0.00	100.00	0.640
14	2	3	0	8	13	61.54	40.00	20.00	0.444
15	2	0	0	11	13	84.62	100.00	100.00	0.000
16	0	2	0	11	13	84.62	0.00	100.00	0.000
17	0	3	0	10	13	76.92	0.00	100.00	0.444
18	1	0	0	12	13	92.31	100.00	100.00	0.000
19	1	1	0	11	13	84.62	50.00	0.00	0.000
20	0	5	0	8	13	61.54	0.00	100.00	0.480

Ave's	Absent	Mode+	IA	ITv
Stage 1	82.54	54.44	80.00	0.179
Stage 2	78.32	26.36	83.64	0.223
Overall	80.22	39.00	82.00	0.203

Table 38 Independent Members' Voting Trends: Yugoslav Crisis

	Mode +	Mode -	Mode 0	Absent /	Members	% Absent	% Mode +	IA	ITv
Stage 1,Vote 1	0	0	0	10	10	100.00			
2	0	0	0	10	10	100.00			
3	3	0	0	9	12	75.00	100.00	100.00	0.444
4	0	0	0	12	12	100.00			
5	0	0	0	12	12	100.00			
6	0	2	1	9	12	75.00	0.00	33.33	0.500
7	1	2	0	9	12	75.00	33.33	33.33	0.000
8	0	0	1	11	12	91.67	0.00	100.00	0.000
9	2	0	0	10	12	83.33	100.00	100.00	0.500
Stage 2,Vote 10	1	0	0	11	12	91.67	100.00	100.00	0.000
11	1	0	0	11	12	91.67	100.00	100.00	0.000
12	0	0	1	11	12	91.67	0.00	100.00	0.000
13	0	0	1	11	12	91.67	0.00	100.00	0.000
14	2	0	0	10	12	83.33	100.00	100.00	0.500
15	1	0	0	11	12	91.67	100.00	100.00	0.000
16	1	0	0	11	12	91.67	100.00	100.00	0.000
17	2	0	0	10	12	83.33	100.00	100.00	0.500
18	1	0	0	11	12	91.67	100.00	100.00	0.000
19	2	0	0	10	12	83.33	100.00	100.00	0.500
20	3	0	0	9	12	75.00	100.00	100.00	0.444

Ave's	Absent	Mode+	IA	ITv
Stage 1	88.89	46.67	73.33	0.289
Stage 2	87.88	81.82	100.00	0.177
Overall	88.33	70.83	91.67	0.212

Table 39 European Parliament Voting Trends: Yugoslav Crisis

	Mode +	Mode -	Mode 0	Absent /	Members	% Absent	% Mode +	IA	ITv
Stage 1,Vote 1	74	22	3	419	518	80.89	74.75	49.49	0.844
2	102	0	1	415	518	80.12	99.03	98.06	0.866
3	101	2	0	415	518	80.12	98.06	96.12	0.891
4	46	157	8	307	518	59.27	21.80	48.82	0.849
5	196	8	11	303	518	58.49	91.16	82.33	0.850
6	208	10	70	230	518	44.40	72.22	44.44	0.869
7	65	82	5	366	518	70.66	42.76	7.89	0.866
8	30	105	4	379	518	73.17	21.58	51.08	0.869
9	100	13	3	402	518	77.61	86.21	72.41	0.851
Stage 2,Vote 10	136	6	4	372	518	71.81	93.15	86.30	0.873
11	131	12	3	372	518	71.81	89.73	79.45	0.872
12	141	9	6	362	518	69.88	90.38	80.77	0.865
13	75	83	7	353	518	68.15	45.45	0.61	0.831
14	145	3	1	369	518	71.24	97.32	94.63	0.880
15	158	3	9	348	518	67.18	92.94	85.88	0.873
16	22	134	16	346	518	66.80	12.79	55.81	0.851
17	61	109	6	342	518	66.02	34.66	23.86	0.849
18	151	19	0	348	518	67.18	88.82	77.65	0.866
19	129	3	8	378	518	72.97	92.14	84.29	0.856
20	156	58	5	299	518	57.72	71.23	42.47	0.867

Ave's	Absent	Mode+	IA	ITv
Stage 1	69.41	67.51	61.18	0.862
Stage 2	68.25	73.51	64.70	0.862
Overall	68.77	70.81	63.12	0.862

Bibliography

A. PRIMARY SOURCES

1. European Parliament Debates

All EP Debates are published in the Annex of the Official Journal of the European Communities.

Aglietta, Maria Adelaide (12 May 1992): 'Situation in Bosnia-Herzegovina', *Debates of the European Parliament, OJEC* 3-418, pp. 71-72.

Alavanos, Alexandros (12 September 1990): 'Explanation of vote (Gulf)', *Debates of the European Parliament, OJEC* 3-393 , pp. 153-154.

Alavanos, Alexandros (11 March 1992): 'Situation in the Former Yugoslav Republics', *Debates of the European Parliament, OJEC* 3-416, p. 95.

Alavanos, Alexandros (12 May 1992): 'Situation in Bosnia-Herzegovina', *Debates of the European Parliament, OJEC* 3-418, p. 73.

Alavanos, Alexandros (7 July 1992): 'Economic Aid to Croatia and Slovenia', *Debates of the European Parliament, OJEC* 3-420, pp. 104-105.

von Alemann, Mechthild (21 February 1991): 'Topical and urgent debate (Yugoslavia)', *Debates of the European Parliament, OJEC* 3-401, p. 270.

von Alemann, Mechthild (14 March 1991): 'Situation in Yugoslavia', *Debates of the European Parliament, OJEC* 3-403, p. 222.

von Alemann, Mechthild (10 September 1991): 'Situation in Yugoslavia', *Debates of the European Parliament, OJEC* 3-408, p. 85.

von Alemann, Mechthild (9 April 1992): 'Topical and urgent debate: Bosnia-Herzegovina', *Debates of the European Parliament, OJEC* 3-417, p. 274.

von Alemann, Mechthild (9 June 1992): 'Relations between the European Community and the Republics of the Former Yugoslavia', *Debates of the European Parliament, OJEC* 3-419, p. 59.

von Alemann, Mechthild (7 July 1992): 'Economic Aid to Croatia and Slovenia', *Debates of the European Parliament, OJEC* 3-420, p. 104.

Alliot-Marie, Michèle (10 September 1991): 'Situation in Yugoslavia', *Debates of the European Parliament, OJEC*, 3-408 p. 87.

Amaral, Rui (12 September 1990): 'Explanation of vote (Gulf)', *Debates of the European Parliament, OJEC* 3-393, pp. 156-157.

Amaral, Rui (15 May 1991): 'Establishing a Middle East Peace Settlement', *Debates of the European Parliament, OJEC* 3-405, pp. 140-141.

Andreotti, Giulio (12 September, 1990): 'Statements by the Council and Commission on the Situation in the Gulf', *Debates of the European Parliament, OJEC* 3-393, pp. 98-103.

Antony, Bernard (23 October 1990): 'Topical political questions in the EC and at international Level', *Debates of the European Parliament, OJEC* 3-395, p. 79.

Antony, Bernard (20 November 1991): 'Situation in Yugoslavia', *Debates of the European Parliament, OJEC* 3-411, p. 158.

Antony, Bernard (12 May 1992): 'Situation in Bosnia-Herzegovina', *Debates of the European Parliament, OJEC* 3-418, p. 72-73.

Antony, Bernard (9 June 1992): 'Relations between the European Community and the Republics of the Former Yugoslavia', *Debates of the European Parliament, OJEC* 3-419, p. 57.

Aulas, Marie-Christine (12 September 1990): 'Statements by the Council and Commission on the Situation in the Gulf', *Debates of the European Parliament, OJEC* 3-393, pp. 111-112.

Aulas, Marie-Christine (23 October 1990): 'Topical political questions in the EC and at international Level', *Debates of the European Parliament, OJEC* 3-395, p. 82.

Avgerinos, Paraskevas (14 March 1991): 'Situation in Yugoslavia', *Debates of the European Parliament, OJEC* 3-403, pp. 218-219.

Avgerinos, Paraskevas (16 May 1991): 'Topical and urgent debate, Situation in Yugoslavia', *Debates of the European Parliament, OJEC* 3-405, pp. 268-269.

Avgerinos, Paraskevas (10 September 1991): 'Situation in Yugoslavia', *Debates of the European Parliament, OJEC* 3-408, p. 84.

Avgerinos, Paraskevas (9 October 1991): 'Topical and urgent debate (Yugoslavia)', *Debates of the European Parliament, OJEC* 3-409, p. 168.

Avgerinos, Paraskevas (11 March 1992): 'Situation in the Former Yugoslav Republics', *Debates of the European Parliament, OJEC* 3-416, p. 94.

Avgerinos, Paraskevas (12 May 1992): 'Situation in Bosnia-Herzegovina', *Debates of the European Parliament, OJEC* 3-418, p. 73.

Barón Crespo, Enrique (16 April 1991): 'Address by Pérez de Cuéllar, Secretary-General of the United Nations', *Debates of the European Parliament, OJEC* 3-404, p. 99.

Baget Bozzo, Gianni (9 October 1991): 'Topical and urgent debate (Yugoslavia)', *Debates of the European Parliament, OJEC* 3-409, p. 174.

Barrera i Costa, Heribert (10 September 1991): 'Situation in Yugoslavia', *Debates of the European Parliament, OJEC* 3-408, p. 87.

Barrera i Costa, Heribert (11 March 1992): 'Situation in the Former Yugoslav Republics', *Debates of the European Parliament, OJEC* 3-416, p. 93.

Beazley, Christopher (16 May 1991): 'Topical and urgent debate, Situation in Yugoslavia', *Debates of the European Parliament, OJEC* 3-405, pp. 267-268.

Belo, Maria (15 May 1991): 'Establishing a Middle East Peace Settlement', *Debates of the European Parliament, OJEC* 3-405, p. 142.

Belo, Maria (15 January 1992): 'Question Time', *Debates of the European Parliament, OJEC* 3-413, p. 70.

Bertens, Jan Willem (16 May 1991): 'Topical and urgent debate, Situation in Yugoslavia', *Debates of the European Parliament, OJEC* 3-405, p. 267.

Bertens, Jan Willem (11 March 1992): 'Situation in the Former Yugoslav Republics', *Debates of the European Parliament, OJEC* 3-416, pp. 91-92.

Bertens, Jan Willem (12 May 1992): 'Situation in Bosnia-Herzegovina', *Debates of European Parliament, OJEC* 3-418, p. 74.

Bertens, Jan Willem (9 June 1992): 'Relations between the European Community and the Republics of the Former Yugoslavia', *Debates of the European Parliament, OJEC* 3-419, pp. 55-56.

Bettini, Virginio (12 September 1990): 'Explanation of vote (Gulf)', *Debates of the European Parliament, OJEC* 3-393, p. 157.

Bettini, Virginio (11 October 1990): 'Commission Statement on Oil Prices', *Debates of the European Parliament, OJEC* 3-394, p. 288.

Blaney, Neil (11 October 1990): 'Commission Statement on Oil Prices', *Debates of the European Parliament, OJEC* 3-394, p. 286.

Blot, Yvan M. (14 March 1991): 'Situation in Yugoslavia', *Debates of the European Parliament, OJEC* 3-403, pp. 217-218.

Blot, Yvan M. (16 May 1991): 'Topical and urgent debate, Situation in Yugoslavia', *Debates of the European parliament, OJEC* 3-405, p. 267.

Blot, Yvan M. (9 July 1991): 'Situation in Yugoslavia', *Debates of the European Parliament, OJEC* 3-407, p. 77.

Blot, Yvan M. (10 September 1991): 'Situation in Yugoslavia', *Debates of the European Parliament, OJEC* 3-408, pp. 87-88.

Blot, Yvan M. (9 October 1991): 'Topical and urgent debate (Yugoslavia)', *Debates of the European Parliament, OJEC* 3-409, pp. 164-165.

Blot, Yvan M. (22 November 1991): 'Explanation of vote - Joint Motion for a Resolution on the Situation in Yugoslavia', *Debates of the European Parliament, OJEC* 3-411, p. 346.

Blot, Yvan M. (16 April 1991): 'Statement by the Chairman of the Committee on Budgets on Emergency Aid for the Kurds', *Debates of the European Parliament, OJEC* 3-404, p. 45.

van den Brink, Mathilde (9 October 1991): 'Topical and urgent debate (Yugoslavia)', *Debates of the European Parliament, OJEC* 3-409, pp. 173-174.

Brok, Elmar (13 March 1991): 'Situation in the Gulf', *Debates of the European Parliament, OJEC* 3-403, p. 91.

Canavarro, Pedro Manuel (12 May 1992): 'Situation in Bosnia-Herzegovina', *Debates of the European Parliament, OJEC* 3-418, p. 72.

Capucho, Antonio (23 October 1990): 'Topical political questions in the EC and at international Level', *Debates of the European Parliament, OJEC* 3-395, p. 82.

Carvalhas, Carlos (12 September 1990): 'Statements by the Council and Commission on the Situation in the Gulf', *Debates of the European Parliament, OJEC* 3-393, pp. 123-124.

Cassanmagnago Cerretti, Maria Luisa (30 January 1991): 'Developments in the Gulf', *Debates of the European Parliament, OJEC* 3-399, p. 5.

Caudron, Gérard (October 1990): 'Commission Statement on Oil Prices', *Debates of the European Parliament, OJEC* 394, p. 284.

Chabert, Henry (20 February 1991): 'Situation in the Gulf', *Debates of the European Parliament, OJEC* 3-401, p. 126.

Cheysson, Claude (11 December 1990): 'Situation in the Gulf', *Debates of the European Parliament, OJEC* 3-397, pp. 74-75.

Cheysson, Claude (13 March 1991): 'Situation in the Gulf', *Debates of the European Parliament, OJEC* 3-403, pp. 75-76.

Cheysson, Claude (9 July 1991): 'Situation in Yugoslavia', *Debates of the European Parliament, OJEC* 3-407, pp. 82-83.

Christensen, Ib (12 September 1990): 'Statements by the Council and Commission on the Situation in the Gulf', *Debates of the European Parliament, OJEC* 3-393, pp. 116-117.

Christensen, Ib (21 January 1991): *Debates of the European Parliament, OJEC* 3-398, p. 22.

Christensen, Ib (15 May 1991): 'Common Foreign and Security Policy', *Debates of the European Parliament, OJEC* 3-405, pp. 151-152.

Christensen, Ib (9 October 1991): 'Topical and urgent debate (Yugoslavia)', *Debates of the European Parliament, OJEC* 3-409, p. 166.

Christensen, Ib (20 November 1991): 'Explanation of vote' on Report A3-323/91 by Cassanmagnago Cerretti, on behalf of the Political Affairs Committee on the proposal for a Council decision C3-389/91 on the Denunciation of the Cooperation Agreement between the European Economic Community and the Socialist Federal Republic of Yugoslavia, *Debates of the European Parliament, OJEC* 3-411, pp. 176-177.

Christensen, Ib (22 November 1991): 'Explanation of vote on the Joint Motion for a Resolution on the Situation in Yugoslavia', *Debates of the European Parliament, OJEC* 3-411, pp. 345-346.

Coates, Kenneth (23 January 1991): 'Explanation of vote (Gulf)', *Debates of the European Parliament, OJEC* 3-398, pp. 155-156.

Colajanni, Luigi (12 September 1990): 'Explanation of vote (Gulf)', *Debates of the European Parliament, OJEC* 3-393, pp. 152-153.

Colajanni, Luigi (12 December 1990): 'Situation in the Gulf', *Debates of the European Parliament, OJEC* 3-397, pp. 71-72.

Colajanni, Luigi (21 January 1991): 'Situation in the Gulf', *Debates of the European Parliament, OJEC* 3-398, pp. 17-18.

Colajanni, Luigi (30 January 1991): 'Developments in the Gulf', *Debates of the European Parliament, OJEC* 3-399, p. 7.

Colajanni, Luigi (13 March 1991): 'Situation in the Gulf', *Debates of the European Parliament, OJEC* 3-403, pp. 79-80.

Collins, Kenneth (21 February 1991): *Debates of the European Parliament, OJEC* 3-401.

Cot, Jean Pierre (12 September 1990): 'Statements by the Council and Commission on the Situation in the Gulf', *Debates of the European Parliament, OJEC* 3-393, pp. 107-108.

Cot, Jean Pierre (23 January 1991) *Debates of the European Parliament, OJEC* 3-398.

Cot, Jean Pierre (21 February 1991): 'Explanation of vote on the Motions for Resolutions on the Gulf', *Debates of the European Parliament, OJEC* 3-401, pp. 311-312.

Crampton, Peter (11 December 1990): 'Situation in the Gulf', *Debates of the European Parliament, OJEC* 3-397, pp. 76-77.

Crampton, Peter (23 January 1991): 'Explanation of vote (Gulf)', *Debates of the European Parliament, OJEC* 3-398, p. 160.

Crawley, Christine (23 January 1991): 'Explanation of vote (Gulf)', *Debates of the European Parliament, OJEC* 3-398, p. 151.

Delors, Jacques (23 January 1991): 'Address to the European Parliament Presenting the Commission's Programme for 1991', *Debates of the European Parliament, OJEC* 3-398, pp. 138-143.

De Clercq, Willy (22 January 1991): 'Situation in the Gulf', *Debates of European Parliament, OJEC* 3-398, pp. 22-23.

De Clercq, Willy (12 May 1992): 'Situation in Bosnia-Herzegovina', *Debates of European Parliament, OJEC* 3-418, p. 71.

de Donnea, François-Xavier (11 October 1990): 'Topical and urgent debate (Gulf)', *Debates of the European Parliament, OJEC* 3-394, p. 273.

de Donnea, François-Xavier (6 February 1991): 'Developments in the Gulf', *Debates of the European Parliament, OJEC* 3-400, p. 5.

De Michelis, Gianni (11 December 1990): 'Situation in the Gulf', *Debates of the European Parliament, OJEC* 3-397, pp. 64-67.

De Montesquiou, Fezensac (13 March 1991): 'Situation in the Gulf', *Debates of the European Parliament, OJEC* 3-403, p. 77.

De Piccoli, Cesare (14 March 1991): 'Situation in Yugoslavia', *Debates of the European Parliament, OJEC* 3-403, p. 216.

De Piccoli, Cesare (9 October 1991): 'Topical and urgent debate (Yugoslavia)', *Debates of the European Parliament, OJEC* 3-409, p. 167.

De Piccoli, Cesare (20 November 1991): 'Situation in Yugoslavia', *Debates of the European Parliament, OJEC* 3-411, p. 157.

De Piccoli, Cesare (11 March 1992): 'Situation in the Former Yugoslav Republics', *Debates of the European Parliament, OJEC* 3-416, p. 92.

Desmond, Barry (21 February 1991): 'Topical and urgent debate (Yugoslavia)', *Debates of the European Parliament, OJEC* 3-401, p. 271.

Dessylas, Dimitrios (10 July 1991): 'Explanation of vote on Joint Motion for a Resolution on the Situation in Yugoslavia', *Debates of the European Parliament, OJEC* 3-407, p. 167.

Dessylas, Dimitrios (11 September 1991): 'Explanation of vote on Joint Motion for a Resolution on Yugoslavia', *Debates of the European Parliament, OJEC* 3-408, p. 162.

Dessylas, Dimitrios (9 June 1992): 'Relations between the European Community and the Republics of the Former Yugoslavia', *Debates of the European Parliament, OJEC* 3-419, p. 59.

de Deus Pinheiro, João (15 January 1992): 'Question Time', *Debates of the European Parliament, OJEC* 3-413, p. 70.

Dillen, Karel (12 September 1990): 'Explanation of vote (Gulf)', *Debates of the European Parliament, OJEC* 3-393, p. 162.

Dillen, Karel (11 October 1990): *Debates of the European Parliament, OJEC* 3-393, 285-286.

Dillen, Karel (11 March 1992): 'Situation in the Former Yugoslav Republics', *Debates of the European Parliament, OJEC* 3-416, pp. 93-94.

Dillen, Karel (9 June 1992): 'Relations between the European Community and the Republics of the Former Yugoslavia', *Debates of the European Parliament, OJEC* 3-419, p. 59.

Di Rupo, Elio (23 January 1991): 'Explanation of vote (Gulf)', *Debates of the European Parliament, OJEC* 3-398, p. 152.

Dury, Raymonde (21 February 1991): *Debates of the European Parliament, OJEC* 3-401.

Elliot, Michael (23 January 1991): 'Explanation of vote (Gulf)', *Debates of the European Parliament, OJEC* 3-398, p. 156.

Ephremidis, Vassilis (14 March 1991): 'Situation in Yugoslavia', *Debates of the European Parliament OJEC*, 3-403, pp. 226-227.

Ephremidis, Vassilis (15 May 1991): *Debates of the European Parliament OJEC*, 3-403 p. 152.

Ephremidis, Vassilis (9 October 1991): 'Topical and urgent debate (Yugoslavia)', *Debates of the European Parliament, OJEC* 3-409, pp. 167-168.

Ephremidis, Vassilis (11 December 1990): 'Situation in the Gulf', *Debates of the European Parliament, OJEC* 3-397, p. 73.

Ephremidis, Vassilis (15 May 1991): *Debates of the European Parliament, OJEC* 3-405.

Ephremidis, Vassilis (11 March 1992): 'Situation in the Former Yugoslav Republics', *Debates of the European Parliament, OJEC* 3-416, p. 95.

Ephremidis, Vassilis (12 May 1992): 'Situation in Bosnia-Herzegovina', *Debates of the European Parliament, OJEC* 3-418, p. 75.

Ephremidis, Vassilis (9 June 1992): 'Relations between the European Community and the Republics of the Former Yugoslavia', *Debates of the European Parliament, OJEC* 3-419, pp. 57-58.

Ephremidis, Vassilis (20 November 1991): 'Situation in Yugoslavia', *Debates of the European Parliament, OJEC* 3-411, pp. 157-158.

Ernst de la Graete, Brigitte (17 April 1991): 'Gulf crisis and arms exports', *Debates of the European Parliament, OJEC* 3-404, p. 142.

Ewing, Winifred (12 September 1990): 'Statements by the Council and Commission on the Situation in the Gulf', *Debates of the European, OJEC* 3-393, p. 124.

Falconer, Alexander (23 January 1991): 'Explanation of vote (Gulf)', *Debates of the European Parliament, OJEC* 3-398, p. 154.

Fernex, Solange (15 May 1991): 'Common Foreign and Security Policy', *Debates of the European Parliament, OJEC* 3-405, p. 155.

Ferri, Enrico (12 September 1990): 'Explanation of vote (Gulf)', *Debates of the European Parliament, OJEC* 3-393, pp. 162-163.

Fontaine, Nicole (12 September 1991): *Debates of the European Parliament, OJEC* 3-393.

Fontaine, Nicole (13 March 1991): 'Situation in the Gulf', *Debates of the European Parliament, OJEC* 3-403, p. 83.

Ford, Glyn (22 November 1990): 'Topical and urgent debate on Kuwait', *Debates of the European Parliament, OJEC* 3-396, p. 249.

Ford, Glyn (21 February 1991) *Debates of the European Parliament, OJEC* 3-401.

Ford, Glyn (13 March 1991): 'Situation in the Gulf', *Debates of the European Parliament, OJEC* 3-403, pp. 90-91.

Formigoni, Roberto (12 September 1990): 'Statements by the Council and Commission on the Situation in the Gulf', *Debates of the European Parliament, OJEC* 3-393, pp. 106-107.

Gaibisso, Gerardo (30 January): *Debates of the European Parliament, OJEC* 3-399, p. 130.

Giscard d'Estaing, Valéry (12 September 1990): 'Statements by the Council and Commission on the Situation in the Gulf', pp. 151-152; 'Explanation of vote (Gulf)', *Debates of the European Parliament, OJEC* 3-393, pp. 109-110.

Giscard d'Estaing, Valéry (20 February 1991): 'Situation in the Gulf', *Debates of the European Parliament, OJEC* 3-401, pp. 122-123.

Giscard d'Estaing, Valéry (9 July 1991): 'Situation in Yugoslavia', *Debates of the European Parliament, OJEC* 3-407, pp. 69-70.

Gollnisch, Bruno J,-J.M. (13 March 1991): 'Situation in the Gulf', *Debates of the European Parliament, OJEC* 3-403, p. 81.

Green, Pauline (23 January 1991): 'Explanation of vote (Gulf)', *Debates of the European Parliament, OJEC* 3-398, p. 155.

Grund, Joanna-Christina (12 September 1990): 'Explanation of vote (Gulf)', *Debates of the European Parliament, OJEC* 3-393, p. 154.

Habsburg, von, Otto (12 September 1990): *Debates of the European Parliament, OJEC* 3-393.

Habsburg, von, Otto (16 May 1991): 'Topical and urgent debate, Situation in Yugoslavia', *Debates of the European Parliament*, 3-405, pp. 266-267.

Habsburg, von, Otto (9 October 1991): 'Topical and urgent debate (Yugoslavia)', *Debates of the European Parliament, OJEC* 3-409, p. 165.

Habsburg, von, Otto (20 November 1991): 'Situation in Yugoslavia', *Debates of the European Parliament, OJEC* 3-411, pp. 159-160.

Habsburg, von, Otto (9 April 1992): 'Topical and urgent debate: Bosnia-Herzegovina', *Debates of the European Parliament, OJEC* 3-417, pp. 273-274.

Habsburg, von, Otto (12 May 1992): 'Situation in Bosnia-Herzegovina', *Debates of the European Parliament, OJEC* 3-418, pp. 73-74.

Habsburg, von, Otto (9 June 1992): 'Relations between the European Community and the Republics of the Former Yugoslavia', *Debates of the European Parliament, OJEC* 3-419, pp. 58-59.

Habsburg, von, Otto (7 July 1992): 'Economic aid to Croatia and Slovenia', *Debates of the European Parliament, OJEC* 3-420.

Herzog, Philippe A.R. (10 September 1991): 'Situation in Yugoslavia', *Debates of the European Parliament, OJEC* 3-408, pp. 88-89.

Howell, Paul F. (12 May 1992): 'Situation in Bosnia-Herzegovina', *Debates of the European Parliament, OJEC* 3-418, pp. 76-77.

Hughes, Stephen (23 January 1991): 'Explanation of vote (Gulf)', *Debates of the European Parliament, OJEC* 3-398, p. 154.

Jackson, Christopher (13 March 1991): 'Situation in the Gulf', *Debates of the European Parliament, OJEC* 3-403, pp. 77-78.

Jackson, Christopher (9 July 1991): 'Situation in Yugoslavia', *Debates of the European Parliament, OJEC* 3-407, p. 70.

Jackson, Christopher (10 September 1991): 'Situation in Yugoslavia', *Debates of the European Parliament, OJEC* 3-408, p. 85.

Jackson, Christopher (9 October 1991): 'Topical and urgent debate (Yugoslavia)', *Debates of the European Parliament, OJEC* 3-409, pp. 168-169.

Jackson, Christopher (20 November 1991): 'Situation in Yugoslavia', *Debates of the European Parliament, OJEC* 3-411, p. 156.

Jepsen, Marie (12 September 1990): *Debates of the European Parliament, OJEC* 3-393.

Klepsch, Egon (21 January 1991): 'Explanation of vote (Gulf)', *Debates of the European Parliament, OJEC* 3-398.

Lacaze, Jeannou (22 November 1990): 'Topical and urgent debate on Kuwait', *Debates of the European Parliament, OJEC* 3-396, p. 252.

Lagorio, Lelio (20 February 1991): 'Situation in the Gulf', *Debates of the European Parliament, OJEC* 3-401, pp. 134-135.

La Malfa, Giorgio (12 September 1990): 'Statements by the Council and Commission on the Situation in the Gulf', *Debates of the European Parliament, OJEC* 3-393, pp. 1201-1210.

Lamassoure, Alain (9 October 1991): 'Topical and urgent debate (Yugoslavia)', *Debates of the European Parliament,* 3-409, pp. 166-167.

300

Lamassoure, Alain (20 November 1991): 'Situation in Yugoslavia', *Debates of the European Parliament, OJEC* 3-411, p. 156.

Lane, Patrick (11 October 1990): 'Commission statement on oil prices', *Debates of the European Parliament, OJEC* 3-394, p. 285.

Lane, Patrick (20 February 1991): 'Situation in the Gulf', *Debates of the European Parliament, OJEC* 3-401, p. 131.

Lane, Patrick (13 March 1991): 'Situation in the Gulf', *Debates of the European Parliament, OJEC* 3-403, p. 86.

Langer, Alexander (20 February 1991): 'Situation in the Gulf', *Debates of the European Parliament, OJEC* 3-401, pp. 124-125.

Langer, Alexander (14 March 1991): 'Situation in Yugoslavia', *Debates of the European Parliament, OJEC* 3-403, pp. 223-224.

Langer, Alexander (10 September 1991): 'Situation in Yugoslavia', *Debates of the European Parliament, OJEC* 3-408, pp. 85-86.

Langer, Alexander (9 October 1991): 'Topical and urgent debate (Yugoslavia)', *Debates of the European Parliament, OJEC* 3-409, pp. 169-170.

Langer, Alexander (11 March 1992): 'Situation in the Former Yugoslav Republics', *Debates of the European Parliament, OJEC* 3-416, p. 93.

Langer, Alexander (12 May 1992): 'Situation in Bosnia-Herzegovina', *Debates of the European Parliament, OJEC* 3-418, p. 74.

Langer, Alexander (9 June 1992): 'Relations between the European Community and the Republics of the Former Yugoslavia', *Debates of the European Parliament, OJEC* 3-419, p. 56.

Laroni, Nereo (14 March 1991): 'Situation in Yugoslavia', *Debates of the European Parliament, OJEC* 3-403, p. 221.

Laroni, Nereo (16 May 1991): 'Topical and urgent debate, Situation in Yugoslavia', *Debates of the European Parliament, OJEC* 3-405.

Léhideux, Martine (11 December 1990): 'Situation in the Gulf', *Debates of the European Parliament, OJEC* 3-397, pp. 72-73.

Lenz, Marlene (15 May 1991): 'Establishing a Middle East Peace Settlement', *Debates of the European Parliament, OJEC* 3-405, p. 140.

Le Pen, Jean-Marie (12 September 1990): 'Statements by the Council and Commission on the Situation in the Gulf', *Debates of the European Parliament, OJEC* 3-393, pp. 114-116.

Le Pen, Jean-Marie (21 January 1991): 'Situation in the Gulf', *Debates of the European Parliament, OJEC* 3-398, pp. 19-20.

Lomas, Alfred (12 September 1990): 'Explanation of vote (Gulf)', *Debates of the European Parliament, OJEC* 3-393, pp. 158-159.

Lucas Pires, Francisco António (20 February 1991): *Debates of the European Parliament, OJEC* 3-399, p. 137.

Lucas Pires, Francisco António (March 1991): 'Situation in the Gulf', *Debates of the European Parliament, OJEC* 3-403, p. 91.

301

de la Malène, Christian (12 September 1990): 'Statements by the Council and Commission on the Situation in the Gulf', *Debates of the European Parliament, OJEC* 3-393, p. 114.

de la Malène, Christian (21 January 1991): 'Situation in the Gulf', *Debates of the European Parliament, OJEC* 3-398, pp. 18-19.

de la Malène, Christian (13 March 1991): *Debates of the European Parliament, OJEC* 3-403.

de la Malène, Christian (9 July 1991): 'Situation in Yugoslavia', *Debates of the European Parliament, OJEC* 3-407, pp. 76-77.

de la Malène, Christian (12 May 1992): 'Situation in Bosnia-Herzegovina', *Debates of the European Parliament, OJEC* 3-418, p. 72.

Martinez, Jean-Claude (12 September 1990): 'Explanation of vote (Gulf)', *Debates of the European Parliament, OJEC* 3-393, p. 153.

Matutes, Abel, Commissioner for Middle East Affairs, (21 January 1991): Address to the European Parliament, *Debates of the European Parliament, OJEC* 3-398, pp. 11-12.

McCubbin, Henry (23 January 1991): 'Explanation of vote (Gulf)', *Debates of the European Parliament, OJEC* 3-398, p. 161.

McGowan, Michael (23 January 1991): 'Explanation of vote (Gulf)', *Debates of the European Parliament, OJEC* 3-398, p. 152.

McMahon, Hugh (11 October 1990): 'Topical and urgent debate (Gulf)', *Debates of the European Parliament, OJEC* 3-394, pp. 273-274.

McMillan-Scott, Edward (12 September 1990): 'Statements by the Council and Commission on the Situation in the Gulf', *Debates of the European Parliament, OJEC* 3-393, pp. 128-129.

McMillan-Scott, Edward (30 January 1991): 'Developments in the Gulf', *Debates of the European Parliament, OJEC* 3-399, p. 6.

McMillan-Scott, Edward (20 February): *Debates of the European Parliament, OJEC* 3-401, p. 133.

McMillan Scott, Edward (11 March 1992): 'Situation in the Former Yugoslav Republics', *Debates of the European Parliament, OJEC* 3-416, p. 92.

McMillan-Scott, Edward (9 June 1992): 'Relations between the European Community and the Republics of the Former Yugoslavia', *Debates of the European Parliament, OJEC 3-419*, pp. 54-55.

Medina Ortega, Manuel (12 May 1992): 'Situation in Bosnia-Herzegovina', *Debates of the European Parliament, OJEC* 3-418, p. 76.

Megret, Bruno (22 November 1990): 'Topical and urgent debate on Kuwait', *Debates of the European Parliament, OJEC* 3-396, p. 249.

Melandri, Eugenio (12 September 1990):, 'Statements by the Council and Commission on the Situation in the Gulf', p. 129, 'Explanation of vote (Gulf)', p. 157, *Debates of the European Parliament, OJEC* 3-393.

Melandri, Eugenio (11 December 1990): 'Situation in the Gulf', *Debates of the European Parliament, OJEC* 3-397, p. 71.

Melandri, Eugenio (21 January 1991): 'Situation in the Gulf', *Debates of the European Parliament, OJEC* 3-398, pp. 2-3.

Melis, Mario (20 February 1991): 'Situation in the Gulf', *Debates of the European Parliament, OJEC* 3-401, pp. 127-128.

Merz, Friedrich (20 February 1991): 'Situation in the Gulf', *Debates of the European Parliament, OJEC* 3-401, pp. 138-139.

Millan, Bruce (16 May 1991): 'Topical and urgent debate, Situation in Yugoslavia', *Debates of the European Parliament, OJEC* 3-405, pp. 269-270.

Monnier-Besombes, Gérard (16 May 1991): 'Topical and urgent debate, Situation in Yugoslavia', *Debates of the European Parliament, OJEC* 3-405, p. 269.

Monnier-Besombes, Gérard (9 October 1991): 'Topical and urgent debate (Yugoslavia)', *Debates of the European Parliament, OJEC* 3-409, p. 167.

De Montesquiou Fezensac, Aymeri (13 March 1991): *Debates of the European Parliament, OJEC* 3-403.

Moorhouse, James (11 October 1990): 'Commission Statement on Oil Prices', *Debates of the European Parliament, OJEC* 3-394, p. 285.

Moorhouse, James (7 July 1992): 'Economic Aid to Croatia and Slovenia', *Debates of the European Parliament, OJEC* 3-420, pp. 103-104.

Morris, David (20 February 1991): 'Situation in the Gulf', *Debates of the European Parliament, OJEC* 3-401, p. 139.

Musso, François (23 October 1990): 'Topical political questions in the EC and at international Level', *Debates of the European Parliament, OJEC* 3-395, p. 78.

Napolitano, Giorgio (20 February 1991): 'Situation in the Gulf', *Debates of the European Parliament, OJEC* 3-401, pp. 125-126.

Napolitano, Giorgio (9 July 1991): 'Situation in Yugoslavia', *Debates of the European Parliament, OJEC* 3-407, p. 76.

Newens, Stanley (23 January 1991): 'Explanation of vote (Gulf)', *Debates of the European Parliament, OJEC* 3-398, p. 150.

Newens, Stanley (9 July 1991): 'Situation in Yugoslavia', *Debates of the European Parliament, OJEC* 3-407, pp. 84-85.

Newton Dunn, William (12 September 1990): 'Statements by the Council and Commission on the Situation in the Gulf', *Debates of the European Parliament, OJEC* 3-393, pp. 137-138.

Nianias, Dimitrios (22 November 1990): 'Topical and urgent debate on Kuwait', *Debates of the European Parliament, OJEC* 3-396, p. 250.

Nianias, Dimitrios (11 December 1990): 'Situation in the Gulf', *Debates of the European Parliament, OJEC* 3-397, p. 72.

Nianias, Dimitrios (20 February 1991): 'Situation in the Gulf', *Debates of the European Parliament, OJEC* 3-401, p. 134.

Nianias, Dimitrios (14 March 1991): 'Situation in Yugoslavia', *Debates of the European Parliament, OJEC* 3-403, pp. 225-226.

Nianias, Dimitrios (10 September 1991): 'Situation in Yugoslavia', *Debates of the European Parliament, OJEC* 3-408, p. 91.

Nianias, Dimitrios (9 October 1991): 'Topical and urgent debate (Yugoslavia)', *Debates of the European Parliament, OJEC* 3-409, p. 170.

Nianias, Dimitrios (20 November 1991): 'Situation in Yugoslavia', *Debates of the European Parliament, OJEC* 3-411, p. 157.

Nianias, Dimitrios (12 May 1992): 'Situation in Bosnia-Herzegovina', *Debates of the European Parliament, OJEC* 3-418, pp. 74-75.

Nianias, Dimitrios (9 June 1992): 'Relations between the European Community and the Republics of the Former Yugoslavia', *Debates of the European Parliament, OJEC* 3-419, pp. 56-57.

Nordmann, Jean-Thomas (12 September 1990): 'Explanation of vote (Gulf)', *Debates of the European Parliament, OJEC* 3-393, p. 155.

Nordmann, Jean-Thomas (22 November 1990): 'Topical and urgent debate on Kuwait', *Debates of the European Parliament, OJEC* 3-396, p. 251.

Occhetto, Achille (12 September 1990): 'Statements by the Council and Commission on the Situation in the Gulf', *Debates of European Parliament, OJEC* 3-393, pp. 112-113.

Oostlander, Arie M. (20 February 1991): *Debates of the European Parliament, OJEC* 3-399, p. 138.

Oostlander, Arie M. (16 May 1991): 'Topical and urgent debate, Situation in Yugoslavia', *Debates of the European Parliament, OJEC* 3-405, p. 269.

Oostlander, Arie M. (9 July 1991): 'Situation in Yugoslavia', *Debates of the European Parliament, OJEC* 3-407, pp. 78-79.

Oostlander, Arie M. (10 September 1991): 'Situation in Yugoslavia', *Debates of the European Parliament, OJEC* 3-408, pp. 89-90.

Oostlander, Arie M. (11 March 1992): 'Situation in the Former Yugoslav Republics', *Debates of the European Parliament, OJEC* 3-416, pp. 89-90.

Oostlander, Arie M. (9 April 1992): 'Topical and urgent debate: Bosnia-Herzegovina', *Debates of the European Parliament, OJEC* 3-417, p. 274.

Oostlander, Arie M. (12 May 1992): 'Situation in Bosnia-Herzegovina', *Debates of the European Parliament, OJEC* 3-418, pp. 70-71.

Oostlander, Arie M. (9 June 1992): 'Relations between the European Community and the Republics of the Former Yugoslavia', *Debates of the European Parliament, OJEC* 3-419, pp. 52-53.

Oostlander, Arie M. (7 July 1992): 'Economic aid to Croatia and Slovenia', *Debates of the European Parliament, OJEC* 3-420, p. 105.

Pack, Doris (21 February 1991): *Debates of the European Parliament, OJEC* 3-401.

Pack, Doris (14 March 1991): 'Situation in Yugoslavia', *Debates of the European Parliament, OJEC* 3-403, pp. 221-222.

Pack, Doris (9 July 1991): 'Situation in Yugoslavia', *Debates of the European Parliament, OJEC* 3-407, p. 69.

304

Pack, Doris (12 May 1992): 'Situation in Bosnia-Herzegovina', *Debates of the European Parliament, OJEC* 3-418, p. 75.

Pack, Doris (7 July 1992): 'Economic aid to Croatia and Slovenia', *Debates of the European Parliament, OJEC* 3-420, p. 105.

Papayannakis, Mihail (12 September 1990): *Debates of the European Parliament, OJEC* 3-393, p. 122.

Papayannakis, Mihail (12 May 1992): 'Situation in Bosnia-Herzegovina', *Debates of European Parliament, OJEC* 3-418, p. 71.

Pagoropoulos, Dimitrios (13 March 1991): 'Situation in the Gulf', *Debates of the European Parliament, OJEC* 3-403, p. 87.

Penders, Jean J.M. (12 September 1991): *Debates of the European Parliament, OJEC* 3-393.

Penders, Jean J.M. (30 January 1991): 'Developments in the Gulf', *Debates of the European Parliament, OJEC* 3-399, p. 9.

Penders, Jean J.M. (20 February 1991): 'Situation in the Gulf', *Debates of the European Parliament, OJEC* 3-401, p. 122.

Pérez Royo, Fernando (22 November 1990): 'Topical and urgent debate on Kuwait', *Debates of the European Parliament, OJEC* 3-396, p. 250.

Perreau de Pinninck, Carlos (12 September 1990): 'Statements by the Council and Commission on the Situation in the Gulf', *Debates of the European Parliament, OJEC* 3-393, pp. 129-130.

Pesmazoglou, Ioannis (December 1990): 'Situation in the Gulf', *Debates of the European Parliament, OJEC* 3-397, p. 70.

Pesmazoglou, Ioannis (20 February 1991): 'Situation in the Gulf', *Debates of the European Parliament, OJEC* 3-401, pp. 132-133.

Piermont, Dorothee (12 September 1990): 'Statements by the Council and Commission on the Situation in the Gulf', p. 13; 'Explanation of vote (Gulf)', p. 155, *Debates of the European Parliament, OJEC* 3-393.

Pinxten, Karel (December 1990): *Debates of the European Parliament, OJEC* 3-397.

Piquet, Réné-Emile (12 September 1990): 'Statements by the Council and Commission on the Situation in the Gulf', *Debates of the European Parliament, OJEC* 3-393, p. 116.

Piquet, Réné-Emile (20-21 February 1991): 'Situation in the Gulf', *Debates of the European Parliament, OJEC* 3-401, p. 128.

Piquet, Réné-Emile (13 March 1991): 'Situation in the Gulf', *Debates of the European Parliament, OJEC* 3-403, p. 82.

Pisoni, Ferruccio (13 March 1991): 'Situation in the Gulf', *Debates of the European Parliament, OJEC* 3-403, p. 90.

Poettering, Hans-Gert (20 February 1991): 'Situation in the Gulf', *Debates of the European Parliament, OJEC* 3-401, p. 135.

Poos, Jacques, EC President-in-office, (21 January 1991): Address to the European Parliament, *Debates of the European Parliament, OJEC* 3-398, pp. 9-11.

305

Porrazzini, Giacomo (11 October 1990): 'Commission statement on oil prices', *Debates of the European Parliament, OJEC* 3-394, p. 286.

Prag, Derek (12 September 1990): 'Statements by the Council and Commission on the Situation in the Gulf', *Debates of the European Parliament, OJEC* 3-393, pp. 135-136.

Prag, Derek (21 January 1991): 'Situation in the Gulf', *Debates of the European Parliament, OJEC* 3-398, p. 22.

Prag, Derek (20 February 1991): 'Situation in the Gulf', *Debates of the European Parliament, OJEC* 3-401, pp. 123-124.

Prag, Derek (14 March 1991): 'Situation in Yugoslavia', *Debates of the European Parliament, OJEC* 3-403, pp. 222-203.

Prag, Derek (10 September 1991): 'Situation in Yugoslavia', *Debates of the European Parliament, OJEC* 3-408, pp. 90-91.

Prag, Derek (11 March 1992): 'Situation in the Former Yugoslav Republics', *Debates of the European Parliament, OJEC* 3-416, p. 94.

Prag, Derek (9 June 1992): 'Relations between the European Community and the Republics of the Former Yugoslavia', *Debates of the European Parliament, OJEC* 3-419, pp. 59-60.

Price, Peter (21 January 1991): 'Situation in the Gulf', *Debates of the European Parliament, OJEC* 3-398, p. 3.

Prout, Christopher (12 September 1990): 'Statements by the Council and Commission on the Situation in the Gulf', *Debates of the European Parliament, OJEC* 3-393, pp. 110-111.

Prout, Christopher (21 January 1991): 'Situation in the Gulf', *Debates of the European Parliament, OJEC* 3-398, p. 16.

Prout, Christopher (30 January 1991): 'Developments in the Gulf', *Debates of the European Parliament, OJEC* 3-399, p. 10.

Prout, Christopher (10 September 1991): 'Situation in Yugoslavia', *Debates of the European Parliament, OJEC* 3-408, pp. 93-94.

van Putten, Maartje (11 October 1990): 'Topical and urgent debate (Gulf)', *Debates of the European Parliament, OJEC* 3-394, p. 274.

Randzio-Plath, Christa (13 March 1991): 'Situation in the Gulf', *Debates of the European Parliament, OJEC* 3-403, pp. 91-92.

Rawlings, Patricia (12 September 1990): 'Explanation of vote (Gulf)', *Debates of the European Parliament, OJEC* 3-393, p. 155.

Rawlings, Patricia (13 March 1991): 'Situation in the Gulf', *Debates of the European Parliament, OJEC* 3-403, p. 88.

Reding, Viviane (20 February 1991): 'Situation in the Gulf', *Debates of the European Parliament, OJEC* 3-401, p. 136.

Ribeiro, Sérgio (20-21 February 1991): 'Situation in the Gulf', *Debates of the European Parliament, OJEC* 3-401, pp. 131-132.

Robles Piquer, Carlos (12 September 1990): *Debates of the European Parliament, OJEC* 3-393.

306

Robles Piquer, Carlos (November 1990): 'Topical and urgent debate on Kuwait', *Debates of the European Parliament, OJEC* 3-396.

Robles Piquer, Carlos (13 March 1991): 'Situation in the Gulf', *Debates of the European Parliament, OJEC* 3-403, p. 92.

Robles Piquer, Carlos (12 May 1992): 'Situation in Bosnia-Herzegovina', *Debates of the European Parliament, OJEC* 3-418, p. 76.

Romeos, Georgios (23 January 1991): 'Explanation of vote (Gulf)', *Debates of the European Parliament OJEC* 3-398, p. 162.

Romeos, Georgios (20 February 1991): 'Situation in the Gulf', *Debates of the European Parliament, OJEC* 3-401, p. 135.

Rossetti, Giorgio (10 September 1991): 'Situation in Yugoslavia', *Debates of the European Parliament, OJEC* 3-408, pp. 86-87.

Rossetti, Giorgio (7 July 1992): 'Economic aid to Croatia and Slovenia', *Debates of the European Parliament, OJEC* 3-420, p. 104.

Sainjon, André (22 November 1990): 'Topical and urgent debate on Kuwait', *Debates of the European Parliament, OJEC* 3-396, p. 251.

Sakellariou, Jannis (11 December 1990): 'Situation in the Gulf', *Debates of the European Parliament, OJEC* 3-397, pp. 69-70.

Sakellariou, Jannis (20 February 1991): 'Situation in the Gulf', *Debates of the European Parliament, OJEC* 3-401, pp. 139-140.

Sakellariou, Jannis (13 March 1991): 'Situation in the Gulf', *Debates of the European Parliament, OJEC* 3-403, pp. 88-89.

Sakellariou, Jannis (9 October 1991): 'Topical and urgent debate (Yugoslavia)', *Debates of the European Parliament, OJEC* 3-409, pp. 165-166.

Sakellariou, Jannis (20 November 1991): 'Situation in Yugoslavia', *Debates of the European Parliament, OJEC* 3-411, p. 155.

Sakellariou, Jannis (11 March 1992): 'Situation in the Former Yugoslav Republics', *Debates of the European Parliament, OJEC* 3-416, p. 91.

Sakellariou, Jannis (12 May 1992): 'Situation in Bosnia-Herzegovina', *Debates of the European Parliament, OJEC* 3-418, p. 77.

Sälzer, Bernhard (11 October 1990): *Debates of the European Parliament, OJEC* 3-394.

Santos, Maria Amélia (12 September 1990): 'Explanation of vote (Gulf)', *Debates of the European Parliament, OJEC* 3-393, p. 152.

Sarlis, Pavlos (14 March 1991): 'Situation in Yugoslavia', *Debates of the European Parliament, OJEC* 3-403, pp. 215-216.

Sarlis, Pavlos (9 October 1991): 'Topical and urgent debate (Yugoslavia)', *Debates of the European Parliament, OJEC* 3-409, p. 168.

Schinzel, Dieter (20 February 1991): 'Situation in the Gulf', *Debates of the European Parliament, OJEC* 3-401, p. 138.

Seligman, Madron Richard (20 February 1991): *Debates of the European Parliament, OJEC* 3-401, 130.

307

Simeoni, Max (11 December 1990): *Debates of the European Parliament, OJEC* 3-397.

Simeoni, Max (23 October 1990): 'Topical political questions in the EC and at international Level', *Debates of the European Parliament, OJEC* 3-395, pp. 82-83.

Simeoni, Max (11 December 1990): *Debates of the European Parliament, OJEC* 3-395, p. 73.

Simeoni, Max (13 March 1991): 'Situation in the Gulf', *Debates of the European Parliament, OJEC* 3-403, pp. 81-82.

Simeoni, Max (14 March 1991): 'Situation in Yugoslavia', *Debates of the European Parliament, OJEC* 3-403, pp. 216-217.

Simeoni, Max (16 May 1991): 'Topical and urgent debate, Situation in Yugoslavia', *Debates of the European Parliament, OJEC* 3-405, p. 268.

Simpson, Brian (12 May 1992): 'Situation in Bosnia-Herzegovina', *Debates of the European Parliament, OJEC* 3-418, pp. 75-76.

Spencer, Thomas N.B. (9 October 1991): 'Topical and urgent debate (Yugoslavia)', *Debates of the European Parliament, OJEC* 3-409, p. 165.

Speroni, Francesco Enrico (12 September 1990): 'Explanation of vote (Gulf)', *Debates of the European Parliament, OJEC* 3-393, p. 154.

Taradash, Marco (12 September 1990): 'Explanation of vote', *Debates of the European Parliament, OJEC* 3-393, p. 159.

Taradash, Marco (20 November 1991): 'Situation in Yugoslavia', *Debates of the European Parliament, OJEC* 3-411, p. 157.

Telkämper, Wilfried (12 September 1990): 'Statements by the Council and Commission on the Situation in the Gulf', *Debates of the European Parliament, OJEC* 3-393, pp. 124-125.

Tomlinson, John (14 May 1991): 'Financial Perspectives - Draft amending budget No. 1/91 Preliminary Draft Budget for 1992', *Debates of the European Parliament, OJEC* 3-405, pp. 80-81.

Tongue, Carole (23 January 1991): 'Explanation of vote (Gulf)', *Debates of the European Parliament, OJEC* 3-398, p. 153.

Trivelli, Renzo (16 May 1991): 'Topical and urgent debate: Situation in Yugoslavia', *Debates of the European Parliament, OJEC* 3-405, p. 268.

Trivelli, Renzo (9 April 1992): 'Topical and urgent debate: Bosnia-Herzegovina', *Debates of the European Parliament, OJEC* 3-417, p. 274.

Vandemeulebroucke, Jaak H. A. (12 September 1990): 'Explanation of vote', *Debates of the European Parliament, OJEC* 3-393, p. 154.

Vandemeulebroucke, Jaak H. A. (January 1991): 'Topical and urgent debate', *Debates of the European Parliament, OJEC* 3-398.

Vandemeulebroucke, Jaak H. A. (21 February 1991): 'Topical and urgent debate', *Debates of the European Parliament, OJEC* 3-401, p. 270.

Vandemeulebroucke, Jaak H. A. (9 July 1991): 'Situation in Yugoslavia', *Debates of the European Parliament, OJEC* 3-407, pp. 75-76.

308

Vandemeulebroucke, Jaak H. A. (9 October 1991): 'Topical and urgent debate (Yugoslavia)', *Debates of the European Parliament, OJEC* 3-409, pp. 166.

Veil, Simone (12 September 1990): *Debates of the European Parliament, OJEC* 3-393.

Veil, Simone (22 November 1990): 'Topical and urgent debate on Kuwait', *Debates of the European Parliament, OJEC* 3-396, pp. 248-249.

Veil, Simone (11 December 1990): 'Situation in the Gulf', *Debates of the European Parliament, OJEC* 3-397, pp. 70-71.

Veil, Simone (23 January 1991): 'Situation in the Gulf', pp. 15; 'Explanation of vote (Gulf)', p. 153, *Debates of the European Parliament, OJEC* 3-398.

Verbeek, Herman (22 November 1990): 'Topical and urgent debate on Kuwait', *Debates of the European Parliament, OJEC* 3-396, p. 250.

Visser, Ben (11 October 1990): 'Topical and urgent debate (Gulf)', *Debates of the European Parliament, OJEC* 3-394, pp. 274-275.

von der Vring, Thomas (11 October 1990): *Debates of the European Parliament, OJEC* 3-394, p. 309.

von Wechmar, Rüdiger (30 January 1991): *Debates of the European Parliament, OJEC* 3-399, pp. 5-6.

Woltjer, Eisso P. (12 September 1990): 'Explanation of vote (Gulf)', *Debates of the European Parliament, OJEC* 3-393, pp. 164-165.

Woltjer, Eisso P. (23 October 1990): 'Topical political questions in the EC and at international level', *Debates of the European Parliament, OJEC* 3-395.

Woltjer, Eisso P. (20 February 1991): 'Situation in the Gulf', *Debates of the European Parliament, OJEC* 3-401, p. 122.

Woltjer, Eisso P. (9 July 1991): 'Situation in Yugoslavia', *Debates of the European Parliament, OJEC* 3-407, pp. 68-69.

Woltjer, Eisso P. (10 September 1991): 'Situation in Yugoslavia', *Debates of the European Parliament, OJEC* 3-408.

Woltjer, Eisso P. (12 May 1992): 'Situation in Bosnia-Herzegovina', *Debates of the European Parliament, OJEC* 3-418, p. 70.

Woltjer, Eisso P. (9 June 1992): 'Relations between the European Community and the Republics of the Former Yugoslavia', *Debates of the European Parliament, OJEC* 3-419, p. 54.

Woltjer, Eisso P. (7 July 1992) 'Economic aid to Croatia and Slovenia', *Debates of the European Parliament, OJEC* 3-420, p. 103.

Woltjer, Eisso P. (9 July 1992) 'Economic Aid to Croatia and Slovenia', *Debates of the European Parliament, OJEC* 3-420, p. 243.

2. European Parliament Resolutions and Motions for Resolutions

All adopted EP Resolutions on the Gulf and Yugoslav crises and related matters respectively between August 1990 and May 1991; January 1991-July 1992 are printed in the Official Journal of the European Communities, Series C. The texts of the non-adopted Motions for Resolutions are not published and are not kept in the libraries of the European Parliament, but only in the Archives of the Translation Division of the Secretariat of the European Parliament in Luxembourg.

2.1 Adopted EP Resolutions on the Gulf Crisis

Joint Resolution replacing B3-1600, B3-1602, B3-1603, B3-1604 and B3-1623 of 12 September 1990 tabled by Cot on behalf of the Socialist Group; Habsburg, Penders, Klepsch and Chanterie on behalf of the EPP Group; d'Estaing and De Clercq on behalf of the LDR Group; McMillan-Scott and Newton Dunn on behalf of the ED Group; Vecchi on behalf of the EUL Group; de la Malène on behalf of the EDA Group; Formigoni, Chairman of the *ad hoc* delegation, *OJEC* C 260 of 15 October 1990, p. 74.

Joint Resolution B3-1844/90 of 12 October 1990 tabled by van Putten and Sakellariou, on behalf of the Socialist Group, Robles Piquer and Verhagen, on behalf of the Group of the European People's Party, Capucho, on behalf of the Liberal, Democratic and Reformist Group, Newton Dunn, on behalf of the European Democratic Group, Aulas on behalf of the Green Group, Vecchi on behalf of the Group for the European Unitarian Left, Wurts, on behalf of the Left Unity Group and Vandemeulebroucke and others on behalf of the Rainbow Group, on the rise in oil prices, *OJEC* C 284 of 12 November 1990, p. 185.

Joint Resolution B3-1881 and 1889/90 of 25 October 1990 tabled by Verde i Aldea, Woltjer and Sakellariou on behalf of the Socialist Group and Colajanni, Gutierrez Diaz, Papayannakis and Iversen on behalf of the EUL Group on topical political issues in the Community and at international level, *OJEC* C 295 of 26 November 1990, p. 186.

Joint Resolution B3-2009, B3-2017, B3-2027, B3-2043, B3-2062, B3-2083/90 of 12 November 1990 tabled by Woltjer and Dury on behalf of the Socialist Group, Robles Piquer on behalf of the EPP Group, Veil and Bertens on behalf of the LDR Group, Newton Dunn on behalf of the ED Group, Vecchi on behalf of the EUL Group, de la Malène on behalf of the EDA Group, Ephremidis, Piquet, Miranda da Silva and De Rossa on behalf of LU Group on the attempt by Iraq to destroy Kuwait, *OJEC* C 324 of 24 December 1990, p. 200.

310

Resolution B3-2023 of 22 November 1990 tabled by Visser and Woltjer on behalf of the Socialist Group and van Ray and Robles Piquer on behalf of the EPP on the effects on the Philippines of the earthquake on 16 July 1990 and the Gulf crisis, *OJEC* C 324 of 24 December 1990, p. 217.

Joint Resolution B3-2188/90, B3-2189/90 and B3-2232/90 of 12 December 1990 tabled by Cot and Sakellariou on behalf of the Socialist Group, Colajanni on behalf the EUL Group, Ephremidis, De Rossa, Piquet, Miranda da Silva on behalf of the LU Group on the Situation in the Gulf, *OJEC* C 19 of 28 January 1991, p. 76.

Resolution B3-2190/90 of 12 December 1990 tabled by Ford on behalf of the Socialist Group on contingency measures in the event of a crisis in the Gulf, *OJEC* C 19 of 28 January 1991, p. 78.

Resolution B3-0120 of 24 January 1991 tabled by Price, Tindemans, von der Vring, Capucho, Beumer, van Velzen, Speroni, de Clercq, Collins, von Wechmar, Herman, Tomlins, Penders, Navarro, Kofoed, Ewing, Ruiz-Gimenez, Vandemeulebroucke, Pronk, Maher, Simpson A., Roth-Behrendt, Tongue, Garcia Amigo, Muntingh, Randzio-Plath, Pimenta, Jepsen, Prag, de Vries, de Donnea, Arias Cañete, Sonneveld, Newton-Dunn, McMillan-Scott, Jackson, C., Welsh, Patterson, Moorhouse, Beazley, C., Beazley, P., Simmonds, Nicholson, Cooney, Cushnahan, Porto, Salema, Carvalho Cardoso, Vohrer, Cox, Bertens, Larive-Groenendaal, Defraigne, Adam, Hughes, McGowan, Elliott, Bowe, van Hemeldonck, Goedmakers, Wynn, Onur, Peter, van Outrive, Cassidy, Daly and Valverde Lopez on the Gulf and the Baltic States, *OJEC* C 48 of 25 February 1991, p. 66.

Joint Motion for a Resolution replacing B3-0123 and B3-0127 of 24 January 1991 tabled by Sakellariou on behalf of the Socialist Group and Ewing, Vandemeulebroucke and Christensen on behalf of the Rainbow, on the Conflict in the Gulf, *OJEC* C 48 of 25 February 1991, pp. 115-116.

Joint Resolution replacing B3-0311, 0334, 0338, 0341, 0343, 0347, 0359 and 0382/91 of 21 February 1991 on the economic and social consequences of the Gulf crisis, *OJEC* C 72 of 18 March 1991, p. 129.

Joint Resolution replacing B3-387, 388, 389 and 392/91 of 21 February 1991 tabled by LU, on the Gulf War, *OJEC* C 72 of 18 March 1991, p. 141.

Joint Motion for a Resolution replacing B3-0398, 0402, 0429, 0450 and 0466/91 of 14 March 1991 tabled by Sakellariou on behalf of the Socialist Group, Cassanmagnago-Cerretti, Penders and Pesmazoglou on behalf of the EPP Group, McMillan-Scott on behalf of the ED Group, Aulas and Langer, on behalf of the Green Group, Vecchi on behalf of the EUL Group, Miranda da Silva, Piquet, Ephremidis and De Rossa on behalf of the LU Group. *OJEC* C 106 of 22 April 1991, p. 122.

Joint Resolution replacing B3-458, 470 and 477/91 of 14 March 1991 tabled by EUL on the Kurds *OJEC* C 106 of 22 April 1991, p. 120.

Joint Motion for a Resolution replacing B3-0552, 0555, 0562, 0564, 0565 and 0660/91 of 18 April 1991 tabled by Sakellariou on behalf of the Socialist Group, Penders, Verhagen and Poettering, on behalf of the EPP Group, Capucho, Lacaze, Bertens and Holzfuss, on behalf of the LDR Group, Jackson, on behalf of the ED Group, Aulas and Langer on behalf of the Green Group, Iversen and Porrazzini, on behalf of the EUL Group, Vandemeulebroucke, on behalf of the LU Group on Gulf crisis and arms trade, *OJEC* C 129 of 20 May 1991, p. 139.

Joint Resolution replacing B3-556-560-618-619-620-621-622-623 and 624/91 of 18 April 1991 tabled by Dury on behalf of the Socialist Group, Penders and Cassanmagnago Cerretti on behalf of the EPP Group, Bertens and Calvo Ortega on behalf of LDR Group, Jackson and McMillan-Scott on behalf of the ED Group, Roth and Langer on behalf of the Green Group, Colajanni on behalf of the EUL Group, de la Malène on behalf of the EDA Group, Vandemeulebroucke of the Rainbow Group and Piquet on behalf of the LU Group on the situation of the Kurds, *OJEC* C 129 of 20 May 1991, p. 141.

Joint Resolution replacing B3-0740, 0746 and 0798/91 of 16 May 1991 on the Situation of the Kurdish Refugees, *OJEC* C 158 of 17 June 1991, p. 247.

Joint Resolution replacing B3-0741, 0744, 0751, 0755, 0765, 0777 and 0811/91 of 16 May 1991, *OJEC* C 158 of 17 June 1991 tabled by Socialist Group, EPP, LDR, Greens, EUL, LU on the Situation in Kuwait, *OJEC* C 158 of 17 June 1991, p. 247.

2.2 Motions for Resolutions on the Gulf Crisis

Motion for a Resolution B3-1618 of 10 September 1990 by Aulas, Telkämper Lannoye, Santos and Langer on behalf of the Green Group on the Gulf crisis.

Motion for a Resolution B3-1624 of 12 September 1990 by Ib Christensen, Vandemeulebroucke, Ewing, Simeoni, Moretti, Blaney, Garaikoetxea Urriza, de los Santos, Speroni, Bjørnvig, Bond and Sandbæk on the behalf of the Rainbow Group.

Motion for a Resolution B3-1843/90 of 12 October 1990 by Metten and others, on behalf of the Socialist Group, on the rise in oil prices.

Motion for a Resolution B3-1821/90 of 8 October 1990 tabled by Aulas, Melandri, Santos, Langer, Tazdait and Telkämper on behalf of the Green Group on the situation in the Gulf.

Motion for a Resolution B3-1816/90 of 8 October 1990 tabled by Jackson and Newton-Dunn on behalf of the ED Group.

Motion for a Resolution B3-1829/90 of 11 October 1990 tabled by de la Malène on behalf of the EDA on humanitarian consequences of the Gulf crisis.

Motion for a Resolution B3-1847/90 of 12 October 1990 tabled by de la Malène and Musso on behalf of the EDA on oil prices.

Motion for a Resolution B3-2032 of 19 November 1990 tabled by Le Pen on behalf of the Technical Group of the European Right on the situation of the hostages in Kuwait and Iraq.

Motion for a Resolution B3-0115/91 of 23 January 1991 tabled by de la Malène on behalf of the EDA Group on the Situation in the Gulf.

Motion for a Resolution B3-0125/91 of 24 January 1991 tabled by the following Members: Aglietta, Ainardi, Alavanos, Aulas, Barros Moura, Barzanti, Bettini, Bontempi, Buchan, Calvo Ortega, Canavarro, Castellina, Cramon Baiber, Crampton, Ceci, Coates, De Rossa, Domingo, Elmalan, Elliott, Ephremidis, Falconer, Fernex, Gutierrez Diaz, Hindley, Hughes, Kostopoulos, Langer, Lannoye, Lomas, Mayer, McCubbin, McMahon, Megahy, Miranda da Silva, Moretti, Morris, Napoletano, Newens, Newman, Papayannakis, Piquet, Puerta, Quistorp, Regge, Ribeiro, Seal, Smith A., Smith L., Speroni, Stewart, Tsimas, Vecchi, West, White and Wurtz on the Gulf War.

2.3 Adopted EP Resolutions on Yugoslavia (February 1991-July 1992)

Joint Resolution B3-0302, 0336 and 0379 of 21 February 1991 tabled by Dury and Sakellariou on behalf of the Socialist Group, Pack on behalf of the EPP Group, von Alemann on behalf of LDR Group, Newton Dunn on behalf of the ED Group, Langer and Monnier-Besombes on behalf of the Green Group, Vandemeulebroucke on behalf of the Rainbow Group on the crisis on Kosovo, *OJEC* C 72 of 18 March 1991, p. 131.

Joint Resolution B3-0395, 0397/fin, 0399, 0403, 0431 and 0482 of 15 March 1991 tabled by Avgerinos on behalf of the Socialist Group, Sarlis and Pack on behalf of the EPP Group, von Alemann on behalf of the LDR Group, Langer on behalf of the Green Group, Rossetti on behalf of the EUL Group de la Malène on behalf of the EDA Group Prag on behalf of the ED Group was also signatory on the Situation in Yugoslavia, *OJEC* C 106 of 22 April 1991, p. 168.

Joint Resolution B3-745, 779, 786, 794, 806, 807, 822 and 826 tabled by Avgerinos, Dury on behalf of the Socialist Group, Habsburg, Pack and Oostlander on behalf of the EPP Group, von Alemann on behalf of the LDR Group , McMillan-Scott on behalf of the ED Group, Langer and Monnier-Besombes on behalf of the Green Group, De Piccoli on behalf of the EUL Group, Alliot-Marie on behalf of the EDA Group, Vandemeulebroucke on behalf of the Rainbow Group of 16 May 1991 on the Situation in Yugoslavia, *OJEC* C 158 of 17 June 1991, p. 242.

Joint Resolution B3-1119, 1216, 1217, 1218, 1220, 1222 and 1223 of 10 July 1991 tabled by EPP, Socialist, Greens, EUL, LDR, ED and LU on the Situation in Yugoslavia, *OJEC* C 240 of 16 September 1991, p. 137.

313

Joint Resolution B3-1325, 1360, 1371, 1372 and 1390 of 11 September 1991 tabled by Socialist, EPP, EUL, EDA and Prag on the Situation in Yugoslavia, *OJEC* C267 of 14 October 1991, p. 100.

Resolution B3-1604 of 10 October 1991, tabled by EPP, LDR, ED, EUL, Greens, Rainbow on the events in Yugoslavia *OJEC* C 280 of 28 October 1991, p. 127.

Joint Resolution B3-1882, 1886, 1890, 1896 of 22 November 1991 signed by Sakellariou and Woltjer on behalf of the Socialist Group, Habsburg and Oostlander on the behalf of the EPP Group, Jackson of the ED Group and De Piccoli, Rossetti and Vecchi on the behalf of the EUL Group, von Alemann cosigned the joint resolution on her own behalf on the situation on Yugoslavia, *OJEC* 326 of 16 December 1991.

Joint Resolution B3-0037, 0038, 0040, 0042, 0045, 0047, 0049 of 17 January 1992, signed by Sakellariou and Woltjer on behalf of the Socialist Group, Habsburg, Pack, Tindemans and Sarlis on behalf of the EPP Group, von Alemann, von Wechmar and Bertens on behalf of the LDR Group, Jackson on behalf of the ED Group, Aglietta and Lannoye on behalf of the Green Group, De Piccoli and Rossetti on behalf of the EDA Group, Vandemeulebroucke, Simeoni and Ewing on behalf of the Rainbow Group. on the decision by the Council to recognize Croatia and Slovenia, *OJEC* 39 of 17 February 1992, p. 130.

Joint Resolution B3-405, 406, 407, 408, 409, 410, 413 of 12 March 1992 (On Bosnian crisis) tabled by Socialist, EPP, LDR, ED, EUL, Greens, EDA and Rainbow on the territory of former Yugoslavia.

Resolution B3-0532 of 9 April 1992 tabled by Oostlander and thirty others signatories on behalf of EPP Group on the situation in Bosnia-Herzegovina, *OJEC* C 125 of 18 May 1992, p. 220.

Resolution B3-0528 of 9 April 1992 tabled by von Alemann on behalf of LDR Group on the crisis in Kosovo, *OJEC* 125 of 18 May 1992, pp. 228-229.

Joint Resolution B3-0675, 677, 679, 680, 681, 682 of 14 May 1992 tabled by Socialist, EPP, LDR, EUL, EDA, Rainbow on the situation in Bosnia-Herzegovina, *OJEC* C 150 of 15 June 1992, pp. 234-235.

Resolution A3-0208 of 11 June 1992 Relations between the European Community and the Republics of the former Yugoslavia (*Oostlander Report*), C 176 of 13 July 1992, p. 198.

Resolution B3-0973 and 1049 of 9 July 1992 on the Situation in Bosnia-Herzegovina tabled by Habsburg and Oostlander on behalf of EPP and de la Malène on behalf of EDA, Vandemeulebroucke on behalf of Rainbow Group and von Alemann on her behalf, *OJEC* C 241 of 21 September 1992, p. 145.

Legislative Resolution A3-0232 of 9 July 1992 embodying the opinion of the EP on the Commission proposal for a Council Regulation amending regulation (EEC) No. 3906/80 in order to extend economic aid to include Croatia and Slovenia, *Stavrou Report*, *OJEC* C 241 of 21 September 1992, p. 170.

Resolution B3-1047/92 of 9 July 1992 tabled by Habsburg, Tindemans, Lenz, McMillan Scott, Oostlander and Pack on behalf of the EPP on the Death Sentences on Croatian Citizens in Belgrade, *OJEC* C 241 of 21 September 1992, p. 147.

2.4 Motions for Resolutions on Yugoslavia

Motion for a Resolution B3-0297 of February 1991 on Yugoslavia tabled by the ER Group. The motion was not incorporated in the topical and urgent debate. Originally the subject should have been on Western Sahara but then it was replaced by Yugoslavia.

Motion for a Resolution B3-0394 of 7 March 1991 tabled by Blot and Léhideux on behalf of ER Group on Yugoslavia.

Motion for a Resolution B3-0396 of 7 March 1991 tabled by Vandemeulebroucke on behalf of Rainbow Group on the situation in Yugoslavia.

Motion for a Resolution B3-0400 of 7 March 1991 tabled by De Piccoli, Rossetti and Papayannkis on behalf of EUL Group on the situation in Yugoslavia.

Motion for a Resolution B3-0252 of 15 March 1991 tabled by Blot on behalf of the Technical Group of the European Right on Yugoslavia.

Motion for a Resolution B3-0782 of 16 May 1991 tabled by Le Pen and others on behalf of the Technical Group of the European Right on Yugoslavia.

Motion for a Resolution B3-1137 of 4 July 1991 tabled by Le Pen, Blot, Le Chevallier, Léhideux, Tauran, Schodruch and Dillen on behalf of the Technical Group of the European Right on Slovene and Croat Independence.

Motion for a Resolution B3-1219 of 9 July 1991 tabled by de la Malène on behalf of the EDA Group on the political situation in Yugoslavia.

Motion for a Resolution B3-1221 of 9 July 1991 tabled by Vandemeulebroucke, Moretti, Ewing, Bjørnvig, Melis, Simeoni, de los Santos, Canavarro, Blaney and Barreca on behalf of the Rainbow Group on the situation in Yugoslavia.

Motion for a Resolution B3-1258 of 8 August 1991 on article 63 of Regulation by Guidolin on independence of Slovenia and Croatia.

Motion for a Resolution B3-1373 of 11 September 1991 tabled by Barreca i Costa, Melis, Simeoni, Ewing and Speroni on behalf of the Rainbow Group on the situation in Yugoslavia.

Motion for a Resolution B3-1383 of 11 September 1991 tabled by the LDR Group.

Motion for a Resolution B3-1391 of 10 September 1991 tabled by Habsburg, Pack and Chanterie on behalf of the EPP Group.

Motion for a Resolution B3-1608 of 11 October 1991 by Vandemeulebroucke on behalf of the Rainbow Group on the situation in Yugoslavia.

Motion for a Resolution B3-1716 of 5 November 1991 tabled by Coates on Freedom of Expression in Yugoslavia (Article 63 of Regulations).

Motion for a Resolution B3-1894 of 22 November 1991 tabled by Monnier-Besombes and Langer on behalf of the Greens on Yugoslavia.

Motion for a Resolution B3-1745 of 15 November 1991 tabled by Muscardini on Recognition of Croatia and Slovenia.

Motion for a Resolution B3-1895 of 22 November 1991 tabled by Antony and Léhideux on behalf of the ER on Croatia.

Motion for a Resolution of 11 December 1991 tabled by Rovsing on behalf of the ED on "Pax Europea" in Yugoslavia.

Motion for a Resolution of 11 December 1991 tabled by Romeos on behalf of the Socialist Group on protection of journalists in Yugoslavia.

Motion for a Resolution B3-0040 of 14 January 1992 tabled by de la Malène on behalf of the EDA Group on the Community's foreign policy on Yugoslavia.

Motion for a Resolution B3-0333/91 of 21 January 1991 on the Ecological Disaster in the Gulf tabled by Amendola, Quistorp, Bettini, Santos Lopez, Langer and Monnier-Besombes on behalf of the Greens.

Motion for a Resolution B3-0411 of 12 March 1991 tabled by the ER Group on humanitarian aid for people in the former Yugoslav Republics who are the victims of military operations.

Motion for a Resolution B3-0678 of 14 May 1992 tabled by Antony and Léhideux on behalf of ER Group on the situation in Bosnia-Herzegovina.

Motion for a Resolution B3-0680 of 12 May 1992 tabled by de la Malène on behalf of the EDA Group on the Civil War in Bosnia-Herzegovina.

3. European Parliament Reports

Blumenfeld Report on European Political Cooperation, 13 December 1977 (Doc. 427/77).

Cassanmagnago Cerretti Report on Denunciation of EEC-Yugoslavia Cooperation Agreement, 20 November 1991 (A3-0323/91).

Lady Elles Report on European Political Cooperation and the Role of the European Parliament, 9 July 1981, EP Resolution of 14 September 1981, *OJEC* C 234.

Crampton Report on the Commission proposal to revise Council Regulation no 2340/90 of 8 August 1990 pertaining the extension of the embargo to Iraq and occupied Kuwait by the Communit, 26 October 1990 (A3-261/90).

Crampton Report on a proposal for a Council regulation on financial aid for the countries most directly affected by the Gulf crisis SEC(90) 1862 C3-0313/90, 23 November 1990 (A3-0321/90).

Herman Report on the strategy of the European Parliament for achieving European Union, 21 December 1988 (A2-322/88).

Langer Report on the European peace caravan in Yugoslavia (25-29 September 1991), unpublished document PE 153.297, 7 October 1991.

Poettering Report on the Prospects for a European Security Policy (A3-107/91).

Poettering Report on the Development of a Common and Defence Policy for the European Union: Objectives, Instruments and Procedures, 23 February 1994 (A3-0109/94).

Roumeliotis Report on behalf of the Committee on Institutional Affairs on the conclusion and adaption of inter-institutional agreements, 2 February 1993 (A3-0043/93).

Toussaint Report on the Democratic Deficit in the European Community, 1 February 1988 (A2-276/87).

Tsatsos Report on the Constitutional Status of the European Political Parties, 10 December 1996 (A4-342/96).

Vedel Report examining the problem of the Enlargement of the Powers of the European Parliament, April 1972.

Verde I Aldea Report on shaping the European Community's Common Foreign Policy, 23 October 1992.

4. European Parliament Press Releases

Europe, Agence Europe 19 September 1990, 14 December 1990 and 19 June 1991 and the communiqués from the Party Federations' Presidential Conferences.

The Week, (9 October 1991): European Parliament Directorate-General for Information and Public Relations, Strasbourg, PE 155.623, p. 29.

The Week, (18-22 November 1991): European Parliament, Directorate-General for Information and Public Relations, Strasbourg, PE 155.639/rev, p. 28.

Briefing, (11-15 March 1996): European Parliament, Directorate-General for Information and Public Relations, pp. 24-25.

5. European Parliament Official Documents

EP Rules of Procedure, February 1992, February 1993, February 1996.
Treaties establishing the European Communities, 1987.
Treaty on European Union, OOPEC, Luxembourg, 1992.
European Union Consolidated Treaties, OOPEC, Luxembourg, 1997.

6. European Parliament Publications

European Parliament, Directorate-General for Research, *The Prospects for a Foreign and Security Policy of the European Union after Maastricht,* Working Paper No. 2, Political Series, Luxembourg, 1992.

European Parliament, Directorate General for Research, *The Crisis in the Former Yugoslavia,* Working Paper No. 18, Political Series, Luxembourg, 1993.

317

7. Political Groups Publications and Press Release

Parti Populaire européen PPE, 'Pour une Constitution fédérale de l'Union européenne', Projet de document de Congrès, Dublin, 15-16 mai 1990, LDR Communiqué de Presse, Bruxelles, 29 August 1990.

Press release by the Socialist group within the European Parliament, *Presse information*, Brussels 28 February 1991.

Lannoye, Paul (1991) 'A Green Group in the European Parliament what for?' *Green Leaves*, Bulletin of the Greens in the European Parliament, No. 1, April, p. 1.

'Greens and the Gulf War', *Green Leaves*, Bulletin of the Greens in the European Parliament, No. 1, April 1991, p. 3.

PPE, *Europe: Securité et Défense*, Bruxelles, Textes et Documents 4, 1991.

EPP Report of the activities, July 1990-July 1991, Luxembourg, September 1991.

Williams, Gareth S (1991): 'Note for the Attention of Jean-Pierre Cot and Eisso Woltjer: Yugoslavia - the Future stance of the Group', Socialist Group European Parliament, Brussels 19 September.

8. EC Member State Statements and Decisions

Statements by the Twelve on the Gulf:
on the Iraqi invasion of Kuwait, Brussels 2 August 1990.
on the Iraqi invasion of Kuwait, Brussels 4 August 1990.
on the Gulf, Extraordinary meeting, Paris, 17 January 1991.
Following an Iraqi attack against Israel, Luxembourg, 18 January 1991.
on the Gulf crisis, EPC ministerial meeting, Luxembourg, 19 February 1991.
on the Gulf, Luxembourg, Brussels, 24 February 1991.
on the Gulf, Brussels, 28 February 1991.
on the situation in Iraq, Brussels, 3 April 1991.

Statements by the Twelve on Yugoslavia:
Report on European Political Cooperation issued by the Foreign Ministers of the Ten on 13 October 1981 Europe No. 5309 of 3 August 1990.
Europe, No. 5310 of 4 September 1990.
Europe, No. 5395 of 19 December 1990.
Europe No. 5404 of 7-8 January 1991.
Statements by the Twelve, 20 August 1991, 27 August 1991.
London Report, *Bulletin of the European Communities*, S.3/81, Part II, Paragraph 13, pp. 14-17.
'Proposals by Hans van den Broek and Lord Carrington for Yugoslavia's future', *Europe*, 15-19 October 1991.

9. Interviews

Aelvoet, Magda, MEP (Green, Belgium), Brussels, 2 February 1996.

Balfe, Richard, MEP (Socialist, UK), London, 3 March 1997.

Barón Crespo, Enrique, MEP (Socialist, Spain) and former President of the European Parliament, Brussels, 23 January 1996.

Caccavale, Ernesto, MEP, (*Forza Italia/Europa*, Italy), Brussels, 24 January 1996.

Castellina, Luciana, MEP (EUL, Italy), Brussels, 31 January 1996.

Crampton, Peter, MEP (Socialist, UK), Brussels, 31 January 1996.

Colajanni, Luigi, MEP (former leader EUL, Italy), Brussels, 31 January 1996.

Corbett, Richard, Deputy Secretary-General Socialist group, 24 January 1996.

De Clercq, Willy, MEP (Belgium LDR), Brussels, 7 February 1996.

Dury, Raymonde, MEP (Belgium, Socialist) Brussels, 1 February 1996.

Elles, James, MEP (UK, ED), Brussels, 24 January 1996.

Grunert, Thomas, EP fonctionnaire, DGIV , Brussels, 24 January 1996.

van Hamme, Nadia, fonctionnaire, Socialist group, Brussels, 7 February 1996.

Hildebrandt, Arthur, fonctionnaire, EPP group, Brussels, 6 February 1996.

Imbeni, Renzo, MEP, (Socialist, Italy EUL Group, subsequently merged with the Socialist group, Brussels, 7 February 1996.

Kranidiotis, Yannos, MEP (Greece, Socialist), Brussels, 1 February 1996.

Kristoffersen, Frode, MEP (Denmark, EPP) Brussels, 24 January 1996.

La Malfa, Giorgio, Liberal MEP, Brussels, 1 February 1996.

Moore, Richard, fonctionnaire, LDR group, Brussels, 25 January 1996.

Moorhouse, James, British ED MEP, London, 26 February 1997.

Newens, Stanley, British Socialist MEP, London, May 1993 and 26 March 1997.

Oostlander, Arie M., Dutch EPP MEP, Brussels, 1 February 1996.

Piquet, Réné-Emile, French MEP, leader of the LU group, Brussels, 31 January 1996.

Poettering, Hans-Gert, German EPP MEP, Brussels, 25 January 1996.

Rehn, Elisabeth, MEP (ELDR, Finland), Brussels, 25 January 1996.

Riess-Passer, Susanne, MEP (Independent, Austria), Brussels, 31 January 1996.

Roubatis, Yiannis, MEP (Socialist Greece), Brussels, 7 February 1996.

Sakellariou, Jannis, MEP (Socialist, Germany), Brussels, 31 January 1996.

Silvestro, Massimo, Director-General DGIV and former Secretary-General of the LDR Group, Luxembourg, 29 January 1996.

Theorin, Maj Britt, MEP (Socialist, Sweden), Brussels, 31 January 1996.

Verde i Aldea, Joseph, (Socialist, Spain), Brussels, 24 January 1996.

van der Water, Rob, fonctionnaire, Socialist group, Brussels, 25 January 1996.

319

10. Written Interviews

Information gathered from responses to letters and questionnaires drafted by the author and completed by the French Socialist MEP and former Prime Minister, Michel Rocard, 22 July 1995, the Greek Communist MEP Alavanos, the Dutch EPP MEP Arie M Oostlander, the Italian Green official Paolo Bergamaschi, the Secretary-General of the EUL Group, Maria D'Alimonte, the British Conservative MEP Edward McMillan-Scott, the British Socialist official Richard Corbett, the Head of the London office, EPP group, Timothy Bainbridge and other officials of the political groups and of the Secretariat of the European Parliament, July-September 1995.

11. Miscellaneous

Committee on Foreign Affairs, Report No. 2 on "Winning the Cold War. The U.S ideological Offensive", 88th Congress, House Report No. 1352, April 27, 1964, pp. 6-7.

Decision of 28 February 1986 adopted by Ministers meeting in the framework of European Political Cooperation on the occasion of the signing of the Single European Act, *European Political Cooperation Bulletin*, Doc. 86/090.

Commission White Paper on Completion of the Internal Market, COM(85) 310fin point 219.

Resolution 678 adopted by the UN Security Council on 29 November 1990.

Info Memo 141, 13 septembre 1991.

Info Memo 173, 25 octobre 1991.

Opinion of the Committee on Foreign Affairs and Security for the Committee on Institutional Affairs on the Treaty on European Union, 21 January 1992 in European Parliament, *Maastricht*, Luxembourg, 1992, p. 23.

Cattet, Dominique (30/8/1990): Note du groupe libéral, démocratique et réformateur relative à la réunion sur la situation dans le Golfe, Bruxelles, Communiqué de presse redigé par le groupe libéral, démocratique et réformateur, Bruxelles.

EPC Secretariat Declaration on foreign citizens in Iraq and Kuwait, Press Release No. 63, 1990.

Appeal of 9 January 1991 addressed by MEPs Birgit Cramon Daiber, Dieter Schinzel, Claude Cheysson, Mechthild Rothe, Hiltrud Breyer, Yves Cochet, Claire Joanny, Alec Falconer, Philippe Herzog, Claudia Roth to the US Congress and Senate as well as to the USSR Parliament.

Letter of 9 January 1991 from the President of the European Parliament, Enrique Barón Crespo addressed to the President of the Iraqi National Parliament, Saadi Mahdi Salih, Brussels.

Letter of 10 January 1991 from the President of the European Parliament Enrique Barón Crespo addressed to MEPs.

Declaration of the Committee of the Political Affairs, Brussels 10 January 1991, Doc PE 147.883/BUR.

Declaration of the Committee of Political Affairs, Brussels 14 January 1991.

European Parliament, Delegation for Relations with Yugoslavia, 'Yugoslavia: The Political Situation', Report drawn up by the Directorate-General for Research of the European Parliament, 16 January 1991, unpublished document PE 146.209.

Déclaration commune du Président du Groupe Socialiste et du Président du Groupe pour la Gauche Unitaire europénne, Bruxelles, 16/1/1991 Doc: PE/GC/08/91.

Report on the visit of European Parliament Delegation to Yugoslavia 10-15 February 1991: 'Summary and Conclusions'.

Women European Parliamentarians' Appeal for Peace in the Gulf, Brussels, drafted by British Labour Crawley, German Green MEP Eva Quistorp and German Socialist Randzio-Plath on 19 December 1991 and signed on 9 January 1991 by the following forty-two MEPs Aglietta (Green Italy) Aulas, (Green France), Belgium (Socialist, Portugal), Braun-Moser, (EPP, Germany), Breyer (Green Germany), Buchan (Socialist, UK), van der Brink, (Socialist, NL), Castellina (EUL, Italy) Catasta (EUL, Italy), Cassanmagnago-Cerretti (EPP, Italy), Crawley (Socialist, UK) Diez de Rivera Icaza (Socialist, Spain), van Dijk (Green, NL), Domingo Segarra (EUL, Spain), Dury (Socialist, Belgium), Ernst de la Graete (Green, Belgium), Fernex (Green France) Ferrer (EPP, Spain), Goedmakers (Socialist, NL), Hoff (Socialist, Germany), Hermans, (PPE, Belgium), Izquierdo Rojo (Socialist, Spain) Jensen (Socialist, DK), Joanny, (Green, France), Junker (Socialist, Germany), Magnani Noya (Socialist, Italy), Llorca Vilaplana (EPP, Spain), Miranda de Lage (Socialist, Spain), Napoletano (EUL, Italy), Pollack (Socialist, UK), Quistorp, (Green Germany), van Putten (Socialist, NL) (Socialist, Germany), Rønn, (Socialist, DK), Roth-Behrendt (Socialist, Germany), Rothe (Socialist, Germany), Sandbæk (Rainbow, DK), Santos (Green, Portugal), Schmidbauer (Socialist, Germany), Tazdait (Green, France), Valent, (EUL, Italy) Van Hemeldonck, (Socialist, Belgium).

Reply of the National Assembly of Iraq to the European Parliament, July 1991, Annex to the letter addressed by the Iraqi Embassy in Brussels to the EP President Enrique Barón Crespo, PE 153.014 (unofficial English translation).

Déclaration de la Commission politique du Parlement européen sur la situation en Yougoslavie. Bruxelles, 12 août 1991.

EP Document C/JN/46/91,'Yougoslavie: Pour contribuer a la recherche d'une solution négociée, le President du Parlement européen invite le President du Parlement fédéral et ceux des Républiques.'

European Parliament *ad hoc* Delegation monitoring the referendum organized in Bosnia-Herzegovina on 29 February and 1 March 1992, Report by Paraskevas Avgerinos, Chairman of the ad hoc Delegation.

European Parliament Declaration on the Situation in the Former Yugoslavia, 10 August 1992, Press Release, EPI/14/92.

1992 'Enlarged Community: Institutional Adaptations', Study on behalf of the European Parliament by Trans-European Policy Studies Association (TEPSA), Working papers, Political Series No. 17, Brussels, Bonn, pp. 13-14.

Assembly of Western European Union (1992) 'Crises and wars in the Gulf 1958-1991', Brief prepared by the Office of the Clerk of the Assembly at the request of De Decker and Pieralli, Rapporteurs of the Political Committee, and De Hoop Scheffer, Rapporteur of the Defence Committee, Thirty-eighty ordinary session, Part I Chronology, pp. 16-26.

European Parliament Resolution on the European Council Report on Progress towards European Union, 11 March 1993, Doc. PE 170.288, p. 39.

Note for the attention of José Maria Gil-Robles Gil-Delgado, President of the European Parliament and Julian Priestley, Secretary-General, on the European Parliament's Priorities for the IGC and the New Amsterdam Treaty: Report and initial evaluation of the results, Document DV\332\457 drafted by the EP task-force on the Intergovernmental Conference, 15 July 1997.

B. SECONDARY SOURCES

The secondary sources include books, articles and other academic materials that have been directly or indirectly useful to this study.

1. Books, Chapters in Books and Pamphlets

Abélès, Marc (1992): *La vie quotidienne au Parlement européen*, Hachette, Paris.

Abelshauser, Werner (1994): ' "Integration a la carte": the primacy of politics and the economic integration of Western Europe in the 1950s' in *The Construction of Europe: Essays in honour of Emile Noel*, edited by Stephen Martin, Kluwer Academic Publishers, Dordrecht, Netherlands, pp. 1-18.

Allen, David, Rummel, Reinhardt and Wessels, Wolfgang, eds. (1982): *European Political Cooperation*, Butterworths, London.

Allen, David and Pijpers, Alfred, eds. (1984): *European Foreign Policy-Making and the Arab-Israeli Conflict*, Martinus Nijhoff, The Hague.

Allum, Percy (1995): *State and Society in Western Europe*, Polity.

Andersen, Svein S and Eliassen, Kjell A, eds. (1996): *The European Union: How Democratic is it?* Sage, London, Thousand Oaks, New Delhi.

Arndt, Rudi (1992): 'The Political Groups in the European Parliament', in *The European Community in the Historical Context of its Parliament*, Proceedings of the 40th Anniversary Symposium, Strasbourg, pp. 65-68.

Arter, David (1993): *The Politics of European Integration in the Twentieth Century*, Dartmouth, Aldershot, Brookfield USA, Hong Kong, Singapore, Sydney.

Attinà, Fulvio (1986): *Il Parlamento europeo e gli interessi comunitari*, Franco Angeli, Milano.

Attinà, Fulvio (1995): 'Partiti ed Elezioni nell'Unione europea' in Attinà, Fulvio, Longo, Francesca and Panebianco, Stefania *Identità, Partiti ed Elezioni nell'Unione europea*, Annali '90 Dipartimento di Studi Politici, Università degli Studi di Catania, Cacucci Editore, Bari, pp. 31-76.

Attinà, Fulvio (1998): 'Party Fragmentation and Discontinuity in the European Union, in *Transnational Parties in the European Union* edited by David S Bell and Christopher Lord, Ashgate, Aldershot, Brookfield USA, Singapore and Sydney.

Bagehot, Walter (1963): *The English Constitution*, Collins, London and Fontana Library.

Banks, Michael (1985): 'The Inter-Paradigm Debate', in *International Relations: A Handbook of Current Theory*, edited by Margot Light and Arthur John Richard Groom, Pinter, London.

Bardi, Luciano (1994): 'Transnational Party Federations, European Parliamentary Party Groups and the Building of Europarties', *How Parties Organize: Change and Adaptation in Party Organisations in Western Democracies*, edited by Richard S. Kats and Peter Mair, Sage, London, pp. 357-372.

Bay Brzinski, Joanne (1995): 'Political Group Cohesion in the European Parliament, 1989-1994', in *The State of the European Union, Vol. 3: Building a European Polity?*, edited by Carolyn Rhodes and Sonia Mazey, Lynne Rienner, Boulder, pp. 135-158.

Beloff, Max (1970): *The New International Actors: The United Nations and the European Economic Community*, edited by Carol Ann Cosgrove and Kenneth Joseph Twitchett, Macmillan, London.

Bennett, Christopher (1995): *Yugoslavia's Bloody Collapse: Causes, Course and Consequences*, Hurst and Company, London.

Brown, Chris (1992): *International Relations Theory. New Normative approaches*, Harvester Wheatsheaf, Hemel Hempstead.

Budd, Stanley Alec and Jones, Alun (1991): *The European Community: A Guide to the Maze*, 4th edition, Kogan Page, London.

Buffotot, Patrice (1994): 'The Security and Defence Policies of European Christian Democracy', in *Christian Democracy in Europe: A Comparative Perspective*, edited by David Hanley, Pinter, London, 202-211.

Bull, Hedley (1977, 1995): *The Anarchical Society*, Macmillan, London.

Bulmer, Simon and Wessels, Wolfgang (1987): *The European Council: Decision-making in European Politics,* Macmillan, London.

Burgess, Michael (1989): *Federalism and European Union : Political ideas, Influences, and Strategies in the European Community, 1972-1987,* Routledge. London and New York.

Burke, Edmund (1774): 'Extract from Speech to electors of Bristol' (3 November), cited in Hill, B, *Edmund Burke on Government, Politics and Society,* Harvester, Hemel Hempstead, 1975, pp. 156-158.

Burton, John Wear (1984): *Global Conflict: The Domestic Sources of International crisis,* Wheatsheaf, Brighton and Centre for International Development, University of Maryland, College Park, MD.

Cameron, D.R. (1992): 'The 1992 Initiative: Causes and Consequences', in *Euro-Politics: Institutions and Policy-Making in the New European Community,* edited by Alberta Sbragia, The Brookings Institution, Washington D.C.

Caporaso James A and Keeler John, T.S. (1995): 'The European Union and Regional Integration Theory', in *The State of the European Union, Vol. 3: Building a European Polity?,* edited by Carolyn Rhodes and Sonia Mazey, Lynne Rienner, Boulder USA and Longman, Harlow, England.

Chryssouchoou, Dimitris N. (1994): *The Consociational Dimension of European Integration: Limits and Possibilities of Transnational Democracy,* Institute of International Relations, Centre for European Affairs, Occasional Research Paper No. 6, Athens, July.

Clark, Alan (1992): 'François Mitterand and the Idea of Europe', in *The Idea of Europe: Problems of National and Transnational Identity,* edited by Brian Nelson, David Roberts and Walter Veit, Berg, New York and Oxford, pp. 152-170.

Claude, Inis Lothair, Jr (1964, 1965, 1971): *Swords into Plowshares: The Problem and Progress of International Organization,* 3rd edition, Random House, New York.

Closa, Carlos (1991): 'EPC and the Gulf crisis: A Case Study of National Constraints on Community Action', University of Hull, Research Paper 1/91.

Colajanni, Luigi (1990): 'Bilancio del vertice di Roma: Il cammino verso l'Unione europea, un passo avanti, *1990 Il cammino verso l'Unione europea,* Dicembre 1990, pp. 61-62.

Coombes, David (1979): *The Future of the European Parliament,* Policy Studies Institute, London.

Corbett, Richard (1994): 'Representing the people', in *Maastricht and Beyond: Building the European Union,* edited by Andrew Duff, John Pinder and Roy Pryce, Routledge, London and New York.

Corbett, Richard (1998): *The European Parliament's Role in Closer EU Integration,* Macmillan, London.

Cotta, Maurizio (1984): 'Direct Elections of the European Parliament: A Supranational Political Elite in the Making? in *European Elections 1979/91 and*

1984; Conclusions and Perspectives form Empirical Research, edited by Reif, K, Berlin: Quorum.

Cram, Laura (1996):'Integration Theory and the Study of the European Policy Process', in *European Union: Power and Policy-making* edited by Jeremy Richardson, London and New York, Routledge, pp. 40-58.

Crnobrnja, Mihailo (1992): *Yugoslavia: A Test Case for EC Foreign Policy*, Centre for European Policy Studies, CEPS, No. 91, 16 June.

Crnobrnja, Milhailo (1994): *The Yugoslav Drama*, I.B. Tauris, London, New York.

Cullen, Holly, Kritziotis, Dino and Wheeler, Nicholas, eds. (1993): *Politics and Law of Former Yugoslavia*, Research Paper 3/93, University of Hull.

Deutsch, Karl (1953 and 1966): *Nationalism and Social Communication: An Inquiry into the Foundation of Nationality*, MIT Press.

Deutsch, Karl (1954): *Political Community at the International Level*, Doubleday, New York.

Deutsch, Karl, Burrel, Sydney A., Kann, Robert A., Lee, Maurice Jr, Lichterman, Martin, Lindgren, Raymond E., Loewenheim Francis L., Van Wagenen, Richard W. (1957): *Political Community in the North Atlantic Area, International Organization in the Light of Historical Experience*, Princeton University Press, Princeton NJ.

Dini, Lamberto (1997): 'The European Union after Amsterdam', Foreword to *The Treaty of Amsterdam. Text and Commentary*, edited by Andrew Duff, Federal Trust, Sweet and Maxwell, London.

Ewing, Winifred (1989): 'The Political Groups in Parliament', in *Towards 1992: The European Parliament and the Single European Act 1989*, edited by Allan Macartney, University of Edinburgh, pp. 19-23.

Fitzmaurice, John (1975): *The Party Groups in the European Parliament*, Saxon House, Farnborough.

Fitzmaurice, John (1978): *The European Parliament*, Saxon House, Farnborough.

Freedman, Lawrence and Karsh, Efraim (1994): *The Gulf Conflict 1990-1991: Diplomacy and War in the New World Order*, updated edition, Faber and Faber, London.

Gaja, Giorgio (1980): 'European Parliament and Foreign Affairs: Political Co-operation among the Nine', in *Parliamentary Control over Foreign Policy*, edited by Antonio Cassese (1980), Sijthoff and Nordhoff, Alpehn aan den Rijn, The Netherlands and Germantown, MD, USA.

George, Stephen (1985): *Politics and Policy in the European Community*, Clarendon Press, Oxford.

Ginsberg, Roy H (1989): *Foreign Policy Actions of the European Community: the Politics of Scale*, Lynne Rienner, Boulder, USA and Adamantine Press, London.

Gnesotto, Nicole and Roper, John, eds. (1992): *Western Europe and the Gulf*, Institute for Security Studies of WEU, Paris.

Gow, James and Smith, James D (1992): *Peace-making, Peace-keeping : European Security and the Yugoslav Wars*, Brassey's for the Centre for Defence Studies (CDS).

Gow, James (1997): *The Triumph of the Lack of Will: Calling International Diplomacy and the Yugoslav War*, Hurst, London.

Greven, Michael Th. (1992): 'Political Parties between National Identity and Europeanification', in *The Idea of Europe: Problems of National and Transnational Identity* edited by Brian Nelson, David Roberts and Walter Veit, Berg, New York and Oxford, pp. 75-95.

Groom, Arthur John Richard and Heraclides, Alexis (1985): 'Integration and disintegration' in *International Relations: A Handbook of Current Theory*, edited by Margot Light and Arthur John Richard Groom, Pinter, London, 174-193.

Groom, Arthur John Richard (1990): 'The setting in world society', edited by A.J.R. Groom and Paul Taylor, pp. 9-10.

Guazzone, Laura (1992): 'Italy in the Gulf crisis' in *Western Europe and the Gulf*, edited by Nicole Gnesotto and John Roper, Institute for Security Studies of WEU, Paris.

Haas, Ernst B. (1958): *The Uniting of Europe: Political, Social and Economical forces 1950-1957*, 1st edition, Stevens and Sons, London, under the auspices of the London institute of World Affairs.

Haas, Ernst B. (1960): *Consensus Formation in the Council of Europe*, Stevens, London.

Haas, Ernst B. (1966): 'International Integration', in *International Political Communities: An Anthology*, New York.

Haas, Ernst B. (1971): 'The Study of Regional Integration: Reflections on the Joy and Anguish of Pretheorizing' in *Regional Integration: Theory and Research*, edited by Lindberg Leon N and Scheingold Stuart A., Harvard University Press, Cambridge, Massachusetts, pp. 3-42.

Haas, Ernst B. (1983): 'Words can hurt you; or who said what to whom about regimes' in *International Regimes*, edited by Stephen Krasner, Cornell University Press, Ithaca N.Y. and London, pp. 23-61.

Halliday, Fred (1994): *Rethinking International Relations*, Macmillan, London.

Halliday, Fred (1995): 'The End of the Cold War and International Relations: some Analytic and Theoretical Conclusions', in *International Relations Theory Today*, edited by Ken Booth and Steve Smith, Polity Press, Cambridge.

Hancock M Donald et al. (1993b): *Politics in Western Europe. An Introduction to the Politics of the United Kingdom, France, Germany, Italy, Sweden and the European Community*, Macmillan, London.

Hänsch, Klaus (1996): cited in Ghiţa Ionescu, in 'Conclusion', *Parliaments and Parties: The European Parliament in the Political Life of Europe* edited by Roger Morgan and Clare Tame, Macmillan, London and Martinus, New York.

Harrison, Reginald James (1974): *Europe in Question: Theories of Regional international integration*, Allen and Unwin, London.

326

Harrison, Reginald James (1990): 'Neo-functionalism' in *Frameworks for International Co-operation*, edited by A.J.R. Groom and Paul Taylor, Pinter, London, pp. 139-150.

Heisbourg, François (1992): 'France and the Gulf crisis' in *Western Europe and the Gulf*, edited by Nicole Gnesotto and A.J.R. Roper, Institute for Security Studies of WEU, Paris.

Hill, Christopher (1983a) *National Foreign Policies and European Political Cooperation*, RIIA and Allen and Unwin, London.

Hill, Christopher (1983b): 'National Interests - the Insuperable Obstacle?', in *National Foreign Policies and European Political Cooperation*, edited by Christopher Hill, RIIA and Allen and Unwin, London, pp. 185-198.

Hill, Christopher (1991): *Cabinet Decisions on Foreign Policy: The British Experience, October 1938 - June 1941*, Cambridge University Press, Cambridge.

Hill, Christopher (1994): 'The Capability-Expectations Gap, or Conceptualizing Europe's International Role', in *Economic and Political Integration in Europe: Internal Dynamics and Global Context*, Simon Bulmer and Andrew Scott, Blackwell, Oxford, 103-126.

Henig, Stanley and Pinder, John (1969): *European Political Parties*, George Allen and Unwin, London.

Henig, Stanley (1979): *Political Parties in the European Community*, George Allen and Unwin, London.

Henig, Stanley (1997): The Uniting of Europe: From Discord to Concord, Routledge, London and New York.

Hodges, Michael (1978): 'Integration Theory' in *Approaches and Theory in International Relations* edited by Trevor Taylor, Longman, London and New York, pp. 237-256.

Holland, Martin, ed. (1991): *The Future of European Political Cooperation*, Macmillan, London.

Holland, Martin (1993): *European Community integration*, Pinter, London.

Hurwitz, Leon, ed. (1980): *Contemporary Perspectives on European Integration: Attitudes, Nongovernmental Behaviour, and Collective Decision Making*, Aldwych Press, London.

Hurwitz, Leon (1983): 'Partisan Ideology or National Interest? An Analysis of the Members of the European Parliament', in *The Harmonization of European Public Policy: Regional Responses to Transnational Challenges*, edited by Leon Hurwitz, Greenwood Press, Westport, pp. 197-217.

Ifestos, Panayiotis (1987): *European Political Cooperation: Towards a Framework of Supranational Diplomacy?*, Avebury, Aldershot, Brookfield USA, Hong Kong, Singapore, Sydney.

Inglehart, Ronald and Rabier, Jacques-Réné (1980): 'Europe Elects a Parliament: Cognitive Mobilization, Political Mobilization, and Pro-European Attitudes as Influences on Voter Turnout', *Contemporary Perspectives on European*

327

Integration: Attitudes, Nongovernmental Behaviour, and Collective Decision Making, edited by Leon Hurwitz, 1980, Aldwych Press, London, pp. 27-51.

Ionescu, Ghiţa (1996): 'Conclusion', *Parliaments and Parties: The European Parliament in the Political Life of Europe*, edited by Roger Morgan and Clare Tame, Macmillan, London and Martinus, New York.

Jacobs, Francis; Corbett, Richard and Shackleton, Michael (1995): *The European Parliament*, 3rd edition, Cartermill, London.

Jørgensen, K.E., ed. (1997): *Reflective Approaches to European Governance*, Macmillan, London.

Johansson, Karl Magnus (1997): *Transnational Party Alliances: Analysing the Hard-Won Alliance Between Conservatives and Christian Democrats in the European Parliament*, Lund University Press, Lund.

Johansson, Karl Magnus (1998): 'The Transnationalization of Party Politics' in *Transnational Parties in the European Union* edited by David S Bell and Christopher Lord, Ashgate, Aldershot, Brookfield USA, Singapore and Sydney.

Kaiser, Karl and Becher, Klaus (1992): 'Germany and the Iraq Conflict' in *Western Europe and the Gulf*, edited by Gnesotto and Roper, Institute for Security Studies of WEU, Paris.

Katz, Richard S. and Mair, Peter, eds. (1994): *How Parties Organize. Change and Adaptation in Party Organizations in Western Democracies*, Sage, London.

Keohane, Robert Owen and Nye, Joseph S. (1975): '*International Interdependence and Integration*, in *Handbook of Political Science* edited by F.I. Freenstein and N.W. Polsby, Vl 8, Addison-Wesley, Reading.

Keohane, Robert Owen (1984): *After Hegemony: Cooperation and Discord in the World Political Economy*.

Keohane, Robert Owen (1986a): 'Theory of World Politics: Structural Realism and Beyond' in *Neorealism and its critics* edited by Keohane, Columbia University Press, New York, pp. 158-203.

Keohane, Robert Owen (1986b): 'Realism, Neorealism and the Study of World Politics', in *Neorealism and its critics* edited by Keohane, Columbia University Press, New York, pp. 1-26.

Keohane, Robert and Hoffmann, Stanley (1990): 'Conclusions: Community Politics and Institutional Change', in *The Dynamics of European Integration*, edited by William Wallace, Pinter for RIIA, London, pp. 276-300.

Keohane, Robert and Hoffmann, Stanley, eds. (1991): *The New European Community: Decision Making and Institutional Change*, Westview Press, Boulder, Colorado.

Keohane, Robert and Nye, Joseph S (1993): 'International Interdependence and Integration', in *International Relations Theory: Realism, Pluralism, Globalism*, 2nd edition, by Viotti and Kauppi, Maxwell, Toronto and Macmillan, New York, pp. 384-401.

Kirchner, Emil Joseph (1992): *Decision-making in the European Community: the Council Presidency and European Integration*, Manchester University Press, Manchester.

Kritziotis, Dino (1993): 'Chronology of events: the Disintegration of Yugoslavia', in *Politics and Law of Former Yugoslavia*, edited by Holly Cullen, Dino Kritziotis, Nicholas Wheeler, Research Paper 3/93, University of Hull.

Ladrech, Robert (1991): 'Political Parties in the European Parliament', in *Political Parties and the European Union*, edited by John Gaffney, Routledge, London and New York, pp. 291-307.

Ladrech, Robert and Brown-Pappamikail, Peter (1995): 'Towards a European Party System', in *Democratie et Construction Européenne*, by Mario Telò, Editions de l'Université de Bruxelles.

Ladrech, Robert (1998): 'Party Networks, Issue Agendas and European Union', in *Transnational Parties in the European Union* edited by David S Bell and Christopher Lord, Ashgate, Aldershot, Brookfield USA, Singapore and Sydney, pp. 51-85.

Lemaignen, R (1964): *L'Europe au Berceau*, Paris.

Lindberg, Leon N. (1963): *The Political Dynamics of European Economic Integration*, Oxford University Press, Oxford.

Lindberg, Leon N. and Scheingold, Stuart A. (1970): *Europe's would-be policy*, Prentice-Hall, Englewoods Cliffs, NJ.

Lipgens, Walter (1968): *Europa-Föderationsplane der Widerstandsbewegungen, 1940-1945: eine Dokumenten*, Munich, cited in Alan Milward.

Little, Richard (1985): 'Structuralism and Neo-Realism', in *International Relations: A Handbook of Current Theory*, edited by Margot Light and Arthur John Richard Groom, Pinter, London, pp. 74-90.

Lijphart, Arend (1977): *Democracies in Plural Societies: A Comparative Exploration*, New Haven: Yale University Press.

Lodge, Juliet (1983a): 'The European Parliament' in *Institutions and Policies of the European Community*, edited by Juliet Lodge, Pinter, London, pp. 27-42.

Lodge, Juliet (1984): 'European Union and the First Elected European Parliament: The Spinelli Initiative', *Journal of Common Market Studies*, Vol. 22, pp. 333-340.

Lodge, Juliet (1983b): 'Integration Theory, Decision-making and institutions in the European Community' in *The European Community: Bibliographical Excursions*, edited by Juliet Lodge, Pinter, London.

Lodge, Juliet, ed. (1986): *European Union: the European Community in Search of a Future*, Macmillan, London.

Lodge, Juliet, ed. (1986b): *Direct Elections of the European Parliament 1984* , Macmillan, London.

Lodge, Juliet (1988): 'The European Parliament and Foreign Policy', in *Foreign policy and Legislatures*, edited by Manohar Sondhi, Abhinav Publications, New Delhi.

Lodge, Juliet (1989): 'EC Policymaking: Institutional Considerations', in *The European Community and the Challenge of the Future* edited by Juliet Lodge, Pinter, London.

Lodge, Juliet (1991): 'The Democratic Deficit and the European Parliament', Discussion Paper, Fabian Society, London.

Lodge, Juliet (1993): 'Introductory Remarks: The EC and Yugoslavia', in *Politics and Law of Former Yugoslavia*, edited by Holly Cullen, Dino Kritziotis, Nicholas Wheeler, Research Paper 3/93, pp. 2-4.

Lodge, Juliet (1996): 'The European Parliament' in *The European Union: How Democratic is it?* edited by Andersen, Svein S and Eliassen, Kjell A, *The European Union: How Democratic is it?* Sage, London, Thousand Oaks, New Delhi.

Ludlow, Peter and Frellesen, Thomas and Jones, Erik (1993): *EC-US Relations: Relations for the Next Four Years*, CEPS Paper No. 53, CEPS, Brussels.

Lucarelli, Sonia (1995a): *The International Community and the Yugoslav crisis: A Chronology of Events*, EUI Working Paper RSC No. 95/8.

Lucarelli, Sonia (1995b): *The European Response to the Yugoslav crisis: Story of a Two-Level Constraint*, EUI Working Paper RSC No. 95/37, Florence: European University Institute.

Mansholt, Sicco (1974), *La Crise*, Stock, cited in Barón Crespo, Enrique (1989): 'Horizon 1992 and the Left', in *Contemporary European Affairs*, Vol. 1, No. 1/2, 1989, pp. 29-44, p. 39.

MacLeod, Iain, Hendry Ian D. and Hyett, Stephen (1996): *The External Relations of the European Communities: A Manual of Law and Practice*, Clarendon Press, Oxford.

Magas, Branka (1993): *The Destruction of Yugoslavia: Tracking the Break-up 1980-92*, Verso, London, New York.

Mair, Peter and Smith, Gordon (1990): *Understanding Party System Change in Western Europe*, Cass, London.

Marquand, David (1979): *Parliament for Europe?*, Jonathan Cape, London, cited in Westlake, 1994a, 7.

Marquand, David (1980): *The European Parliament and European integration: Have direct elections made a difference?*, Manchester Statistical Society.

Matthews, Ken (1993): *The Gulf Conflict and International Relations*, Routledge, London and New York.

Michelmann, Hans J. and Soldatos, Panayotis, eds. (1994): *European Integration: Theories and Approaches*, University Press of America, Lanham, New York, London.

Miles, Lee (1993): 'The Political Groups in the European Parliament', University of Hull, Research Paper 1/91, January.

Millar, David (1991): 'European Political Co-operation' in *Parliament and International Relations*, edited by Charles Carstairs and Richard Ware, Open University Press, Milton Keynes, pp. 140-159.

330

Milward, Alan S. (1992): *The European Rescue of the Nation State*, Routledge, London.

Mitrany, David (1966): *A Working Peace System*, Quadrangle Books, Chicago.

Monnet, Jean (1978): *Memoirs*, (trans R. Mayne), Doubleday and Company, New York.

Moravcsik, Andrew (1993): 'Preferences and Power in the European Community: A Liberal Intergovernmental Approach', *Journal of Common Market Studies*, Vol. 31, pp. 473-524.

Moravcsik, Andrew (1991): 'Negotiating the Single European Act', in *The New European Community Decision-making and institutional change*, edited by Robert O. Keohane and Stanley Hoffmann, Westview Press, Boulder, Colorado, pp. 41-84.

Morgenthau, Hans (1973): *Politics Among Nations*, 5th edition, Knopf, New York.

Mutimer, David (1994): 'Theories of Political Integration', in *European Integration: Theories and Approaches*, edited by Hans Michelmann and Panayotis Soldatos, University Press of America, Lanham, New York, London, pp. 3-42.

Neunreither, Karlheinz (1960): 'Le Rôle du Parlement dans la Formation de Décision des Communautés européennes', Paper to the Colloque on 'La Décision dans les Organisations européennes?, Lyons, cited in *European Political Parties*, (1969), edited by Stanley Henig and John Pinder, George Allen and Unwin, London.

Neunreither, Karlheinz (1990): 'The European Parliament: An Emerging Political Role?', in *Europe's Global Links*, edited by Geoffrey Edwards and Elfriede Regelsberder, Pinter, London, pp. 169-187.

Nugent, Neill (1994): *The Government and Politics of the European Union*, Macmillan, Basingstoke.

Nuttall, Simon (1981-1987): 'European Political Cooperation' in Jacobs, F.G., ed. *Yearbook of European Law*, The Clarendon Press, Oxford.

Nuttall, Simon (1992a): *European Political Cooperation*, Clarendon, Oxford.

Nuttall, Simon (1992b): 'The Institutional Network and the Instruments of Action', in *Towards Political Union: Planning a Common Foreign and Security Policy in the European Community*, edited by Reinhardt Rummel, Westview Press, Boulder, Colorado and Oxford pp. 55-76.

Nuttall, Simon (1993): 'The Foreign and Security Policy Provisions of the Maastricht Treaty: Their Potential for the Future' in *The Maastricht Treaty on European Union*, edited by Jörg Monar, European Inter-University Press, Brussels.

Owen, David (1995): *Balkan Odyssey*, Victor Gollancz, London.

O'Neill, Michael (1996): *The Politics of European Integration: A Reader*, Routledge, London and New York.

Oppenheim, A.N. (1985): 'Psychological Aspects', in *International Relations: A Handbook of Current Theory*, edited by Margot Light and Arthur John Richard Groom, Pinter, London, pp. 201-213.

Palmer, Michael (1981): *The European Parliament: What it is, What is does, How it works*, Pergamon Press, Oxford.

Pedersen, Mogens N (1996): 'Euro-parties and European Parties: New Arenas, new Challenges and New Strategies' in *The European Union: How Democratic is it?* edited by Svein S Andersen and Kjell a Eliassen, Sage, London, Thousand Oaks, New Delhi.

Pentland, Charles (1973): *International Theory and European Integration*, The Free Press, New York.

Pflimlin, Pierre (1992): 'Comments', in *The European Community in the Historical Context of its Parliament*, Proceedings of the 40th Anniversary Symposium, Strasbourg, pp. 69-70.

Pijpers, Alfred, Regelsberger, Elfriede, Wessels, Wolfgang (eds.) with the collaboration of Edwards, Geoffrey (1988): *European Political Cooperation in the 1980s: A Common Foreign Policy for Western Europe?*, Martinus Nijhoff, Dordrecht.

Pridham, Geoffrey and Pridham, Pippa (1981): *Transnational Party Co-Operation and European Integration: The Process Towards Direct Elections*, Allen and Unwin, London.

Pridham, Geoffrey and Pridham, Pippa (1979): 'Transnational Parties in the European Community I: The Party Groups in the European Parliament', *Political Parties in the European Community*, edited by Stanley Henig, pp. 245-278.

Rae, Douglas W. (1967): *The Political Consequences of Electoral Laws*, Yale UP, New Haven.

Raunio, Tapio and Wiberg, Matti (1995): 'Controlling voting power in the European Parliament 1979-1995, in *National Interest and Integrative Politics in Transnational Assemblies*, edited by Ernst Kuper.

Raunio, Tapio (1997): *The European Perspective: Transnational Party Groups in the 1989-1994 European Parliament*, Ashgate, Aldershot, Brookfield USA, Singapore and Sydney.

Raunio, Tapio (1998): 'Cleavages and Alignments in the European Parliament: MEP Voting Behaviour, 1989-1994', in *Transnational Parties in the European Union* edited by David S Bell and Christopher Lord, Ashgate, Aldershot, Brookfield USA, Singapore and Sydney, pp. 168-188.

Rémacle, Eric (1992): 'Les Douze dans la crise yougoslave', in *La politique étrangère: de Maastricht à la Yougoslavie*, Le dossier du GRIP, Brussels.

Regelsberger, Elfriede, Schoutheete de Tervarent, Philippe de and Wessels, Wolfgang, eds. (1997): *Foreign Policy of the European Union: From EPC To CSPS and Beyond*, Lynne Rienner, Boulder, Colorado and London.

Rice, Stuart A. (1928): *Quantitative Methods in Politics*, Knopf, New York.

Rosenau, J.N. (1967): 'Foreign Policy as an Issue Area, *Domestic Sources of Foreign Policy*, edited by J.N. Rosenau, New York.

Rossi, Ernesto and Spinelli, Altiero (1941): The Ventotene Manifesto, published in different versions and several languages including Associazione italiana per il Consiglio dei Comuni d'Europa, Centre Italiano Formazione Europea and Movimento Federalista Europea, 1981.

de Rougemont, Denis (1965): *The Meaning of Europe*, Sidgwick and Jackson, London cited in Hodges (1978).

Sbragia, Alberta (1992): 'Thinking about the European Future: the uses of comparison', in A. Sbragia (ed) *Euro-politics: institutions and policymaking in the New European Community*, Brookings.

Schmuck, Otto (1991): 'The European Parliament as an Institutional Actor', in *The State of the European Community. Policies, Institutions and Debates in the Transition Years*, edited by Leon Hurwitz and Christian Lequesne, Boulder (USA) Lynne Rienner, Harrow (England), Longman.

de Schoutheete, Philippe (1980, 1986): *La Coopération politique européenne*, Editions Labor, Brussels, 1st and 2nd editions.

Sjøstedt, Gunnar (1977): *The External Role of the European Community*, Saxon House, Farnborough.

Sked, Alan (1991): 'Cheap Excuses or Life, Death and European Unity' Target Paper 1, The Bruges Group: London, February.

Smith, Gordon (1972): *Politics in Western Europe*, Heinemann, London, 5th edition, Gower, Aldershot, 1989.

Snidal, Duncan (1993): 'Relative Gains and the Pattern of International Cooperation', in *Neorealism and Neoliberalism: The Contemporary Debate*, edited by David Baldwin, Columbia University Press, New York.

Spinelli, Altiero (1957): 'Une Constituante Européenne', *Pensée Française*, Fédération, Nos. 9-10.

Spinelli, Altiero (1958): 'La Méthode Constitutionelle: Méthodes et Mouvements pour unir l'Europe', *Bulletin du Centre européen de la Culture*, Geneva.

Spinelli, Altiero (1960): *L'Europa non cade dal cielo*, Il Mulino, Bologna.

Spinelli, Altiero, ed. (1963): *Che fare per l'Europa?*, Edizione di Comunità, Milano.

Spinelli, Altiero (1966): *The Eurocrats: Conflict and Crisis in the European Community*, John Hopkins University, Baltimore.

Spinelli, Altiero (1972): *L'Avventura europea*, Il Mulino, Bologna.

Stein, Arthur (1993): 'Coordination and Collaboration', in *Neorealism and Neoliberalism: the Contemporary Debate*, edited by David Baldwin, Columbia University Press, New York, pp. 29-59.

Steinberg, James B. (1993): 'The Response of International Institutions to the Yugoslav Conflict: Implications and Lessons', in *Europe's Volatile Powderkeg; Balkan Security After the Cold War*, cited in Lucarelli, Sonia (1995b): 'The European Response to the Yugoslav Crisis: Story of a Two-Level Constraint', EUI Working Paper RSC No. 95/37, Florence: European University Institute.

Sweeney, Jane (1984): *The First European Elections: Neo-functionalism and the European Parliament*, Westview Press, Boulder.

Taylor, Paul (1968): 'Concept of Community and the European Integration Process', *Journal of Common Market Studies*, Vol. 7, No. 2, pp. 83-101.

Taylor, Paul (1975): 'The Politics of the European Communities: the Confederal Phase', *World Politics*, April, pp. 336-360.

Taylor, Paul (1983): *The Limits of European Integration*, Croom Helm, London.

Taylor, Paul (1990): 'Functionalism: the Approach of David Mitrany' in *Frameworks for International Co-operation*, edited by A.J.R. Groom and Paul Taylor, Pinter, London, pp. 125-138.

Taylor, Paul (1990b): 'Supranationalism: the Power and Authority of International Institutions', in *Frameworks for International Co-operation*, edited by A.J.R. Groom and Paul Taylor, Pinter, London, pp. 109-122.

Taylor, Paul (1990c): 'Consociationalism and Federalism as Approaches to International Integration, in *Frameworks for International Co-operation* edited by A.J. Groom and Paul Taylor, Pinter, London, pp. 172-184.

Taylor, Paul and Groom, Arthur John Richard (1992): 'The United Nations and the Gulf War, 1990-1991: Back to the Future?', RIIA Discussion Paper No. 38, The Royal Institute of International Affairs, London.

Taylor, Paul (1993): *International Organization and in the Modern World: the Regional and the Global Process*, Pinter, London and New York.

Taylor, Paul (1993): *International Organization and in the Modern World: the Regional and the Global Process*, Pinter, London and New York.

Taylor, Trevor (1978): *Approaches and Theory in International Relations*, Longman, London and New York.

Telò, Mario (1994): 'National Democracy and Supranational Democracy', *Quaderni Forum*, n. 1, Anno VIII, pp. 45-58.

Vance, Cyrus (1994): 'Foreword' in *Crimes without punishment: Humanitarian Action in Former Yugoslavia*, by Michèle Mercier, Pluto Press, East Haven, Connecticut and London.

Viola, Donatella Maria (1997): 'Forging European Union: What Role for the European Parliament?', in *Rethinking the European Union: Institutions, Interests and Identities*, edited by Alice Landau and Richard Whitman, Macmillan, London, pp. 111-125.

Viotti, Paul and Kauppi, Mark (1993): *International Relations Theory: Realism, Pluralism, Globalism*, 2nd edition, Macmillan, New York and Maxwell Macmillan, Toronto.

Von Beyme, Klaus (1985): *Political Parties in Western Democracies*, St Martin's Press, New York (German editions 1975, 1977).

Waltz, Kenneth (1979): *Theory of International Politics*, Addison-Wesley, Reading, Mass (USA).

Wallace, William and Smith, Julie (1995): 'Democracy or Technocracy? European integration and the Problem of Popular Consent', in *The Crisis of Representation in Europe* edited by Jack Hayward, Frank Cass, London, pp. 137-157.

Ware, Alan (1996): *Political Parties ad Party Systems*, Oxford University Press, Oxford.

Webb, Carol (1983): 'Theoretical Perspectives and Problems', in Wallace, William, Wallace, Helen and Webb, Carol, 2nd edition, *Policy-Making in the European Community*, John Wiley, Chichester.

Weiler, Joseph H.H. and Wessels, Wolfgang (1988): 'EPC and the Challenge of Theory', in *European Political Cooperation in the 1980s: a Common Foreign Policy for Western Europe*, edited by Alfred Pijpers, Elfriede Regelsberger, Wolfgang Wessels in collaboration with George Edwards, M. Nijhoff, Dordrecht, Netherlands, published in cooperation with the Trans European Policy Studies Association (TEPSA), pp. 229-258.

Weiler, Joseph H.H. (1992): 'After Maastricht: Community legitimacy in Post-1992 Europe', in *Singular Europe: Economy and Policy of the European Community after 1992* edited by William James Adams, Ann Arbor, MI, University of Michigan Press.

Weiler, Joseph H.H. (1980): 'The European Parliament and Foreign Affairs: External Relations of the European Community' in *Parliamentary Control over Foreign Policy* edited by Antonio Cassese, Sijthoff and Nordhoff, Alpehn aan den Rijn, The Netherlands and Germantown, MD, USA.

Westlake, Martin (1994a): *Britain's Emerging Euro-elites? The British in the Directly-Elected European Parliament, 1979-1992*, Dartmouth, Aldershot.

Westlake, Martin (1994b): *A Modern Guide to the European Parliament*, Pinter, London, New York.

Wheare, Kenneth (1963): *Federal Government*, Oxford University Press, Oxford.

Wight, Gabriele and Porter, Brian, eds. (1991): *International Theory: The Three Traditions by Martin Wight*, Leicester University Press, Leicester and RIIA, London.

Williams, Shirley (1991): 'Sovereignty and Accountability in the European Community', in *The New European Community: Decision-making and Institutional Change*, edited by Robert Keohane and Stanley Hoffmann Westview Press, Boulder pp. 155-177.

Wistrich, Ernest (1989): *After 1992: The United States of Europe*, Routledge, London.

Wistrich, Ernest (1994): *The United States of Europe*, Routledge, London.

2. Articles in Periodicals

Alendar, Branislava (1992): 'The European Community and the Yugoslav crisis', *Review of International Affairs*, Vol. XLIII, No. 100911, Belgrade, pp. 18-2.

Allott, Philip (1997): 'The Crisis of European Constitutionalism: Reflections in the Revolution in Europe', *Common Market Law Review*, Vol. 34.

Ashdown, Paddy (19 June 1991): 'Europe's Security and Worldwide Responsibility', A Citizens' Europe Liberal Democrats, *Federal Green Paper*, No. 20.

Attinà, Fulvio (1990): 'The Voting Behaviour of European Parliament Members and the Problem of Europarties', *European Journal of Political Research*, Vol. 18, pp. 557-579.

Attinà, Fulvio (1992): 'Parties, Party System and Democracy in the European Union', *International Spectator*, Vol. 27, No. 3, pp. 67-86.

Attinà, Fulvio (1996): 'La Prima Repubblica in Europa', *Europa Europe*, Anno V, Vol. 1.

Bardi, Luciano (1996): 'Transnational Trends in European Parties and the 1994 European Elections of the European Parliament', *Party Politics*, Vol. 2, No. 1, pp. 99-113.

Barón Crespo, Enrique (1989): 'Horizon 1992 and the Left', *Contemporary European Affairs*,'1992 and After', Vol. 1, No. 1/2, pp. 29-44.

Bogdanor, Vernon (1989): 'Direct Elections, Representative Democracy and European Integration', *Electoral Studies*, Vol. 8, pp. 205-16, cited in Holland, 1993, p. 146.

Bonvincini, Gianni (1992): 'The Future of the EC Institutions', *The International Spectator*, Vol. XXVII, No. 1, pp. 3-16.

Bowler, Shaun and Farrell, David M. (1992): 'Profile: the Greens at the European level', *Environmental Politics*, Vol. 1, No. 1, pp. 132-137.

Bulmer, Simon J. (1998): 'New Institutionalism and the Governance of the Single European Market', *Journal of European Public Policy*, Vol. 5, No. 3, pp. 365-386.

Coëme, Guy (1991) 'Préface' in Dury, Raymonde (1991).

Corbett, Richard (1988): 'The European Parliament's New Single Act Powers', *Niew Europa*, Jrg 15, nr. 1, pp. 11-17.

De Michelis, Gianni (1991): 'Italy's Term as EC President', *European Affairs*, Vol.5.

de Rougemont, Denis (1967): 'The Campaign of the European Congresses', *Government and Opposition*, Vol. 2, No. 3.

Disraeli, Benjamin *Hansard Third Series*, Vol. LXXXIII, cols. 1319.

Dury, Raymonde (1991): 'La Communauté européenne et la Guerre du Golfe', Bruxelles: Institut Emile Vandervelde, Notes de Documentation, No. 27.

Duverger, Maurice, 'Italy's Search for a Second Republic', *Contemporary European Affairs*, Vol. 4, No. 2/3, pp. 124-137.

Elles, James (1990): 'The Foreign Policy Role of the European Parliament', *The Washington Quarterly*, Vol. 13, No. 4, pp. 69-78.

Gosalbo, Bono, Ricardo (1992): 'The International Powers of the European Parliament, the Democratic Deficit and the Treaty on European Union', *Yearbook of European Law*, Vol. 12, pp. 85-138.

Groux, Jean and Manin, Philippe (1985): *The European Communities in the international order*, Office for Official Publications of the European Communities, Luxembourg.

Haahr, Jens Henrik (1992) 'European integration and the Left in Britain and Denmark', *Journal of Common Market Studies*, Vol. 30, No. 1, pp. 77-100.

Haas, Ernst B. (1961): 'International Integration: The European and Universal Process', *International Organization*, Vol. 15, No. 3.

Hancock, Landon (1993): 'One Nation or Many? A Critical Approach to the Yugoslav Crisis', *The International Relations Journal*, Vol. 15, No. 1, pp. 47-53.

Hayward, Jack (1995): 'Preface' to 'The Crisis of Representation in Europe' edited by Jack Hayward, Jack, Special issue of *West European Politics*, Vol. 18, No. 3, July.

Hix, Simon (1993): 'The Emerging EC Party System? The European Party Federations in the Intergovernmental Conferences', *Politics*, Vol. 13, No. 2, pp. 38-46.

Hix, Simon (1994): 'The Study of the European Community: The Challenge to Comparative Politics', *West European Politics*, Vol. 17, No. 1, pp. 1-30.

Hix, Simon (1995b): 'Parties at the European level and the Legitimacy of EU Socio-Economic Policy', *Journal of Common Market Studies*, Vol. 33, No. 4, pp. 527-554.

Hix, Simon (1998): 'The Study of the European Union II: The 'New Governance' Agenda and its Rival', *Journal of European Public Policy*, Vol. 5, No. 1, 38-65.

Hoffman, Stanley (1964-5): 'The European Process at Atlantic Co-purposes', *Journal of Common Market Studies*, Vol. 3, pp. 85-101.

Hoffmann, Stanley (1966): 'Obstinate of Obsolete? The Fate of the Nation State and the Case of Western Europe' *Daedalus*, Vol. 95, pp. 862-915.

Johnson, Paul (1991): 'Why Britain Balks', *European Affairs*, Vol. 5.

Judge, David, Earnshaw, David and Cowan Ngaire (1994): 'Ripples or Waves: the European Parliament in the European Community Policy Process', *Journal of European Public Policy*, Vol. 1, No. 1, June, pp. 27-52.

Landgraf, Martin (1994): 'The Impact of the Second Gulf War on the Middle Eastern Policy of the European Union', *Orient*, Vol. 35, No. 1, pp. 81-94.

Levi, Arrigo (1990): 'I riflessi globali di una crisi regionale', *Affari esteri*, N. 88, pp. 622-629.

Marsh, Michael and Norris, Pippa (1997): 'Political Representation in the European Parliament', *European Journal of Political Research*, Vol. 32, No. 2, pp. 153-164.

Mearsheimer, John (1990): 'Back to the Future: Instability in Europe After the Cold War', *International Security*, Vol. 15.

Merkl, Peter H (1964): 'European Assembly Parties and National Delegations', *Journal of Conflict Resolution*, Vol. VIII.

Moïsi, Dominique (1991): 'The Causes of War', *European Affairs*, February-March, Vol. 1, pp. 10-11.

Nel, Philip (1992): 'Underestimating Insecurity: the International Community and Yugoslavia', *Review of International Affairs*.

Neunreither, Karlheinz (1994): 'The Democratic Deficit of the European Union: Towards Closer Cooperation between the European Parliament and the National Parliaments', *Government and Opposition*, Vol. 29, No. 3, Summer, pp. 299-315.

Nuttall, Simon (1994): 'The EC and Yugoslavia - Deus ex Machina or Machina sine Deo', *Journal of Common Market Studies*, Vol. 32, in *Annual Review of Activities, The European Union 1993*, edited by Neil Nugent, pp. 11-25.

Øhrgaard, Jakob C. (1997): '"Less than Supranational, More than Intergovernmental": European Political Cooperation and the Dynamics of Intergovernmental Integration', *Millennium*, Vol. 26, No. 1, pp. 1-29.

Peel, Robert, *Hansard Third Series*, Vol. LXXXIII, cols. 92 and 95.

Penders, Jean (1988): 'European Parliament and European Political Co-operation', *Irish Studies in International Affairs*, Vol. 2, No. 1.

Rémacle, Eric (1991): 'What Future for European Security?' in The Gulf Crisis, *Contemporary European Affairs*, Vol. 4, No. 1, pp. 27-46.

Risse-Kappen, Thomas (1996): 'Exploring the Nature of the Beast: International Relations Theory and Comparative Policy Analysis meet the European Union', *Journal of Common Market Studies*, Vol. 34, No. 1, pp. 53-80.

Salmon, Trevor C. (1992): 'Testing Times for European Political Cooperation: the Gulf and Yugoslavia, 1990-1992', *International Affairs*, April, Vol. 68, No. 2, pp. 233-253.

Silvestro, Massimo (1989): 'Des groupes politiques du parlement européen aux partis européens', *Revue du Marché Commun*, No. 327.

Silvestro, Massimo (1996): 'Le Parlement européen et les droits de l'homme', *Revue du Marché Commun et de l'Union européenne*, No. 394, janvier.

Sweeney, Jane P. (1984b): 'The Left in Europe's Parliament: The Problematic Effects of Integration Theory', *Comparative Politics*, Vol. 16, No. 2, pp. 171-190.

Taylor, Paul (1991): 'The European Community and the State: Assumptions, Theories and Propositions', *Review of international Studies*, Vol. 17, No. 2.

Tranholm-Mikkelsen, Jeppe (1991): 'Neo-functionalism: Obstinate or Obsolete? A Reappraisal in the Light of the New Dynamism of the EC', *Millennium*, Vol. 20, No. 1, Spring, pp. 1-22.

Wallace, William (1982): 'Europe as a Confederation: the Community and the Nation-State', *Journal of Common Market Studies*, Vol. 20, pp. 59-68.

Young, Oran (1969): 'Interdependencies in World Politics', *International Journal*, vol. 24, pp. 726-750 cited in Keohane and Nye (1975).

3. Conference Papers

Attinà, Fulvio (1994): 'On Political Representation in the European Union: Party Politics, Electoral System and Territorial Representation', Paper to the ECPR Madrid Joint Sessions of Workshops.

Bale, Tim (1996): 'Cultural Theory and the Parliamentary Labour Party', Paper presented at ECPR Oslo Joint Sessions of Workshops.

Bowler, Shaun and Farrell, David M. (1993): 'Parliamentary Norms of Behaviour: the Case of the European Parliament: Committees, Specialization and Co-ordination', EPRU Paper 4 and 93, University of Manchester.

Greco, Ettore (1993): 'Italy's Policy towards the Yugoslav Crisis', Paper to the Rhodes, Halki International Seminars, September.

Guicherd, Catherine (1992): 'The Hour of Europe: Lessons from the Yugoslav Conflict', *The Fletcher Forum*, Summer, pp. 159-181.

Hagevi, Magnus (1996): 'Party Activity Among the Members of the Swedish Riksdag', Paper presented to the ECPR Oslo Joint Session of Workshops.

Heidar, Knut and Koole, Ruud A. (1996): 'Approaches to the Study of Parliamentary Party Groups', Paper to the ECPR Oslo Joint Sessions of Workshops.

Hix, Simon (1995a): 'Political Parties in the European Union: a Comparative Politics Approach to the Organizational Development of the European Party Federations', Paper to the Conference on Party Politics in the Year 2000, Manchester, 13-15 January.

Kopecký, Petr (1996): 'Limits of Whips and Watchdogs: Cohesion of Parliamentary Parties in the First Czech Parliament (1992-1996)', Paper presented at ECPR Oslo Joint Sessions of Workshops.

Ladrech, Robert (1996): 'Party Networks, Issues Agendas and European Union Governance', Paper presented at ECPR Oslo Joint Sessions of Workshops.

Leonardi, Robert (1993): 'The Convergence Model of European integration', Paper to the Economic and Social Cohesion Network, London School of Economics, 20-21 November.

Monar, Jörg (1993): 'The European Parliament as an Actor in the Sphere of EPC/CFSP', Paper to the Conference on 'The Community, the Member States and Foreign Policy: Coming Together or Drifting Apart?', European Policy Unit, European University Institute, Badia Fiesolana, Firenze, Italy, 1-3 July.

Maor, Moshe (1994): 'Strategies of European Political Union', London School of Economics and Political Science.

Prout, Christopher (1992): 'The European Parliament and European Foreign Policy', Paper to the All Souls' College, Foreign Policy Studies, 21 February.

339

Simić, Predrag (1993): 'International Community and Yugoslavia: Lessons from a Failure', Paper to the 14th Biannual Conference of Directors of European Institutes of International Relations, 4 September.

Silvestro, Massimo (1974): 'Les Groupes politiques au parlement européen', Paper to the Conférence de Luxembourg, 1 April.

Sprokkereef, Annemarie (1993): 'The EC and the Fall of Yugoslavia: The Community's Decision-making Process in Times of Crisis', Paper to the ECPR Leiden Joint Sessions of Workshops.

Thiébault, Jean-Louis and Doles, Bernard (1996): 'Parliamentary Parties in the French Fifth Republic', Paper to the ECPR Oslo Joint Sessions of Workshops.

Viola, Donatella Maria (1994): 'Foreign Policy of the European Union: A Future Role for the European Parliament?' Paper to the ECPR Madrid Joint Sessions of Workshops.

Wiberg, Hakan (1992): 'Peace Order in Europe - Lessons from Yugoslavia', Paper to the Conference on 'Challenges for Peace and Security' at the International Institute for Peace, Vienna, 21-22 November, cited in Simić, Predrag (1993): 'International Community and Yugoslavia: Lessons from a Failure', 14th Biannual Conference of Directors of European Institutes of International Relations, 4 September.

Worre, Torben (1996): 'Parliamentary Party Groups in Denmark', Paper to the ECPR Oslo Joint Sessions of Workshops.

4. Press

Altichieri, Alessio (1987): 'Il dramma jugoslavo in tre anni', *Il Corriere della Sera*, 27 March.

Ascherson, Neal (1991): 'British cheers for America conspire to muffle Europe's dissent', *The Independent on Sunday*, 3 February.

Benetazzo, Piero (1990): 'Le ondate nazionaliste affondano la Jugoslavia', *La Repubblica*, 4 luglio.

Binyon, Michael (1990): 'Out for a count of Twelve as EC falls to Saddam', *The Times*, 17 September.

Brock, George and Guildford, Peter (18 January 1991): 'Response to conflict shows up divisions on Continent; Gulf conflict', *The Times*.

Buchan, David (1991): 'The Gulf War: European Parliament urges a greater role for Community', *The Financial Times*, 23 January.

Buchan, David (1991): 'The Gulf War: Common EC defence policy vital, says Nato chief', *The Financial Times*, 25 January.

Buchan, David (1991): 'EC asks UN about trial for Saddam', *The Financial Times*, 16 April.

Butler, Katherine (1998): 'Euro-MPs are expelled from Socialist Group', *The Independent*, 7 January.

Claveloux, Denise (1991): 'Soap opera takes colourful turn', *The European*, 8 February.

Comfort, Nicholas, Castle, Tim, Mather, Ian, Melcher, Robert, Watson, Rory, Paterson, Tony, Conradi, Peter, Endean, Chris and Silver, Eric (1991): 'Recoiling from war', *The European*, 11 January.

Barón Crespo, Enrique (1990): 'L'Europe d'une seule voix', *Le Monde*, 9 octobre.

Counsell, Gail (1990): 'Oilwatch: European MPs demand price-fixing inquiry', *The Independent*, 13 October.

Elles, James (1991): *The European*, 25 January.

Johnson, Boris (1991): 'The Gulf War: MEPs squabble on the sidelines - The reactions of a Community apparently outflanked by events', *The Daily Telegraph*, 23 January.

Lucas, Edward and Usborne, David (1991): 'Turmoil in the Soviet Union: Gulf crisis highlights problems of EC union', *The Independent*, 23 January.

Maitland, Sir Donald (1990): 'Sovereignty: Why British flesh need not creep', *The Financial Times*, 28 August.

Palmer, John (1990): 'The Gulf Crisis: Action raises Community demand for joint force', *The Guardian*, 13 September.

Palmer, John (1991): 'War in the Gulf: Pro-West Arabs "risk rebellions" ', *The Guardian*, 22 January.

Palmer, John (1991): 'The Gulf War: EC's war weakness threatens dream, says Delors', *The Guardian*, 24 January.

Philip, Alan (1991): 'The Gulf War: Coalition's Relief Behind the Ritual Expressions of Regret' *The Daily Telegraph*, 22 February.

Rees-Mogg, William and Davies, G (1992): 'Kohl calls for swift European Union', *The Independent*, 8 June, pp. 19, 23.

Smith, Alison (1990): 'Heath gains Iraqi pledge to free some hostages: Saddam hears former PM's appeal for the release of sick and elderly Britons', *The Financial Times*, 22 October.

Tanner, Marcus (1991): 'Yugoslav Presidency fails to solve crisis', *The Independent*, 17 May.

Tutt, Nigel (1991): 'Gulf War: EC blames Saddam for hostilities', *Lloyd's List*, 18 January.

Usborne, David (1990): 'Europe seeking to try Saddam', *The Independent*, 16 April.

Usborne, David (1991): 'Crisis in the Gulf: EC to seek closer Arab ties when war is over', *The Independent*, 22 January.

Watson, Rory (1991): 'The Gulf War: Bonn ready to increase aid by Dollars 3bn', *The European*, 25 January.

Webster, Philip (1994): 'Manifesto summary', in *The Times Guide to the European Parliament 1989*, edited by Alan Wood.

Wood, Nicholas (1990): 'Thatcher likely to break her self-imposed silence: Iraq invasion of Kuwait', *The Times,* 21 August.

Le Monde, 'Les députés européens réclament plus de pouvoir', 25 novembre 1989.

Libération 'Parlement cherche pouvoir', 16 mars 1990.

'Nouvelle offensive des parlementaires européens', 17 mars 1990.

'The Gulf Crisis: Action raises Community demand for joint force', *The Guardian*, 13 September 1990.

'Pygmy roars: Europe and the Gulf', *The Economist*, 22 December 1990.

'Gulf Crisis and European Parliament' in PR Newswire, 10 January, 1991, Extracts from the speech given by Enrique Barón Crespo, President of the European Parliament, Florence: European University Institute, 4 February 1991.

'Gulf War: Firm stand by some members of the European Parliament', *European Report*, 19 January 1991.

'The Gulf War: Bonn ready to increase aid by Dollars 3bn', *The European*, 25 January 1991.

'Crisis in the Gulf: MEPs support allied forces', *The Independent*, 25 January 1991.

New York Times, 29 June 1991.

The Financial Times, 29-30 June 1991, as cited in Lucarelli, Sonia (1995b): 'The European Response to the Yugoslav Crisis: Story of a Two-Level Constraint', EUI Working Paper RSC No. 95/37, Florence: European University Institute.

'EC finalises co-operation deals with the United States', *The Guardian*, 24 September 1991 cited in Arter, David, 1993, *The Politics of European Integration in the Twentieth Century*, Dartmouth, Aldershot, Brookfield USA, Hong Kong, Singapore, Sydney, p. 7.

'The Gulf: Euro-MPs urge joint policy on security', *The Daily Telegraph*, 13 September 1990.

'The Gulf War: European Parliament urges a greater role for Community', *Financial Times*, 23 January 1991.

5. Doctoral Theses and Dissertations

Corbett, Richard (1994b): 'The Elected European Parliament and its Impact on the Process of European Integration', Doctoral Thesis, University of Hull.

Dupagny, Séverine (1992): 'Les compétences du Parlement européen relatives à la Politique extérieure', Mémoire pour le DEA de Droit Communautaire, Université de Droit, d'Economie et de Sciences sociales de Paris, Paris II.

McDaniel, Gerald R (1969): 'The Danish Unicameral Parliament', Doctoral Thesis, University of California, Berkeley, cited in Chryssochou, 1994, pp. 20-21.

Scalingi, Paula Louise (1978): 'Towards Representative Democracy: The European Parliament, 1952-1958', Doctoral Thesis, The Florida State University College of Arts and Science, USA.

Stavridis, Stylianos (1991): 'Foreign Policy and Democratic Principles: the Case of European Political Co-operation', Doctoral Thesis, London School of Economics.

6. Lectures

Crnobrnja, Mihailo (1991): Extraits de l'Exposé auprès de la CE, 20 juin.

Nuttall, Simon (1995): 'The European Union and Yugoslavia', Lecture given at the London School of Economics and Political Science, 14 February.

Prout, Christopher (1993): 'Foreign Affairs and the European Parliament', The *William Elland Memorial* Lecture, London.

Prout, Christopher (1993b): 'Political Alignments and Constitutional Developments in the European Parliament', 2 November.

Weiler, Joseph (1997): 'New Forms of European Citizenship', The Jean Monnet Lecture, 20 March.